THE INVISIBLES

Apocalipstick

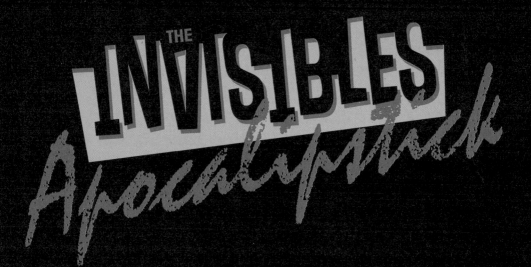

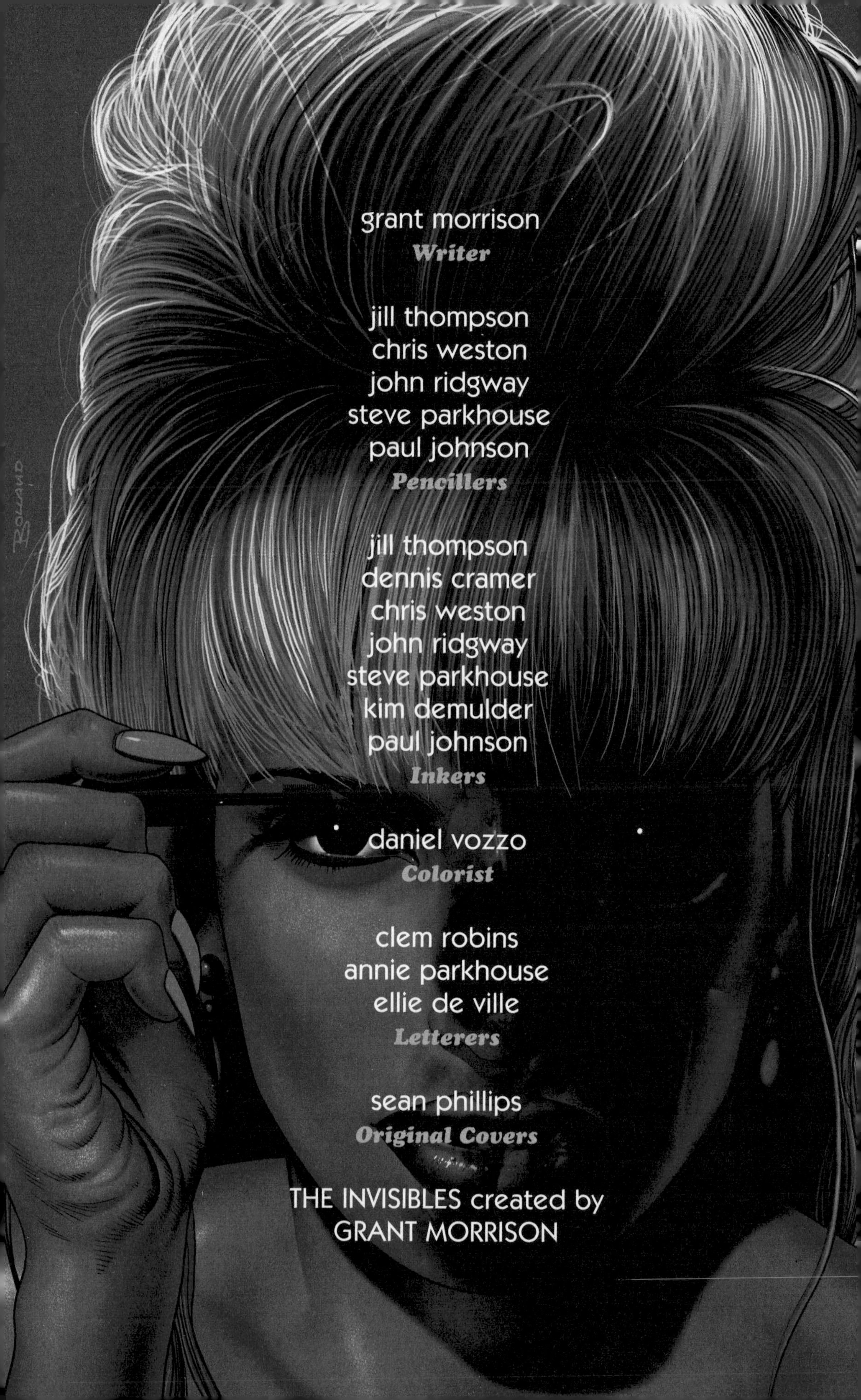

grant morrison
Writer

jill thompson
chris weston
john ridgway
steve parkhouse
paul johnson
Pencillers

jill thompson
dennis cramer
chris weston
john ridgway
steve parkhouse
kim demulder
paul johnson
Inkers

daniel vozzo
Colorist

clem robins
annie parkhouse
ellie de ville
Letterers

sean phillips
Original Covers

THE INVISIBLES created by
GRANT MORRISON

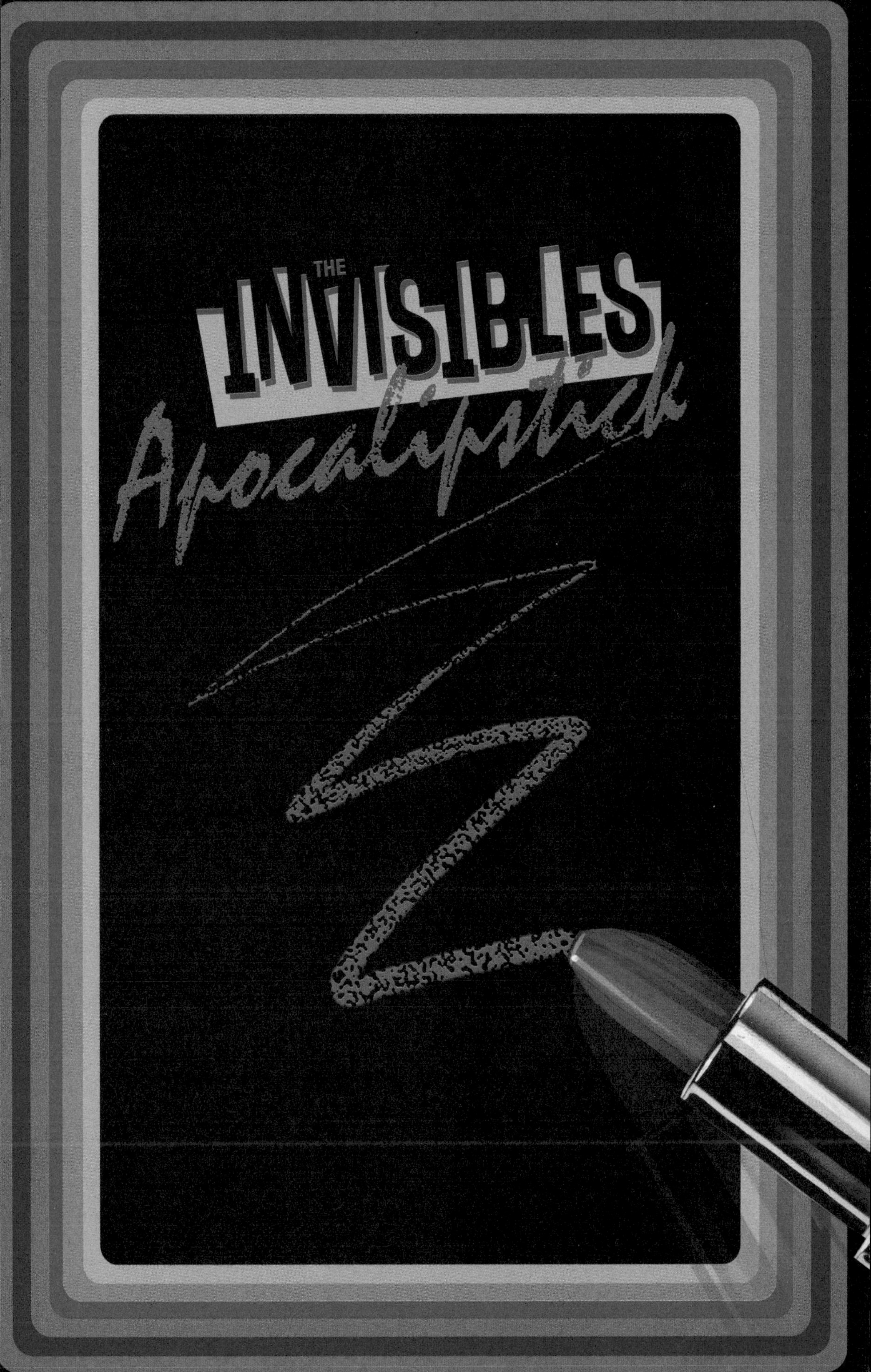
THE
INVISIBLES
Apocalipstick

THE INVISIBLES: APOCALIPSTICK

Published by DC Comics. Cover and compilation Copyright © 2001 DC Comics.
All Rights Reserved.

Originally published in single magazine form as THE INVISIBLES Vol.1 9-16.
Copyright © 1995, 1996 Grant Morrison. All Rights Reserved.
All characters, their distinctive likenesses and related elements featured in this publication
are trademarks of Grant Morrison. VERTIGO is a trademark of DC Comics.
The stories, characters and incidents featured in this publication are entirely fictional.
DC Comics does not read or accept unsolicited submissions of ideas, stories or artwork.

DC Comics, 1700 Broadway, New York, NY 10019
A Warner Bros. Entertainment Company
Printed in the USA. Sixth Printing.
ISBN: 978-1-56389-702-3
Cover illustration by Brian Bolland.

SUSTAINABLE
FORESTRY
INITIATIVE

Certified Chain of Custody
Promoting Sustainable Forestry
www.sfiprogram.org
SFI-01042
APPLIES TO TEXT STOCK ONLY

KING MOB

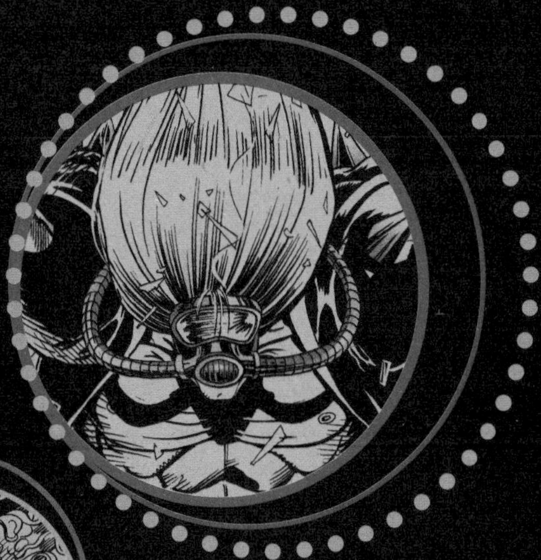

The leader of the pack — trained in physical and psychic combat at the Invisible College and versed in all things occult and Tantric, King Mob is a silver bullet aimed at the heart of the Conspiracy.

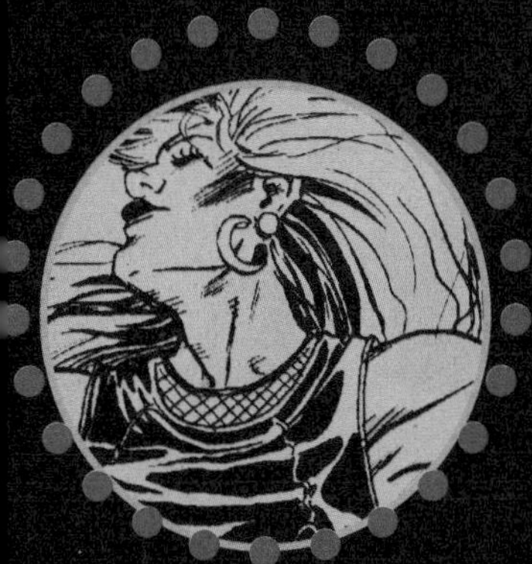

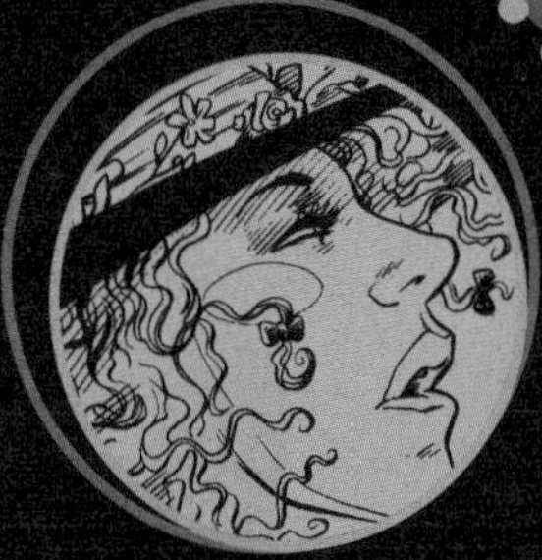

Ragged Robin

A red-headed herald from the future, Robin is a telepathic witch with a mission. But what is her mission, and how much does she know about what's to come?

Lord Fanny

What do you call a transvestite shaman from Brazil? Anything she wants you to, that's what. In this case, it's Lord Fanny, the latest in a long line of native sorceresses who came to the Invisibles via Rio.

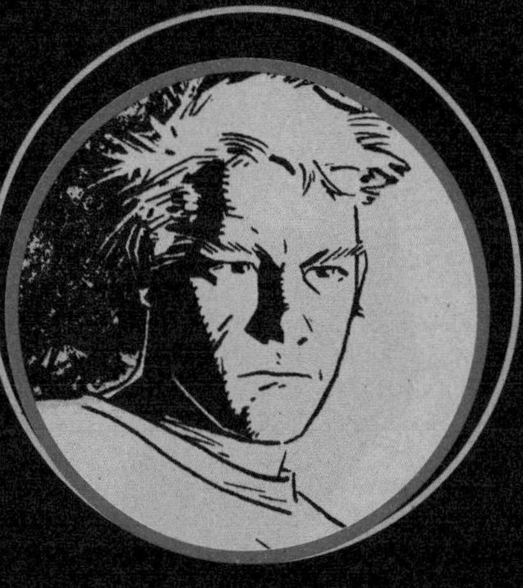

JACK FROST

The raw recruit, still learning what the Invisibles are all about — yet he may be the most powerful force on either side. Some call this former street punk the future Buddha, but he'd rather you call him Dane.

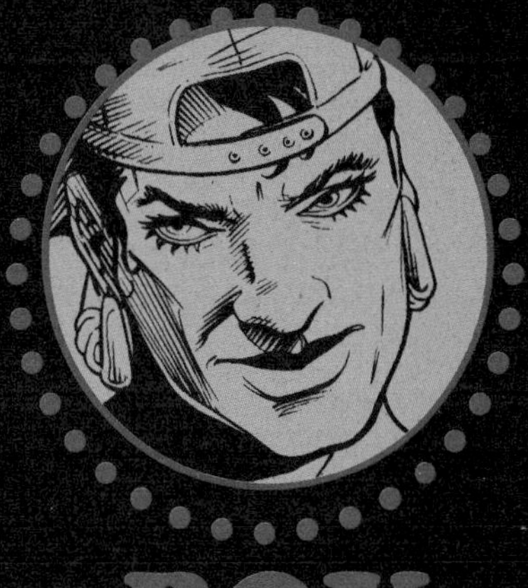

BOY

An ex-cop and martial artist from Harlem, Boy brought her street smarts with her to the fight against the Conspiracy. She doesn't look much like a boy, but hey, if things were simple we wouldn't need the Invisibles, would we?

The Story So Far...

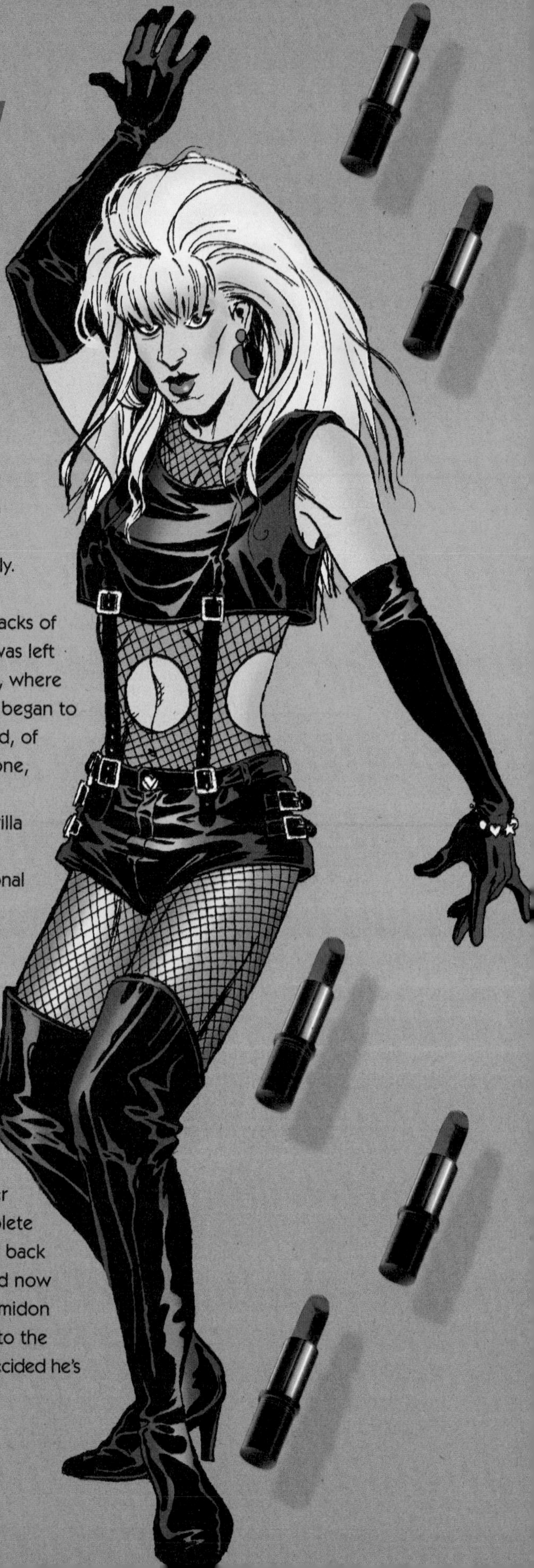

Dane McGowan couldn't see a way out of the dead end that life had led him to except to try to blow it up and burn it down. So the judge sent him down to Harmony House to "correct" him into his proper role in the world's order — which didn't involve keeping a mind of his own. That might have been all she wrote for Dane McGowan, except that he had already been marked as a recruit for something called the Invisibles, and they weren't giving up so easily.

Taken from Harmony over the bloody backs of his jailers by Invisible King Mob, Dane was left to fend for himself on the streets of London, where a man named Tom O'Bedlam found him and began to teach him about the true nature of the world, of magic, and of himself. By the time he was done, Dane had become Jack Frost, newest of the Invisibles — a centerless, revolutionary guerrilla society bent on liberating humanity from its unknowing slavery to a hideous extradimensional conspiracy.

Even for the newest recruit, though, there was no time to try to make sense of all that he had learned before he was pulled into a psychic-projection journey through time to revolutionary France and a meeting with the Marquis de Sade. Across space and time and place, however, the agents of the Conspiracy — human and otherwise — never rest. The Invisibles were barely able to complete their mission in the past before being pulled back to defeat the unfleshed demon Orlando, and now they await an attack by the Conspiracy's Myrmidon shock troops. And after losing a finger joint to the demon, the boy who was called Dane has decided he's had just about enough of all of this...

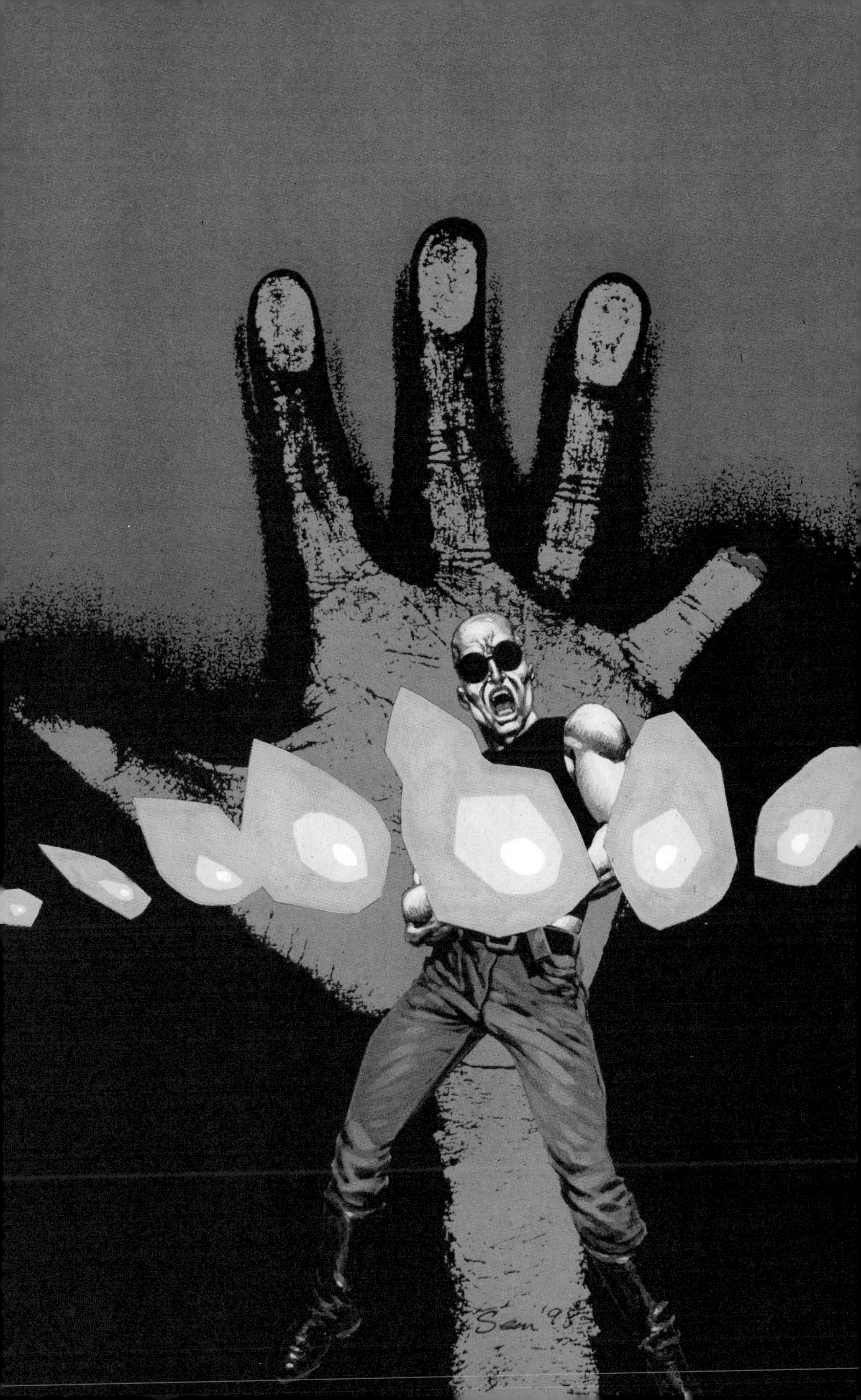

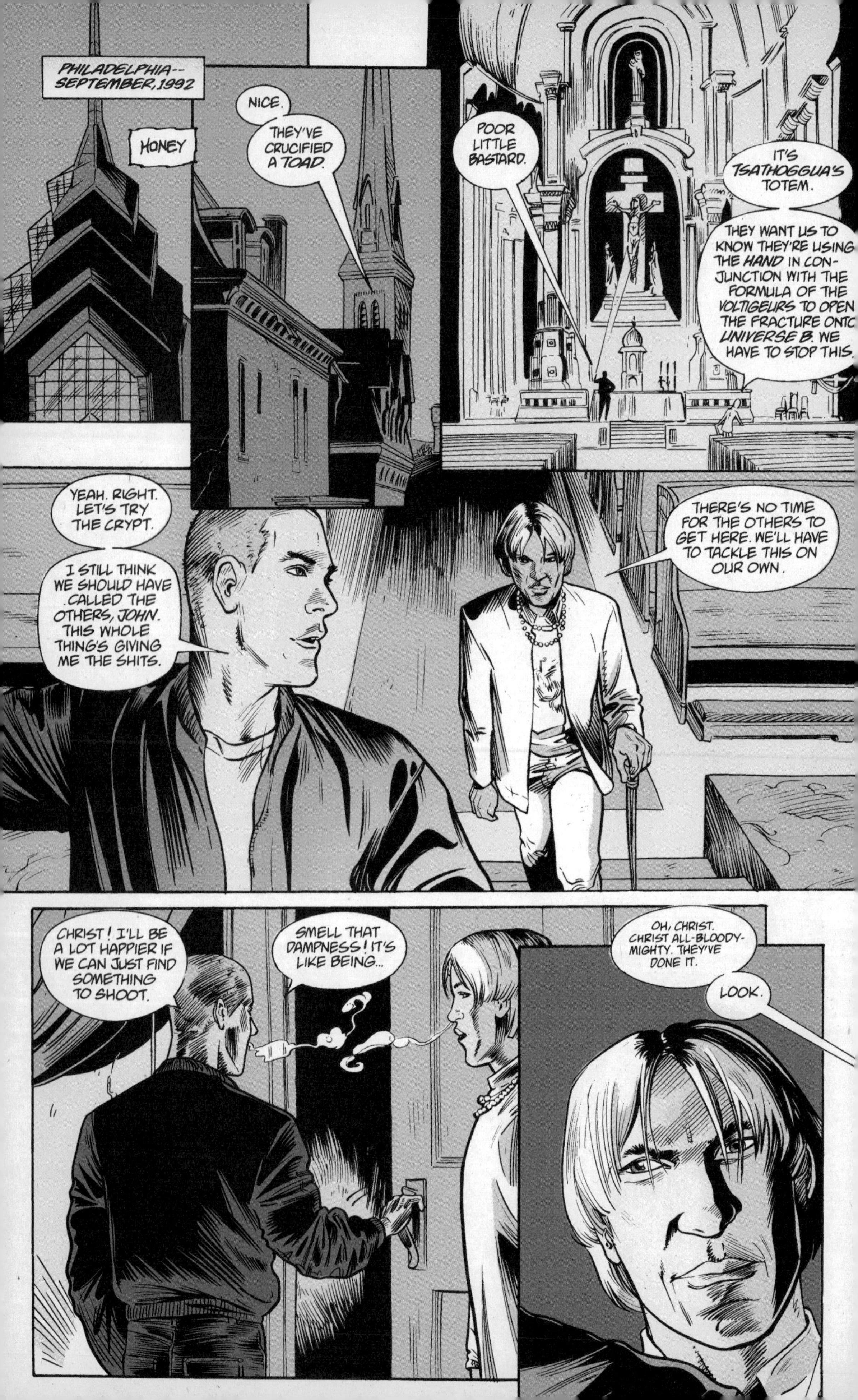
PHILADELPHIA-- SEPTEMBER, 1992
HONEY
NICE.
THEY'VE CRUCIFIED A TOAD.
POOR LITTLE BASTARD.
IT'S TSATHOGGUA'S TOTEM.
THEY WANT US TO KNOW THEY'RE USING THE HAND IN CONJUNCTION WITH THE FORMULA OF THE VOLTIGEURS TO OPEN THE FRACTURE ONTO UNIVERSE B. WE HAVE TO STOP THIS.
YEAH. RIGHT. LET'S TRY THE CRYPT.
I STILL THINK WE SHOULD HAVE CALLED THE OTHERS, JOHN. THIS WHOLE THING'S GIVING ME THE SHITS.
THERE'S NO TIME FOR THE OTHERS TO GET HERE. WE'LL HAVE TO TACKLE THIS ON OUR OWN.
CHRIST! I'LL BE A LOT HAPPIER IF WE CAN JUST FIND SOMETHING TO SHOOT.
SMELL THAT DAMPNESS! IT'S LIKE BEING...
OH, CHRIST. CHRIST ALL-BLOODY-MIGHTY. THEY'VE DONE IT.
LOOK.

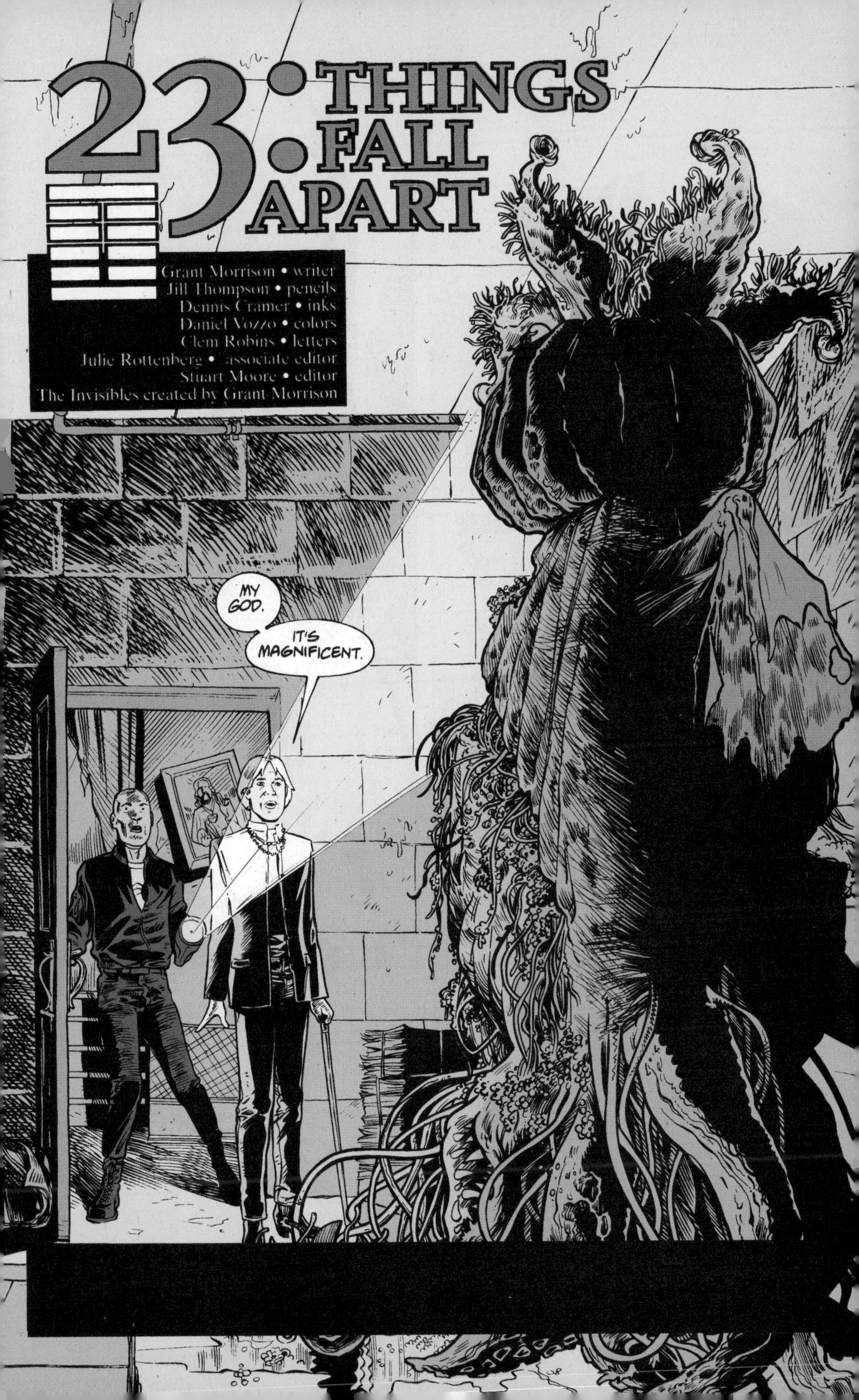
23: THINGS FALL APART
Grant Morrison • writer
Jill Thompson • pencils
Dennis Cramer • inks
Daniel Vozzo • colors
Clem Robins • letters
Julie Rottenberg • associate editor
Stuart Moore • editor
The Invisibles created by Grant Morrison
MY GOD.
IT'S MAGNIFICENT.

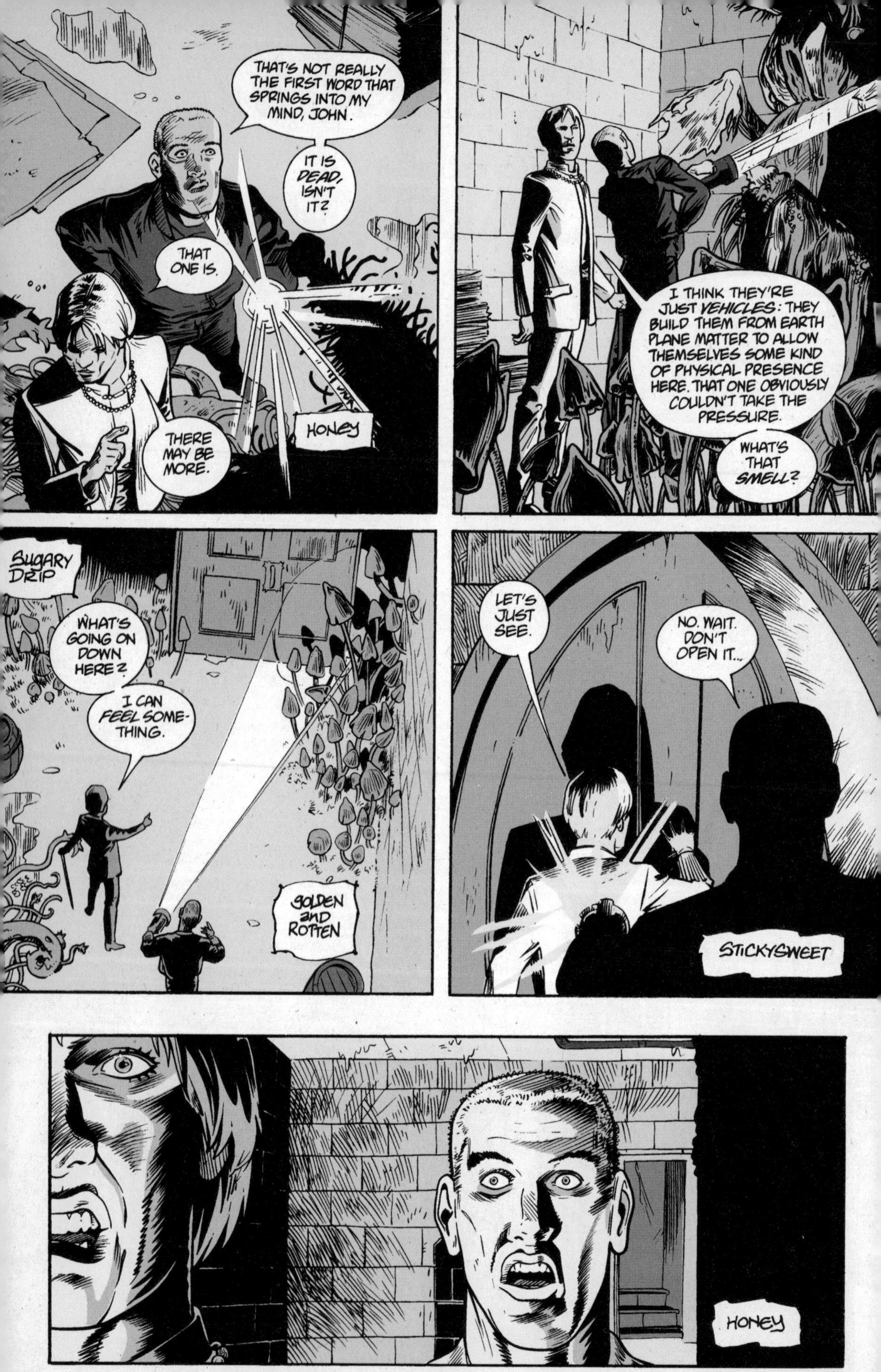
THAT'S NOT REALLY THE FIRST WORD THAT SPRINGS INTO MY MIND, JOHN.
IT IS DEAD, ISN'T IT?
THAT ONE IS.
THERE MAY BE MORE.
HONEY
I THINK THEY'RE JUST VEHICLES: THEY BUILD THEM FROM EARTH PLANE MATTER TO ALLOW THEMSELVES SOME KIND OF PHYSICAL PRESENCE HERE. THAT ONE OBVIOUSLY COULDN'T TAKE THE PRESSURE.
WHAT'S THAT SMELL?
SUGARY DRIP
WHAT'S GOING ON DOWN HERE?
I CAN FEEL SOMETHING.
GOLDEN AND ROTTEN
LET'S JUST SEE.
NO. WAIT. DON'T OPEN IT...
STICKYSWEET
HONEY

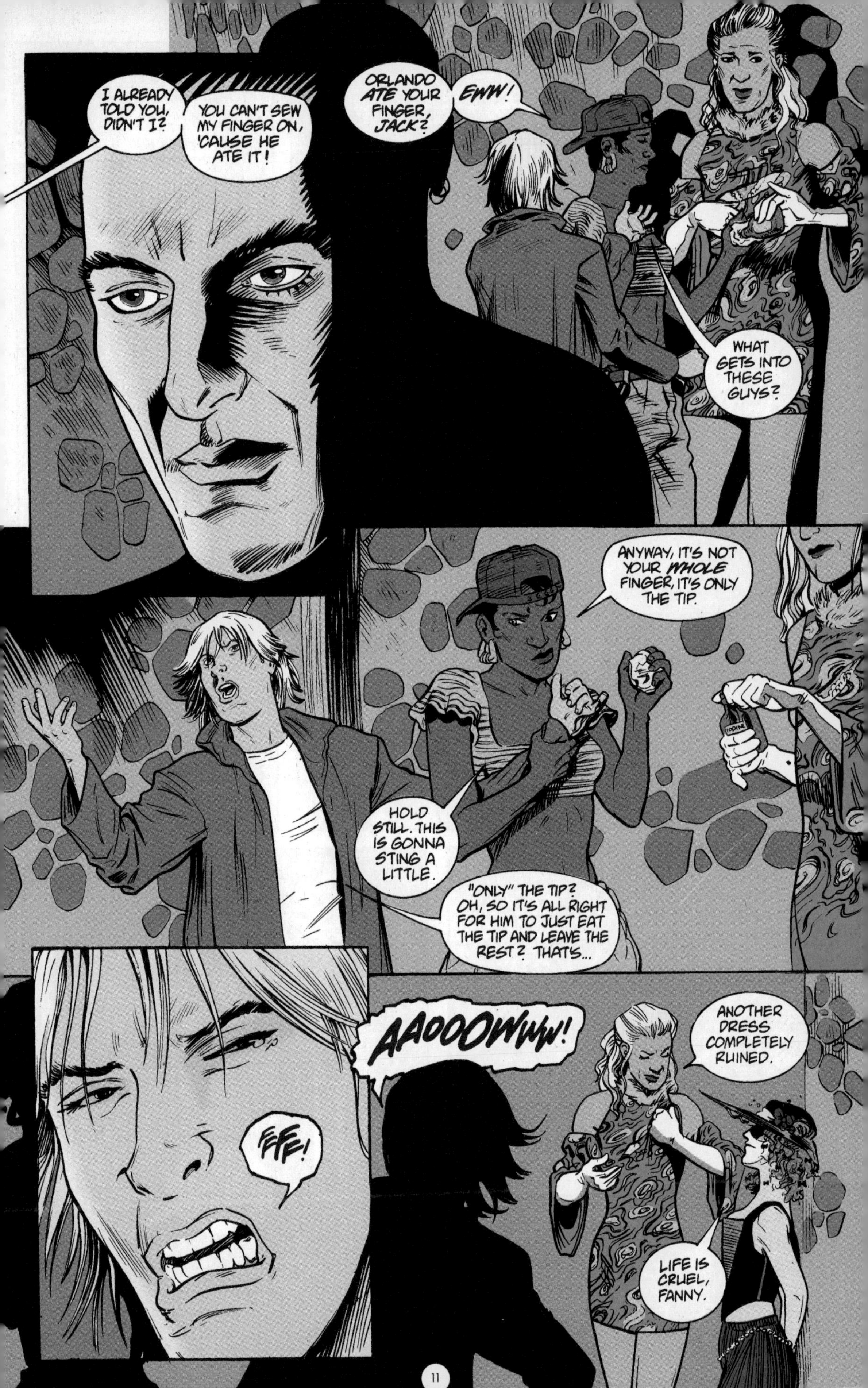
I ALREADY TOLD YOU, DIDN'T I?
YOU CAN'T SEW MY FINGER ON, 'CAUSE HE ATE IT!
ORLANDO ATE YOUR FINGER, JACK?
EWW!
WHAT GETS INTO THESE GUYS?
ANYWAY, IT'S NOT YOUR WHOLE FINGER, IT'S ONLY THE TIP.
HOLD STILL. THIS IS GONNA STING A LITTLE.
"ONLY" THE TIP? OH, SO IT'S ALL RIGHT FOR HIM TO JUST EAT THE TIP AND LEAVE THE REST? THAT'S...
AAOOOWWW!
FFFF!
ANOTHER DRESS COMPLETELY RUINED.
LIFE IS CRUEL, FANNY.

I'VE JUST BEEN THINKING.

I THINK WE'RE IN TROUBLE, MUCH WORSE TROUBLE THAN WE IMAGINED.

WELL, IT'S *YOUR* TROUBLE, MAN, NOT MINE! AND YOU CAN KEEP YOUR FUCKING TROUBLE TO YOURSELF. MAYBE IT'LL BE *YOU* THAT GETS CUT UP NEXT TIME!

I'M FINISHED WITH THIS! I'M GOING HOME!

LOOK AT THAT! LOOK AT MY FUCKING HAND!

THAT'S WHAT I CALL TROUBLE!

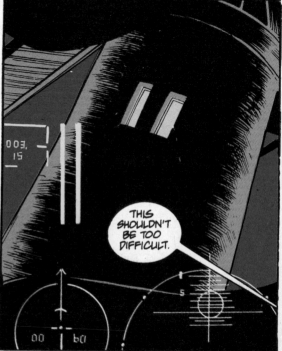

THIS SHOULDN'T BE TOO DIFFICULT.

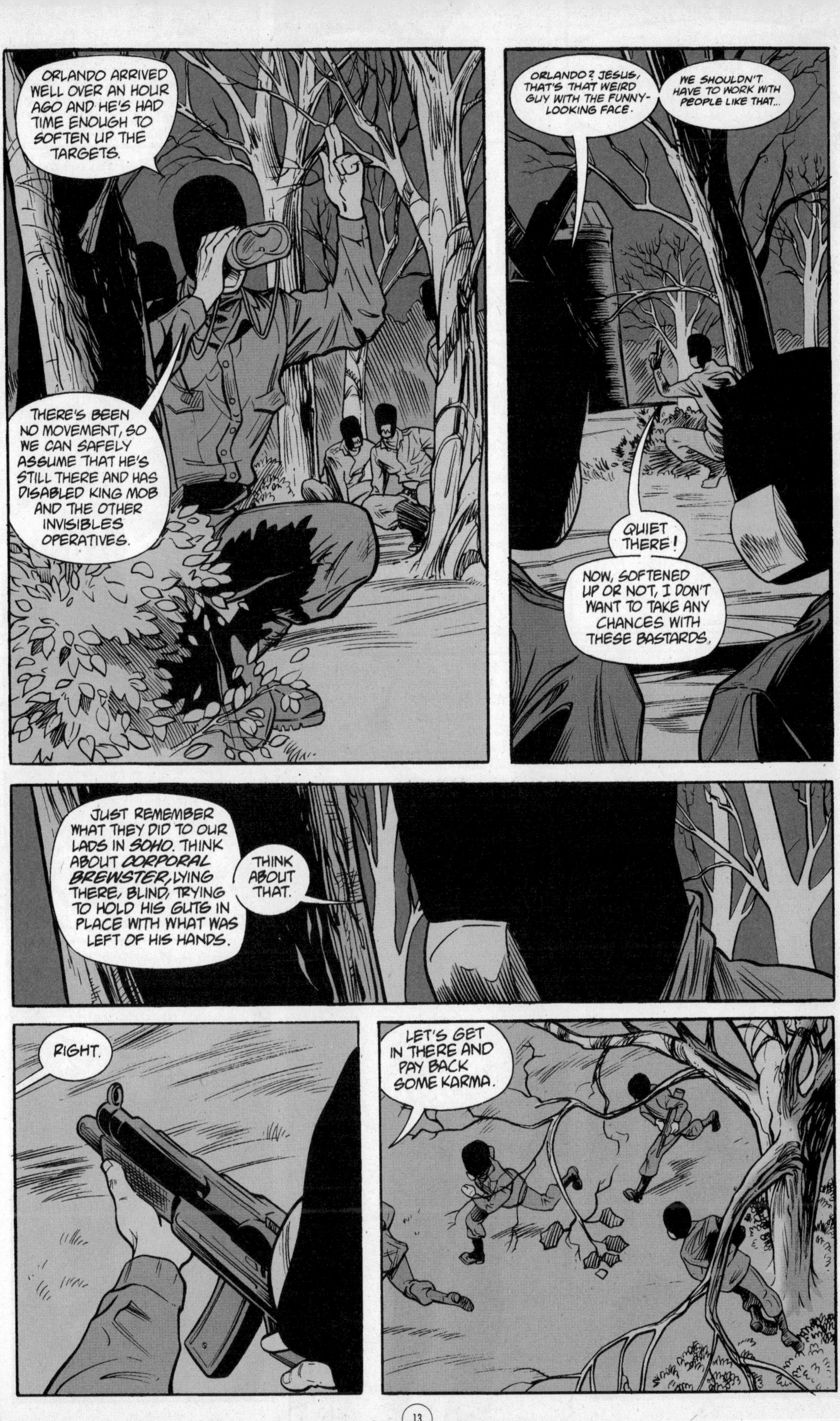
ORLANDO ARRIVED WELL OVER AN HOUR AGO AND HE'S HAD TIME ENOUGH TO SOFTEN UP THE TARGETS.
THERE'S BEEN NO MOVEMENT, SO WE CAN SAFELY ASSUME THAT HE'S STILL THERE AND HAS DISABLED KING MOB AND THE OTHER INVISIBLES OPERATIVES.
ORLANDO? JESUS, THAT'S THAT WEIRD GUY WITH THE FUNNY-LOOKING FACE.
WE SHOULDN'T HAVE TO WORK WITH PEOPLE LIKE THAT...
QUIET THERE!
NOW, SOFTENED UP OR NOT, I DON'T WANT TO TAKE ANY CHANCES WITH THESE BASTARDS.
JUST REMEMBER WHAT THEY DID TO OUR LADS IN SOHO. THINK ABOUT CORPORAL BREWSTER, LYING THERE, BLIND, TRYING TO HOLD HIS GUTS IN PLACE WITH WHAT WAS LEFT OF HIS HANDS.
THINK ABOUT THAT.
RIGHT.
LET'S GET IN THERE AND PAY BACK SOME KARMA.

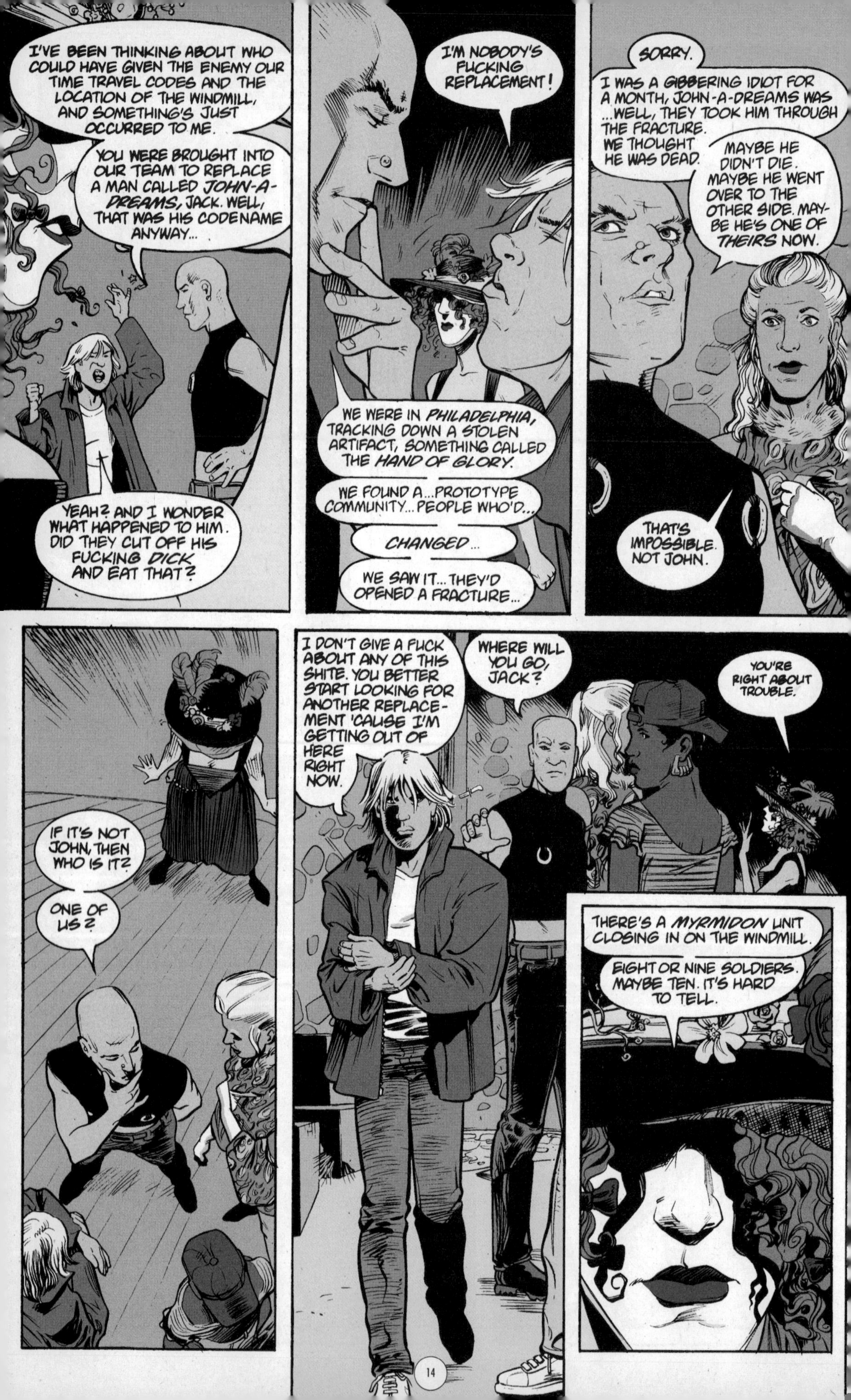
I'VE BEEN THINKING ABOUT WHO COULD HAVE GIVEN THE ENEMY OUR TIME TRAVEL CODES AND THE LOCATION OF THE WINDMILL, AND SOMETHING'S JUST OCCURRED TO ME.
YOU WERE BROUGHT INTO OUR TEAM TO REPLACE A MAN CALLED JOHN-A-DREAMS, JACK. WELL, THAT WAS HIS CODENAME ANYWAY...
YEAH? AND I WONDER WHAT HAPPENED TO HIM. DID THEY CUT OFF HIS FUCKING DICK AND EAT THAT?
I'M NOBODY'S FUCKING REPLACEMENT!
WE WERE IN PHILADELPHIA, TRACKING DOWN A STOLEN ARTIFACT, SOMETHING CALLED THE HAND OF GLORY.
WE FOUND A...PROTOTYPE COMMUNITY...PEOPLE WHO'D...
CHANGED...
WE SAW IT... THEY'D OPENED A FRACTURE...
SORRY.
I WAS A GIBBERING IDIOT FOR A MONTH, JOHN-A-DREAMS WAS ...WELL, THEY TOOK HIM THROUGH THE FRACTURE.
WE THOUGHT HE WAS DEAD.
MAYBE HE DIDN'T DIE. MAYBE HE WENT OVER TO THE OTHER SIDE. MAYBE HE'S ONE OF THEIRS NOW.
THAT'S IMPOSSIBLE. NOT JOHN.
IF IT'S NOT JOHN, THEN WHO IS IT?
ONE OF US?
I DON'T GIVE A FUCK ABOUT ANY OF THIS SHITE. YOU BETTER START LOOKING FOR ANOTHER REPLACEMENT 'CAUSE I'M GETTING OUT OF HERE RIGHT NOW.
WHERE WILL YOU GO, JACK?
YOU'RE RIGHT ABOUT TROUBLE.
THERE'S A MYRMIDON UNIT CLOSING IN ON THE WINDMILL.
EIGHT OR NINE SOLDIERS. MAYBE TEN. IT'S HARD TO TELL.

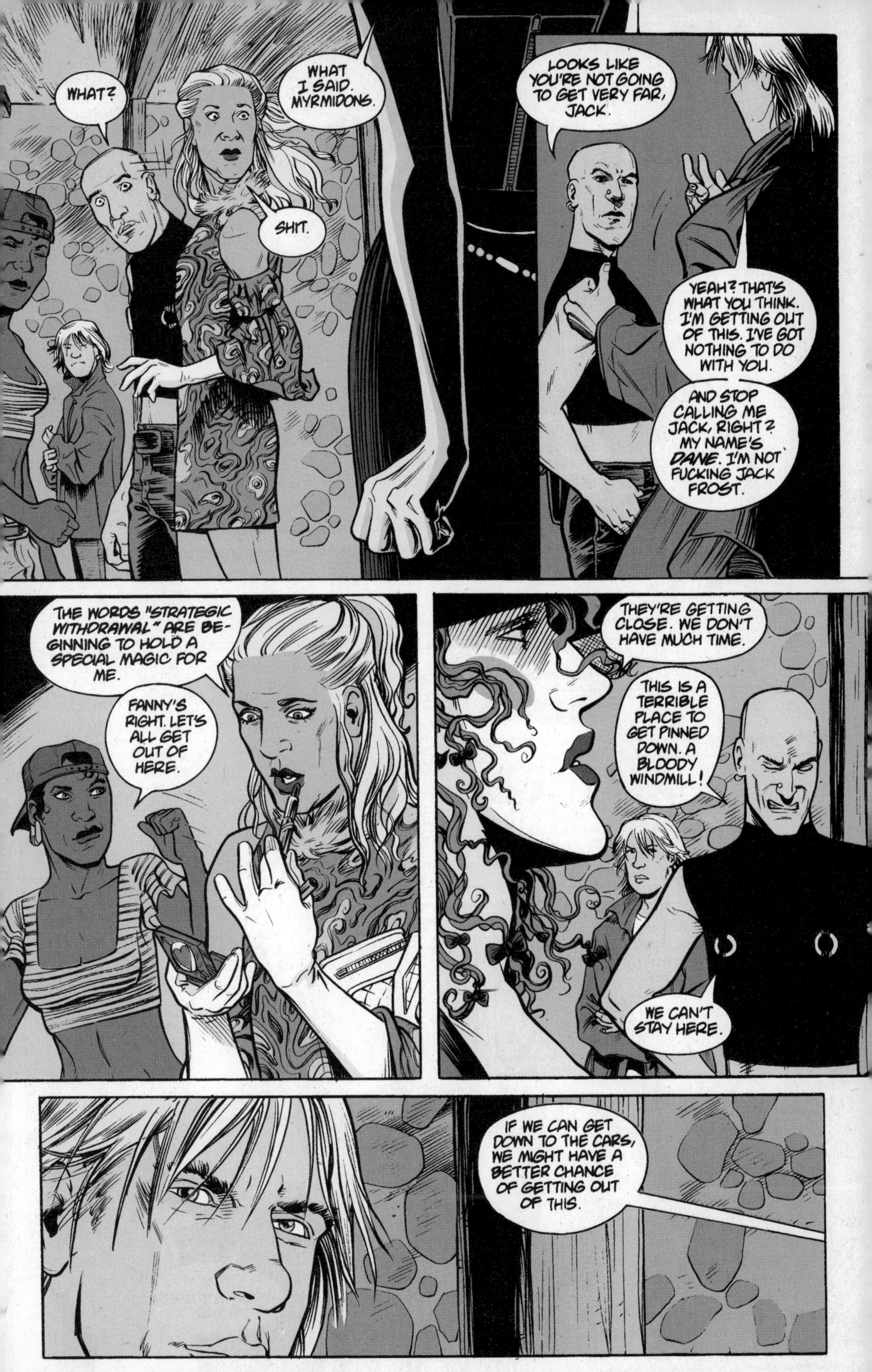
WHAT?
WHAT I SAID. MYRMIDONS.
SHIT.
LOOKS LIKE YOU'RE NOT GOING TO GET VERY FAR, JACK.
YEAH? THAT'S WHAT YOU THINK. I'M GETTING OUT OF THIS. I'VE GOT NOTHING TO DO WITH YOU.
AND STOP CALLING ME JACK, RIGHT? MY NAME'S DANE. I'M NOT FUCKING JACK FROST.
THE WORDS "STRATEGIC WITHDRAWAL" ARE BEGINNING TO HOLD A SPECIAL MAGIC FOR ME.
FANNY'S RIGHT. LET'S ALL GET OUT OF HERE.
THEY'RE GETTING CLOSE. WE DON'T HAVE MUCH TIME.
THIS IS A TERRIBLE PLACE TO GET PINNED DOWN. A BLOODY WINDMILL!
WE CAN'T STAY HERE.
IF WE CAN GET DOWN TO THE CARS, WE MIGHT HAVE A BETTER CHANCE OF GETTING OUT OF THIS.

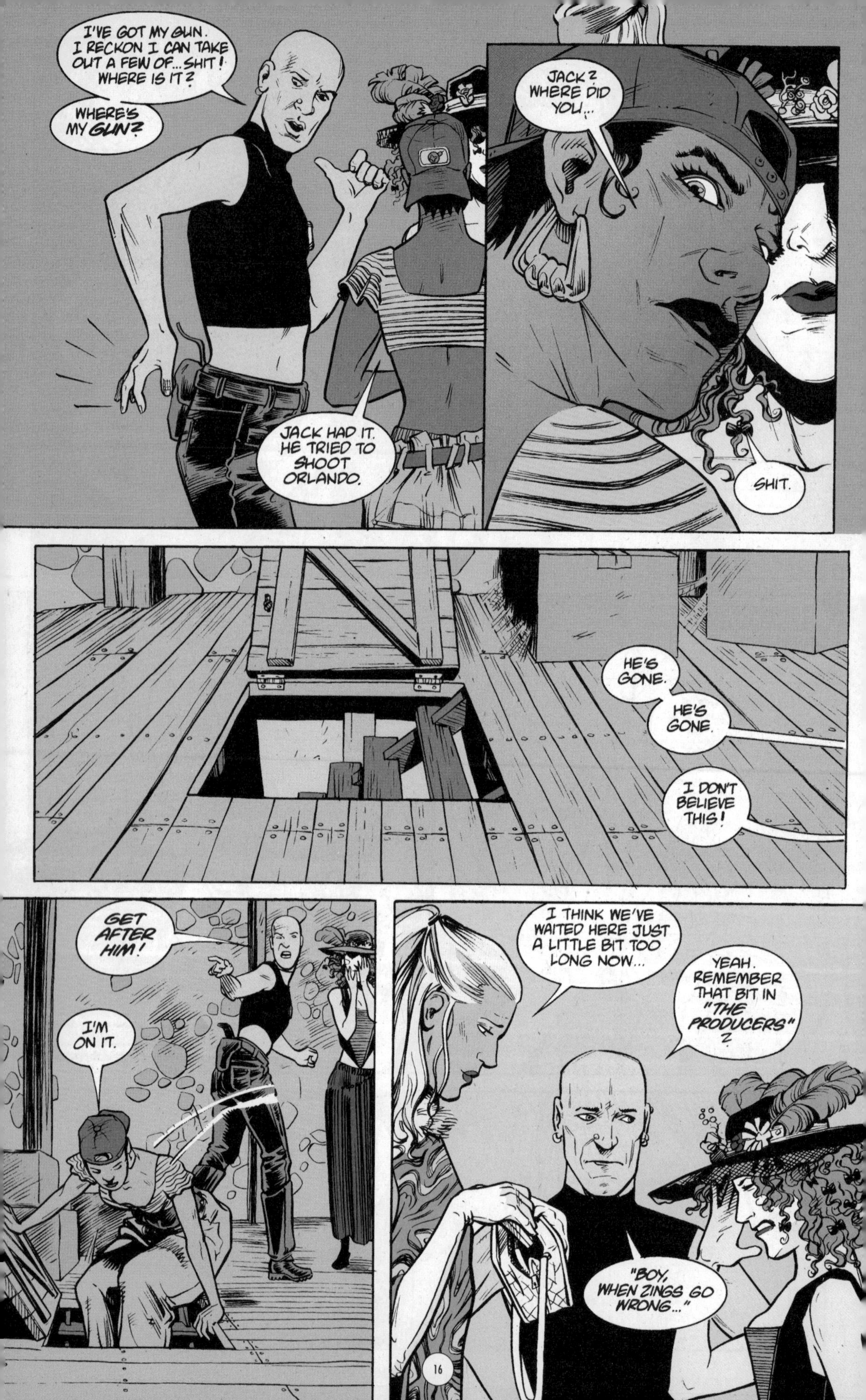
I'VE GOT MY GUN. I RECKON I CAN TAKE OUT A FEW OF... SHIT! WHERE IS IT?
WHERE'S MY GUN?
JACK HAD IT. HE TRIED TO SHOOT ORLANDO.
JACK? WHERE DID YOU...
SHIT.
HE'S GONE.
HE'S GONE.
I DON'T BELIEVE THIS!
GET AFTER HIM!
I'M ON IT.
I THINK WE'VE WAITED HERE JUST A LITTLE BIT TOO LONG NOW...
YEAH. REMEMBER THAT BIT IN "THE PRODUCERS"?
"BOY, WHEN ZINGS GO WRONG..."

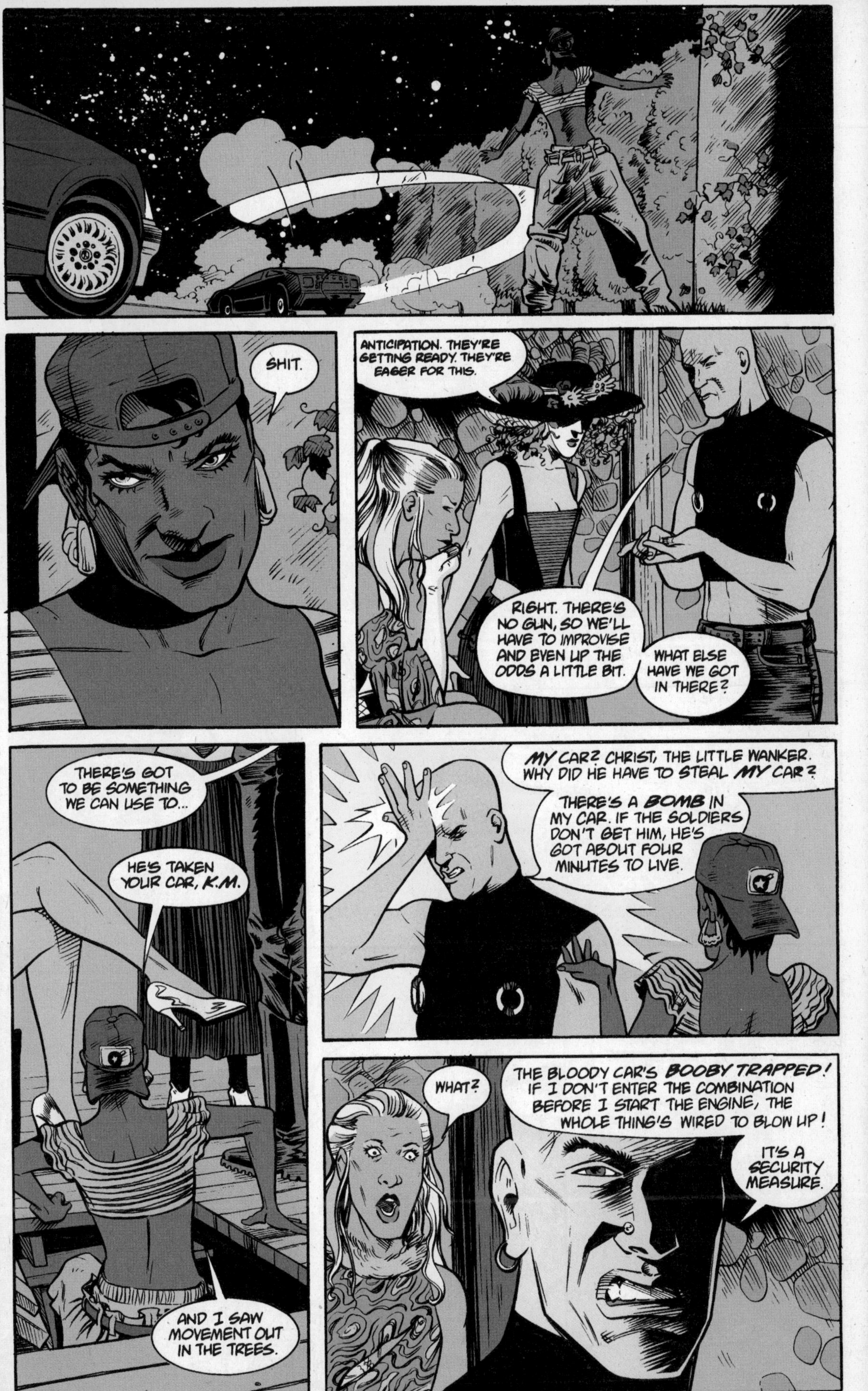
SHIT.
ANTICIPATION. THEY'RE GETTING READY. THEY'RE EAGER FOR THIS.
RIGHT. THERE'S NO GUN, SO WE'LL HAVE TO IMPROVISE AND EVEN UP THE ODDS A LITTLE BIT.
WHAT ELSE HAVE WE GOT IN THERE?
THERE'S GOT TO BE SOMETHING WE CAN USE TO...
HE'S TAKEN YOUR CAR, K.M.
AND I SAW MOVEMENT OUT IN THE TREES.
MY CAR? CHRIST, THE LITTLE WANKER. WHY DID HE HAVE TO STEAL MY CAR?
THERE'S A BOMB IN MY CAR. IF THE SOLDIERS DON'T GET HIM, HE'S GOT ABOUT FOUR MINUTES TO LIVE.
WHAT?
THE BLOODY CAR'S BOOBY TRAPPED! IF I DON'T ENTER THE COMBINATION BEFORE I START THE ENGINE, THE WHOLE THING'S WIRED TO BLOW UP!
IT'S A SECURITY MEASURE.

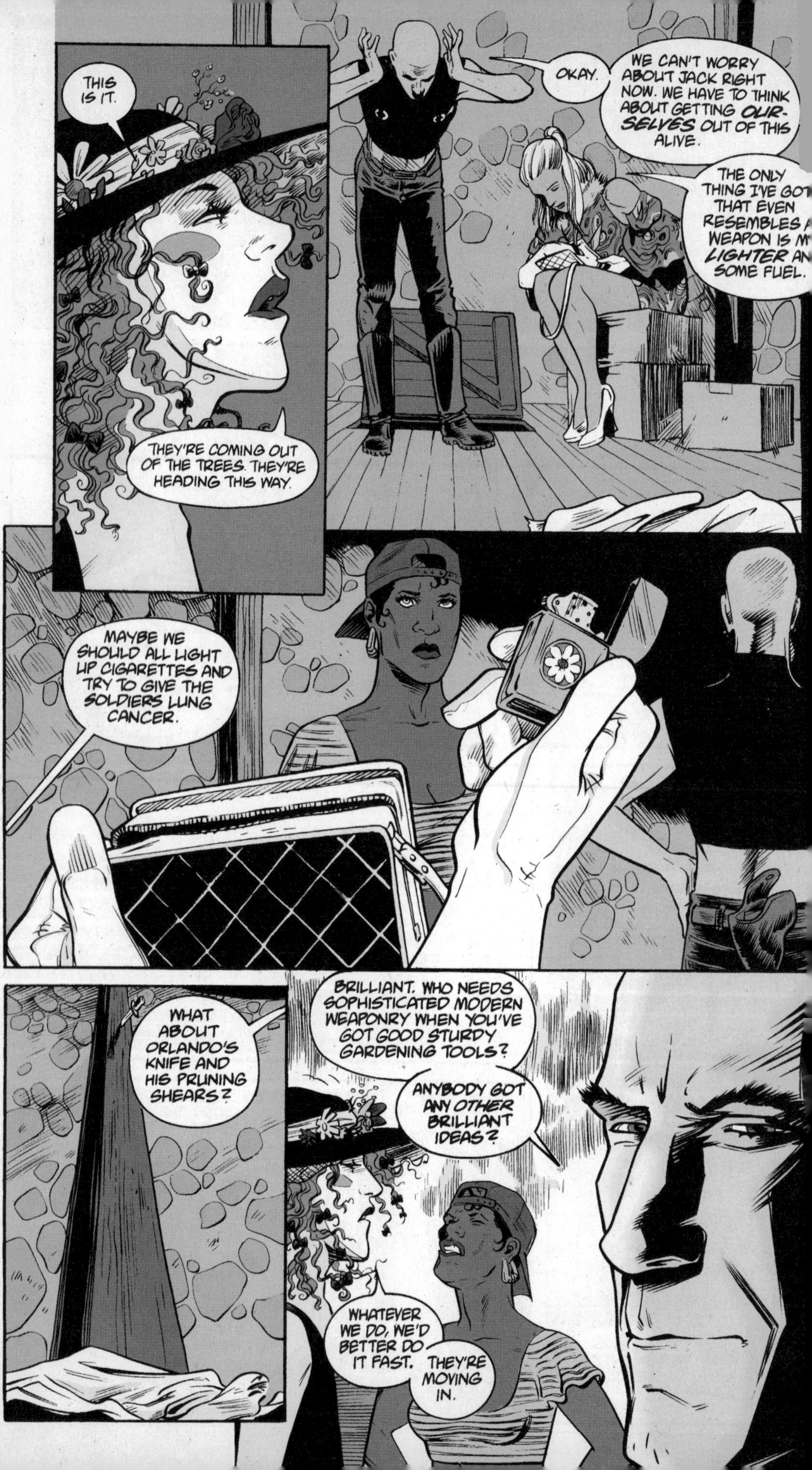
THIS IS IT.
OKAY.
WE CAN'T WORRY ABOUT JACK RIGHT NOW. WE HAVE TO THINK ABOUT GETTING OURSELVES OUT OF THIS ALIVE.
THE ONLY THING I'VE GOT THAT EVEN RESEMBLES A WEAPON IS MY LIGHTER AND SOME FUEL.
THEY'RE COMING OUT OF THE TREES. THEY'RE HEADING THIS WAY.
MAYBE WE SHOULD ALL LIGHT UP CIGARETTES AND TRY TO GIVE THE SOLDIERS LUNG CANCER.
WHAT ABOUT ORLANDO'S KNIFE AND HIS PRUNING SHEARS?
BRILLIANT. WHO NEEDS SOPHISTICATED MODERN WEAPONRY WHEN YOU'VE GOT GOOD STURDY GARDENING TOOLS?
ANYBODY GOT ANY OTHER BRILLIANT IDEAS?
WHATEVER WE DO, WE'D BETTER DO IT FAST.
THEY'RE MOVING IN.

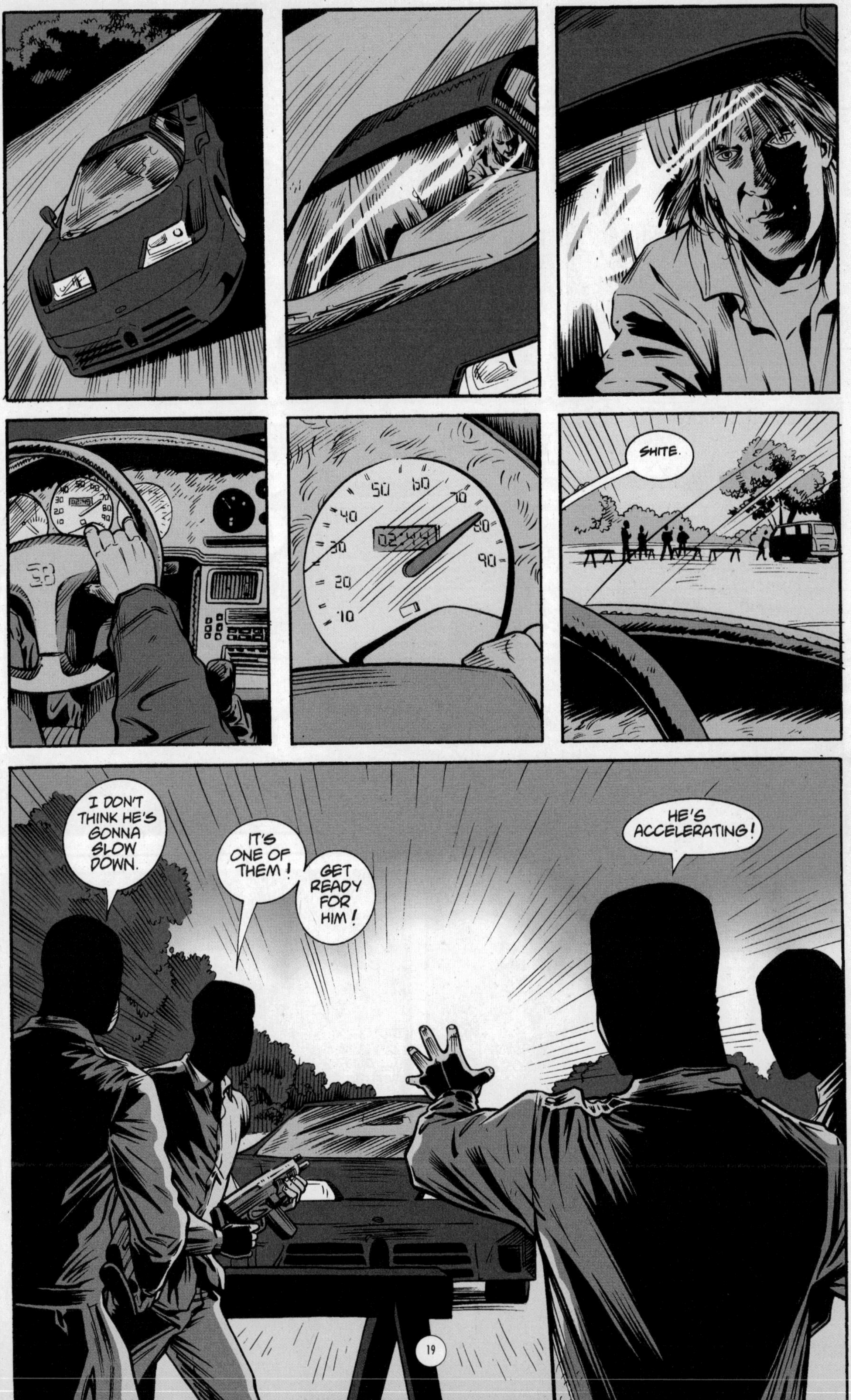
SHITE.
I DON'T THINK HE'S GONNA SLOW DOWN.
IT'S ONE OF THEM!
GET READY FOR HIM!
HE'S ACCELERATING!

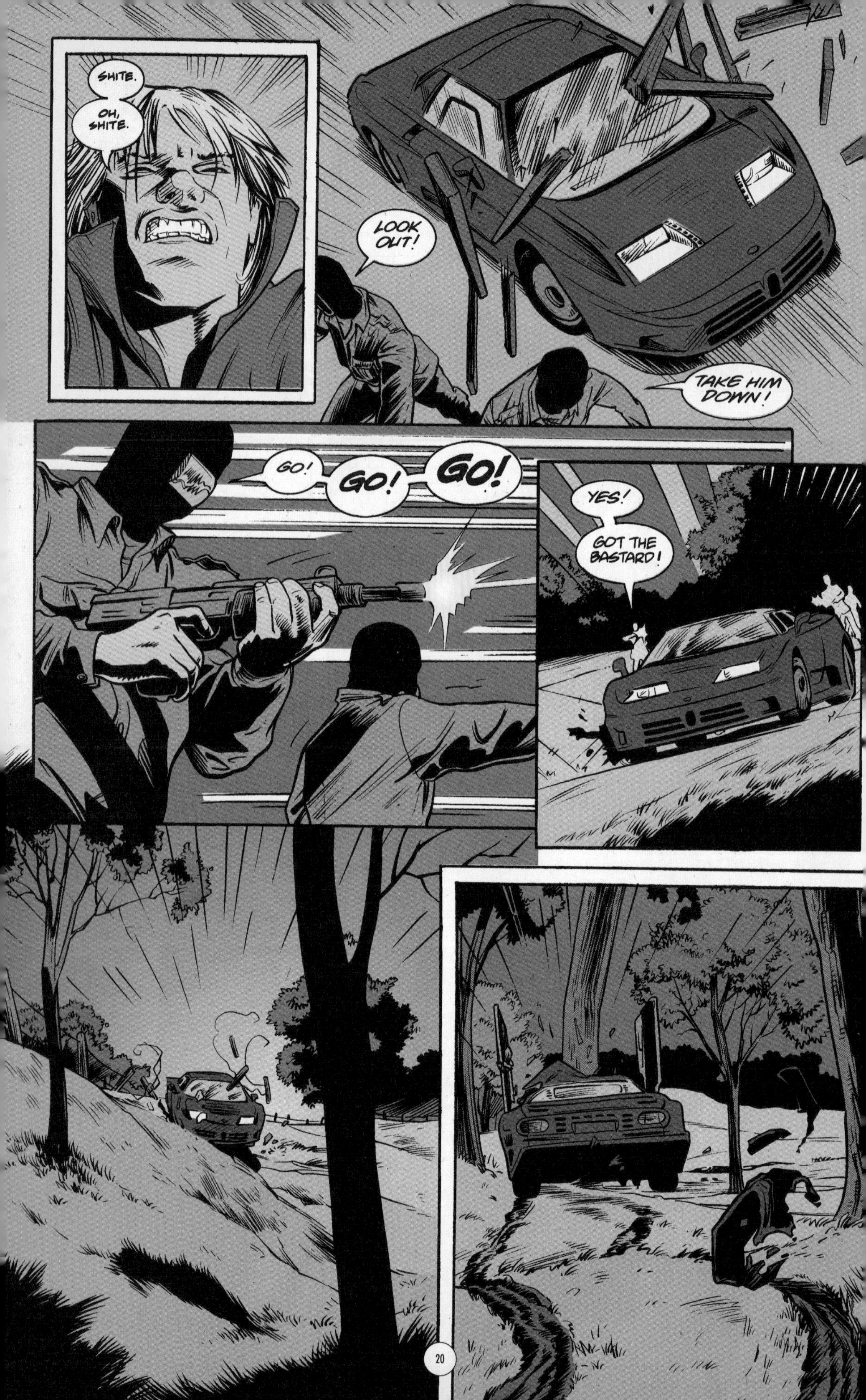
SHITE.
OH, SHITE.
LOOK OUT!
TAKE HIM DOWN!
GO!
GO!
GO!
YES!
GOT THE BASTARD!

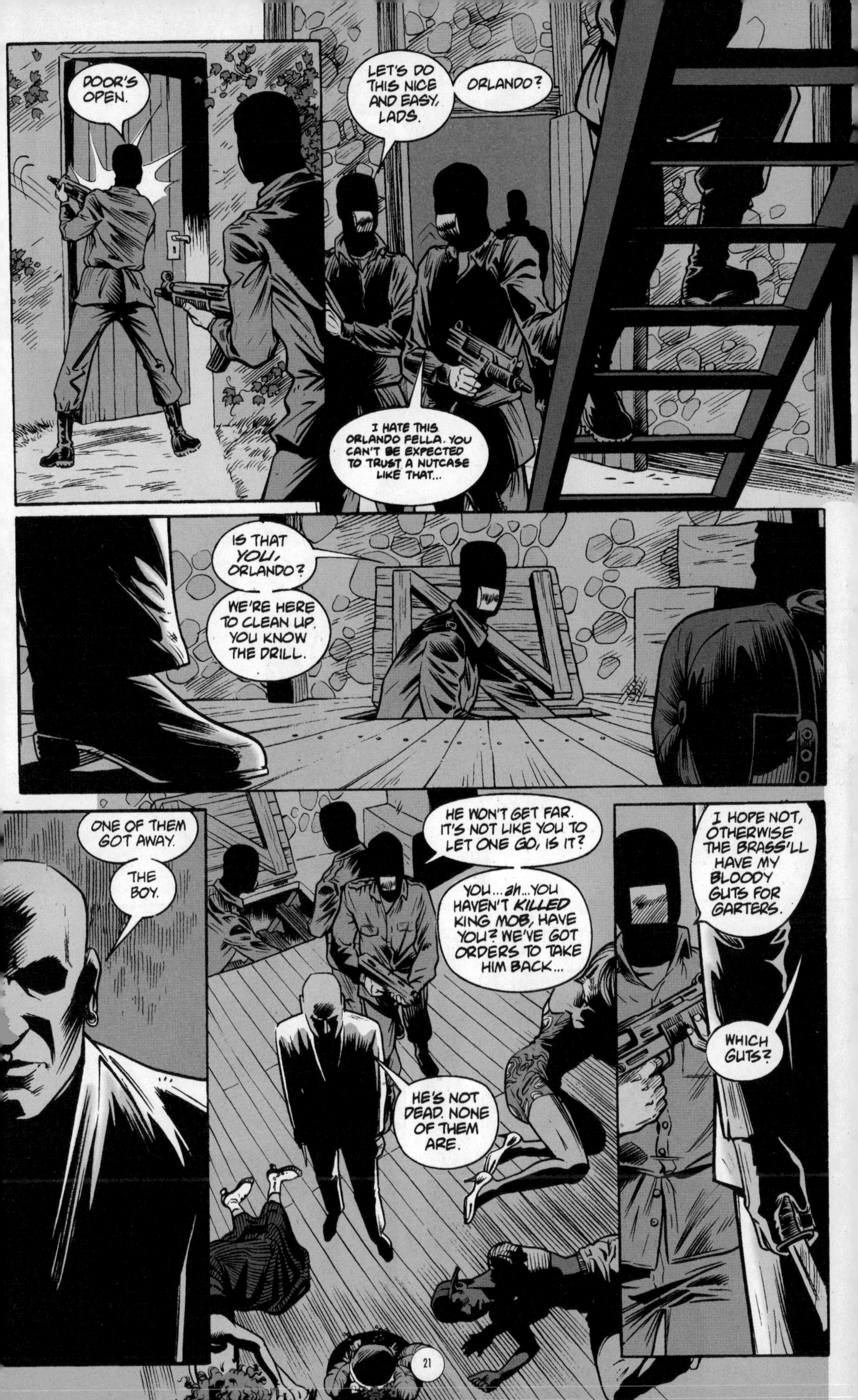
DOOR'S OPEN.
LET'S DO THIS NICE AND EASY, LADS.
ORLANDO?
I HATE THIS ORLANDO FELLA. YOU CAN'T BE EXPECTED TO TRUST A NUTCASE LIKE THAT...
IS THAT YOU, ORLANDO?
WE'RE HERE TO CLEAN UP. YOU KNOW THE DRILL.
ONE OF THEM GOT AWAY.
THE BOY.
HE WON'T GET FAR. IT'S NOT LIKE YOU TO LET ONE GO, IS IT?
YOU...ah...YOU HAVEN'T KILLED KING MOB, HAVE YOU? WE'VE GOT ORDERS TO TAKE HIM BACK...
HE'S NOT DEAD. NONE OF THEM ARE.
I HOPE NOT, OTHERWISE THE BRASS'LL HAVE MY BLOODY GUTS FOR GARTERS.
WHICH GUTS?

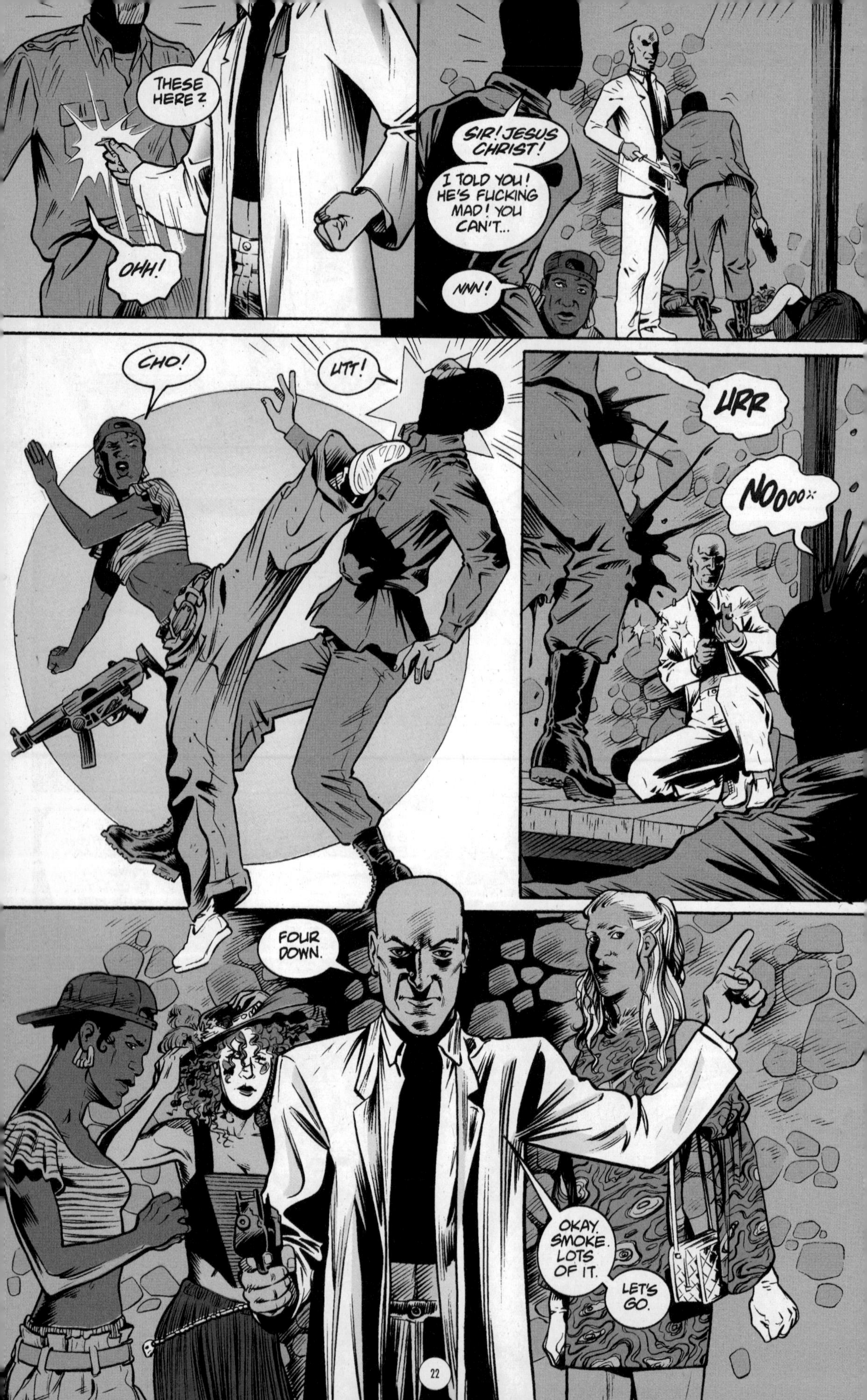
THESE HERE?
OHH!
SIR! JESUS CHRIST!
I TOLD YOU! HE'S FUCKING MAD! YOU CAN'T...
NNN!
CHO!
UTT!
URR
NOOOO
FOUR DOWN.
OKAY. SMOKE. LOTS OF IT.
LET'S GO.

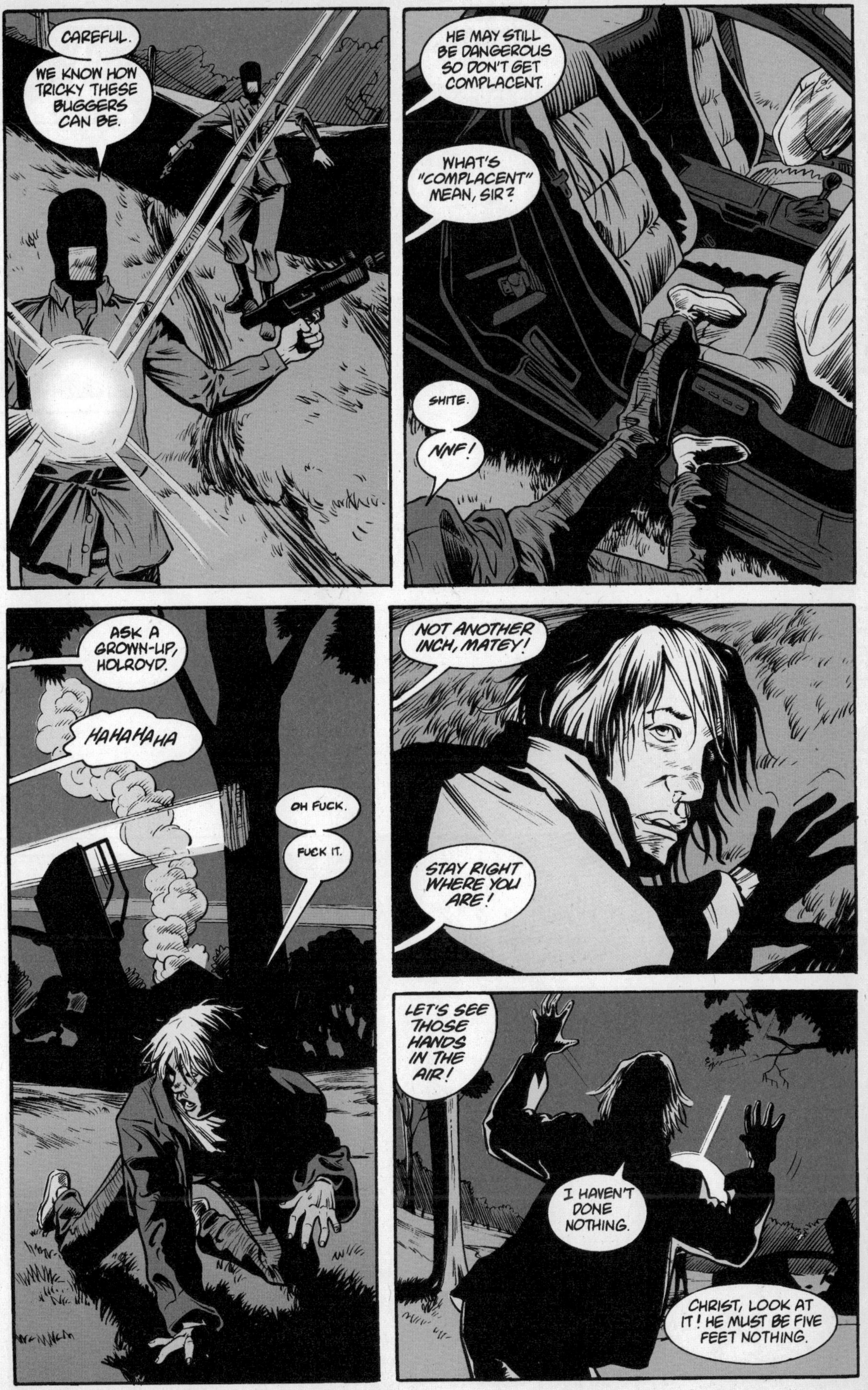
CAREFUL.
WE KNOW HOW TRICKY THESE BUGGERS CAN BE.
HE MAY STILL BE DANGEROUS SO DON'T GET COMPLACENT.
WHAT'S "COMPLACENT" MEAN, SIR?
SHITE.
NNF!
ASK A GROWN-UP, HOLROYD.
HAHAHAHA
OH FUCK.
FUCK IT.
NOT ANOTHER INCH, MATEY!
STAY RIGHT WHERE YOU ARE!
LET'S SEE THOSE HANDS IN THE AIR!
I HAVEN'T DONE NOTHING.
CHRIST, LOOK AT IT! HE MUST BE FIVE FEET NOTHING.

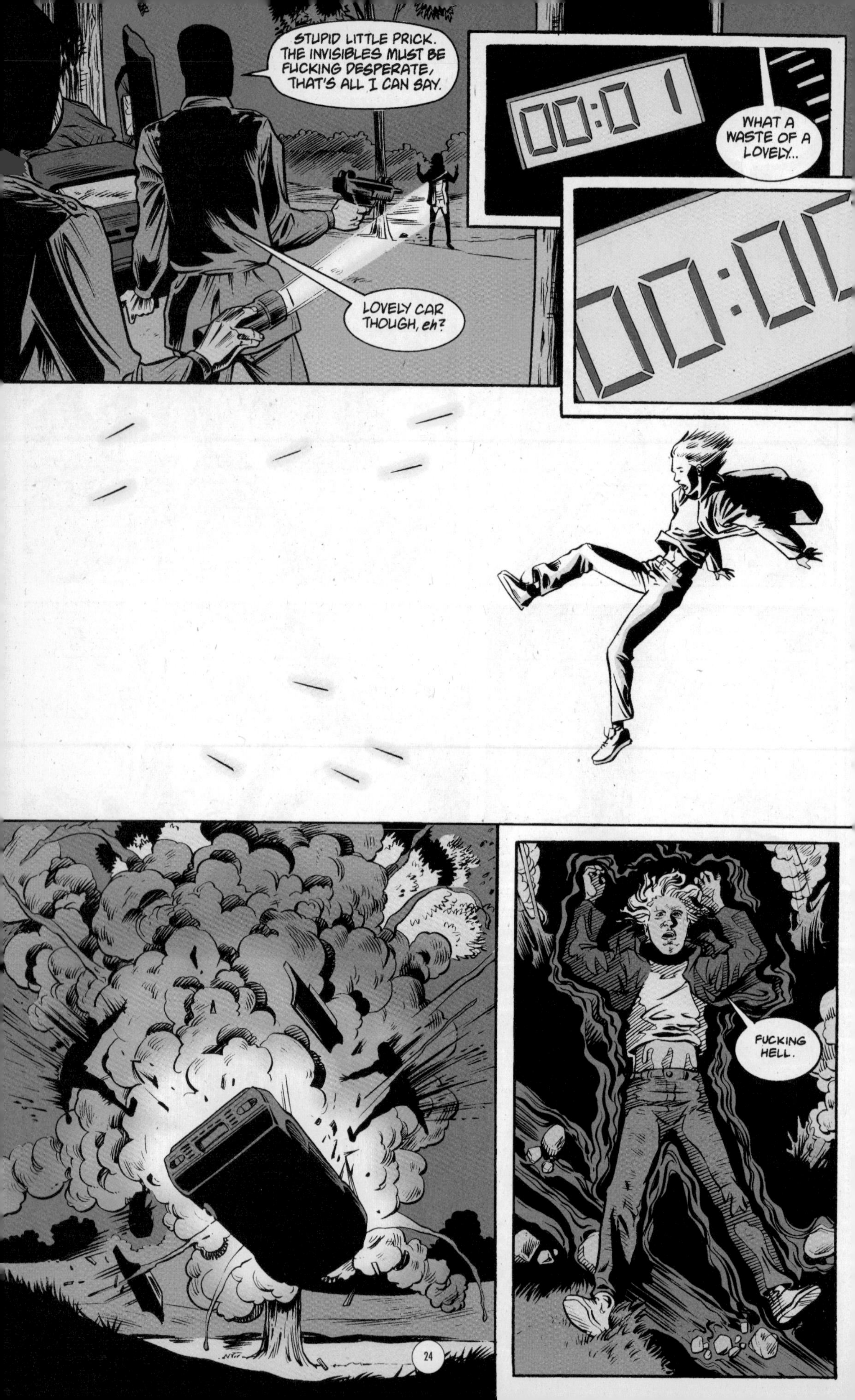
STUPID LITTLE PRICK. THE INVISIBLES MUST BE FUCKING DESPERATE, THAT'S ALL I CAN SAY.
LOVELY CAR THOUGH, eh?
00:01
WHAT A WASTE OF A LOVELY...
00:00
FUCKING HELL.

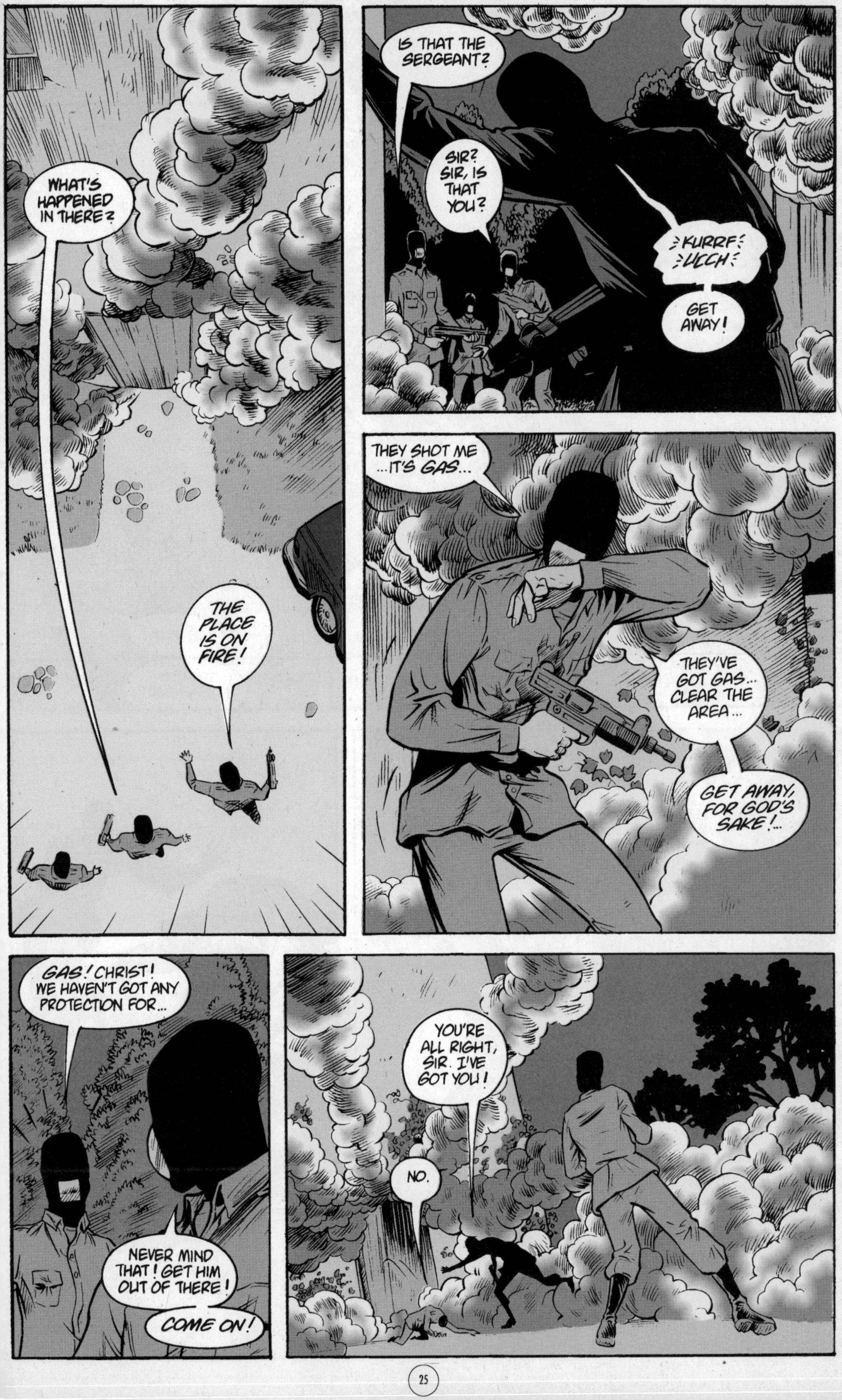
WHAT'S HAPPENED IN THERE?
THE PLACE IS ON FIRE!
IS THAT THE SERGEANT?
SIR? SIR, IS THAT YOU?
KURRF UCCH
GET AWAY!
THEY SHOT ME ...IT'S GAS...
THEY'VE GOT GAS... CLEAR THE AREA...
GET AWAY, FOR GOD'S SAKE!...
GAS! CHRIST! WE HAVEN'T GOT ANY PROTECTION FOR...
NEVER MIND THAT! GET HIM OUT OF THERE!
COME ON!
YOU'RE ALL RIGHT, SIR. I'VE GOT YOU!
NO.

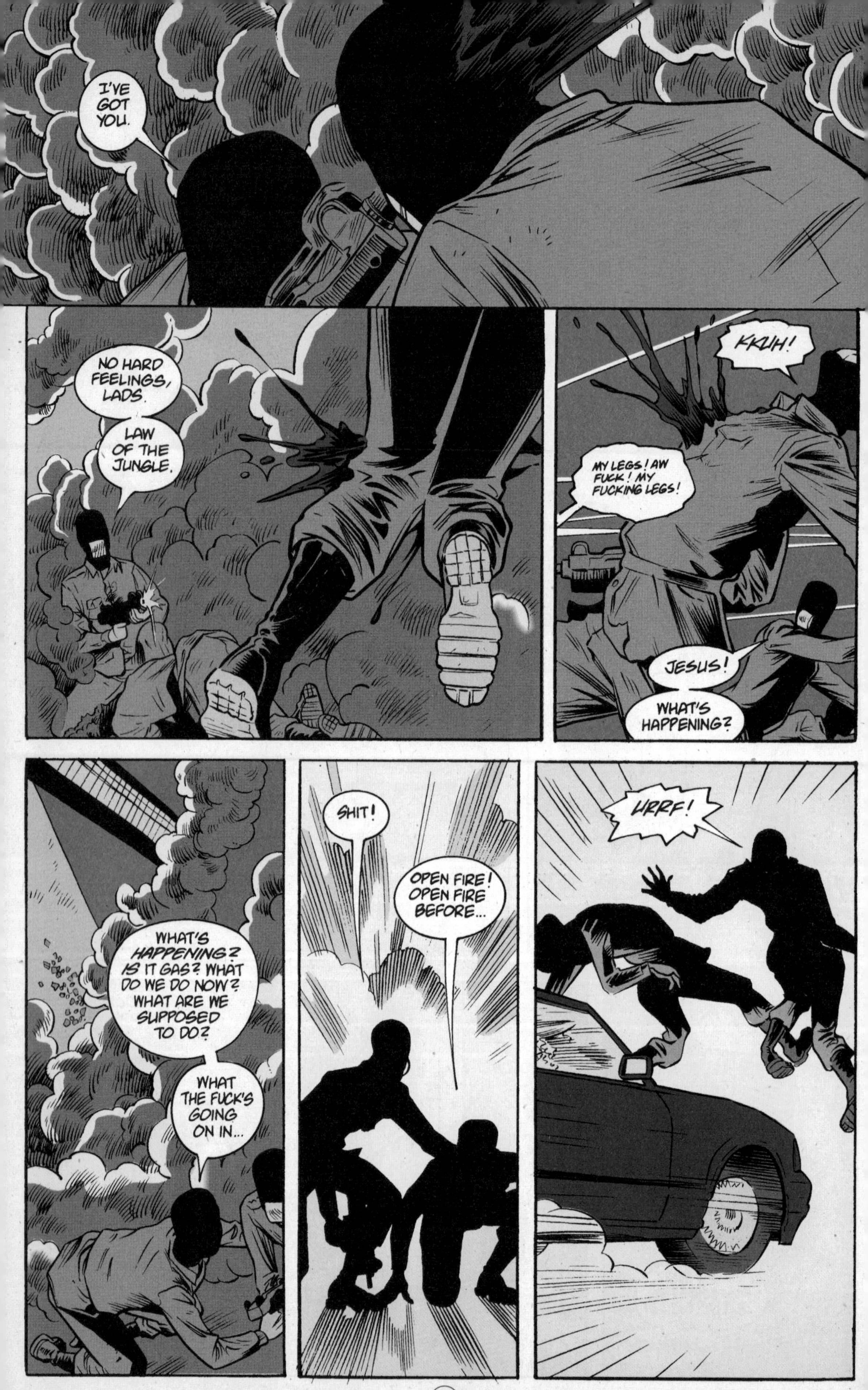
I'VE GOT YOU.
NO HARD FEELINGS, LADS.
LAW OF THE JUNGLE.
KKUH!
MY LEGS! AW FUCK! MY FUCKING LEGS!
JESUS!
WHAT'S HAPPENING?
WHAT'S HAPPENING? IS IT GAS? WHAT DO WE DO NOW? WHAT ARE WE SUPPOSED TO DO?
WHAT THE FUCK'S GOING ON IN...
SHIT!
OPEN FIRE! OPEN FIRE BEFORE...
URRF!

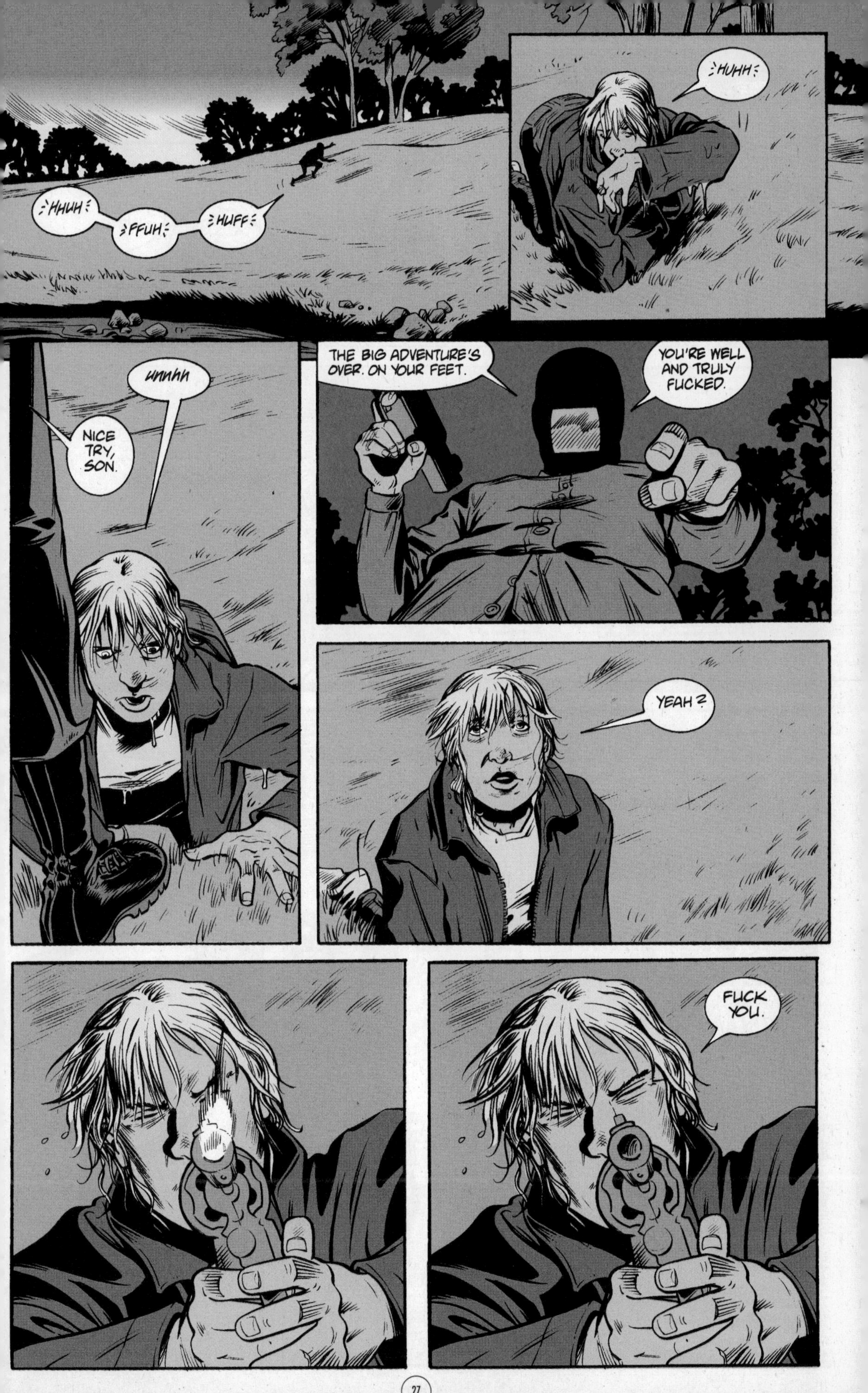
HHUH
FFUH
HUFF
HUHH
unnhh
NICE TRY, SON.
THE BIG ADVENTURE'S OVER. ON YOUR FEET.
YOU'RE WELL AND TRULY FUCKED.
YEAH?
FUCK YOU.

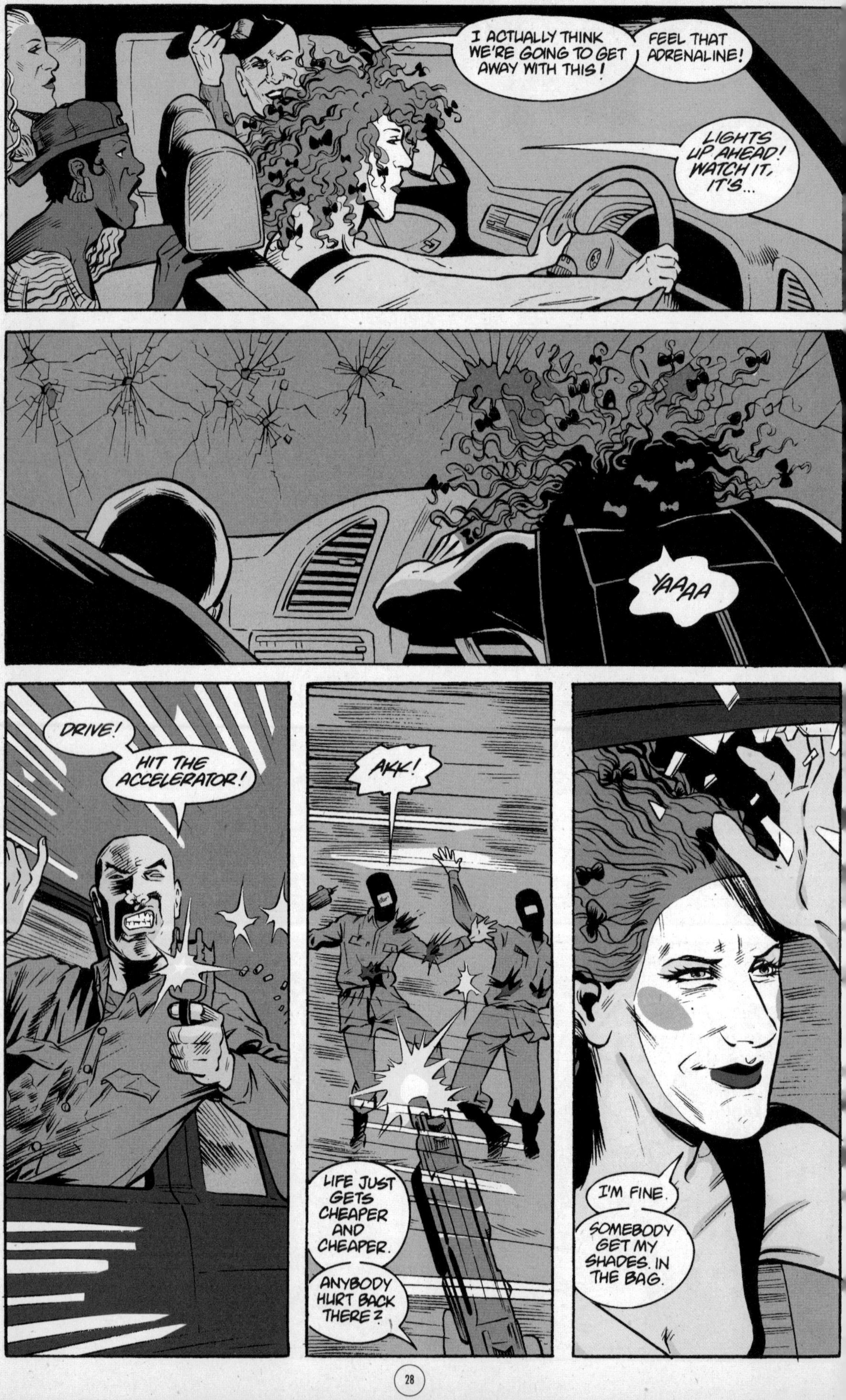
I ACTUALLY THINK WE'RE GOING TO GET AWAY WITH THIS!
FEEL THAT ADRENALINE!
LIGHTS UP AHEAD! WATCH IT, IT'S...
YAAAA
DRIVE!
HIT THE ACCELERATOR!
AKK!
LIFE JUST GETS CHEAPER AND CHEAPER.
ANYBODY HURT BACK THERE?
I'M FINE.
SOMEBODY GET MY SHADES. IN THE BAG.

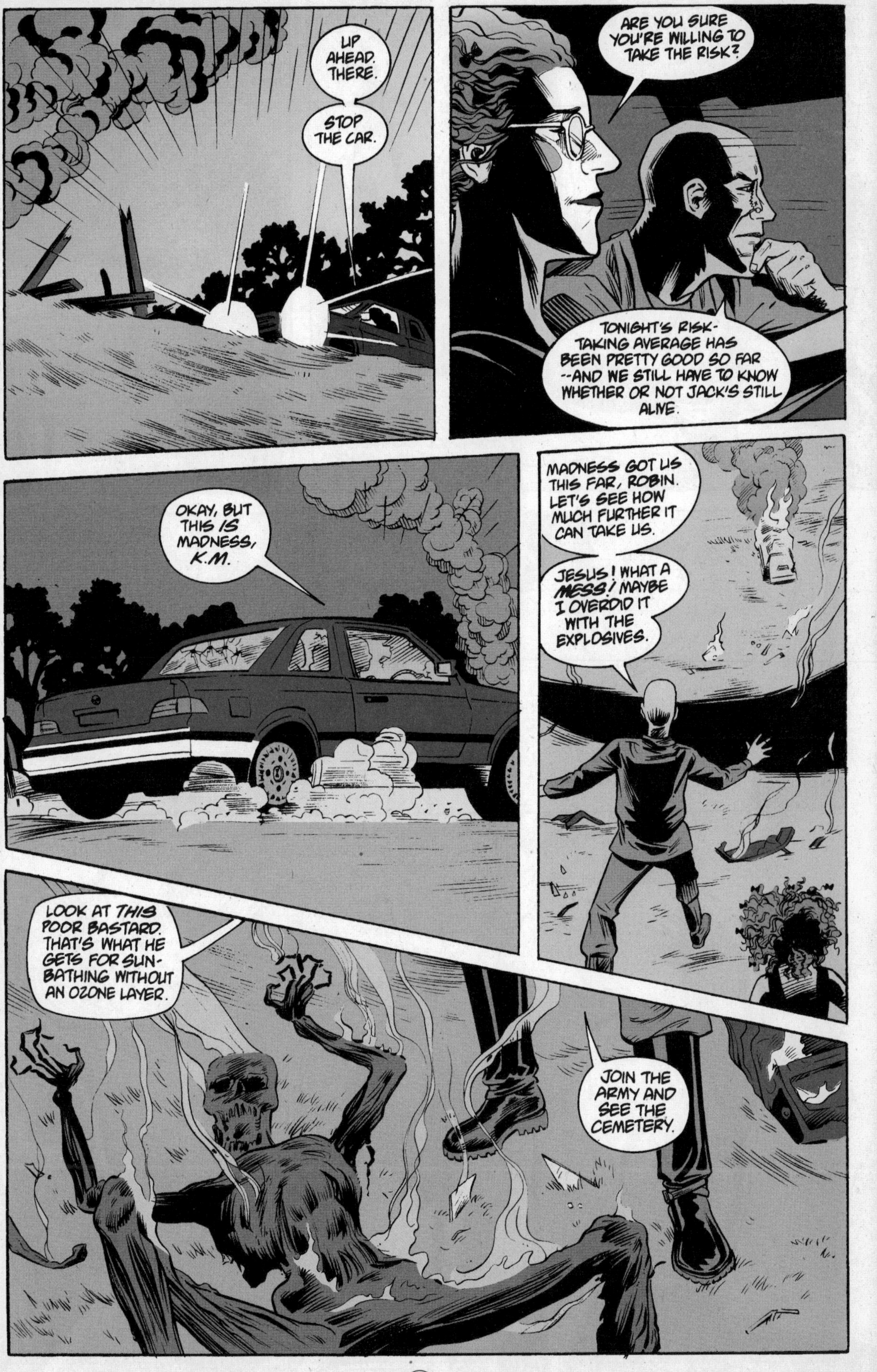
UP AHEAD. THERE.
STOP THE CAR.
ARE YOU SURE YOU'RE WILLING TO TAKE THE RISK?
TONIGHT'S RISK-TAKING AVERAGE HAS BEEN PRETTY GOOD SO FAR --AND WE STILL HAVE TO KNOW WHETHER OR NOT JACK'S STILL ALIVE.
OKAY, BUT THIS *IS* MADNESS, K.M.
MADNESS GOT US THIS FAR, ROBIN. LET'S SEE HOW MUCH FURTHER IT CAN TAKE US.
JESUS! WHAT A *MESS!* MAYBE I OVERDID IT WITH THE EXPLOSIVES.
LOOK AT *THIS* POOR BASTARD. THAT'S WHAT HE GETS FOR SUN-BATHING WITHOUT AN OZONE LAYER.
JOIN THE ARMY AND SEE THE CEMETERY.

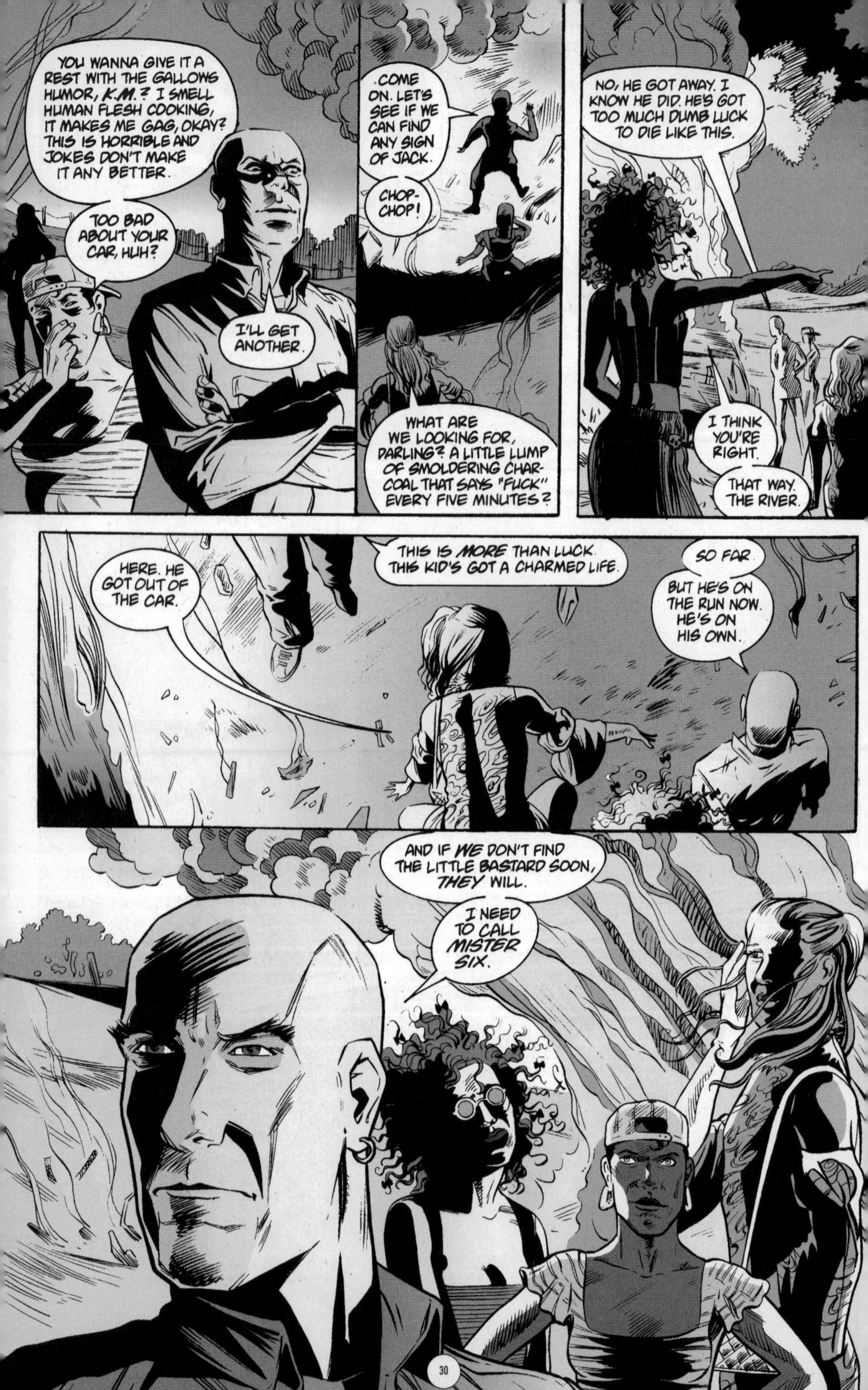

YOU WANNA GIVE IT A REST WITH THE GALLOWS HUMOR, K.M.? I SMELL HUMAN FLESH COOKING, IT MAKES ME GAG, OKAY? THIS IS HORRIBLE AND JOKES DON'T MAKE IT ANY BETTER.
TOO BAD ABOUT YOUR CAR, HUH?
I'LL GET ANOTHER.
COME ON. LET'S SEE IF WE CAN FIND ANY SIGN OF JACK.
CHOP-CHOP!
WHAT ARE WE LOOKING FOR, DARLING? A LITTLE LUMP OF SMOLDERING CHARCOAL THAT SAYS "FUCK" EVERY FIVE MINUTES?
NO, HE GOT AWAY. I KNOW HE DID. HE'S GOT TOO MUCH DUMB LUCK TO DIE LIKE THIS.
I THINK YOU'RE RIGHT.
THAT WAY. THE RIVER.
HERE. HE GOT OUT OF THE CAR.
THIS IS MORE THAN LUCK. THIS KID'S GOT A CHARMED LIFE.
SO FAR.
BUT HE'S ON THE RUN NOW. HE'S ON HIS OWN.
AND IF WE DON'T FIND THE LITTLE BASTARD SOON, THEY WILL.
I NEED TO CALL MISTER SIX.

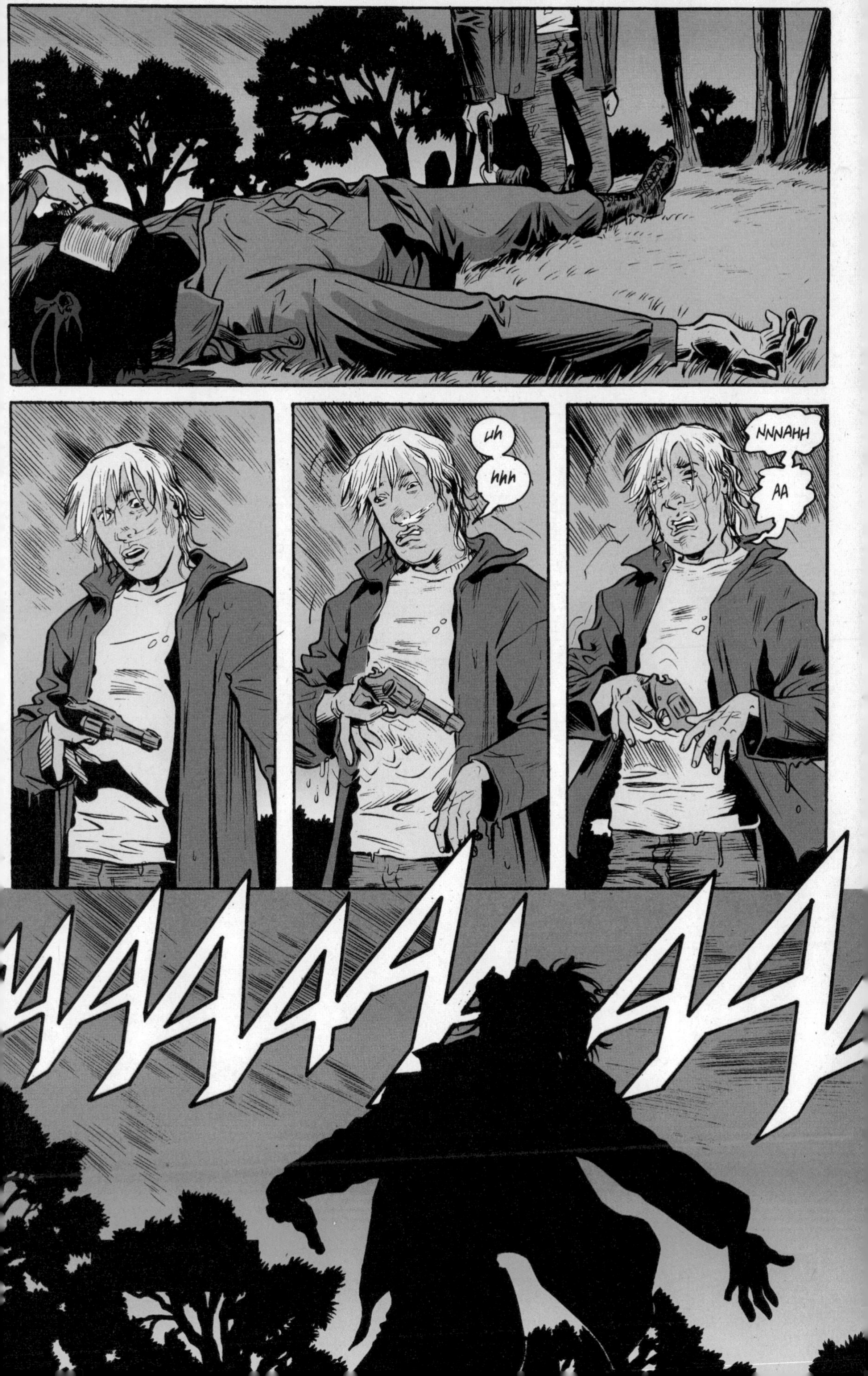
uh
hhh
NNNAHH
AA
AAAAAA AAAA

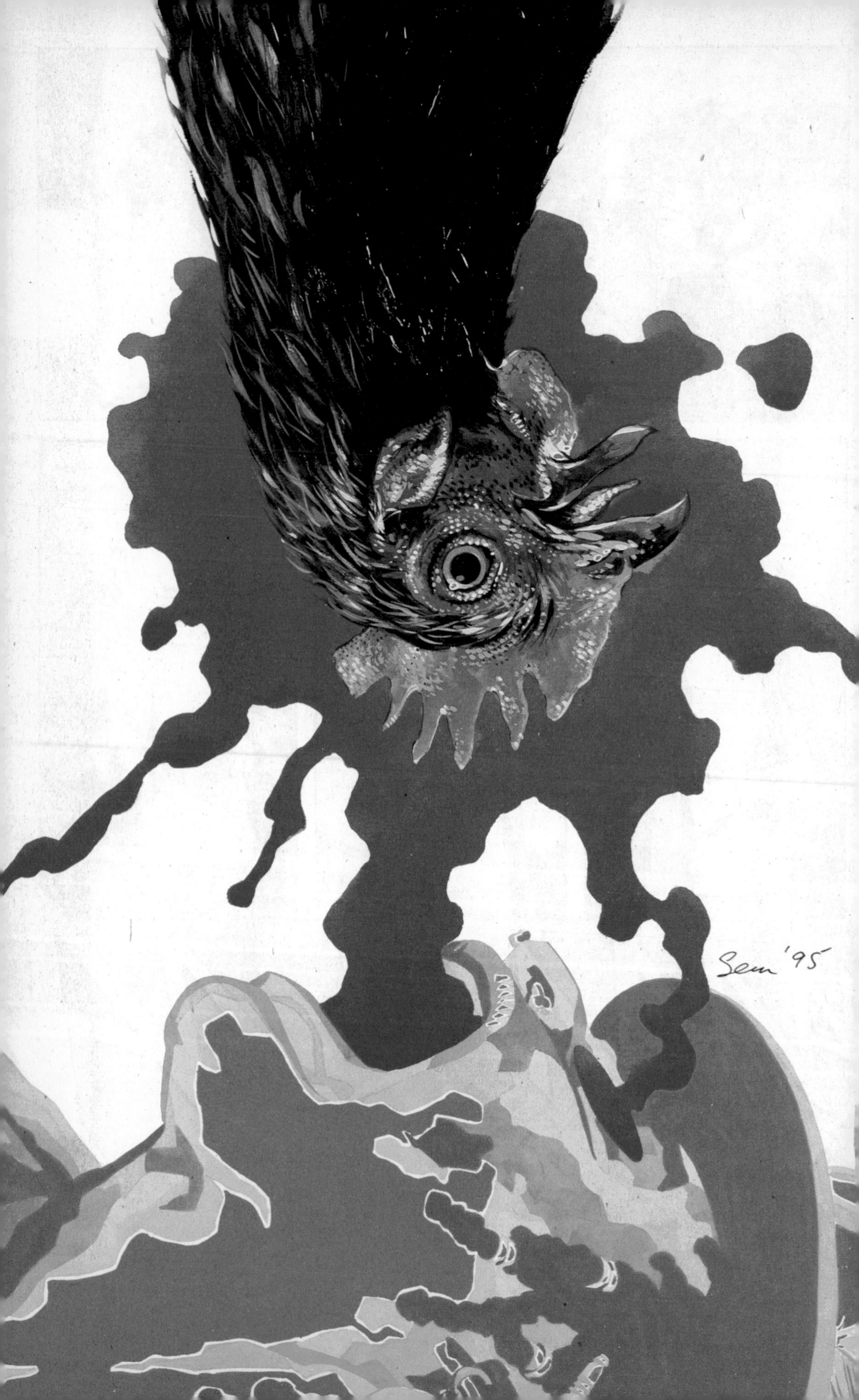
Sem '95

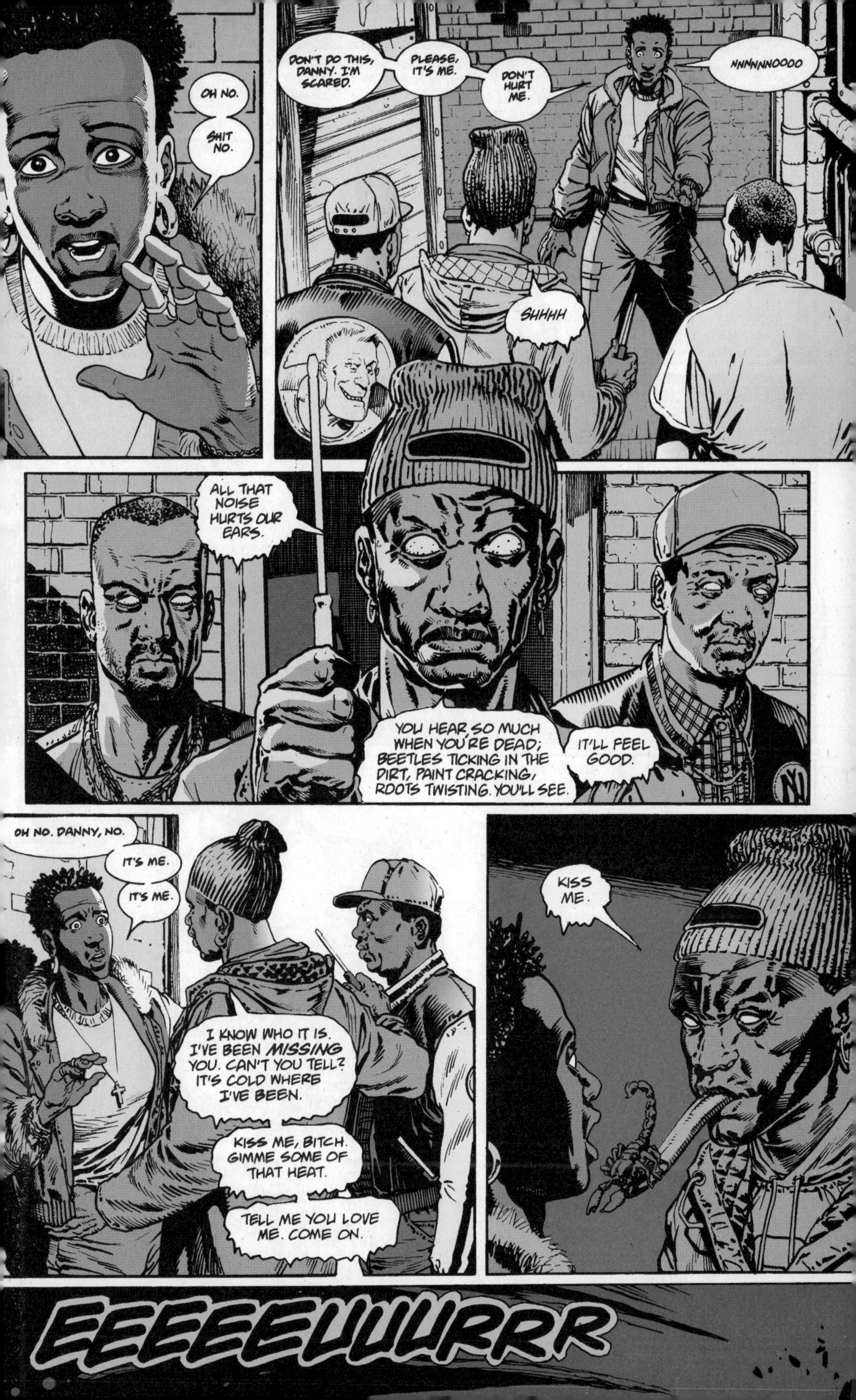
OH NO.
SHIT NO.
DON'T DO THIS, DANNY. I'M SCARED.
PLEASE, IT'S ME.
DON'T HURT ME.
NNNNNNOOOO
SHHHH
ALL THAT NOISE HURTS OUR EARS.
YOU HEAR SO MUCH WHEN YOU'RE DEAD; BEETLES TICKING IN THE DIRT, PAINT CRACKING, ROOTS TWISTING. YOU'LL SEE.
IT'LL FEEL GOOD.
OH NO. DANNY, NO.
IT'S ME.
IT'S ME.
I KNOW WHO IT IS. I'VE BEEN MISSING YOU. CAN'T YOU TELL? IT'S COLD WHERE I'VE BEEN.
KISS ME, BITCH. GIMME SOME OF THAT HEAT.
TELL ME YOU LOVE ME. COME ON.
KISS ME.
EEEEEUUURRR

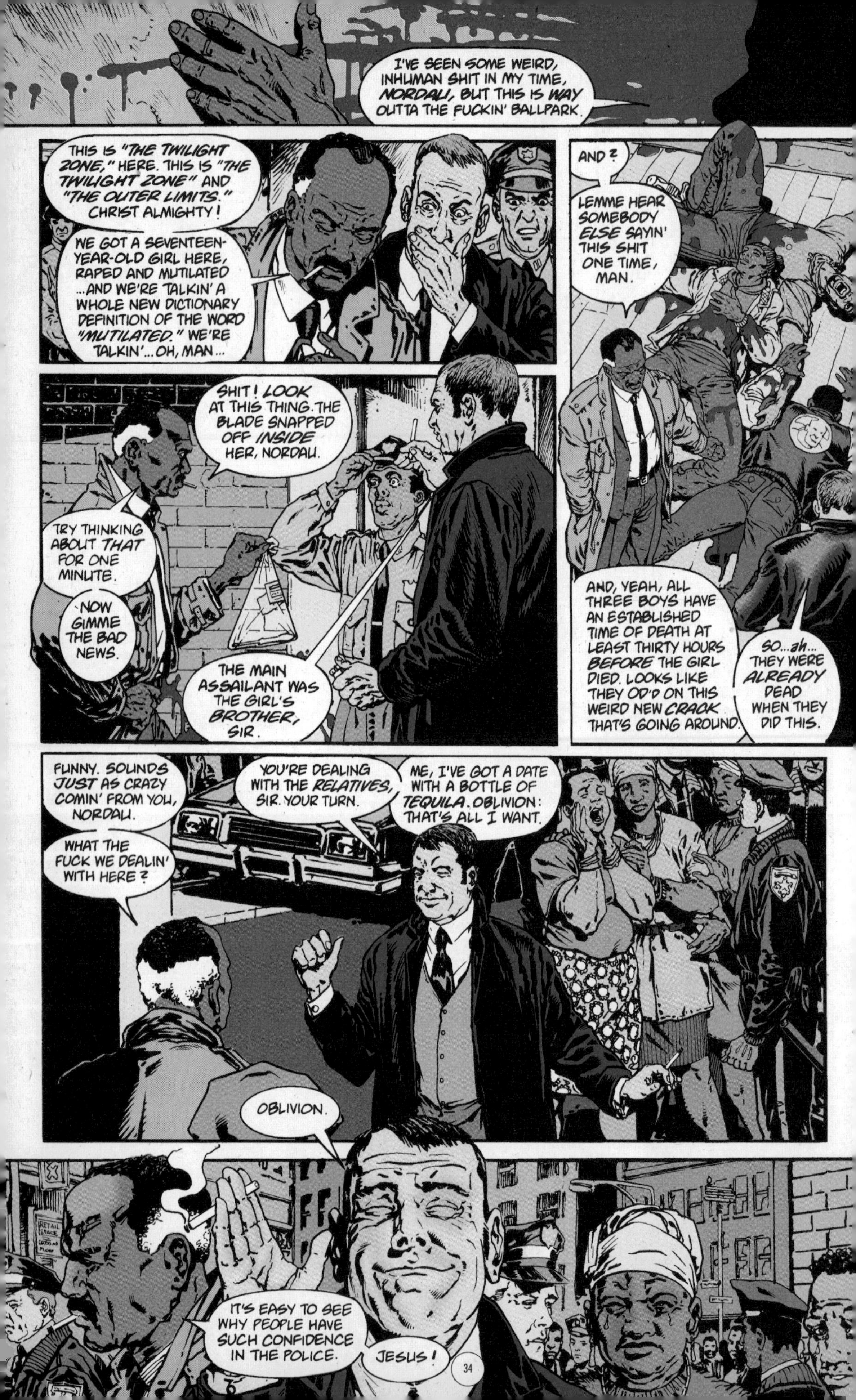
I'VE SEEN SOME WEIRD, INHUMAN SHIT IN MY TIME, NORDAU, BUT THIS IS WAY OUTTA THE FUCKIN' BALLPARK.
THIS IS "THE TWILIGHT ZONE," HERE. THIS IS "THE TWILIGHT ZONE" AND "THE OUTER LIMITS." CHRIST ALMIGHTY!
WE GOT A SEVENTEEN-YEAR-OLD GIRL HERE, RAPED AND MUTILATED ...AND WE'RE TALKIN' A WHOLE NEW DICTIONARY DEFINITION OF THE WORD "MUTILATED." WE'RE TALKIN'...OH, MAN...
AND?
LEMME HEAR SOMEBODY ELSE SAYIN' THIS SHIT ONE TIME, MAN.
AND, YEAH, ALL THREE BOYS HAVE AN ESTABLISHED TIME OF DEATH AT LEAST THIRTY HOURS BEFORE THE GIRL DIED. LOOKS LIKE THEY OD'D ON THIS WEIRD NEW CRACK THAT'S GOING AROUND.
SO...ah... THEY WERE ALREADY DEAD WHEN THEY DID THIS.
SHIT! LOOK AT THIS THING. THE BLADE SNAPPED OFF INSIDE HER, NORDAU.
TRY THINKING ABOUT THAT FOR ONE MINUTE.
NOW GIMME THE BAD NEWS.
THE MAIN ASSAILANT WAS THE GIRL'S BROTHER, SIR.
FUNNY. SOUNDS JUST AS CRAZY COMIN' FROM YOU, NORDAU.
WHAT THE FUCK WE DEALIN' WITH HERE?
YOU'RE DEALING WITH THE RELATIVES, SIR. YOUR TURN.
ME, I'VE GOT A DATE WITH A BOTTLE OF TEQUILA. OBLIVION: THAT'S ALL I WANT.
OBLIVION.
IT'S EASY TO SEE WHY PEOPLE HAVE SUCH CONFIDENCE IN THE POLICE.
JESUS!

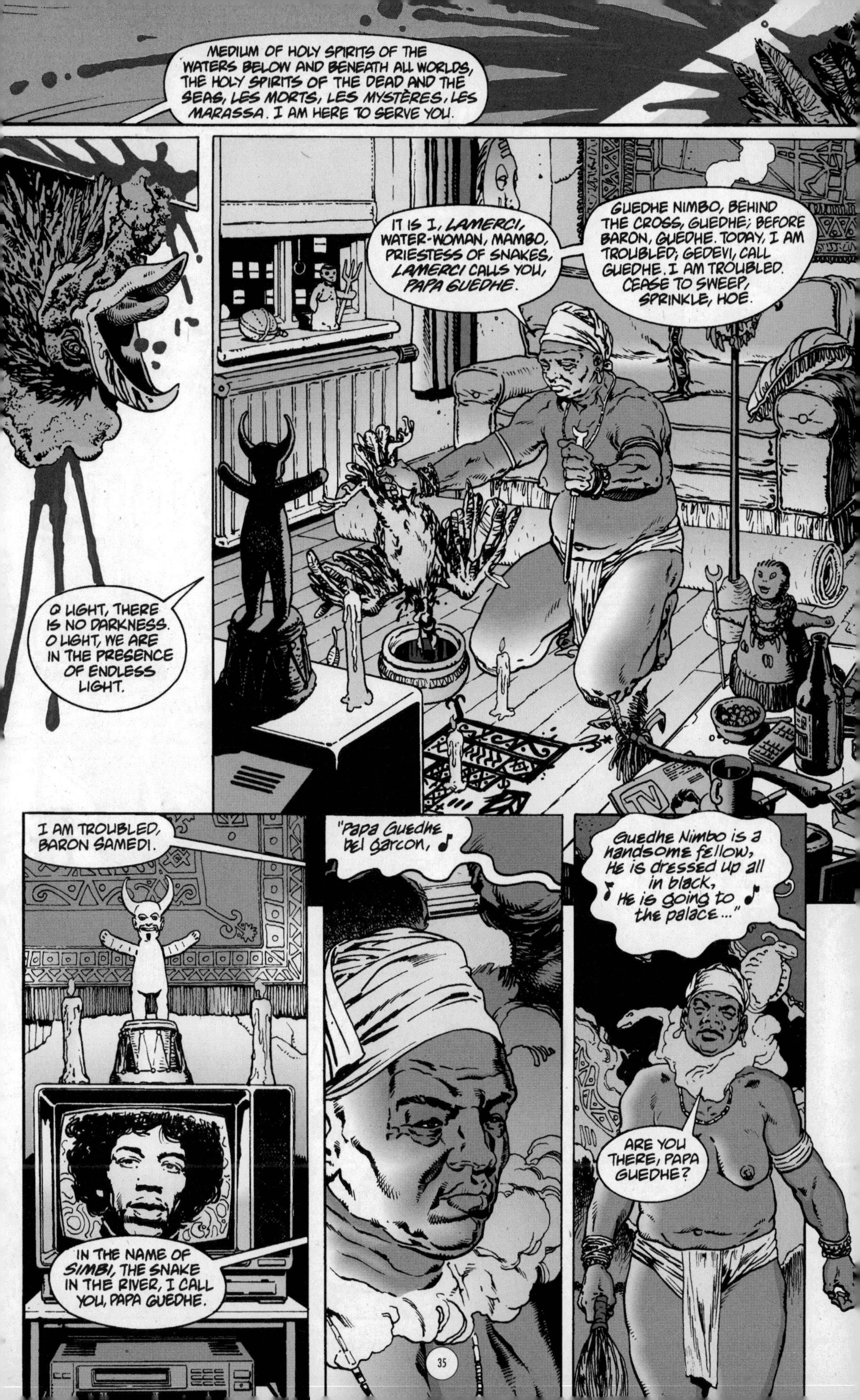

MEDIUM OF HOLY SPIRITS OF THE WATERS BELOW AND BENEATH ALL WORLDS, THE HOLY SPIRITS OF THE DEAD AND THE SEAS, LES MORTS, LES MYSTÈRES, LES MARASSA. I AM HERE TO SERVE YOU.
O LIGHT, THERE IS NO DARKNESS. O LIGHT, WE ARE IN THE PRESENCE OF ENDLESS LIGHT.
IT IS I, LAMERCI, WATER-WOMAN, MAMBO, PRIESTESS OF SNAKES, LAMERCI CALLS YOU, PAPA GUEDHE.
GUEDHE NIMBO, BEHIND THE CROSS, GUEDHE; BEFORE BARON, GUEDHE. TODAY, I AM TROUBLED; GEDEVI, CALL GUEDHE. I AM TROUBLED. CEASE TO SWEEP, SPRINKLE, HOE.
I AM TROUBLED, BARON SAMEDI.
IN THE NAME OF SIMBI, THE SNAKE IN THE RIVER, I CALL YOU, PAPA GUEDHE.
"Papa Guedhe bel garcon,
Guedhe Nimbo is a handsome fellow, He is dressed up all in black, He is going to the palace..."
ARE YOU THERE, PAPA GUEDHE?

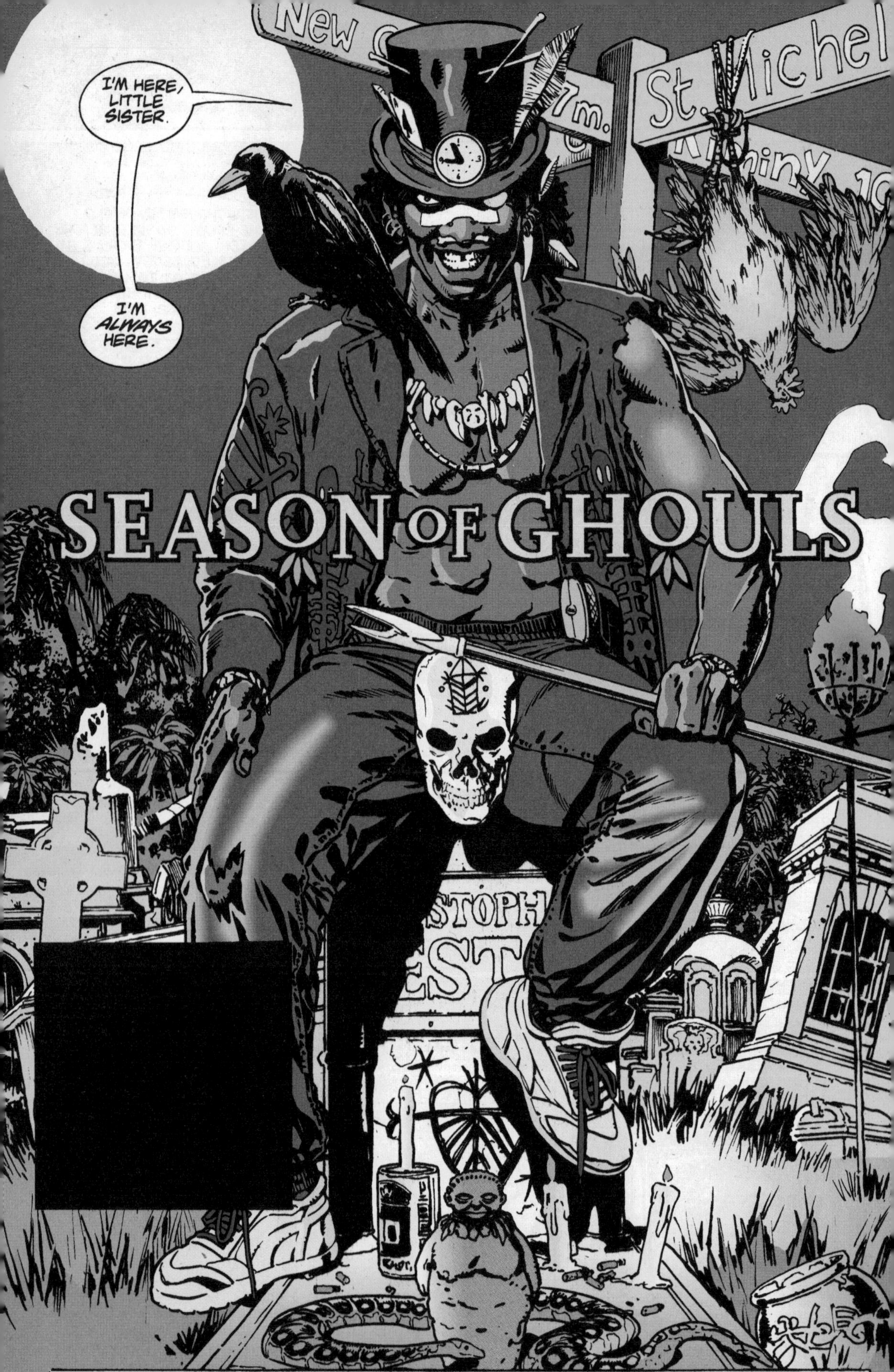
I'M HERE, LITTLE SISTER.
I'M ALWAYS HERE.
SEASON OF GHOULS

GRANT MORRISON writer • CHRIS WESTON artist
DANIEL VOZZO colorist • CLEM ROBINS letterer • JULIE ROTTENBERG associate editor • STUART MOORE editor
The Invisibles created by GRANT MORRISON

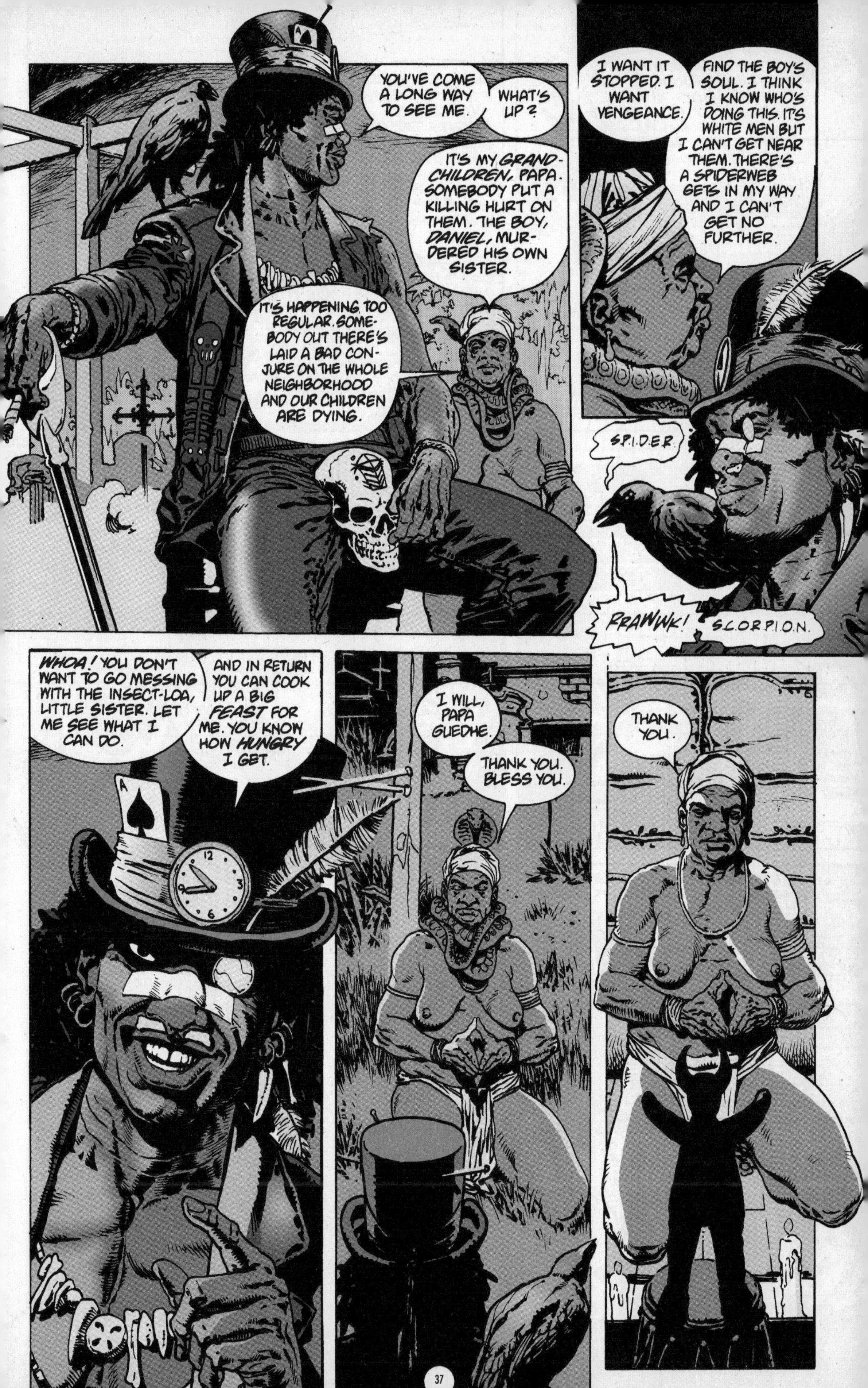

YOU'VE COME A LONG WAY TO SEE ME.
WHAT'S UP?
IT'S MY GRAND-CHILDREN, PAPA. SOMEBODY PUT A KILLING HURT ON THEM. THE BOY, DANIEL, MUR-DERED HIS OWN SISTER.
IT'S HAPPENING TOO REGULAR. SOME-BODY OUT THERE'S LAID A BAD CON-JURE ON THE WHOLE NEIGHBORHOOD AND OUR CHILDREN ARE DYING.
I WANT IT STOPPED. I WANT VENGEANCE.
FIND THE BOY'S SOUL. I THINK I KNOW WHO'S DOING THIS. IT'S WHITE MEN BUT I CAN'T GET NEAR THEM. THERE'S A SPIDERWEB GETS IN MY WAY AND I CAN'T GET NO FURTHER.
S.P.I.D.E.R.
RRAWWK!
S.C.O.R.P.I.O.N.
WHOA! YOU DON'T WANT TO GO MESSING WITH THE INSECT-LOA, LITTLE SISTER. LET ME SEE WHAT I CAN DO.
AND IN RETURN YOU CAN COOK UP A BIG FEAST FOR ME. YOU KNOW HOW HUNGRY I GET.
I WILL, PAPA GUEDHE.
THANK YOU. BLESS YOU.
THANK YOU.

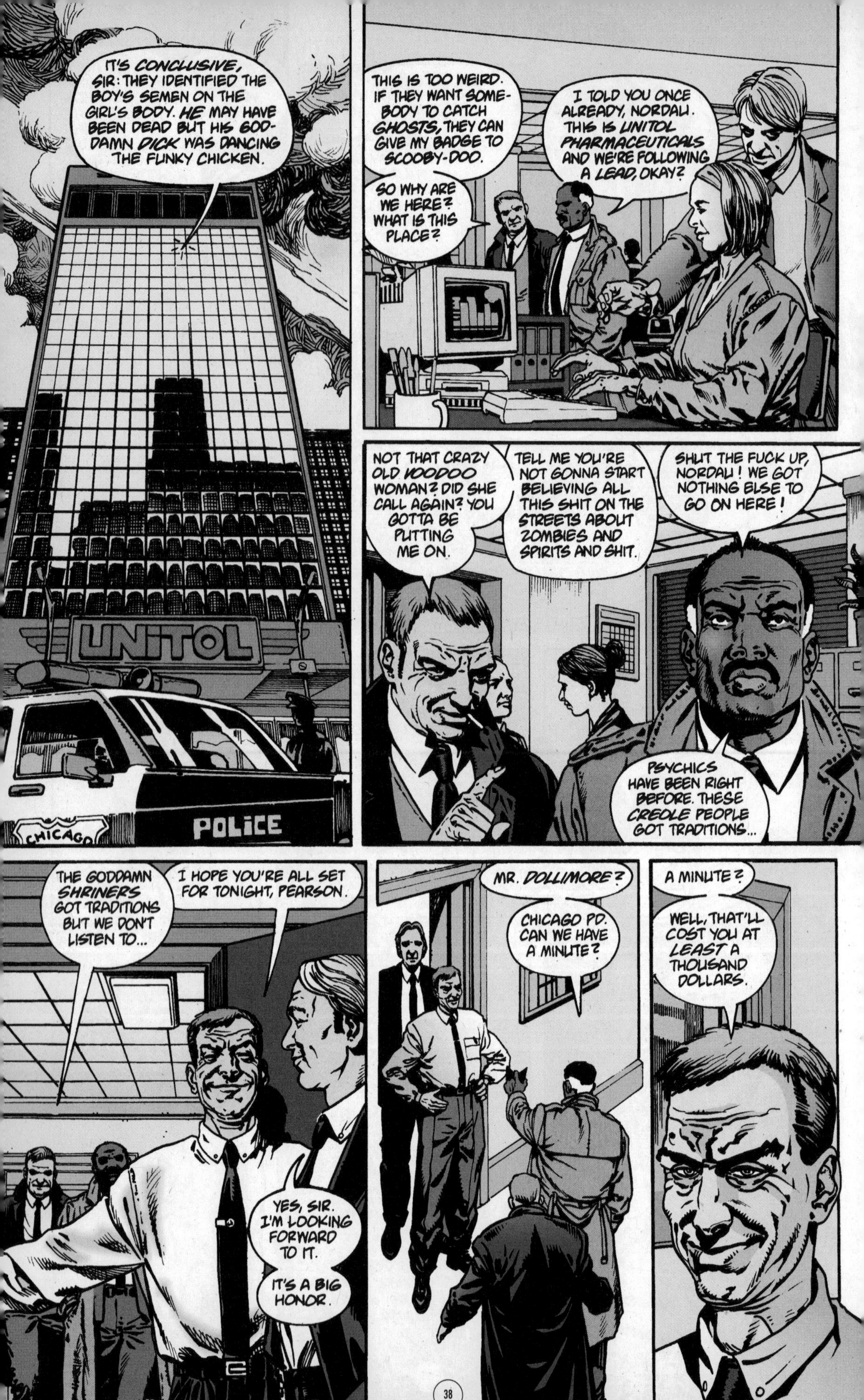
IT'S CONCLUSIVE, SIR: THEY IDENTIFIED THE BOY'S SEMEN ON THE GIRL'S BODY. HE MAY HAVE BEEN DEAD BUT HIS GOD-DAMN DICK WAS DANCING THE FUNKY CHICKEN.
UNITOL
POLICE
CHICAGO
THIS IS TOO WEIRD. IF THEY WANT SOME-BODY TO CATCH GHOSTS, THEY CAN GIVE MY BADGE TO SCOOBY-DOO.
SO WHY ARE WE HERE? WHAT IS THIS PLACE?
I TOLD YOU ONCE ALREADY, NORDAU. THIS IS UNITOL PHARMACEUTICALS AND WE'RE FOLLOWING A LEAD, OKAY?
NOT THAT CRAZY OLD VOODOO WOMAN? DID SHE CALL AGAIN? YOU GOTTA BE PUTTING ME ON.
TELL ME YOU'RE NOT GONNA START BELIEVING ALL THIS SHIT ON THE STREETS ABOUT ZOMBIES AND SPIRITS AND SHIT.
SHUT THE FUCK UP, NORDAU! WE GOT NOTHING ELSE TO GO ON HERE!
PSYCHICS HAVE BEEN RIGHT BEFORE. THESE CREOLE PEOPLE GOT TRADITIONS...
THE GODDAMN SHRINERS GOT TRADITIONS BUT WE DON'T LISTEN TO...
I HOPE YOU'RE ALL SET FOR TONIGHT, PEARSON.
YES, SIR. I'M LOOKING FORWARD TO IT.
IT'S A BIG HONOR.
MR. DOLLIMORE?
CHICAGO PD. CAN WE HAVE A MINUTE?
A MINUTE?
WELL, THAT'LL COST YOU AT LEAST A THOUSAND DOLLARS.

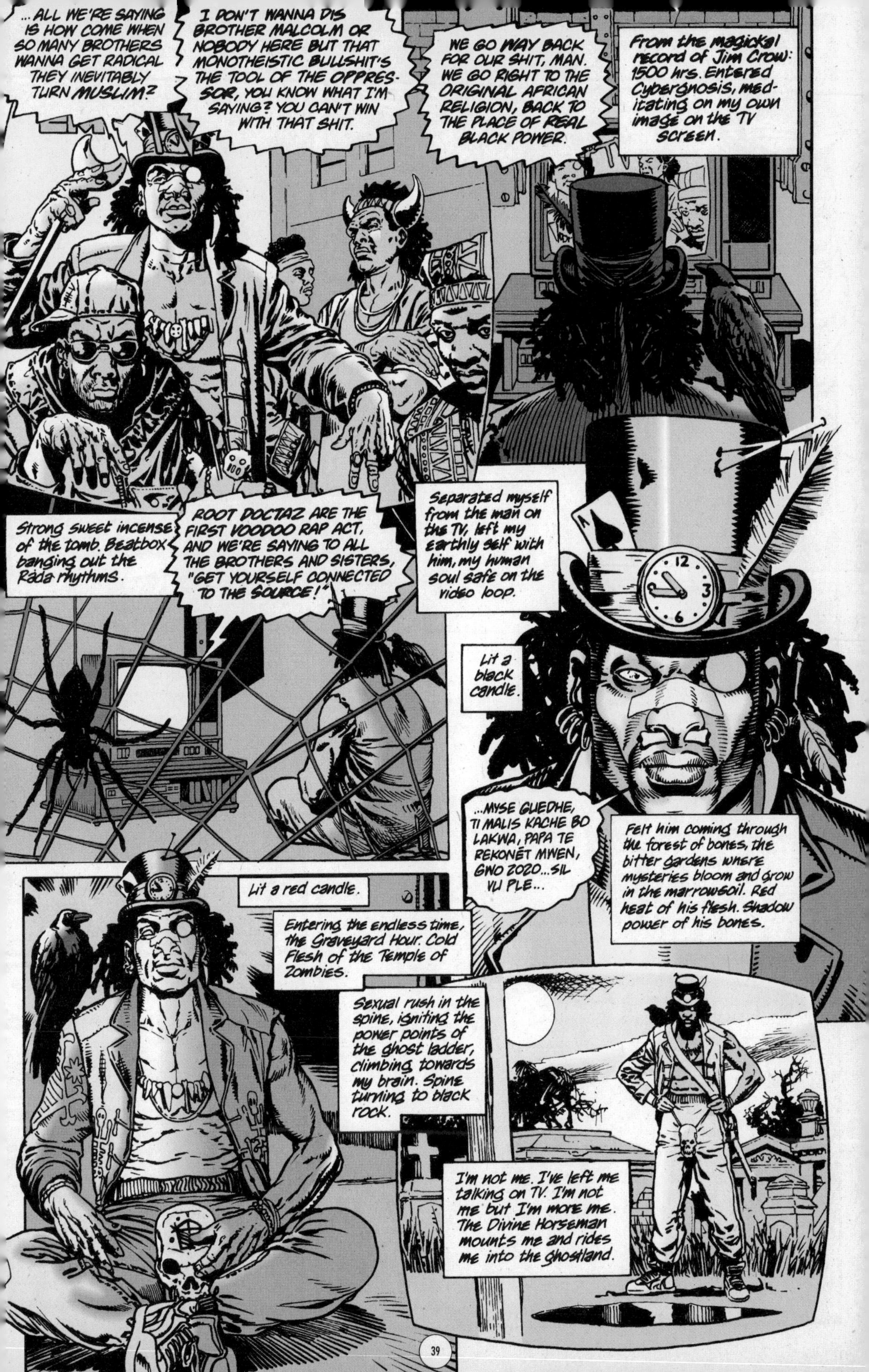
...ALL WE'RE SAYING IS HOW COME WHEN SO MANY BROTHERS WANNA GET RADICAL THEY INEVITABLY TURN MUSLIM?
I DON'T WANNA DIS BROTHER MALCOLM OR NOBODY HERE BUT THAT MONOTHEISTIC BULLSHIT'S THE TOOL OF THE OPPRESSOR, YOU KNOW WHAT I'M SAYING? YOU CAN'T WIN WITH THAT SHIT.
WE GO WAY BACK FOR OUR SHIT, MAN. WE GO RIGHT TO THE ORIGINAL AFRICAN RELIGION, BACK TO THE PLACE OF REAL BLACK POWER.
From the magickal record of Jim Crow: 1500 hrs. Entered Cybergnosis, meditating on my own image on the TV screen.
Strong sweet incense of the tomb. Beatbox banging out the Rada rhythms.
ROOT DOCTAZ ARE THE FIRST VOODOO RAP ACT, AND WE'RE SAYING TO ALL THE BROTHERS AND SISTERS, "GET YOURSELF CONNECTED TO THE SOURCE!"
Separated myself from the man on the TV, left my earthly self with him, my human soul safe on the video loop.
Lit a black candle.
...MYSE GUEDHE, TI MALIS KACHE BO LAKWA, PAPA TE REKONÈT MWEN, GWO ZOZO...SIL VU PLE...
Felt him coming through the forest of bones, the bitter gardens where mysteries bloom and grow in the marrowsoil. Red heat of his flesh. Shadow power of his bones.
Lit a red candle.
Entering the endless time, the Graveyard Hour. Cold Flesh of the Temple of Zombies.
Sexual rush in the spine, igniting the power points of the ghost ladder, climbing towards my brain. Spine turning to black rock.
I'm not me. I've left me talking on TV. I'm not me but I'm more me. The Divine Horseman mounts me and rides me into the Ghostland.

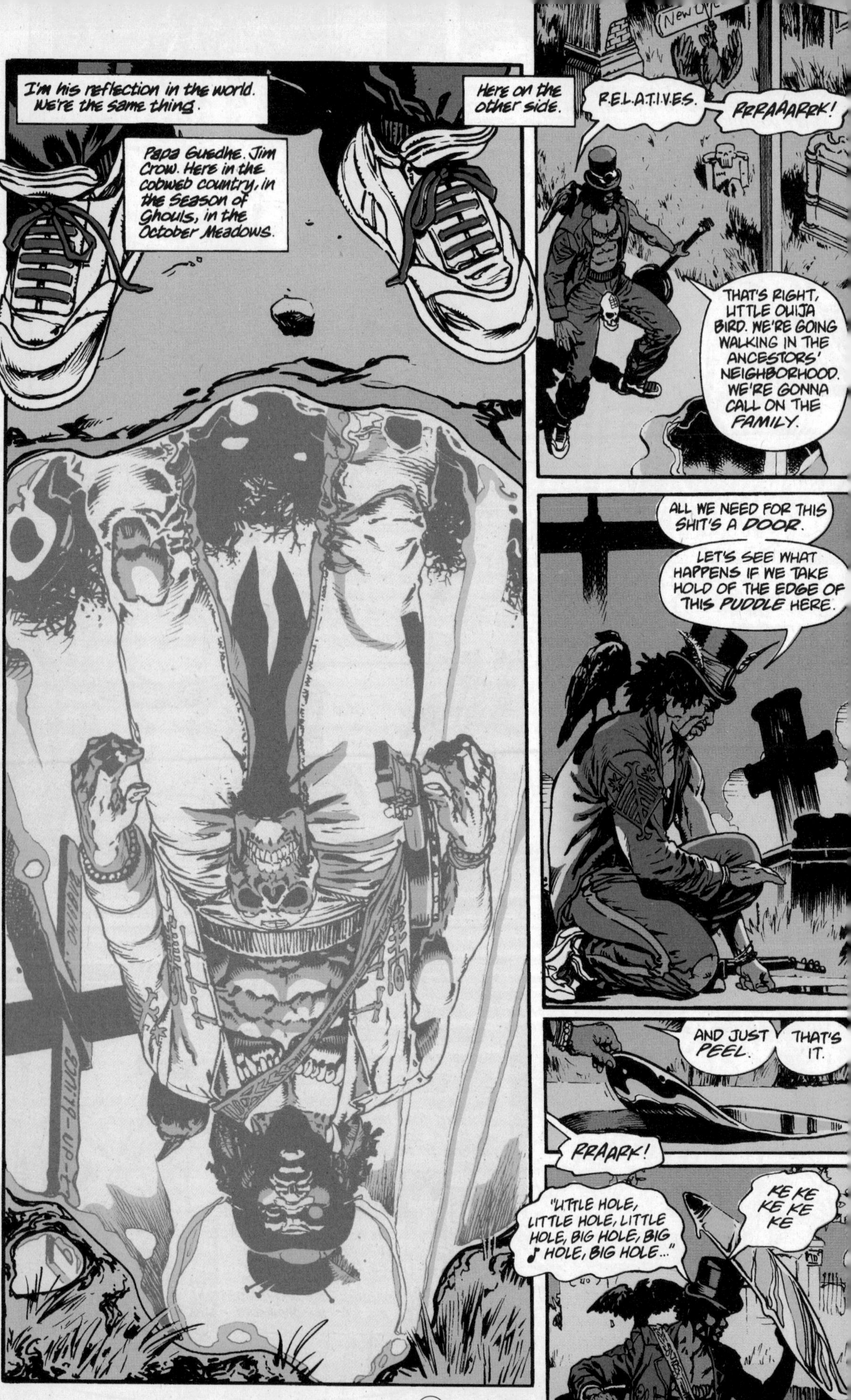
I'm his reflection in the world. We're the same thing.
Papa Guedhe. Jim Crow. Here in the cobweb country, in the Season of Ghouls, in the October Meadows.
Here on the other side.
R.E.L.A.T.I.V.E.S.
RRRAAARRK!
THAT'S RIGHT, LITTLE OUIJA BIRD. WE'RE GOING WALKING IN THE ANCESTORS' NEIGHBORHOOD. WE'RE GONNA CALL ON THE FAMILY.
ALL WE NEED FOR THIS SHIT'S A DOOR.
LET'S SEE WHAT HAPPENS IF WE TAKE HOLD OF THE EDGE OF THIS PUDDLE HERE.
AND JUST PEEL.
THAT'S IT.
RRAARK!
"LITTLE HOLE, LITTLE HOLE, LITTLE HOLE, BIG HOLE, BIG ♪ HOLE, BIG HOLE..."
KE KE KE KE KE

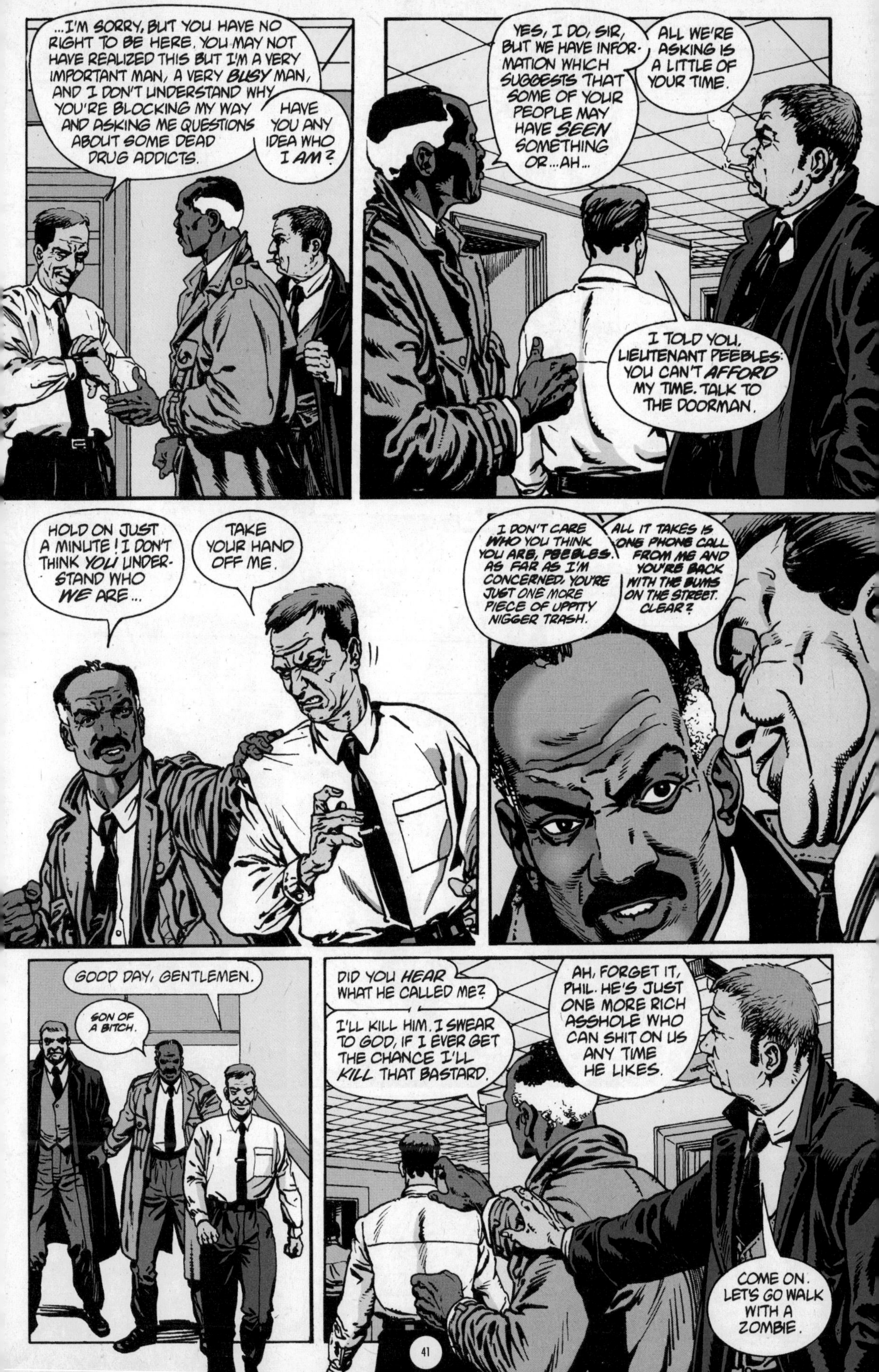
...I'M SORRY, BUT YOU HAVE NO RIGHT TO BE HERE. YOU MAY NOT HAVE REALIZED THIS BUT I'M A VERY IMPORTANT MAN, A VERY BUSY MAN, AND I DON'T UNDERSTAND WHY YOU'RE BLOCKING MY WAY AND ASKING ME QUESTIONS ABOUT SOME DEAD DRUG ADDICTS.
HAVE YOU ANY IDEA WHO I AM?
YES, I DO, SIR, BUT WE HAVE INFORMATION WHICH SUGGESTS THAT SOME OF YOUR PEOPLE MAY HAVE SEEN SOMETHING OR...AH...
ALL WE'RE ASKING IS A LITTLE OF YOUR TIME.
I TOLD YOU, LIEUTENANT PEEBLES: YOU CAN'T AFFORD MY TIME. TALK TO THE DOORMAN.
HOLD ON JUST A MINUTE! I DON'T THINK YOU UNDERSTAND WHO WE ARE...
TAKE YOUR HAND OFF ME.
I DON'T CARE WHO YOU THINK YOU ARE, PEEBLES. AS FAR AS I'M CONCERNED, YOU'RE JUST ONE MORE PIECE OF UPPITY NIGGER TRASH.
ALL IT TAKES IS ONE PHONE CALL FROM ME AND YOU'RE BACK WITH THE BUMS ON THE STREET. CLEAR?
GOOD DAY, GENTLEMEN.
SON OF A BITCH.
DID YOU HEAR WHAT HE CALLED ME?
I'LL KILL HIM. I SWEAR TO GOD, IF I EVER GET THE CHANCE I'LL KILL THAT BASTARD.
AH, FORGET IT, PHIL. HE'S JUST ONE MORE RICH ASSHOLE WHO CAN SHIT ON US ANY TIME HE LIKES.
COME ON. LET'S GO WALK WITH A ZOMBIE.

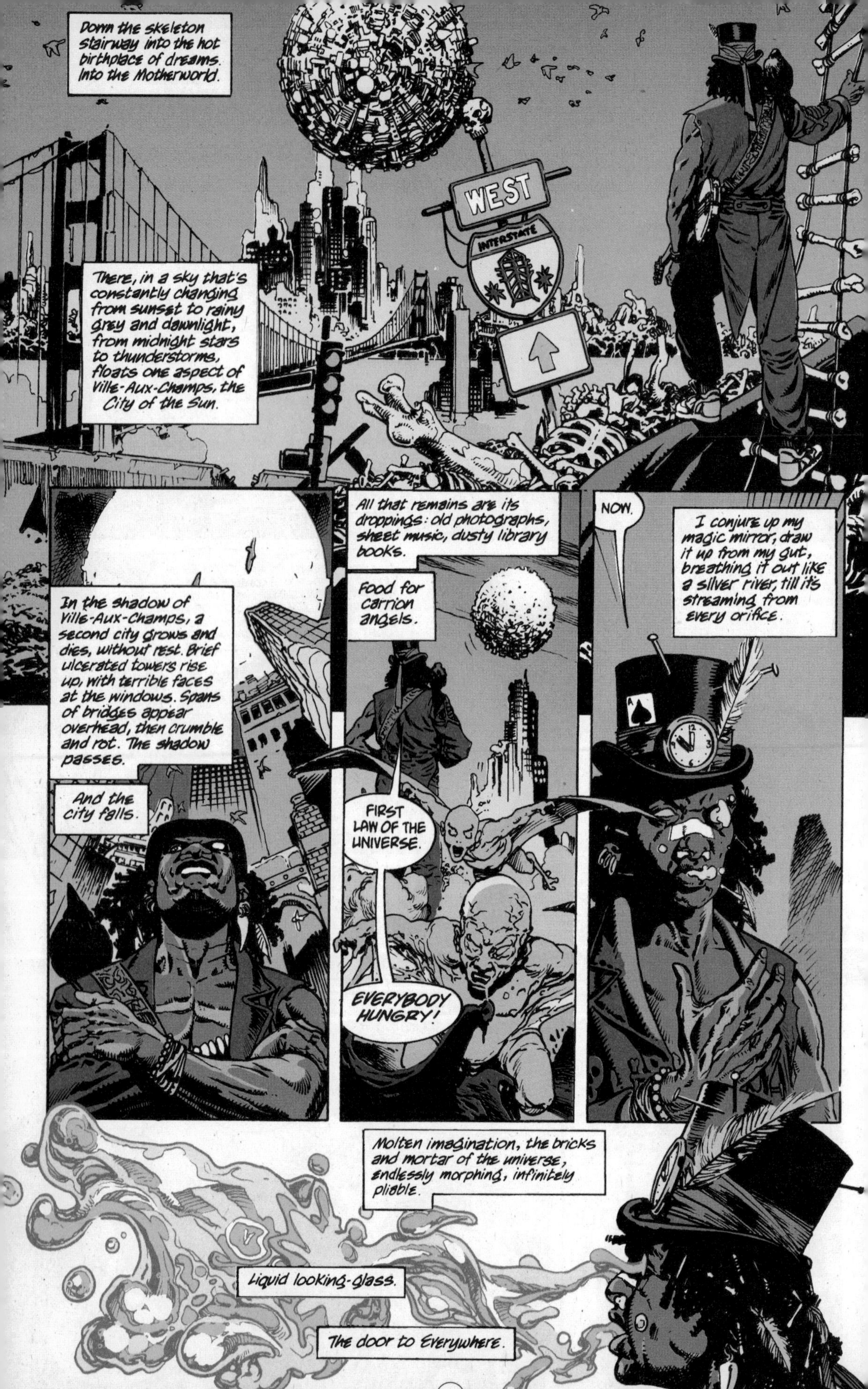
Down the skeleton stairway into the hot birthplace of dreams. Into the Motherworld.
WEST
INTERSTATE
There, in a sky that's constantly changing from sunset to rainy grey and dawnlight, from midnight stars to thunderstorms, floats one aspect of Ville-Aux-Champs, the City of the Sun.
In the shadow of Ville-Aux-Champs, a second city grows and dies, without rest. Brief ulcerated towers rise up, with terrible faces at the windows. Spans of bridges appear overhead, then crumble and rot. The shadow passes.
And the city falls.
All that remains are its droppings: old photographs, sheet music, dusty library books.
Food for carrion angels.
FIRST LAW OF THE UNIVERSE.
EVERYBODY HUNGRY!
NOW.
I conjure up my magic mirror, draw it up from my gut, breathing it out like a silver river, till it's streaming from every orifice.
Molten imagination, the bricks and mortar of the universe, endlessly morphing, infinitely pliable.
Liquid looking-glass.
The door to Everywhere.

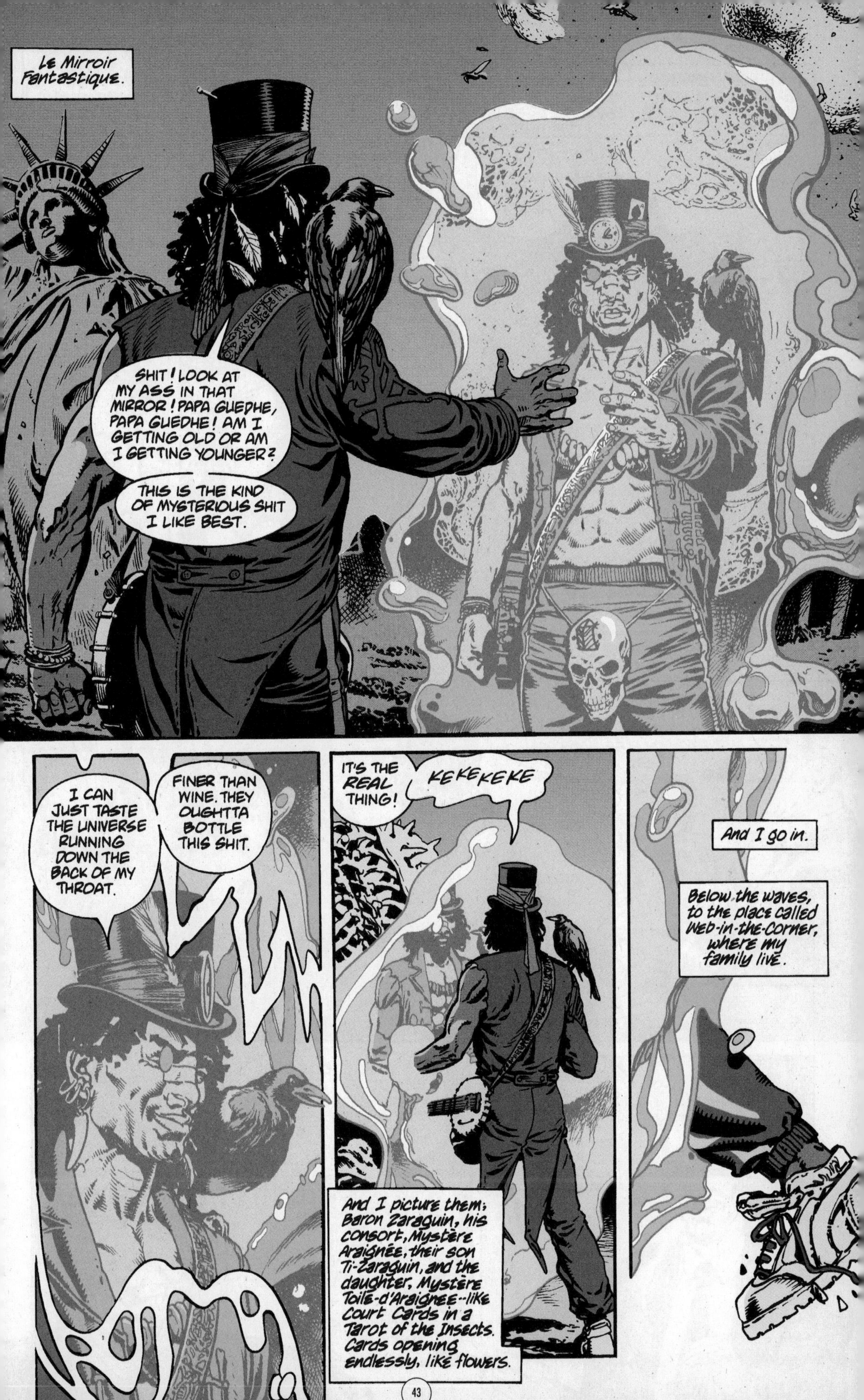
Le Miroir Fantastique.
SHIT! LOOK AT MY ASS IN THAT MIRROR! PAPA GUEDHE, PAPA GUEDHE! AM I GETTING OLD OR AM I GETTING YOUNGER?
THIS IS THE KIND OF MYSTERIOUS SHIT I LIKE BEST.
I CAN JUST TASTE THE UNIVERSE RUNNING DOWN THE BACK OF MY THROAT.
FINER THAN WINE. THEY OUGHTTA BOTTLE THIS SHIT.
IT'S THE *REAL* THING!
KEKEKEKEKE
And I picture them; Baron Zaraguin, his consort, Mystère Araignée, their son Ti-Zaraguin, and the daughter, Mystère Toile-d'Araignee--like Court Cards in a Tarot of the Insects. Cards opening endlessly, like flowers.
And I go in.
Below the waves, to the place called Web-in-the-Corner, where my family live.

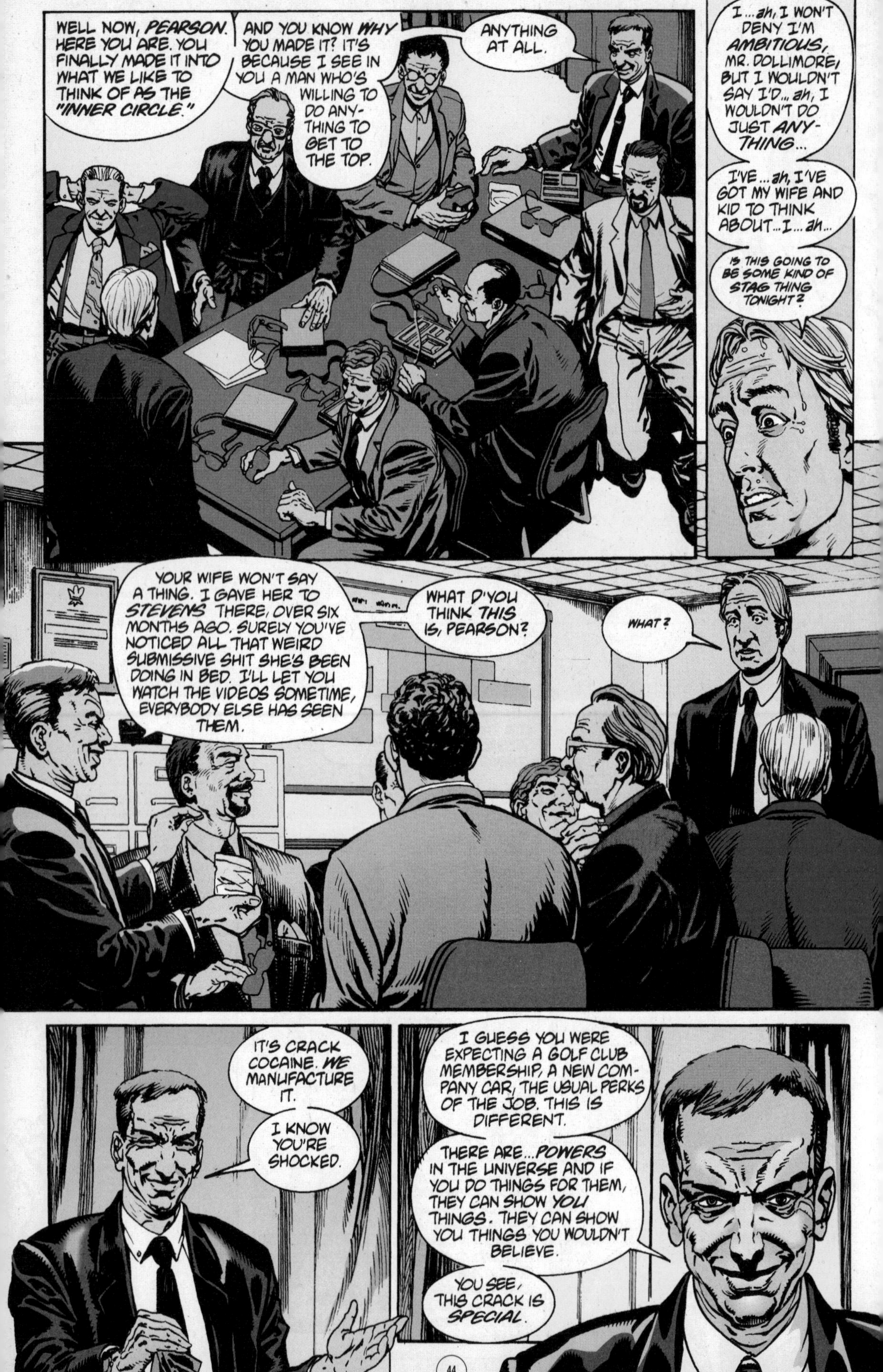
WELL NOW, PEARSON. HERE YOU ARE. YOU FINALLY MADE IT INTO WHAT WE LIKE TO THINK OF AS THE "INNER CIRCLE."
AND YOU KNOW WHY YOU MADE IT? IT'S BECAUSE I SEE IN YOU A MAN WHO'S WILLING TO DO ANY-THING TO GET TO THE TOP.
ANYTHING AT ALL.
I...ah, I WON'T DENY I'M AMBITIOUS, MR. DOLLIMORE, BUT I WOULDN'T SAY I'D... ah, I WOULDN'T DO JUST ANY-THING...
I'VE...ah, I'VE GOT MY WIFE AND KID TO THINK ABOUT...I...ah...
IS THIS GOING TO BE SOME KIND OF STAG THING TONIGHT?
WHAT D'YOU THINK THIS IS, PEARSON?
WHAT?
YOUR WIFE WON'T SAY A THING. I GAVE HER TO STEVENS THERE, OVER SIX MONTHS AGO. SURELY YOU'VE NOTICED ALL THAT WEIRD SUBMISSIVE SHIT SHE'S BEEN DOING IN BED. I'LL LET YOU WATCH THE VIDEOS SOMETIME, EVERYBODY ELSE HAS SEEN THEM.
IT'S CRACK COCAINE. WE MANUFACTURE IT.
I KNOW YOU'RE SHOCKED.
I GUESS YOU WERE EXPECTING A GOLF CLUB MEMBERSHIP, A NEW COM-PANY CAR, THE USUAL PERKS OF THE JOB. THIS IS DIFFERENT.
THERE ARE...POWERS IN THE UNIVERSE AND IF YOU DO THINGS FOR THEM, THEY CAN SHOW YOU THINGS. THEY CAN SHOW YOU THINGS YOU WOULDN'T BELIEVE.
YOU SEE, THIS CRACK IS SPECIAL.

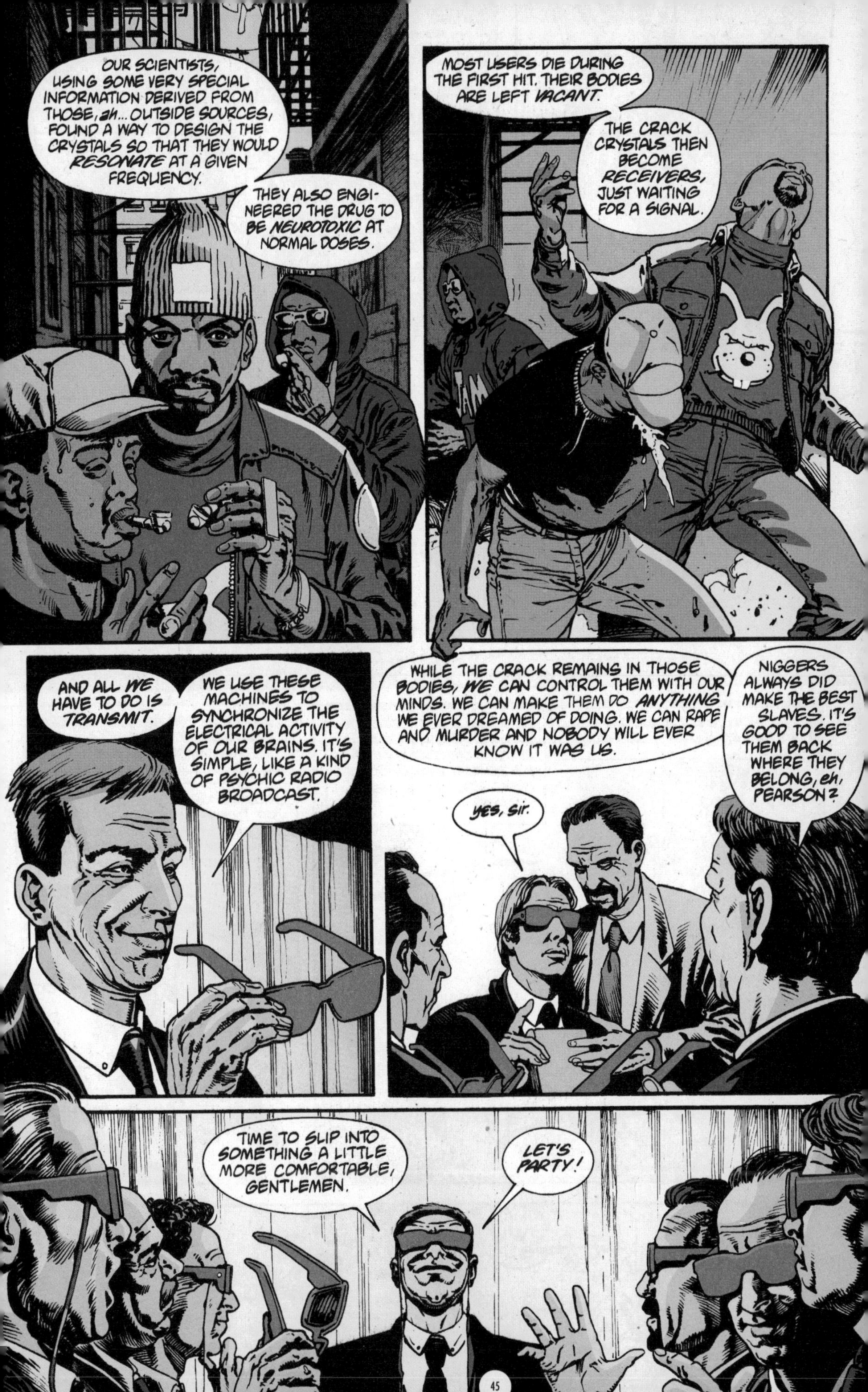
OUR SCIENTISTS, USING SOME VERY SPECIAL INFORMATION DERIVED FROM THOSE, ah... OUTSIDE SOURCES, FOUND A WAY TO DESIGN THE CRYSTALS SO THAT THEY WOULD RESONATE AT A GIVEN FREQUENCY.
THEY ALSO ENGINEERED THE DRUG TO BE NEUROTOXIC AT NORMAL DOSES.
MOST USERS DIE DURING THE FIRST HIT. THEIR BODIES ARE LEFT VACANT.
THE CRACK CRYSTALS THEN BECOME RECEIVERS, JUST WAITING FOR A SIGNAL.
AND ALL WE HAVE TO DO IS TRANSMIT.
WE USE THESE MACHINES TO SYNCHRONIZE THE ELECTRICAL ACTIVITY OF OUR BRAINS. IT'S SIMPLE, LIKE A KIND OF PSYCHIC RADIO BROADCAST.
WHILE THE CRACK REMAINS IN THOSE BODIES, WE CAN CONTROL THEM WITH OUR MINDS. WE CAN MAKE THEM DO ANYTHING WE EVER DREAMED OF DOING. WE CAN RAPE AND MURDER AND NOBODY WILL EVER KNOW IT WAS US.
NIGGERS ALWAYS DID MAKE THE BEST SLAVES. IT'S GOOD TO SEE THEM BACK WHERE THEY BELONG, eh, PEARSON?
yes, sir.
TIME TO SLIP INTO SOMETHING A LITTLE MORE COMFORTABLE, GENTLEMEN.
LET'S PARTY!

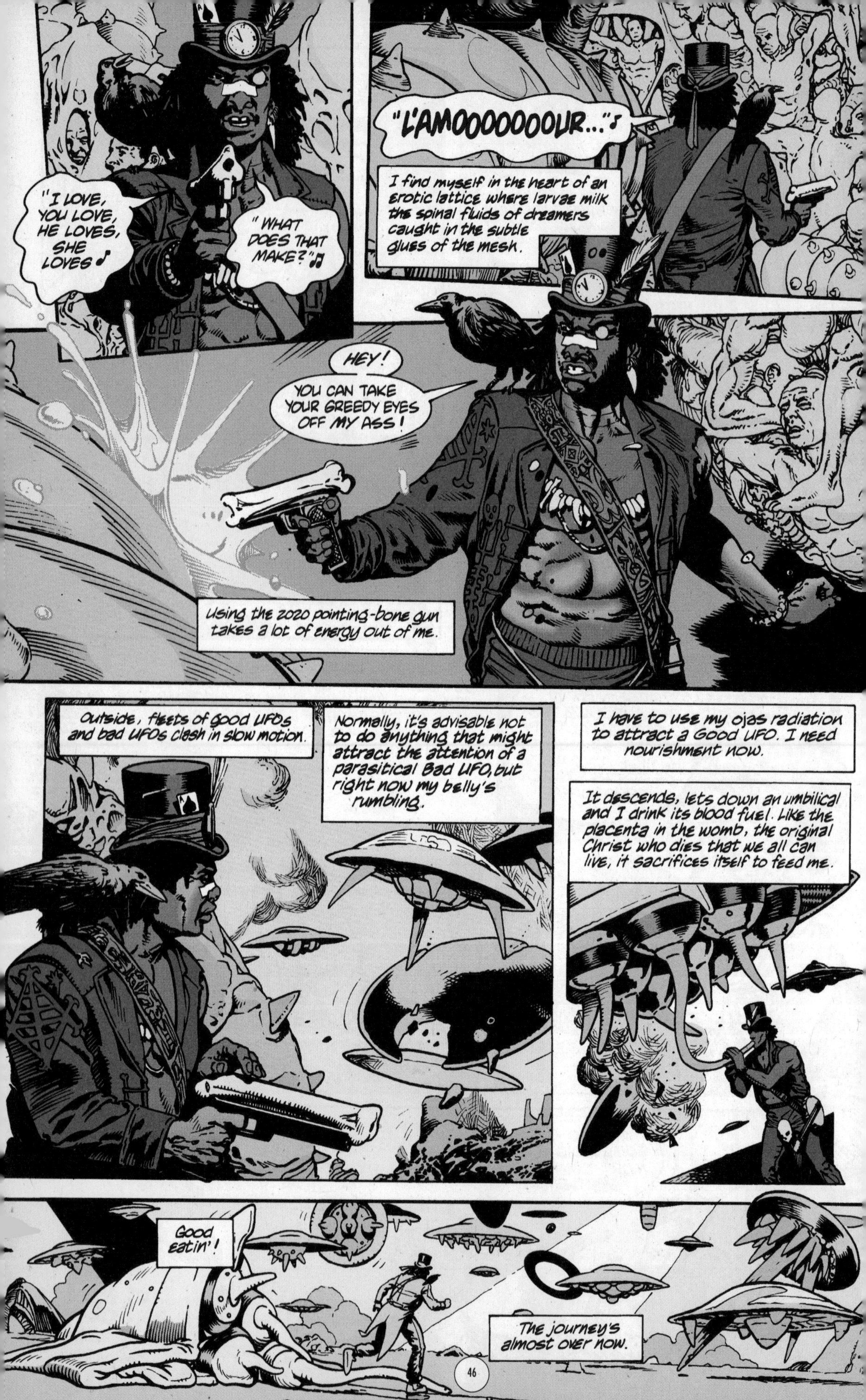
"I LOVE, YOU LOVE, HE LOVES, SHE LOVES ♪
"WHAT DOES THAT MAKE?"♫
"L'AMOOOOOOOUR..."♪
I find myself in the heart of an erotic lattice where larvae milk the spinal fluids of dreamers caught in the subtle glues of the mesh.
HEY! YOU CAN TAKE YOUR GREEDY EYES OFF MY ASS!
Using the 2020 pointing-bone gun takes a lot of energy out of me.
Outside, fleets of Good UFOs and bad UFOs clash in slow motion.
Normally, it's advisable not to do anything that might attract the attention of a parasitical Bad UFO, but right now my belly's rumbling.
I have to use my ojas radiation to attract a Good UFO. I need nourishment now.
It descends, lets down an umbilical and I drink its blood fuel. Like the placenta in the womb, the original Christ who dies that we all can live, it sacrifices itself to feed me.
Good eatin'!
The journey's almost over now.

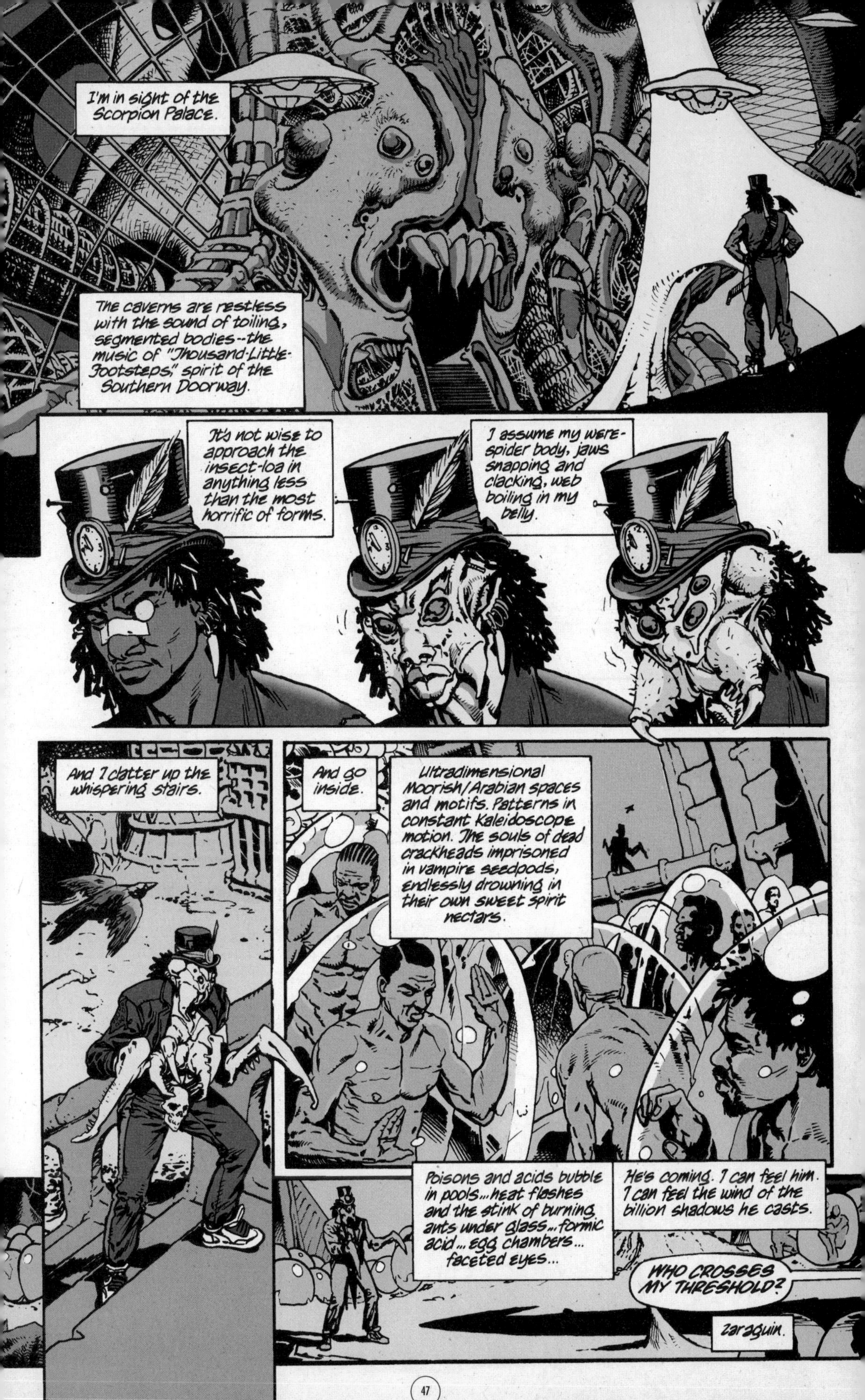
I'm in sight of the Scorpion Palace.
The caverns are restless with the sound of toiling, segmented bodies--the music of "Thousand-Little-Footsteps," spirit of the Southern Doorway.
It's not wise to approach the insect-loa in anything less than the most horrific of forms.
I assume my were-spider body, jaws snapping and clacking, web boiling in my belly.
And I clatter up the whispering stairs.
And go inside.
Ultradimensional Moorish/Arabian spaces and motifs. Patterns in constant kaleidoscope motion. The souls of dead crackheads imprisoned in vampire seedpods, endlessly drowning in their own sweet spirit nectars.
Poisons and acids bubble in pools... heat flashes and the stink of burning ants under glass... formic acid... egg chambers... faceted eyes...
He's coming. I can feel him. I can feel the wind of the billion shadows he casts.
WHO CROSSES MY THRESHOLD?
Zaraguin.

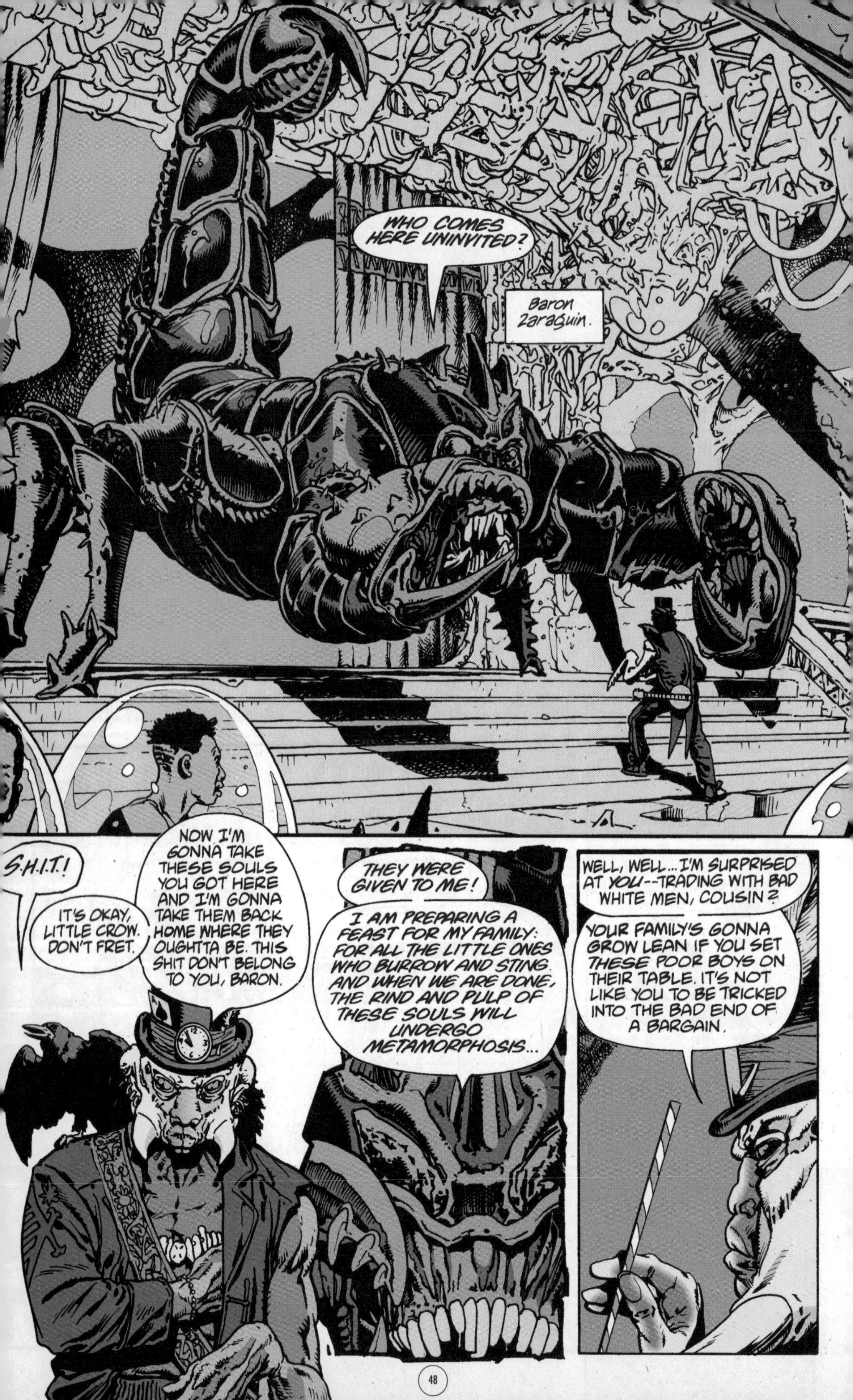

WHO COMES HERE UNINVITED?
Baron Zaraguin.
S.H.I.T.!
IT'S OKAY, LITTLE CROW. DON'T FRET.
NOW I'M GONNA TAKE THESE SOULS YOU GOT HERE AND I'M GONNA TAKE THEM BACK HOME WHERE THEY OUGHTTA BE. THIS SHIT DON'T BELONG TO YOU, BARON.
THEY WERE GIVEN TO ME!
I AM PREPARING A FEAST FOR MY FAMILY: FOR ALL THE LITTLE ONES WHO BURROW AND STING. AND WHEN WE ARE DONE, THE RIND AND PULP OF THESE SOULS WILL UNDERGO METAMORPHOSIS...
WELL, WELL... I'M SURPRISED AT YOU--TRADING WITH BAD WHITE MEN, COUSIN?
YOUR FAMILY'S GONNA GROW LEAN IF YOU SET THESE POOR BOYS ON THEIR TABLE. IT'S NOT LIKE YOU TO BE TRICKED INTO THE BAD END OF A BARGAIN.

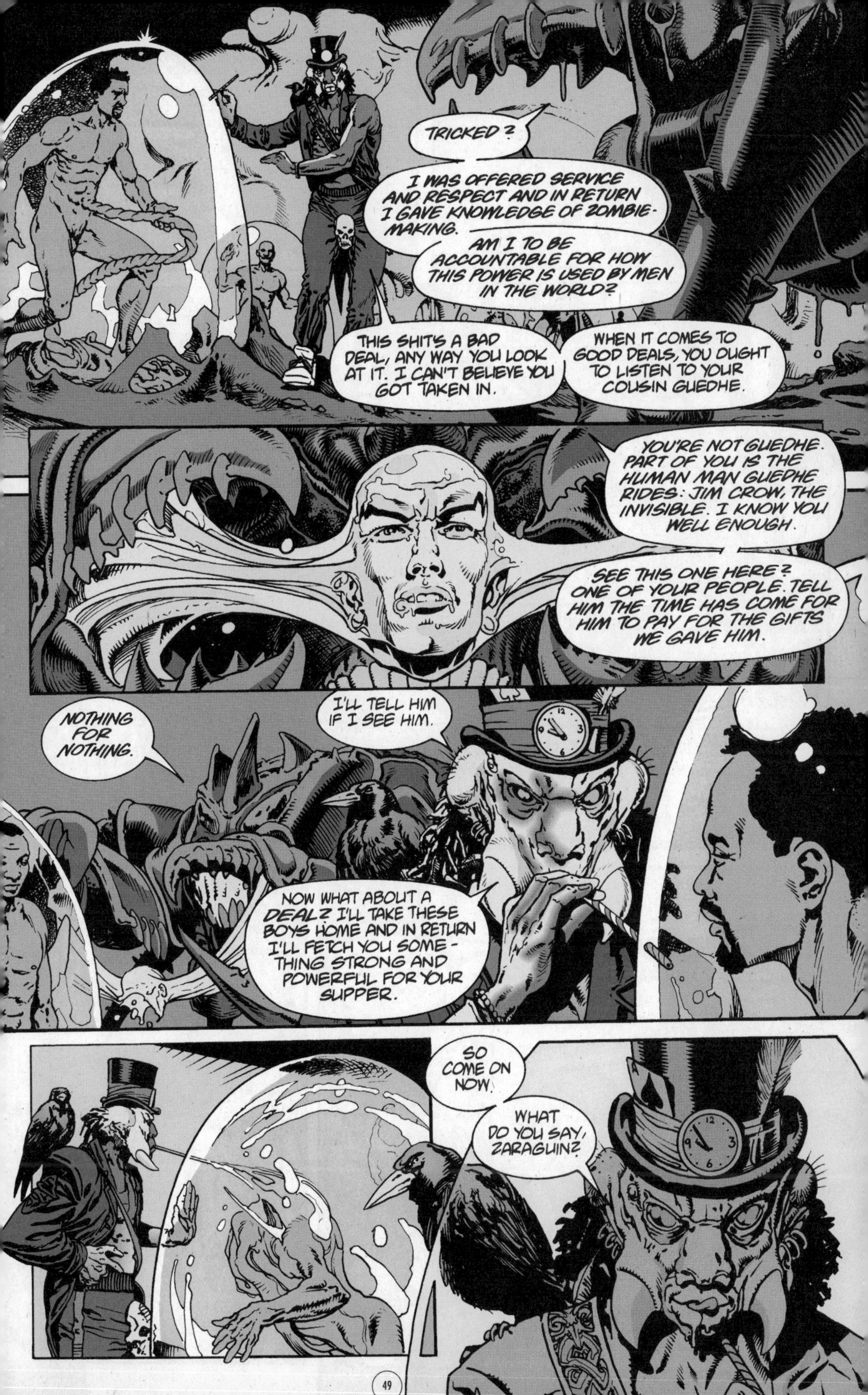
TRICKED?
I WAS OFFERED SERVICE AND RESPECT AND IN RETURN I GAVE KNOWLEDGE OF ZOMBIE-MAKING.
AM I TO BE ACCOUNTABLE FOR HOW THIS POWER IS USED BY MEN IN THE WORLD?
THIS SHIT'S A BAD DEAL, ANY WAY YOU LOOK AT IT. I CAN'T BELIEVE YOU GOT TAKEN IN.
WHEN IT COMES TO GOOD DEALS, YOU OUGHT TO LISTEN TO YOUR COUSIN GUEDHE.
YOU'RE NOT GUEDHE. PART OF YOU IS THE HUMAN MAN GUEDHE RIDES: JIM CROW, THE INVISIBLE. I KNOW YOU WELL ENOUGH.
SEE THIS ONE HERE? ONE OF YOUR PEOPLE. TELL HIM THE TIME HAS COME FOR HIM TO PAY FOR THE GIFTS WE GAVE HIM.
NOTHING FOR NOTHING.
I'LL TELL HIM IF I SEE HIM.
NOW WHAT ABOUT A DEAL? I'LL TAKE THESE BOYS HOME AND IN RETURN I'LL FETCH YOU SOME-THING STRONG AND POWERFUL FOR YOUR SUPPER.
SO COME ON NOW.
WHAT DO YOU SAY, ZARAGUIN?

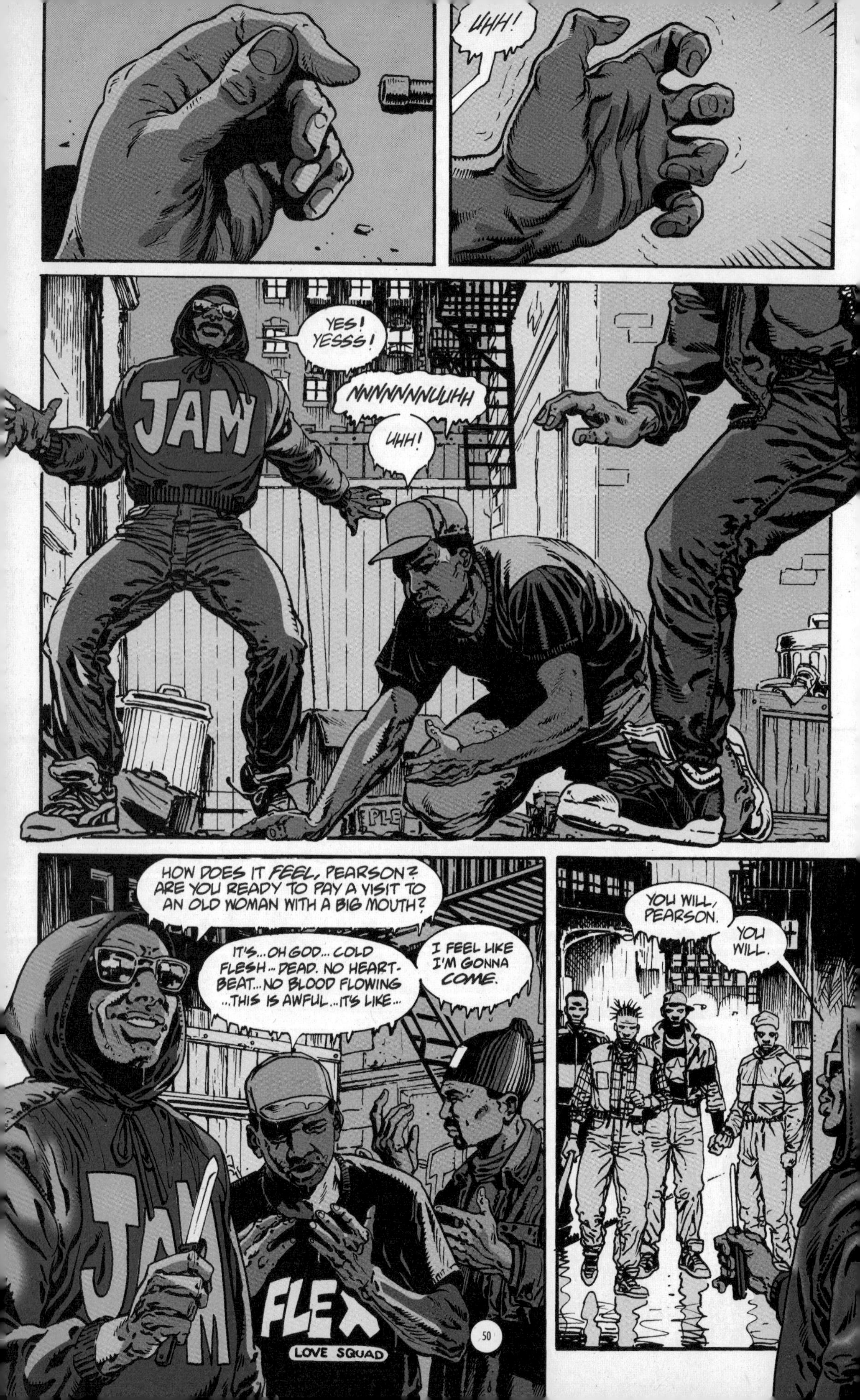
UHH!
YES! YESSS!
NNNNNNNUUHH
UHH!
PLE
HOW DOES IT FEEL, PEARSON? ARE YOU READY TO PAY A VISIT TO AN OLD WOMAN WITH A BIG MOUTH?
IT'S... OH GOD... COLD FLESH... DEAD. NO HEART-BEAT... NO BLOOD FLOWING ...THIS IS AWFUL... IT'S LIKE...
I FEEL LIKE I'M GONNA COME.
JAM
FLEX
LOVE SQUAD
YOU WILL, PEARSON.
YOU WILL.

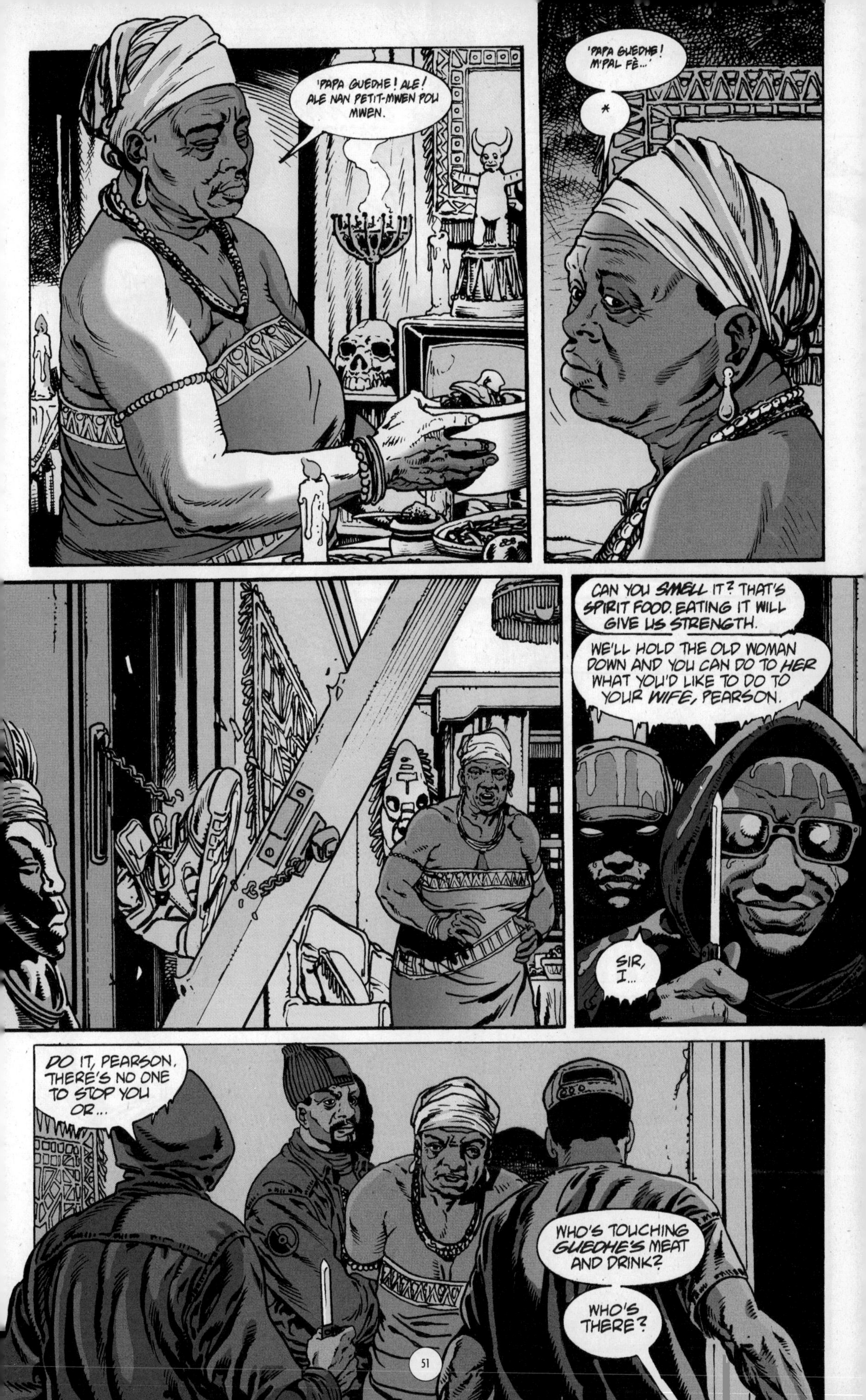
'PAPA GUEDHE! ALE! ALE NAN PETIT-MWEN POU MWEN.
'PAPA GUEDHE! M'PAL FÈ...'
*
CAN YOU SMELL IT? THAT'S SPIRIT FOOD. EATING IT WILL GIVE US STRENGTH.
WE'LL HOLD THE OLD WOMAN DOWN AND YOU CAN DO TO HER WHAT YOU'D LIKE TO DO TO YOUR WIFE, PEARSON.
SIR, I...
DO IT, PEARSON. THERE'S NO ONE TO STOP YOU OR...
WHO'S TOUCHING GUEDHE'S MEAT AND DRINK?
WHO'S THERE?

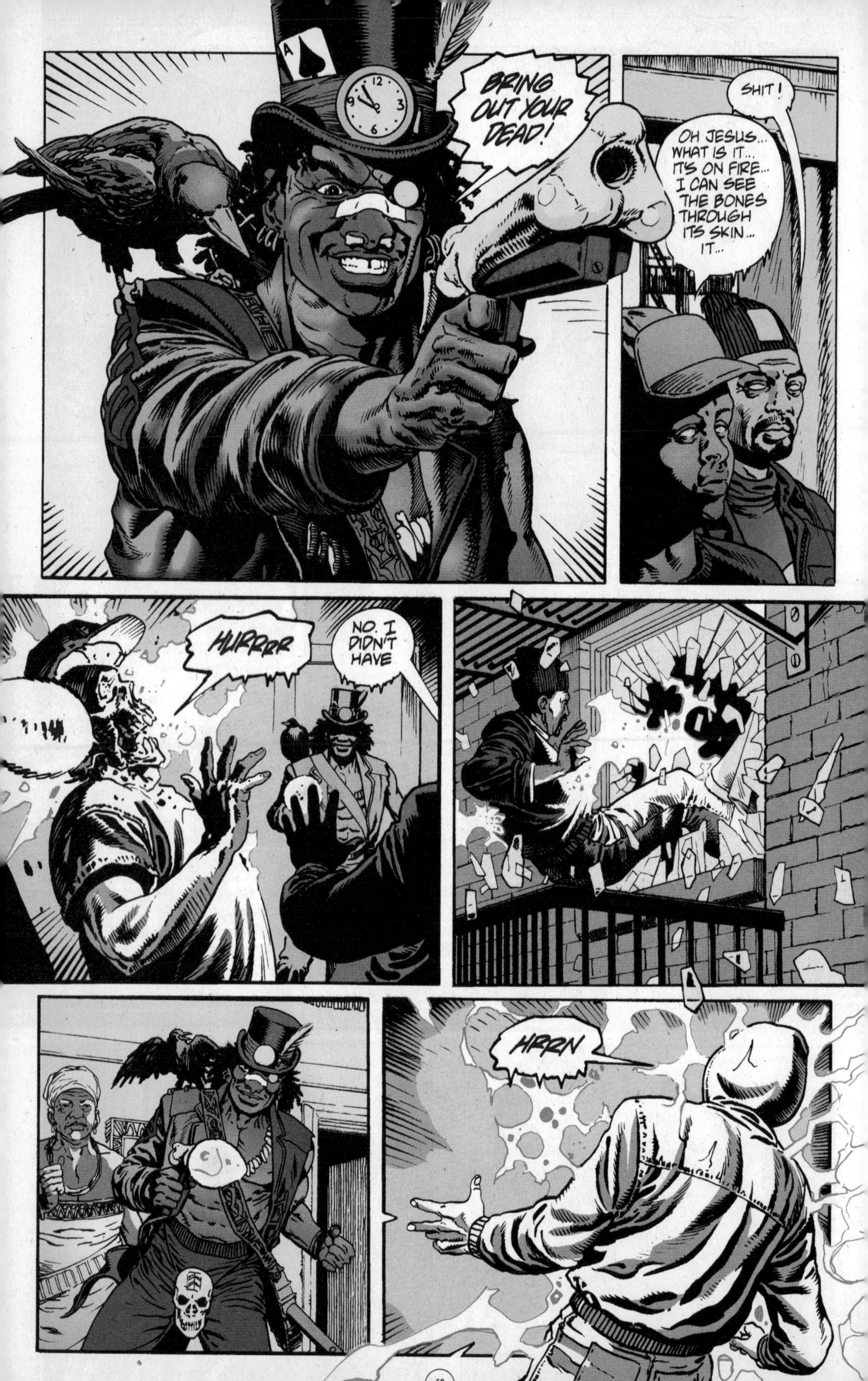
BRING OUT YOUR DEAD!
SHIT!
OH JESUS... WHAT IS IT... IT'S ON FIRE... I CAN SEE THE BONES THROUGH ITS SKIN... IT...
HURRRR
NO. I DIDN'T HAVE
HRRN

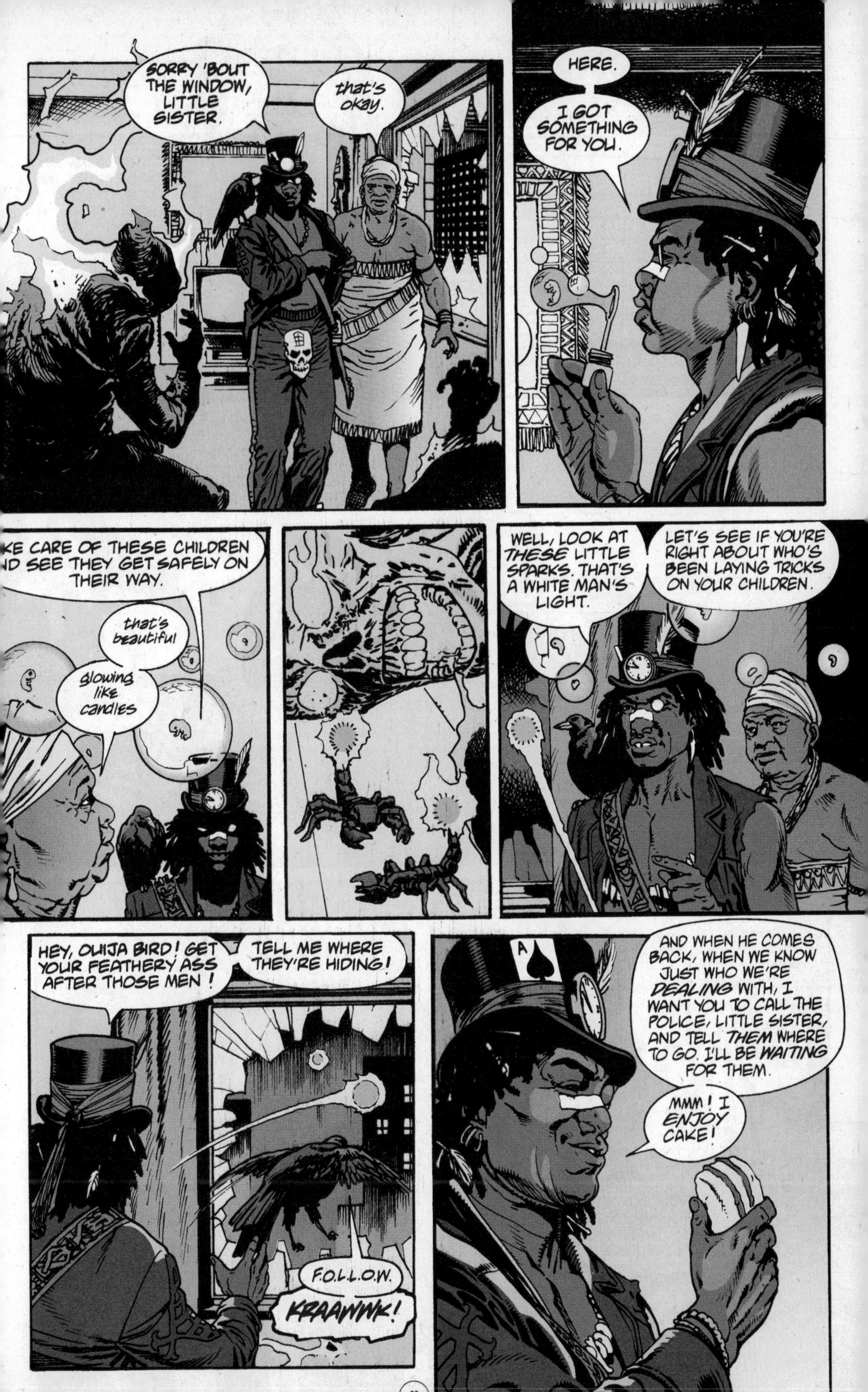

SORRY 'BOUT THE WINDOW, LITTLE SISTER.
that's okay.
HERE.
I GOT SOMETHING FOR YOU.
KE CARE OF THESE CHILDREN ND SEE THEY GET SAFELY ON THEIR WAY.
that's beautiful
glowing like candles
WELL, LOOK AT THESE LITTLE SPARKS. THAT'S A WHITE MAN'S LIGHT.
LET'S SEE IF YOU'RE RIGHT ABOUT WHO'S BEEN LAYING TRICKS ON YOUR CHILDREN.
HEY, OUIJA BIRD! GET YOUR FEATHERY ASS AFTER THOSE MEN!
TELL ME WHERE THEY'RE HIDING!
F.O.L.L.O.W.
KRAAWWK!
AND WHEN HE COMES BACK, WHEN WE KNOW JUST WHO WE'RE DEALING WITH, I WANT YOU TO CALL THE POLICE, LITTLE SISTER, AND TELL THEM WHERE TO GO. I'LL BE WAITING FOR THEM.
MMM! I ENJOY CAKE!

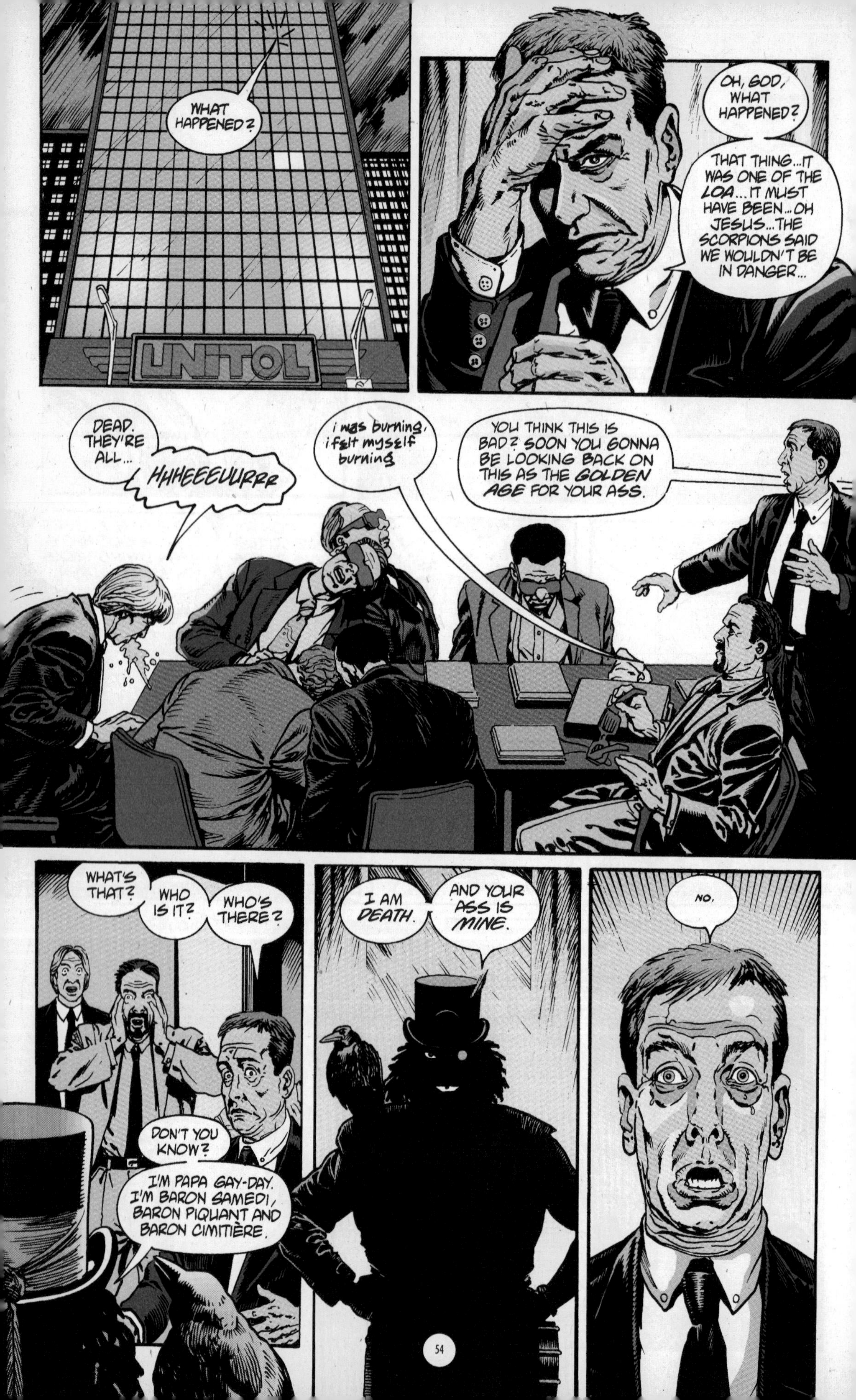
WHAT HAPPENED?
OH, GOD, WHAT HAPPENED?
THAT THING...IT WAS ONE OF THE LOA... IT MUST HAVE BEEN...OH JESUS...THE SCORPIONS SAID WE WOULDN'T BE IN DANGER...
DEAD. THEY'RE ALL...
HHHEEEUURRR
i was burning, i felt myself burning
YOU THINK THIS IS BAD? SOON YOU GONNA BE LOOKING BACK ON THIS AS THE GOLDEN AGE FOR YOUR ASS.
WHAT'S THAT?
WHO IS IT?
WHO'S THERE?
DON'T YOU KNOW?
I'M PAPA GAY-DAY. I'M BARON SAMEDI, BARON PIQUANT AND BARON CIMITIÈRE.
I AM DEATH.
AND YOUR ASS IS MINE.
NO.

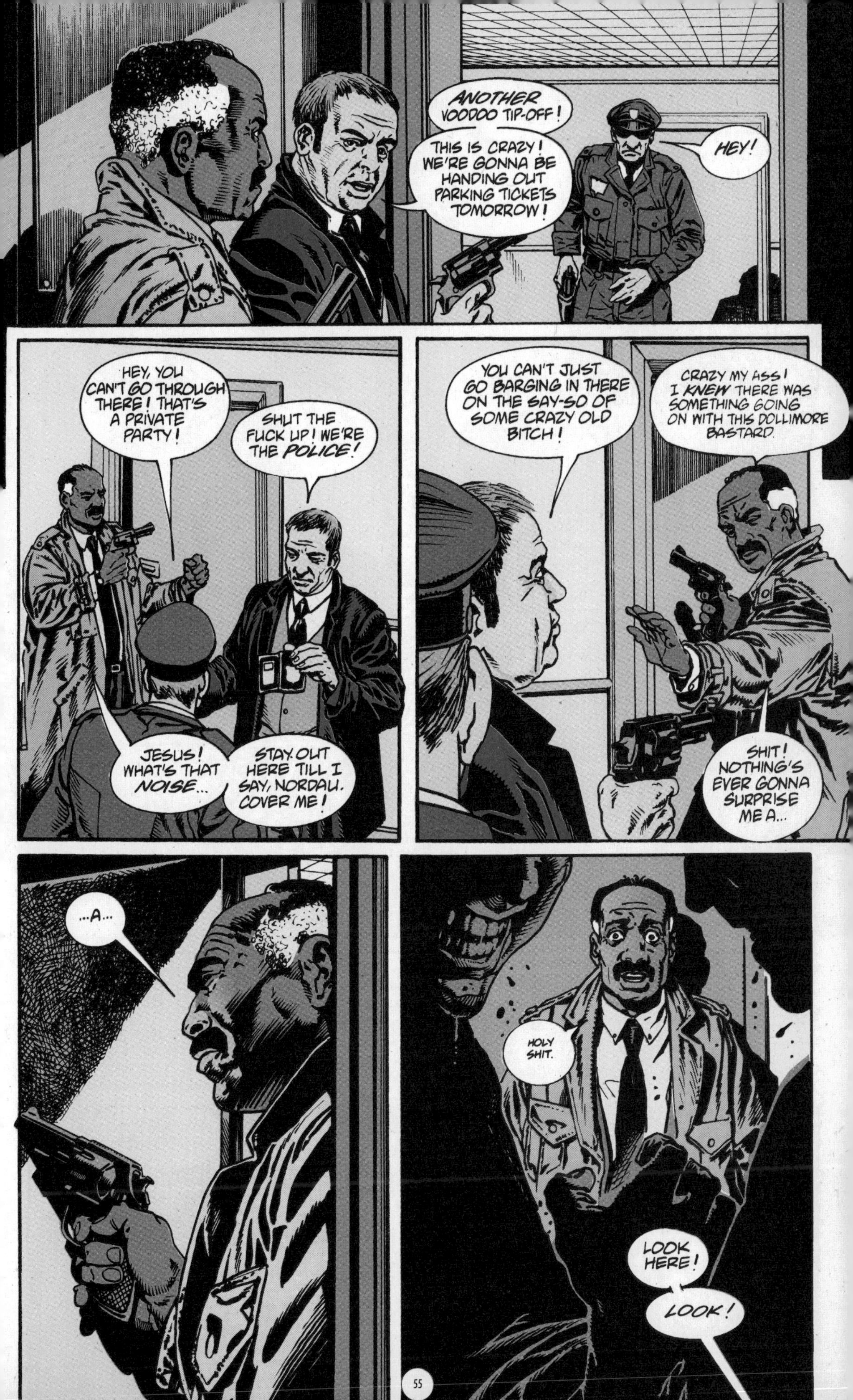
ANOTHER VOODOO TIP-OFF!
THIS IS CRAZY! WE'RE GONNA BE HANDING OUT PARKING TICKETS TOMORROW!
HEY!
HEY, YOU CAN'T GO THROUGH THERE! THAT'S A PRIVATE PARTY!
SHUT THE FUCK UP! WE'RE THE POLICE!
JESUS! WHAT'S THAT NOISE...
STAY OUT HERE TILL I SAY, NORDAU. COVER ME!
YOU CAN'T JUST GO BARGING IN THERE ON THE SAY-SO OF SOME CRAZY OLD BITCH!
CRAZY MY ASS! I KNEW THERE WAS SOMETHING GOING ON WITH THIS DOLLIMORE BASTARD.
SHIT! NOTHING'S EVER GONNA SURPRISE ME A...
...A...
HOLY SHIT.
LOOK HERE!
LOOK!

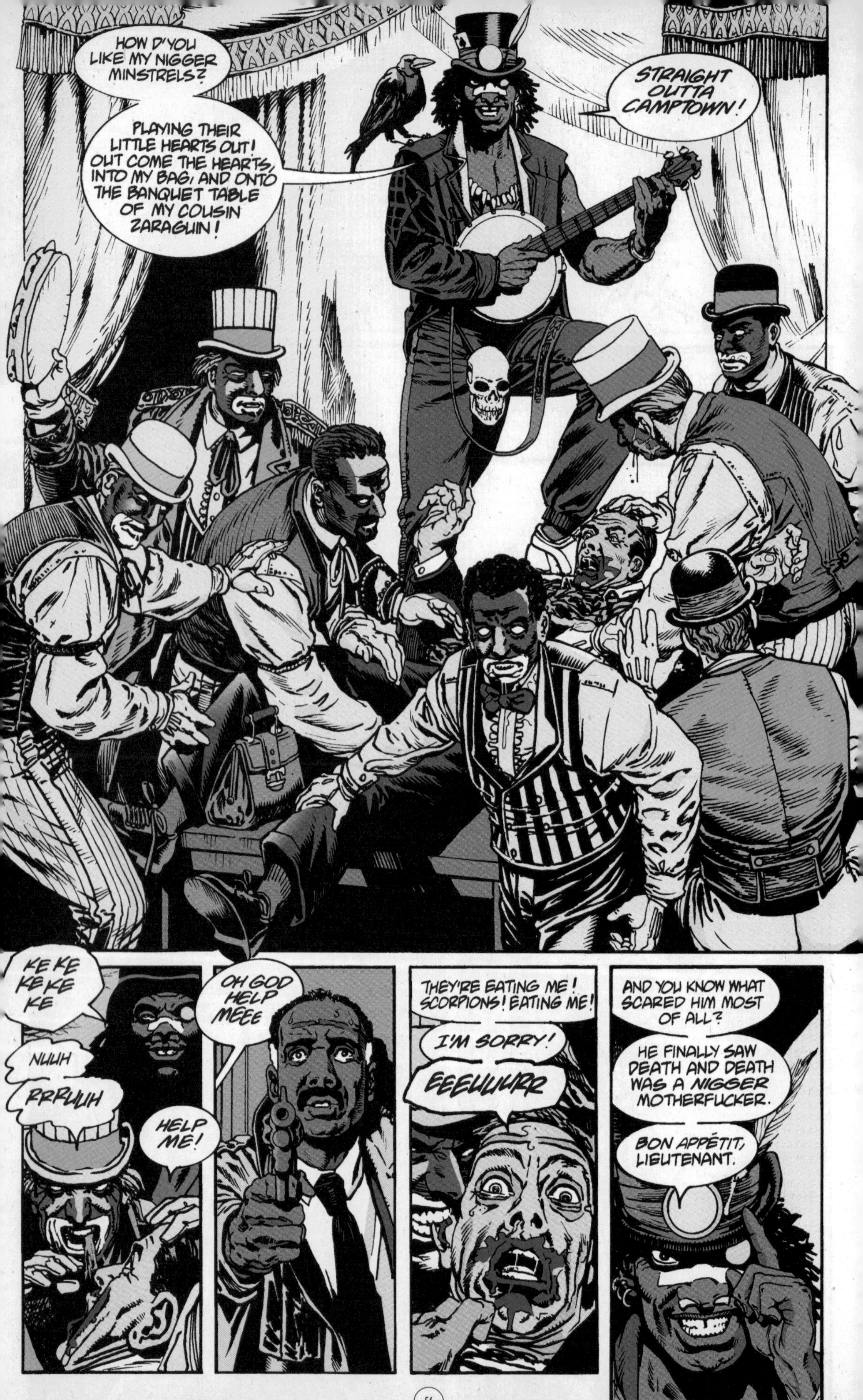

HOW D'YOU LIKE MY NIGGER MINSTRELS?
PLAYING THEIR LITTLE HEARTS OUT! OUT COME THE HEARTS, INTO MY BAG, AND ONTO THE BANQUET TABLE OF MY COUSIN ZARAGUIN!
STRAIGHT OUTTA CAMPTOWN!
KE KE KE KE KE
NUUH
RRRUUH
HELP ME!
OH GOD HELP MEEE
THEY'RE EATING ME! SCORPIONS! EATING ME!
I'M SORRY!
EEEUUURR
AND YOU KNOW WHAT SCARED HIM MOST OF ALL?
HE FINALLY SAW DEATH AND DEATH WAS A NIGGER MOTHERFUCKER.
BON APPÉTIT, LIEUTENANT.

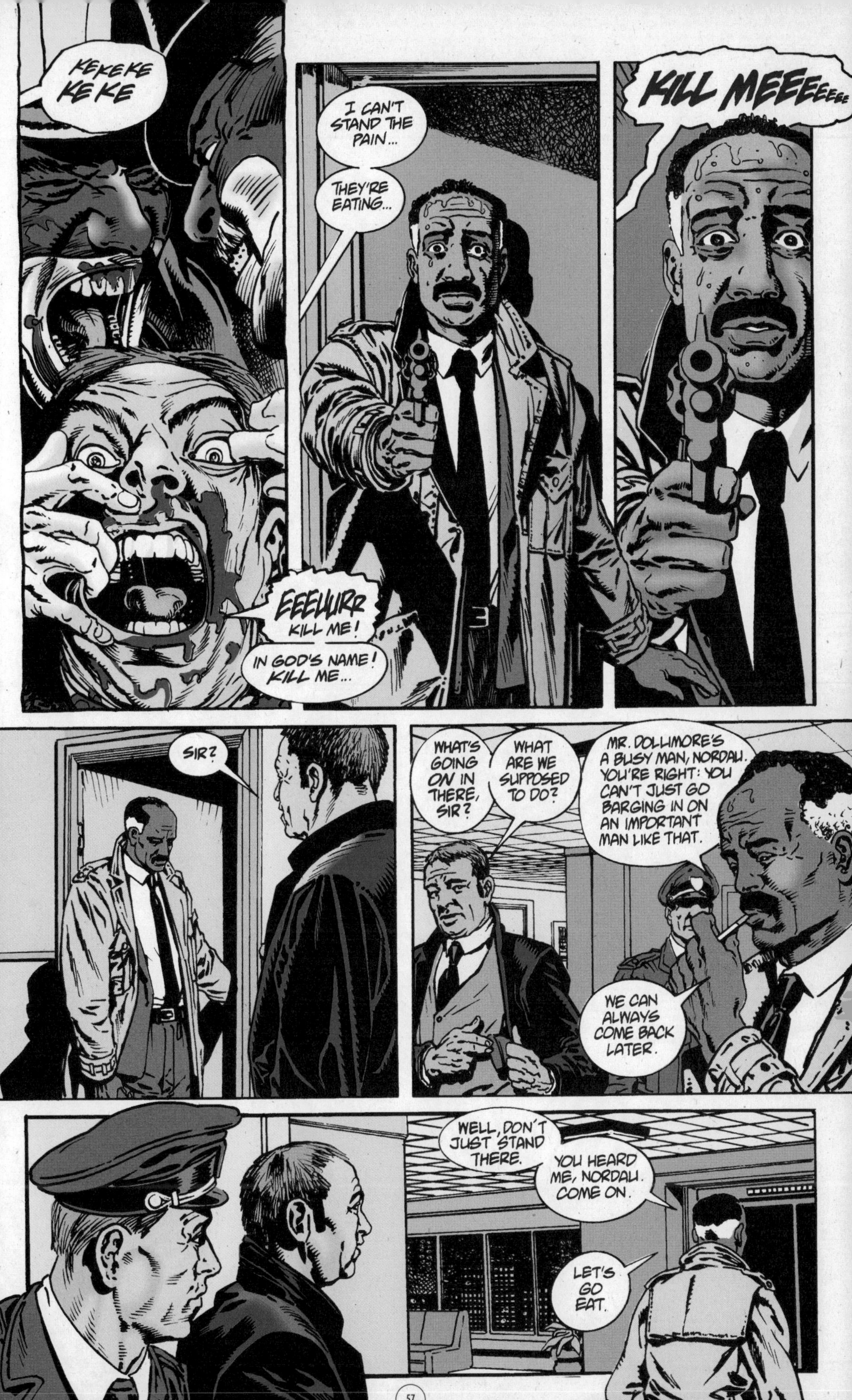
KEKEKE
KEKE
I CAN'T STAND THE PAIN...
THEY'RE EATING...
KILL MEEEeeee
EEEUURR
KILL ME!
IN GOD'S NAME! KILL ME...
SIR?
WHAT'S GOING ON IN THERE, SIR?
WHAT ARE WE SUPPOSED TO DO?
MR. DOLLIMORE'S A BUSY MAN, NORDAU. YOU'RE RIGHT: YOU CAN'T JUST GO BARGING IN ON AN IMPORTANT MAN LIKE THAT.
WE CAN ALWAYS COME BACK LATER.
WELL, DON'T JUST STAND THERE.
YOU HEARD ME, NORDAU. COME ON.
LET'S GO EAT.

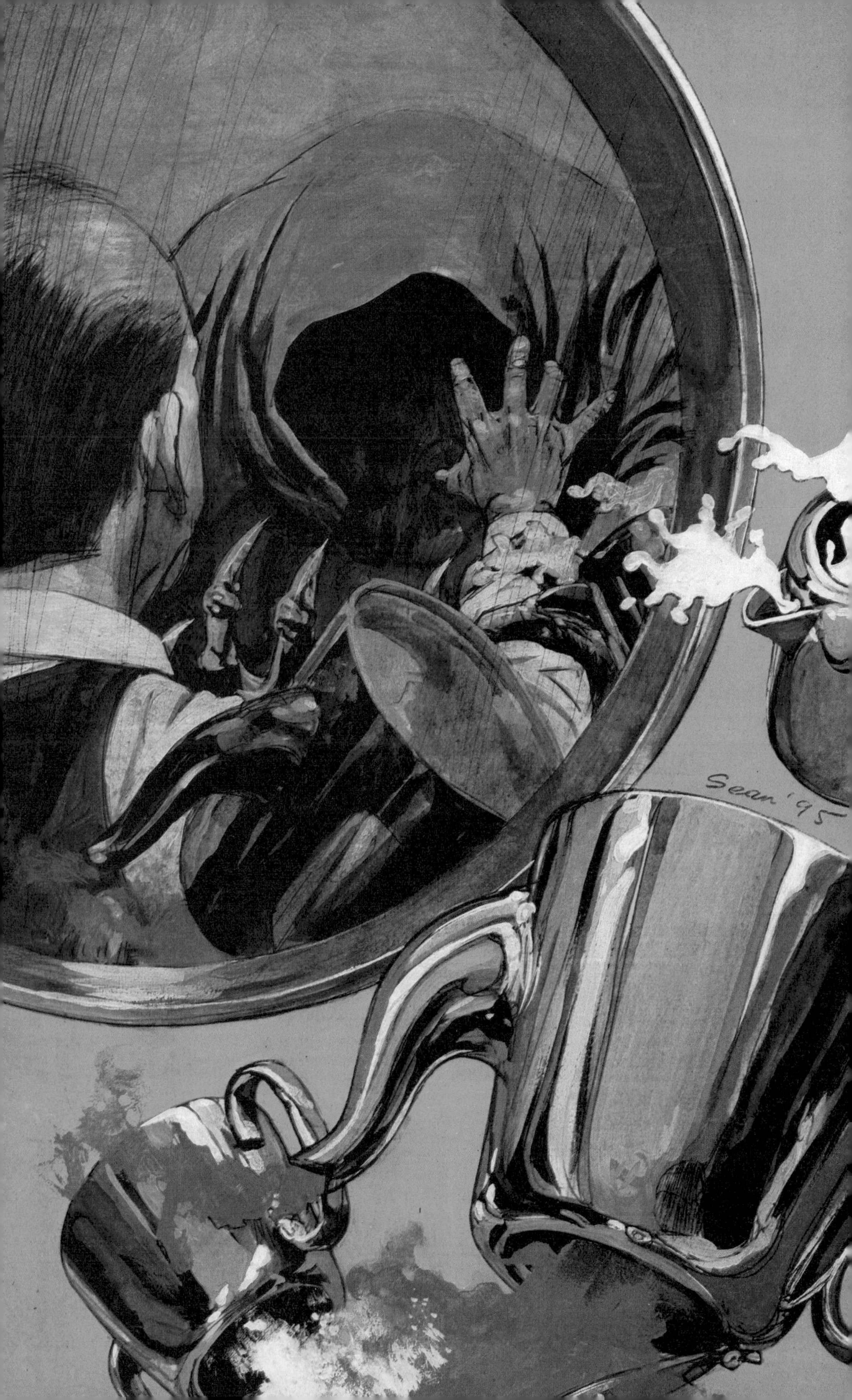
Sean '95

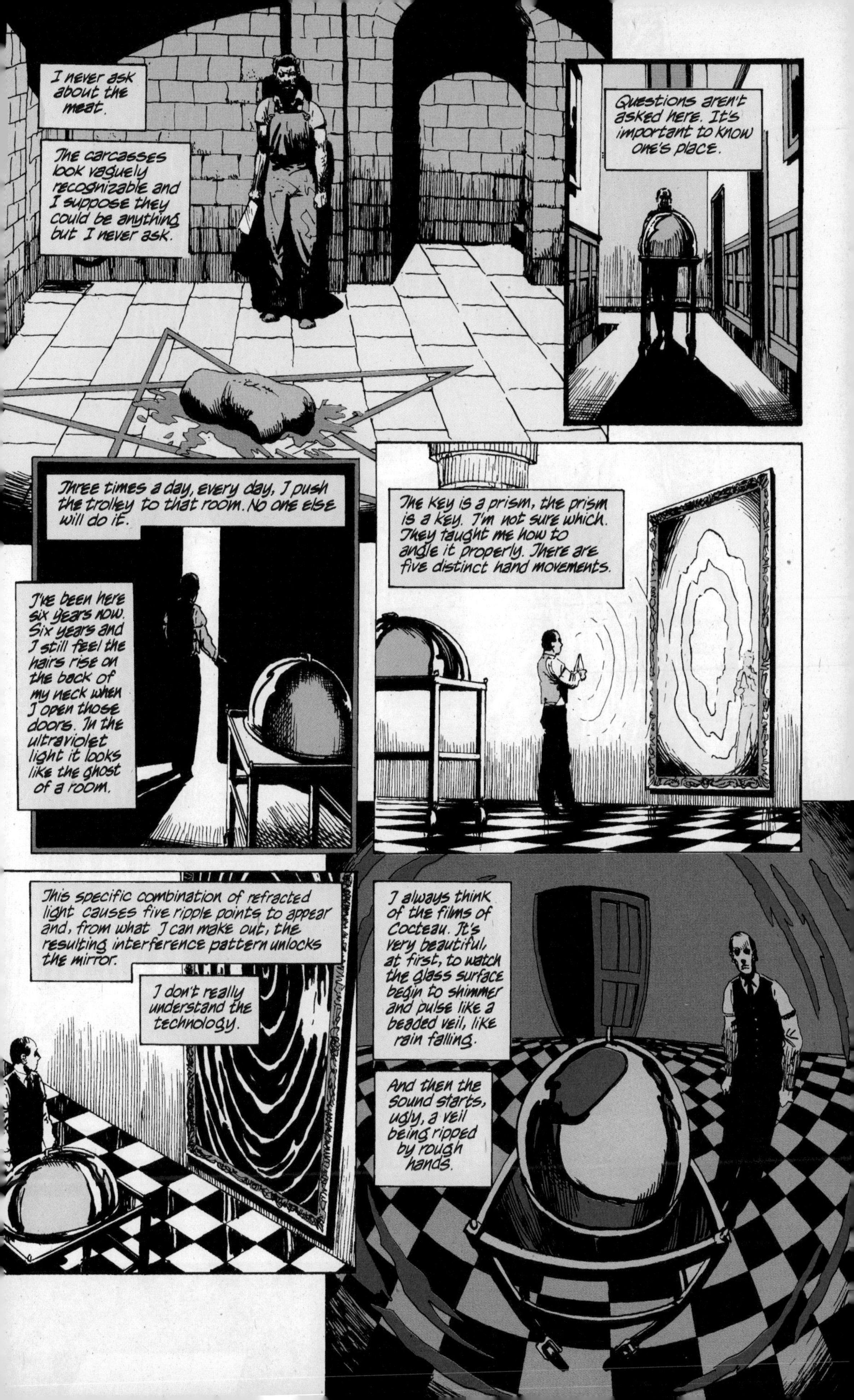
I never ask about the meat.
The carcasses look vaguely recognizable and I suppose they could be anything but I never ask.
Questions aren't asked here. It's important to know one's place.
Three times a day, every day, I push the trolley to that room. No one else will do it.
I've been here six years now. Six years and I still feel the hairs rise on the back of my neck when I open those doors. In the ultraviolet light it looks like the ghost of a room.
The key is a prism, the prism is a key. I'm not sure which. They taught me how to angle it properly. There are five distinct hand movements.
This specific combination of refracted light causes five ripple points to appear and, from what I can make out, the resulting interference pattern unlocks the mirror.
I don't really understand the technology.
I always think of the films of Cocteau. It's very beautiful, at first, to watch the glass surface begin to shimmer and pulse like a beaded veil, like rain falling.
And then the sound starts, ugly, a veil being ripped by rough hands.

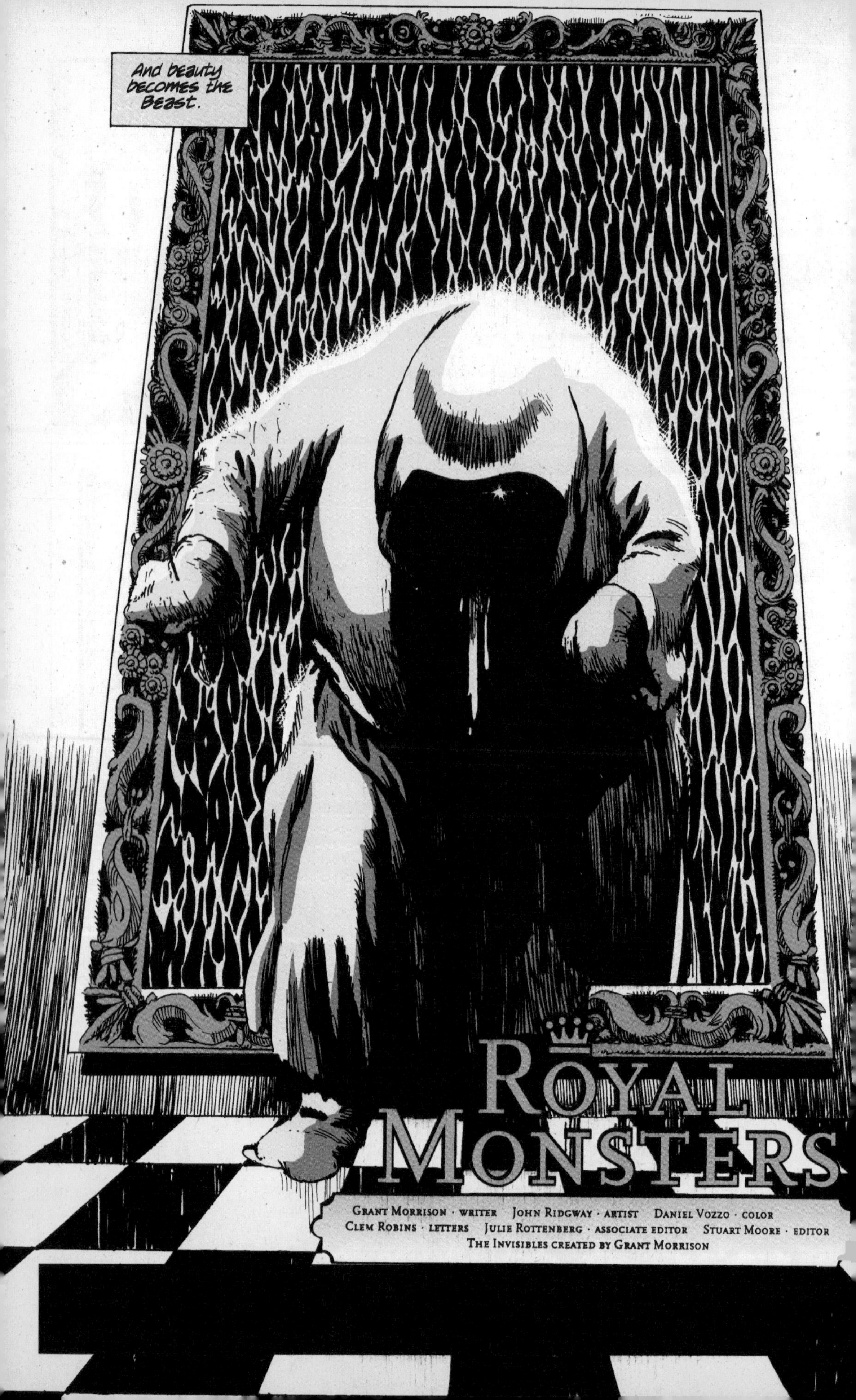
And beauty becomes the Beast.
ROYAL MONSTERS
GRANT MORRISON · WRITER JOHN RIDGWAY · ARTIST DANIEL VOZZO · COLOR
CLEM ROBINS · LETTERS JULIE ROTTENBERG · ASSOCIATE EDITOR STUART MOORE · EDITOR
THE INVISIBLES CREATED BY GRANT MORRISON

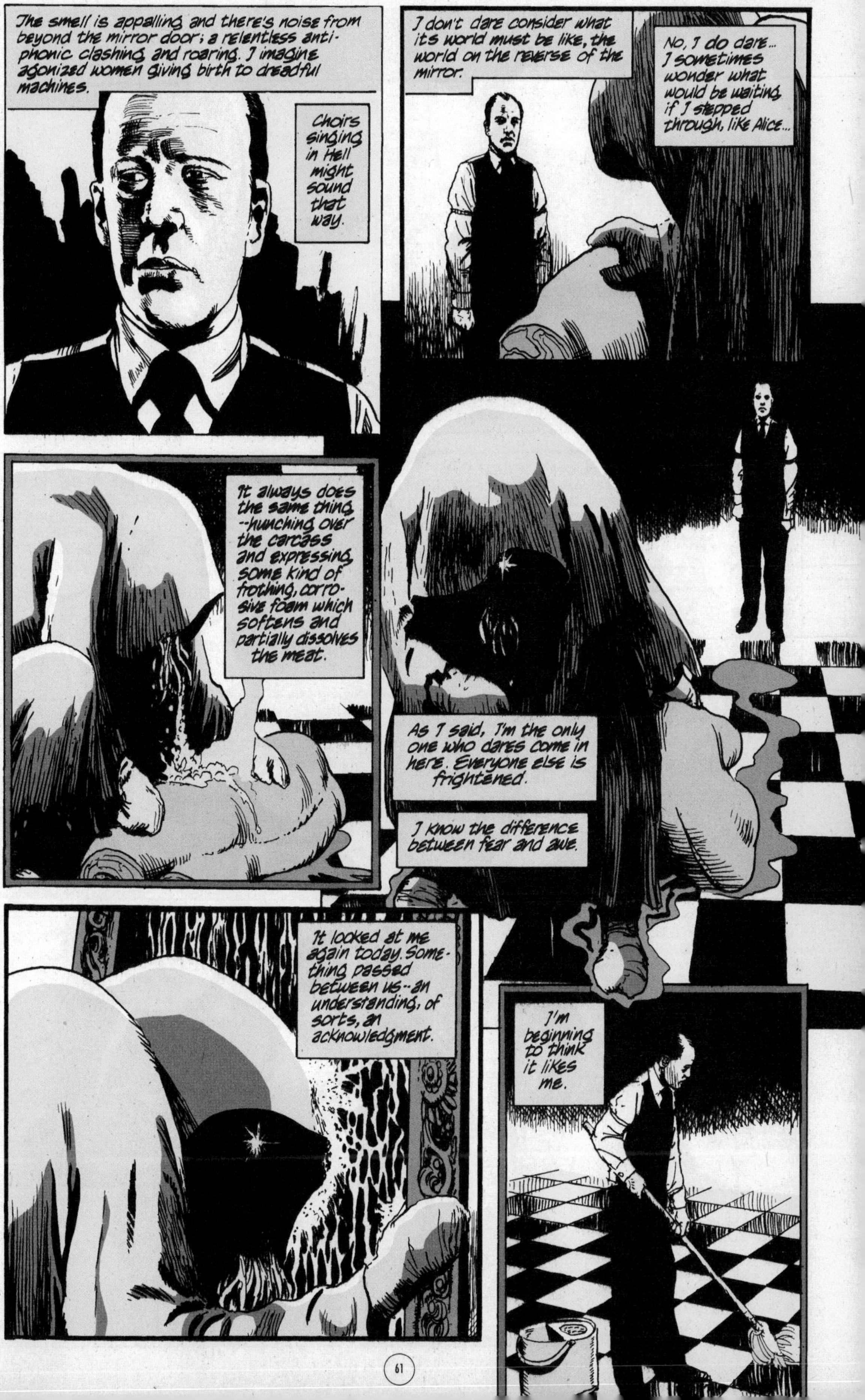

The smell is appalling and there's noise from beyond the mirror door; a relentless antiphonic clashing and roaring. I imagine agonized women giving birth to dreadful machines.
Choirs singing in Hell might sound that way.
I don't dare consider what its world must be like, the world on the reverse of the mirror.
No, I do dare... I sometimes wonder what would be waiting if I stepped through, like Alice...
It always does the same thing --hunching over the carcass and expressing some kind of frothing, corrosive foam which softens and partially dissolves the meat.
As I said, I'm the only one who dares come in here. Everyone else is frightened.
I know the difference between fear and awe.
It looked at me again today. Something passed between us--an understanding, of sorts, an acknowledgment.
I'm beginning to think it likes me.

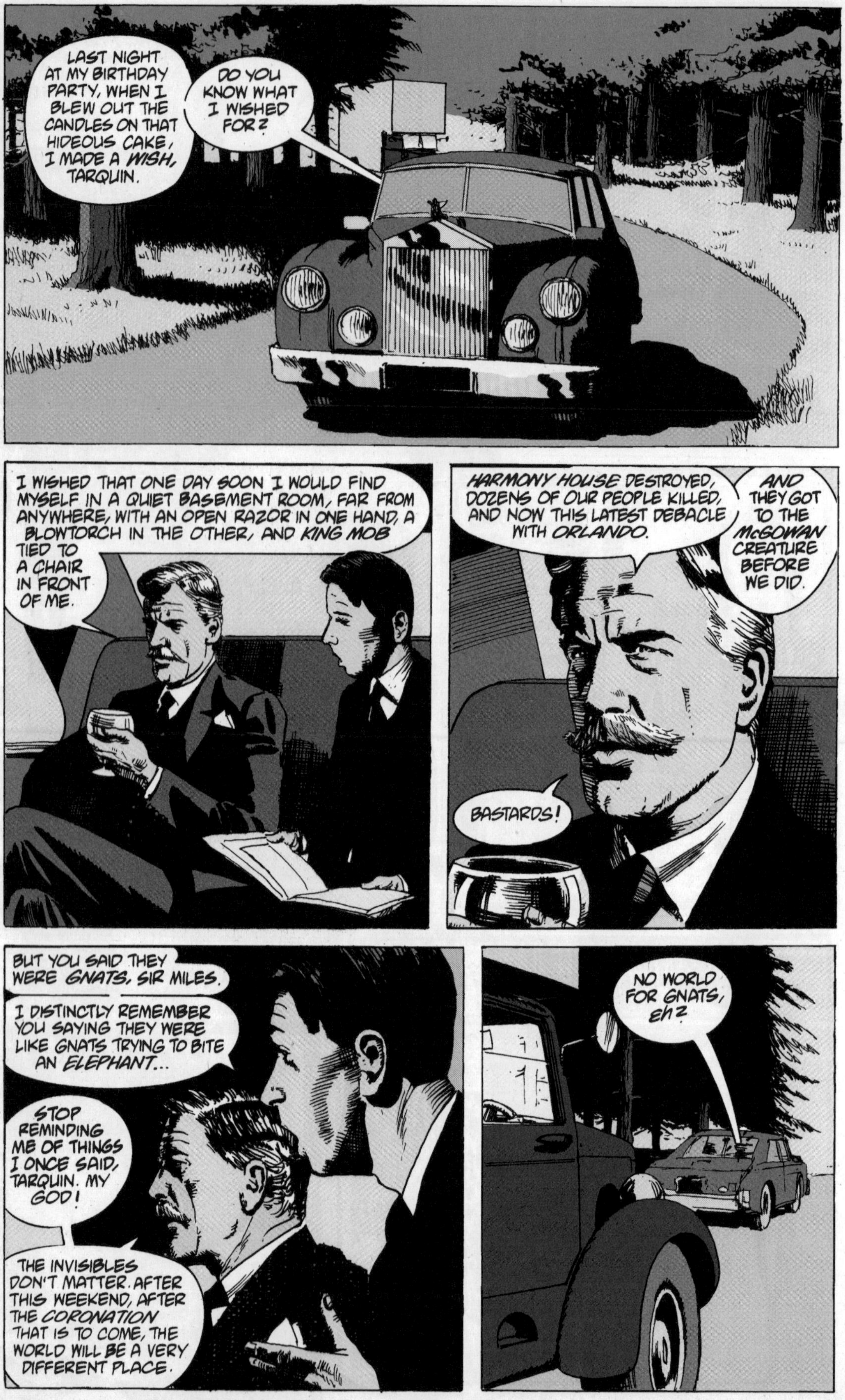
LAST NIGHT AT MY BIRTHDAY PARTY, WHEN I BLEW OUT THE CANDLES ON THAT HIDEOUS CAKE, I MADE A WISH, TARQUIN.
DO YOU KNOW WHAT I WISHED FOR?
I WISHED THAT ONE DAY SOON I WOULD FIND MYSELF IN A QUIET BASEMENT ROOM, FAR FROM ANYWHERE, WITH AN OPEN RAZOR IN ONE HAND, A BLOWTORCH IN THE OTHER, AND KING MOB TIED TO A CHAIR IN FRONT OF ME.
HARMONY HOUSE DESTROYED, DOZENS OF OUR PEOPLE KILLED, AND NOW THIS LATEST DEBACLE WITH ORLANDO.
AND THEY GOT TO THE McGOWAN CREATURE BEFORE WE DID.
BASTARDS!
BUT YOU SAID THEY WERE GNATS, SIR MILES.
I DISTINCTLY REMEMBER YOU SAYING THEY WERE LIKE GNATS TRYING TO BITE AN ELEPHANT...
STOP REMINDING ME OF THINGS I ONCE SAID, TARQUIN. MY GOD!
THE INVISIBLES DON'T MATTER. AFTER THIS WEEKEND, AFTER THE CORONATION THAT IS TO COME, THE WORLD WILL BE A VERY DIFFERENT PLACE.
NO WORLD FOR GNATS, EH?

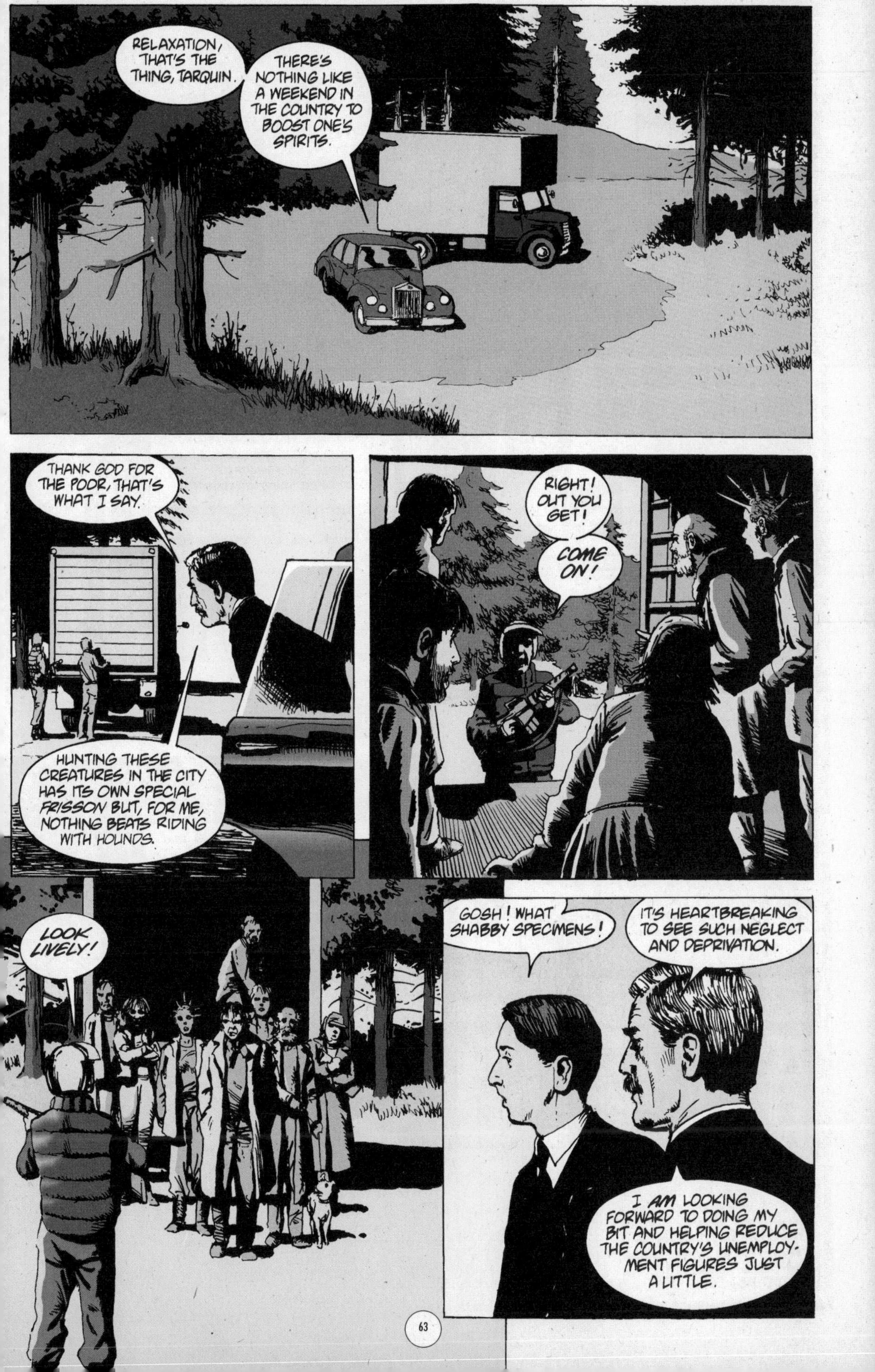
RELAXATION, THAT'S THE THING, TARQUIN.
THERE'S NOTHING LIKE A WEEKEND IN THE COUNTRY TO BOOST ONE'S SPIRITS.
THANK GOD FOR THE POOR, THAT'S WHAT I SAY.
HUNTING THESE CREATURES IN THE CITY HAS ITS OWN SPECIAL FRISSON BUT, FOR ME, NOTHING BEATS RIDING WITH HOUNDS.
RIGHT! OUT YOU GET!
COME ON!
LOOK LIVELY!
GOSH! WHAT SHABBY SPECIMENS!
IT'S HEARTBREAKING TO SEE SUCH NEGLECT AND DEPRIVATION.
I AM LOOKING FORWARD TO DOING MY BIT AND HELPING REDUCE THE COUNTRY'S UNEMPLOYMENT FIGURES JUST A LITTLE.

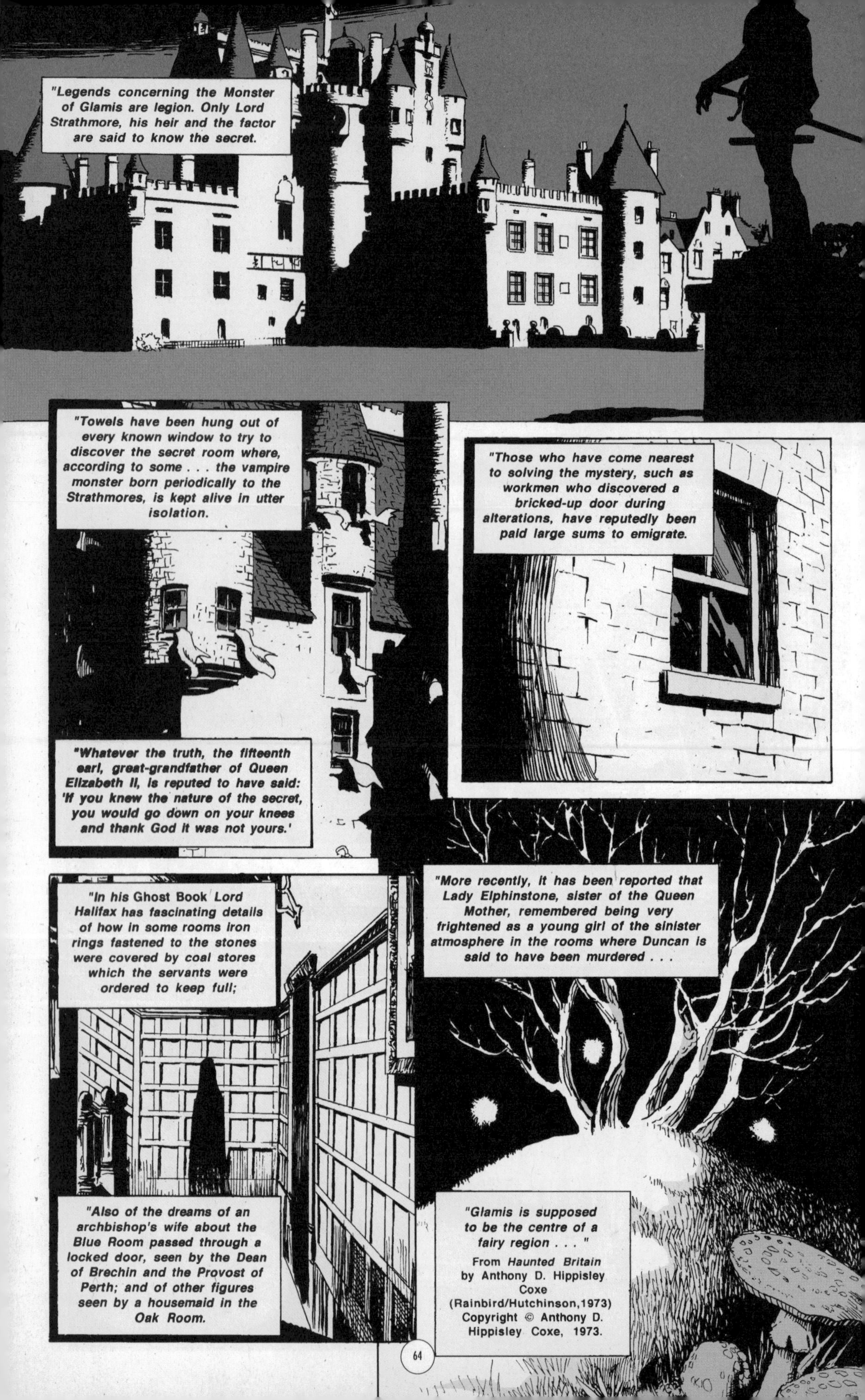
"Legends concerning the Monster of Glamis are legion. Only Lord Strathmore, his heir and the factor are said to know the secret.
"Towels have been hung out of every known window to try to discover the secret room where, according to some . . . the vampire monster born periodically to the Strathmores, is kept alive in utter isolation.
"Those who have come nearest to solving the mystery, such as workmen who discovered a bricked-up door during alterations, have reputedly been paid large sums to emigrate.
"Whatever the truth, the fifteenth earl, great-grandfather of Queen Elizabeth II, is reputed to have said: 'If you knew the nature of the secret, you would go down on your knees and thank God it was not yours.'
"In his Ghost Book Lord Halifax has fascinating details of how in some rooms iron rings fastened to the stones were covered by coal stores which the servants were ordered to keep full;
"More recently, it has been reported that Lady Elphinstone, sister of the Queen Mother, remembered being very frightened as a young girl of the sinister atmosphere in the rooms where Duncan is said to have been murdered . . .
"Also of the dreams of an archbishop's wife about the Blue Room passed through a locked door, seen by the Dean of Brechin and the Provost of Perth; and of other figures seen by a housemaid in the Oak Room.
"Glamis is supposed to be the centre of a fairy region . . . "
From Haunted Britain by Anthony D. Hippisley Coxe (Rainbird/Hutchinson, 1973) Copyright © Anthony D. Hippisley Coxe, 1973.

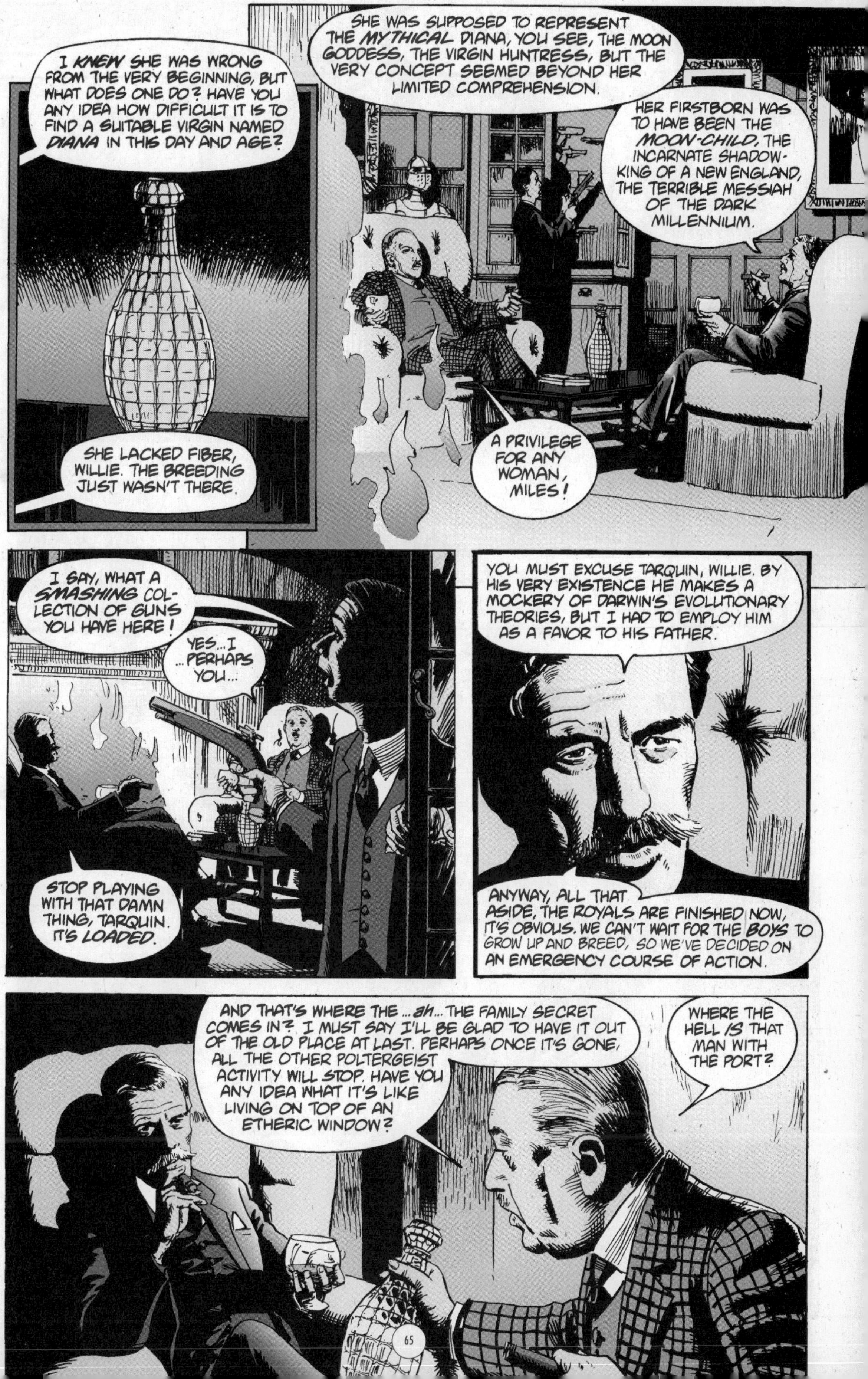
I KNEW SHE WAS WRONG FROM THE VERY BEGINNING, BUT WHAT DOES ONE DO? HAVE YOU ANY IDEA HOW DIFFICULT IT IS TO FIND A SUITABLE VIRGIN NAMED DIANA IN THIS DAY AND AGE?
SHE WAS SUPPOSED TO REPRESENT THE MYTHICAL DIANA, YOU SEE, THE MOON GODDESS, THE VIRGIN HUNTRESS, BUT THE VERY CONCEPT SEEMED BEYOND HER LIMITED COMPREHENSION.
HER FIRSTBORN WAS TO HAVE BEEN THE MOON-CHILD, THE INCARNATE SHADOW-KING OF A NEW ENGLAND, THE TERRIBLE MESSIAH OF THE DARK MILLENNIUM.
SHE LACKED FIBER, WILLIE. THE BREEDING JUST WASN'T THERE.
A PRIVILEGE FOR ANY WOMAN, MILES!
I SAY, WHAT A SMASHING COLLECTION OF GUNS YOU HAVE HERE!
YES...I ...PERHAPS YOU...
STOP PLAYING WITH THAT DAMN THING, TARQUIN. IT'S LOADED.
YOU MUST EXCUSE TARQUIN, WILLIE. BY HIS VERY EXISTENCE HE MAKES A MOCKERY OF DARWIN'S EVOLUTIONARY THEORIES, BUT I HAD TO EMPLOY HIM AS A FAVOR TO HIS FATHER.
ANYWAY, ALL THAT ASIDE, THE ROYALS ARE FINISHED NOW, IT'S OBVIOUS. WE CAN'T WAIT FOR THE BOYS TO GROW UP AND BREED, SO WE'VE DECIDED ON AN EMERGENCY COURSE OF ACTION.
AND THAT'S WHERE THE ...ah... THE FAMILY SECRET COMES IN? I MUST SAY I'LL BE GLAD TO HAVE IT OUT OF THE OLD PLACE AT LAST. PERHAPS ONCE IT'S GONE, ALL THE OTHER POLTERGEIST ACTIVITY WILL STOP. HAVE YOU ANY IDEA WHAT IT'S LIKE LIVING ON TOP OF AN ETHERIC WINDOW?
WHERE THE HELL IS THAT MAN WITH THE PORT?

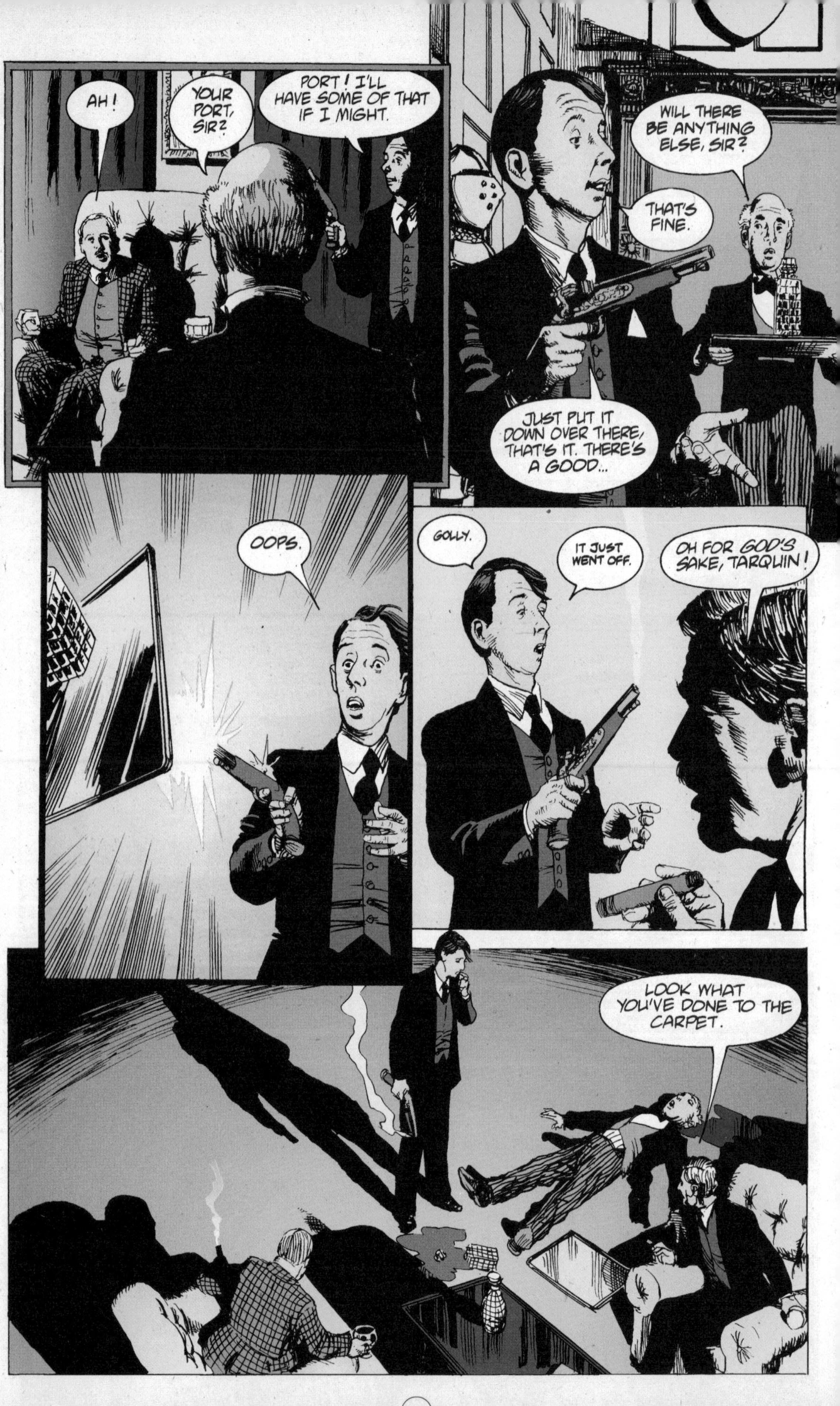
AH!
YOUR PORT, SIR?
PORT! I'LL HAVE SOME OF THAT IF I MIGHT.
WILL THERE BE ANYTHING ELSE, SIR?
THAT'S FINE.
JUST PUT IT DOWN OVER THERE, THAT'S IT. THERE'S A GOOD...
OOPS.
GOLLY.
IT JUST WENT OFF.
OH FOR GOD'S SAKE, TARQUIN!
LOOK WHAT YOU'VE DONE TO THE CARPET.

I tried to do it again today.

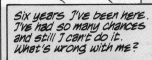

Six years I've been here. I've had so many chances and still I can't do it. What's wrong with me?

Six years. It was just after I split up with Emma. That was when Kate ran away. That last phone call. "I HATE YOU AND I'M NEVER COMING BACK!"

Six years. Talk about deep cover.

The last communication I had with one of the Invisibles was two years ago next month.

Perhaps I'm punishing myself for Kate. I don't know. Maybe Emma and I should have tried a little harder to get on. Perhaps when I look at the Monster I'm simply seeing another trapped and confused creature, like myself.

I feel sorry for it.

I promised I'd do it then. Two years later and I'm still here, still here. I can hardly remember when I wasn't a servant.

I'm the Thing on the far side of its mirror. We're both the same.

God help me, but I can't fulfill my mission. I'll be here for the rest of my life, I know I will. I just cannot do it.

I can't kill the Monster.

I feel sorry for it. I think it likes me.

I can't kill it.

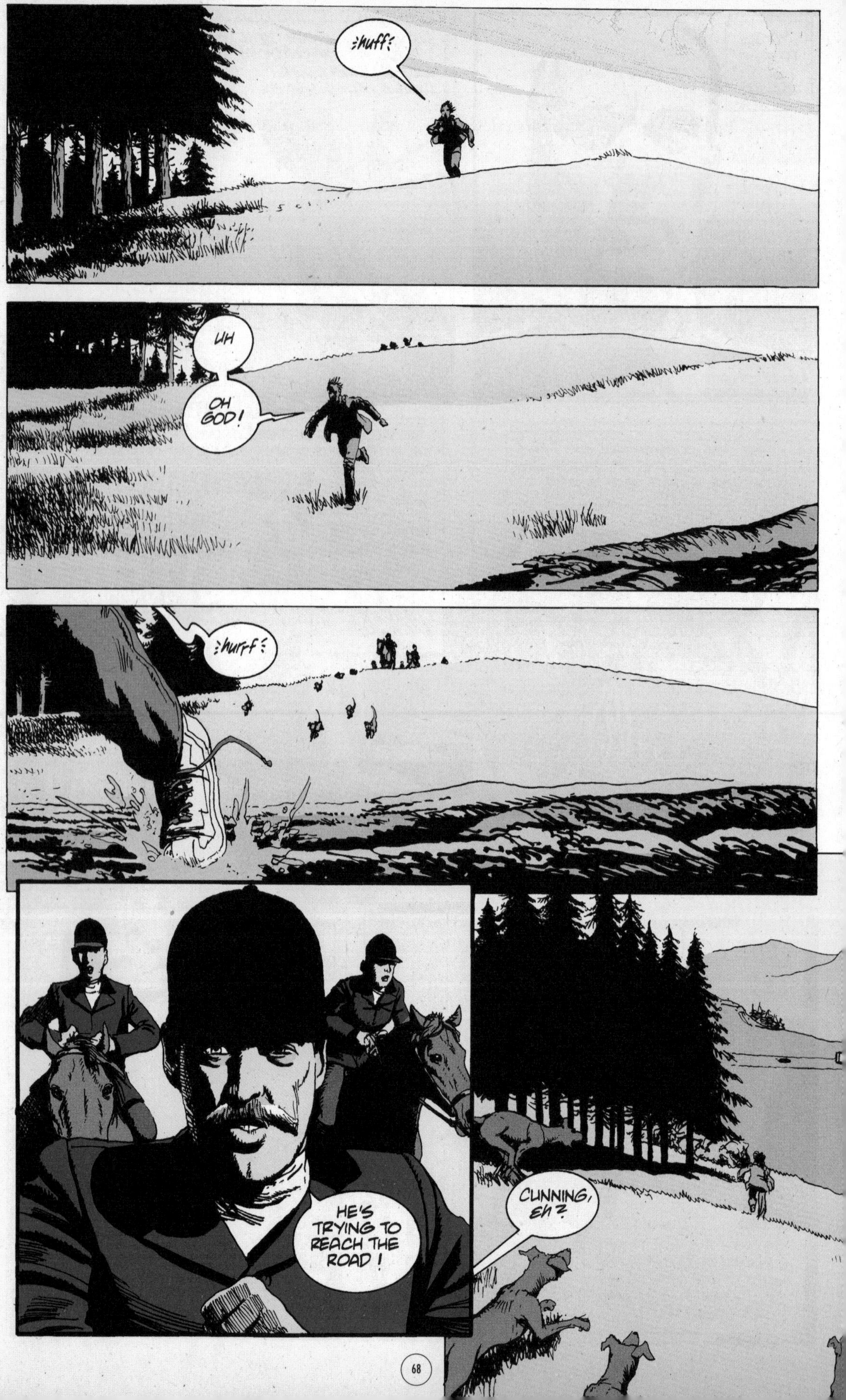

:huff:
UH
OH GOD!
:hurrf:
HE'S TRYING TO REACH THE ROAD!
CUNNING, EH?

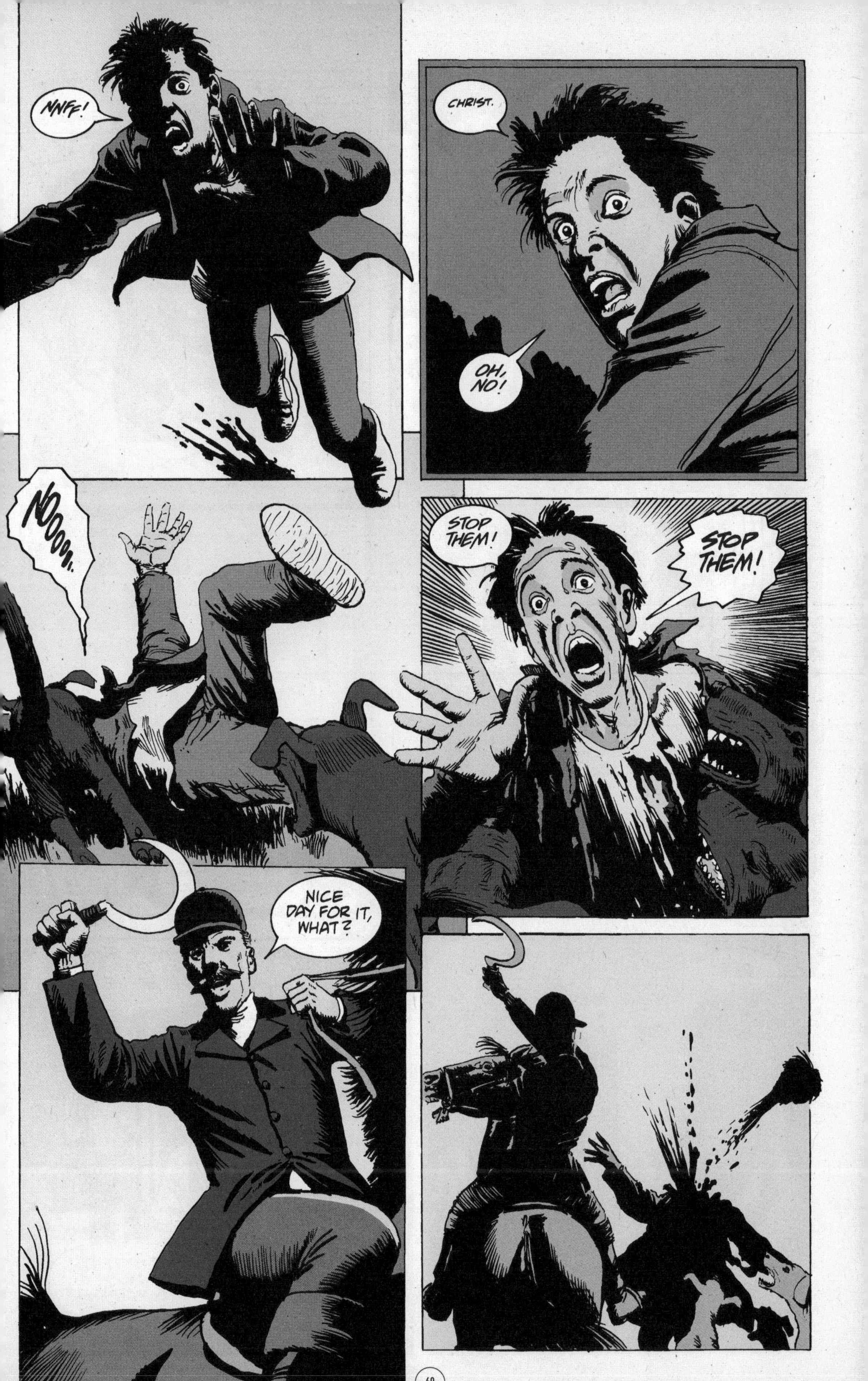
NNFF!
CHRIST.
OH, NO!
NOOOOO...
STOP THEM!
STOP THEM!
NICE DAY FOR IT, WHAT?

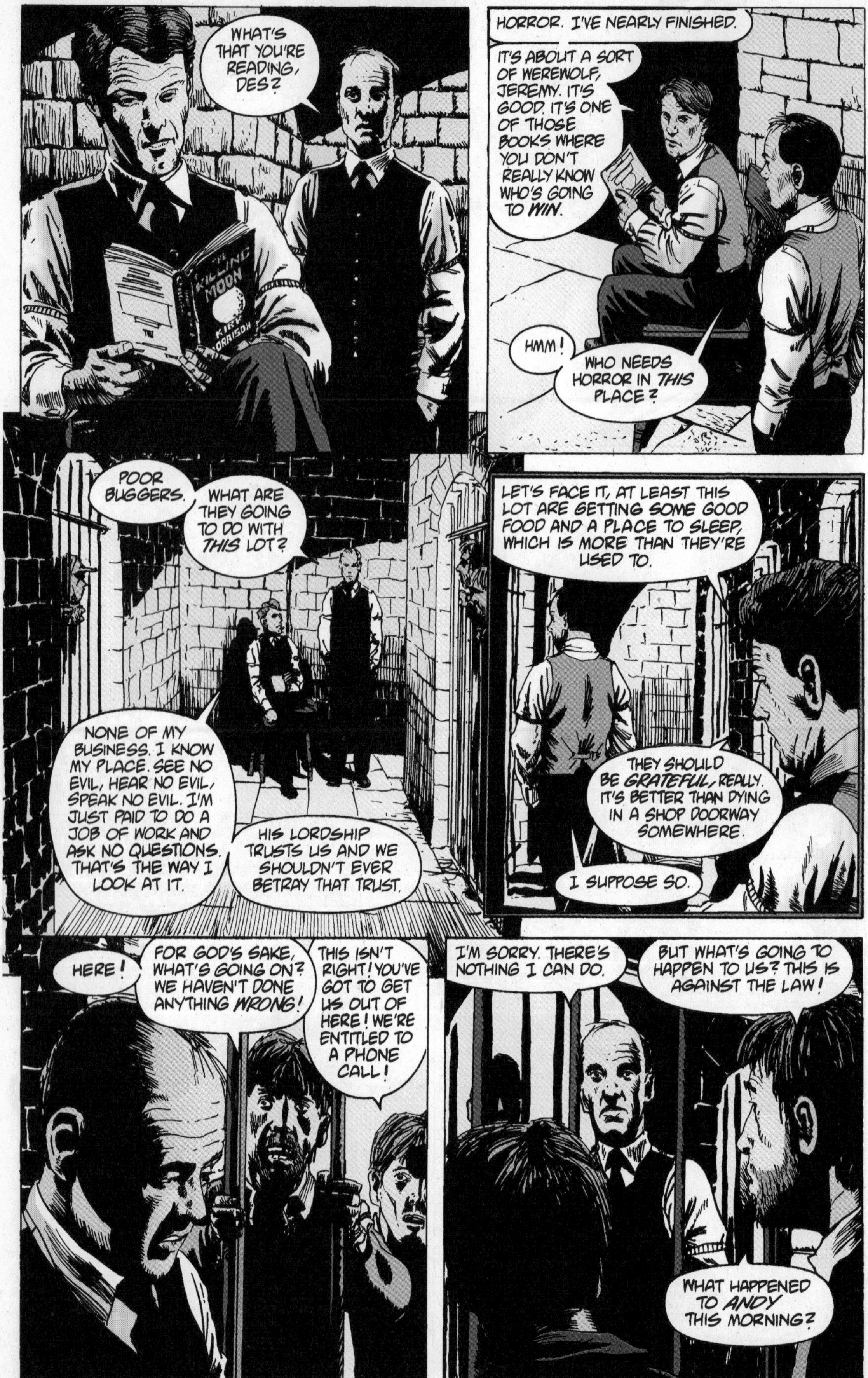

WHAT'S THAT YOU'RE READING, DES?
THE KILLING MOON
KIRK MORRISON
HORROR. I'VE NEARLY FINISHED.
IT'S ABOUT A SORT OF WEREWOLF, JEREMY. IT'S GOOD. IT'S ONE OF THOSE BOOKS WHERE YOU DON'T REALLY KNOW WHO'S GOING TO *WIN*.
HMM!
WHO NEEDS HORROR IN *THIS* PLACE?
POOR BUGGERS.
WHAT ARE THEY GOING TO DO WITH *THIS* LOT?
NONE OF MY BUSINESS. I KNOW MY PLACE. SEE NO EVIL, HEAR NO EVIL, SPEAK NO EVIL. I'M JUST PAID TO DO A JOB OF WORK AND ASK NO QUESTIONS. THAT'S THE WAY I LOOK AT IT.
HIS LORDSHIP TRUSTS US AND WE SHOULDN'T EVER BETRAY THAT TRUST.
LET'S FACE IT, AT LEAST THIS LOT ARE GETTING SOME GOOD FOOD AND A PLACE TO SLEEP, WHICH IS MORE THAN THEY'RE USED TO.
THEY SHOULD BE *GRATEFUL*, REALLY. IT'S BETTER THAN DYING IN A SHOP DOORWAY SOMEWHERE.
I SUPPOSE SO.
HERE!
FOR GOD'S SAKE, WHAT'S GOING ON? WE HAVEN'T DONE ANYTHING *WRONG*!
THIS ISN'T RIGHT! YOU'VE GOT TO GET US OUT OF HERE! WE'RE ENTITLED TO A PHONE CALL!
I'M SORRY. THERE'S NOTHING I CAN DO.
BUT WHAT'S GOING TO HAPPEN TO US? THIS IS AGAINST THE LAW!
WHAT HAPPENED TO *ANDY* THIS MORNING?

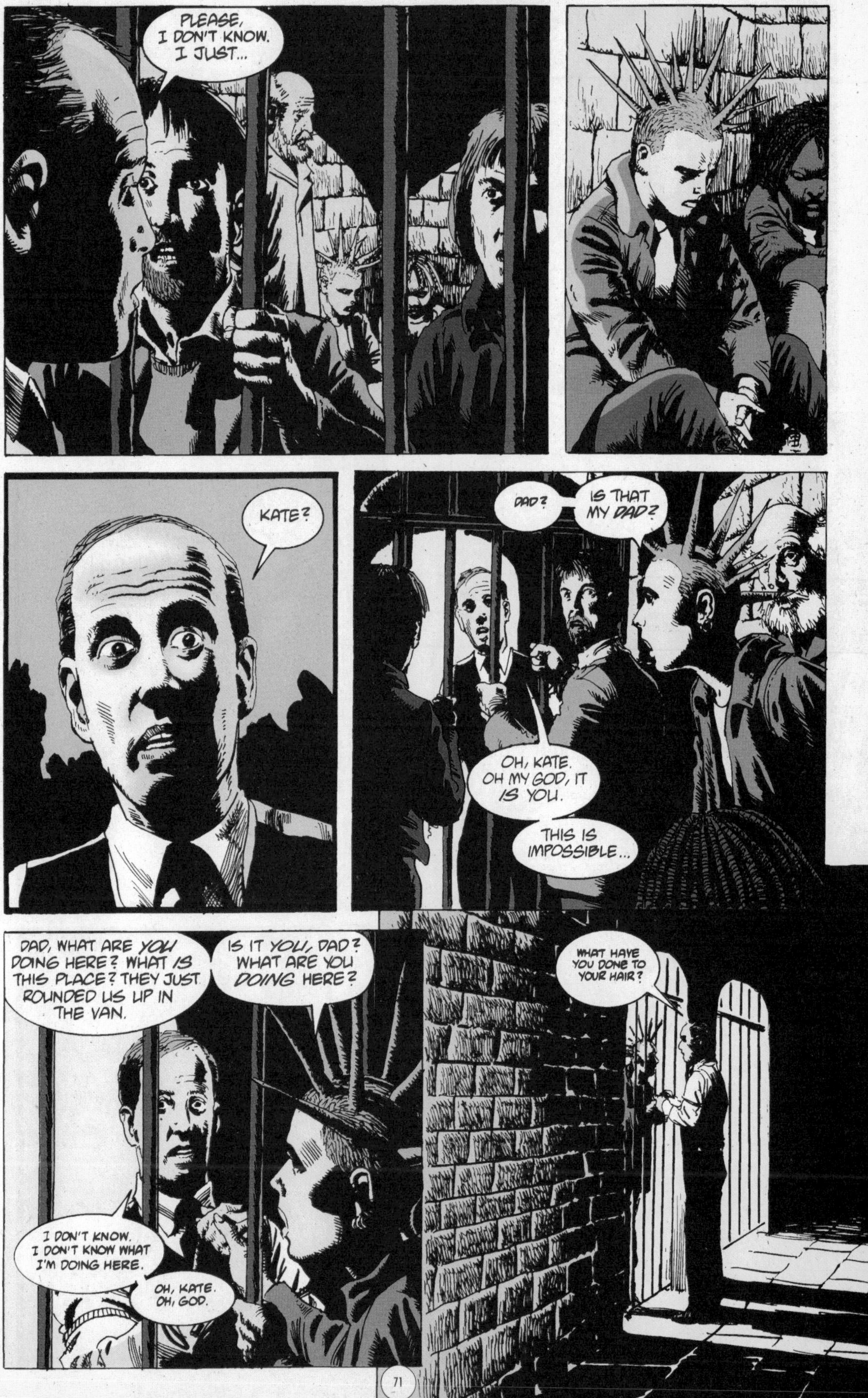
PLEASE, I DON'T KNOW. I JUST...
KATE?
DAD?
IS THAT MY DAD?
OH, KATE. OH MY GOD, IT IS YOU.
THIS IS IMPOSSIBLE...
DAD, WHAT ARE YOU DOING HERE? WHAT IS THIS PLACE? THEY JUST ROUNDED US UP IN THE VAN.
IS IT YOU, DAD? WHAT ARE YOU DOING HERE?
I DON'T KNOW. I DON'T KNOW WHAT I'M DOING HERE.
OH, KATE. OH, GOD.
WHAT HAVE YOU DONE TO YOUR HAIR?

"AND BEFORE THAT I'M GOING TO DO WHAT I CAME TO DO; TOMORROW MORNING I'M GOING TO KILL THE MONSTER..."

THRILLING STUFF.

"I CAN FIX EVERYTHING. I'M GOING TO FIX EVERYTHING. KATE'S IN THE BATCH THEY INTEND TO HUNT TONIGHT BUT I'M GOING TO GET HER OUT. BY TOMORROW NIGHT WE'LL BE FREE AND TOGETHER AGAIN."

THIS MAN *SUTTON* WAS RECRUITED BY THE *INVISIBLES* IN *1988*, HE STARTED WORK HERE IN *'89*, AND WE'VE ONLY *JUST* DISCOVERED HE'S BEEN WORKING FOR THE INVISIBLES?

GOOD GOD, D'YOU REALIZE THE DAMAGE HE COULD HAVE DONE IF HE WASN'T SO SPINELESS?

WELL, WE *HAVE* BEEN MONITORING HIM FOR FOUR MONTHS...

WHO'D HAVE THOUGHT HE'D BE STUPID ENOUGH TO START KEEPING A *DIARY* AFTER ALL THIS TIME?

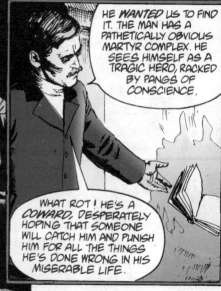

HE *WANTED* US TO FIND IT. THE MAN HAS A PATHETICALLY OBVIOUS MARTYR COMPLEX. HE SEES HIMSELF AS A TRAGIC HERO, RACKED BY PANGS OF CONSCIENCE.

WHAT ROT! HE'S A *COWARD*, DESPERATELY HOPING THAT SOMEONE WILL CATCH HIM AND PUNISH HIM FOR ALL THE THINGS HE'S DONE WRONG IN HIS MISERABLE LIFE.

HA!

IT'S A LUCKY MAN WHO GETS TO LIVE OUT HIS DREAM!

THE GAME'S AFOOT, WHAT?

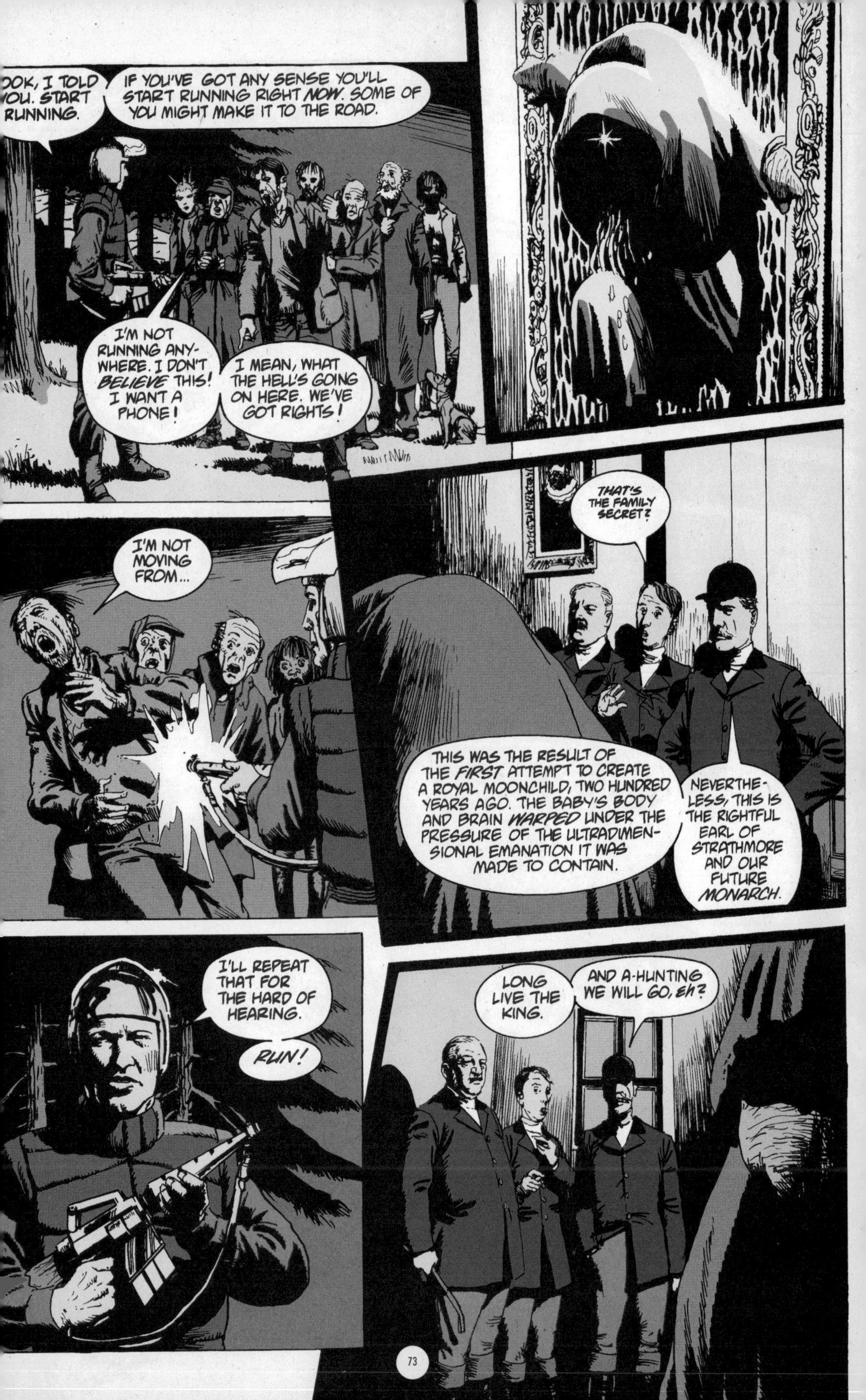

OOK, I TOLD YOU. START RUNNING.
IF YOU'VE GOT ANY SENSE YOU'LL START RUNNING RIGHT *NOW*. SOME OF YOU MIGHT MAKE IT TO THE ROAD.
I'M NOT RUNNING ANYWHERE. I DON'T *BELIEVE* THIS! I WANT A PHONE!
I MEAN, WHAT THE HELL'S GOING ON HERE. WE'VE GOT RIGHTS!
THAT'S THE FAMILY SECRET?
I'M NOT MOVING FROM...
THIS WAS THE RESULT OF THE *FIRST* ATTEMPT TO CREATE A ROYAL MOONCHILD, TWO HUNDRED YEARS AGO. THE BABY'S BODY AND BRAIN *WARPED* UNDER THE PRESSURE OF THE ULTRADIMENSIONAL EMANATION IT WAS MADE TO CONTAIN.
NEVERTHELESS, THIS IS THE RIGHTFUL EARL OF STRATHMORE AND OUR FUTURE *MONARCH*.
I'LL REPEAT THAT FOR THE HARD OF HEARING.
RUN!
LONG LIVE THE KING.
AND A-HUNTING WE WILL GO, *EH*?

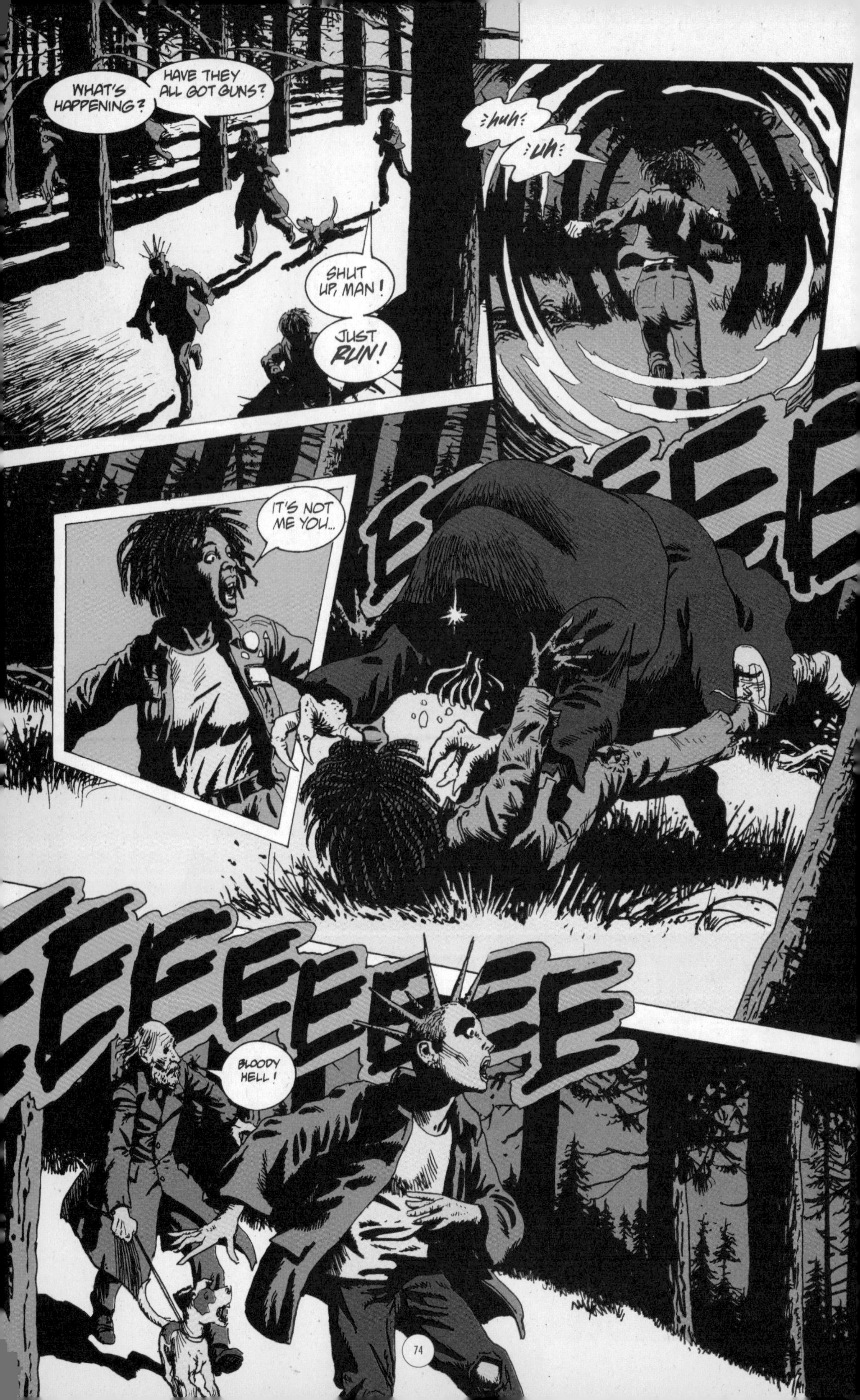
WHAT'S HAPPENING?
HAVE THEY ALL GOT GUNS?
SHUT UP, MAN!
JUST RUN!
huh
uh
IT'S NOT ME YOU...
BLOODY HELL!

IIIIIWAAAAAAAAAAAAAA

KATE!

KATE!

WHAT?

IT'S OKAY. IT'S ME. YOU'RE SAFE.

IT'S ALL RIGHT.

DAD! OH, DAD, IT'S KILLING THEM! IT'S LIKE SOME KIND OF ANIMAL!

IT'S KILLING THEM!

IT WON'T GET YOU. THEY WON'T GET YOU.

OH, KATE. OH, LOVE. I'M SORRY IT ALL WENT WRONG. I THOUGHT I'D LOST YOU FOREVER.

I'M SORRY.

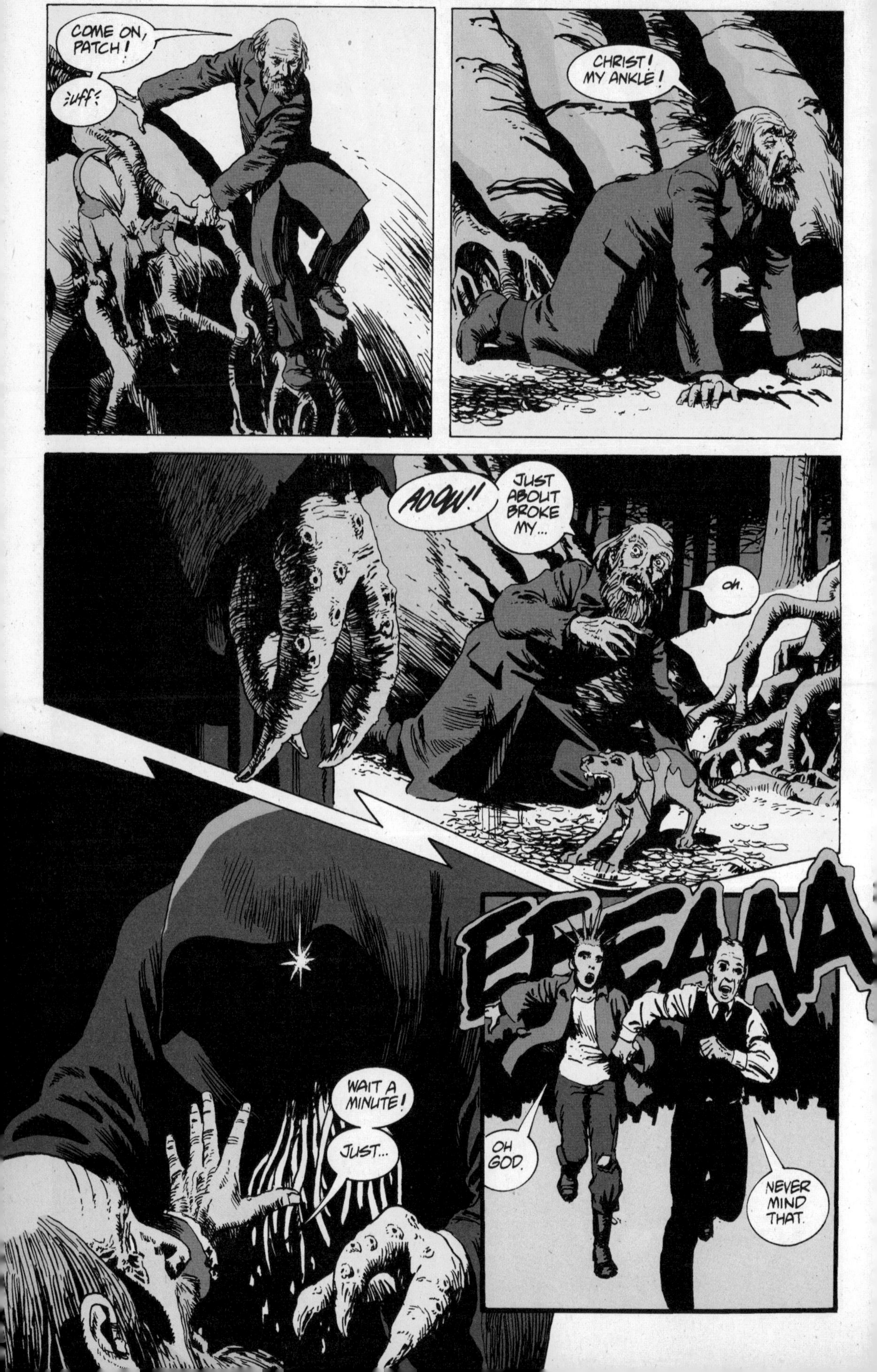
COME ON, PATCH!
:UFF:
CHRIST! MY ANKLE!
AOOW!
JUST ABOUT BROKE MY...
OH.
WAIT A MINUTE!
JUST...
OH GOD.
NEVER MIND THAT.

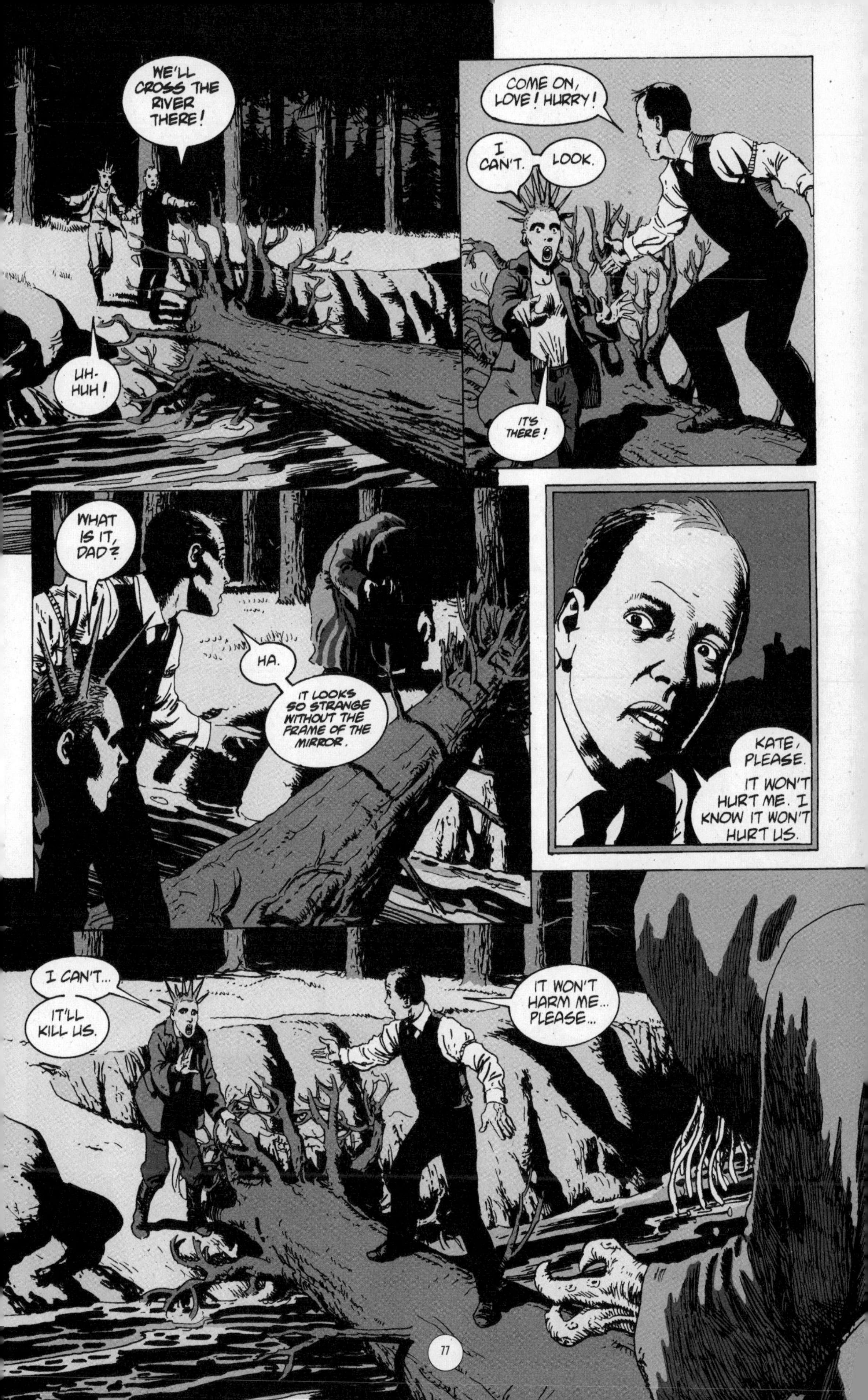
WE'LL CROSS THE RIVER THERE!
UH-HUH!
COME ON, LOVE! HURRY!
I CAN'T.
LOOK.
IT'S THERE!
WHAT IS IT, DAD?
HA.
IT LOOKS SO STRANGE WITHOUT THE FRAME OF THE MIRROR.
KATE, PLEASE.
IT WON'T HURT ME. I KNOW IT WON'T HURT US.
I CAN'T...
IT'LL KILL US.
IT WON'T HARM ME... PLEASE...

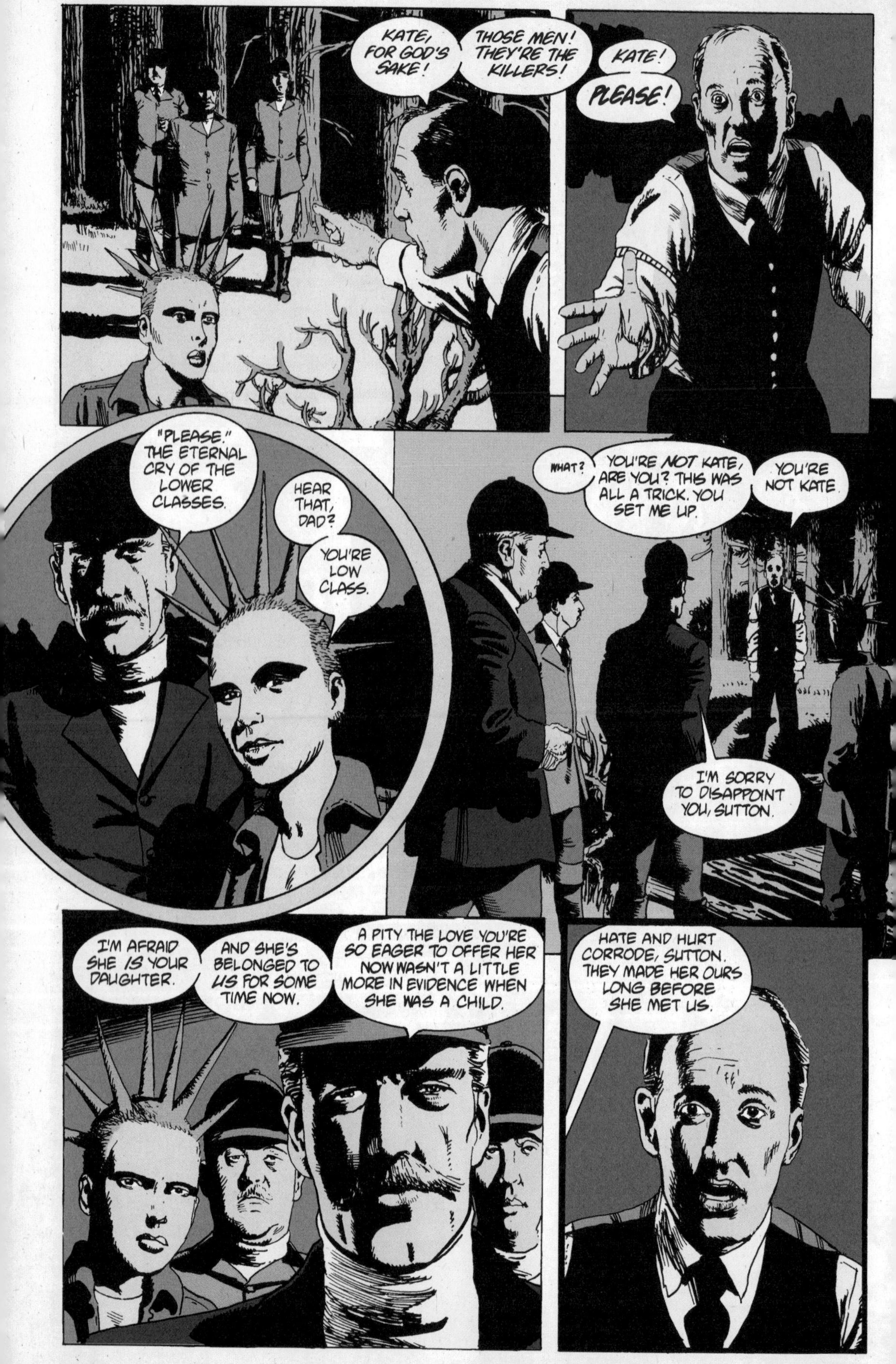
KATE, FOR GOD'S SAKE!
THOSE MEN! THEY'RE THE KILLERS!
KATE!
PLEASE!
"PLEASE." THE ETERNAL CRY OF THE LOWER CLASSES.
HEAR THAT, DAD?
YOU'RE LOW CLASS.
WHAT?
YOU'RE NOT KATE, ARE YOU? THIS WAS ALL A TRICK. YOU SET ME UP.
YOU'RE NOT KATE.
I'M SORRY TO DISAPPOINT YOU, SUTTON.
I'M AFRAID SHE IS YOUR DAUGHTER.
AND SHE'S BELONGED TO US FOR SOME TIME NOW.
A PITY THE LOVE YOU'RE SO EAGER TO OFFER HER NOW WASN'T A LITTLE MORE IN EVIDENCE WHEN SHE WAS A CHILD.
HATE AND HURT CORRODE, SUTTON. THEY MADE HER OURS LONG BEFORE SHE MET US.

DON'T LOOK THERE FOR HELP. YOU WERE ONLY EVER ITS *SERVANT*. IT'S ALL TO DO WITH PRIVILEGE.

AND NOW YOU'RE CENTER STAGE, SUTTON. IT'S YOUR BIG SCENE.

TARQUIN.

RIGHTO, SIR MILES.

BOO!

WHAT'S THIS?

IS THIS A JOKE?

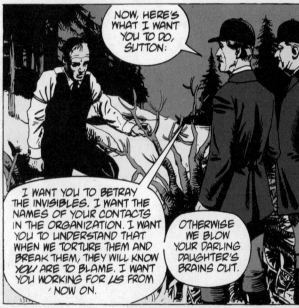

NOW, HERE'S WHAT I WANT YOU TO DO, SUTTON:

I WANT YOU TO BETRAY THE INVISIBLES. I WANT THE NAMES OF YOUR CONTACTS IN THE ORGANIZATION. I WANT YOU TO UNDERSTAND THAT WHEN WE TORTURE THEM AND BREAK THEM, THEY WILL KNOW *YOU* ARE TO BLAME. I WANT YOU WORKING FOR *US* FROM NOW ON.

OTHERWISE WE BLOW YOUR DARLING DAUGHTER'S BRAINS OUT.

QUICKLY, MR. SUTTON.

ALL RIGHT.

ALL RIGHT. I'LL TELL YOU EVERYTHING I KNOW.

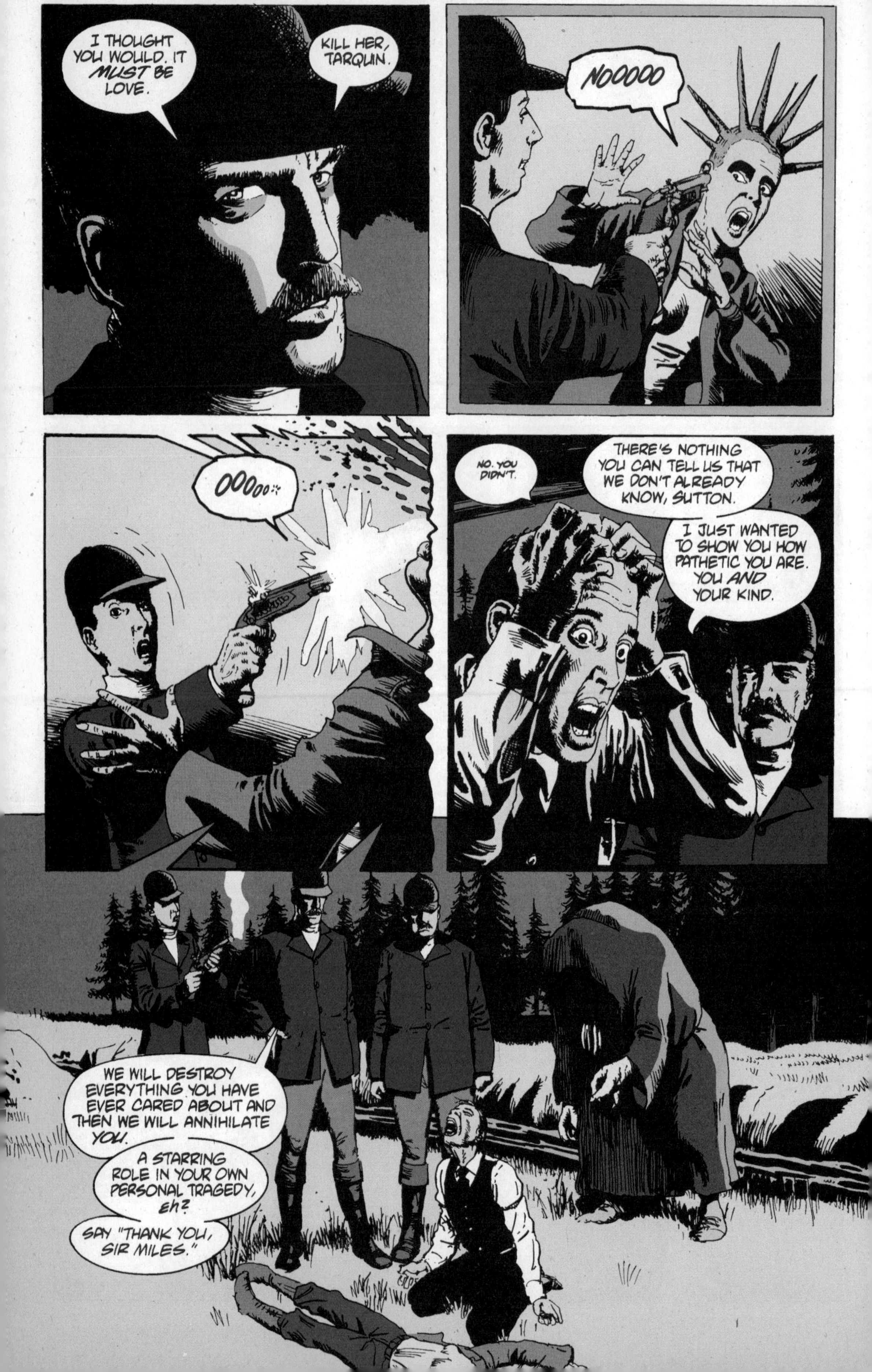
I THOUGHT YOU WOULD. IT MUST BE LOVE.
KILL HER, TARQUIN.
NOOOOO
OOOoo
NO. YOU DIDN'T.
THERE'S NOTHING YOU CAN TELL US THAT WE DON'T ALREADY KNOW, SUTTON.
I JUST WANTED TO SHOW YOU HOW PATHETIC YOU ARE. YOU AND YOUR KIND.
WE WILL DESTROY EVERYTHING YOU HAVE EVER CARED ABOUT AND THEN WE WILL ANNIHILATE YOU.
A STARRING ROLE IN YOUR OWN PERSONAL TRAGEDY, eh?
SAY "THANK YOU, SIR MILES."

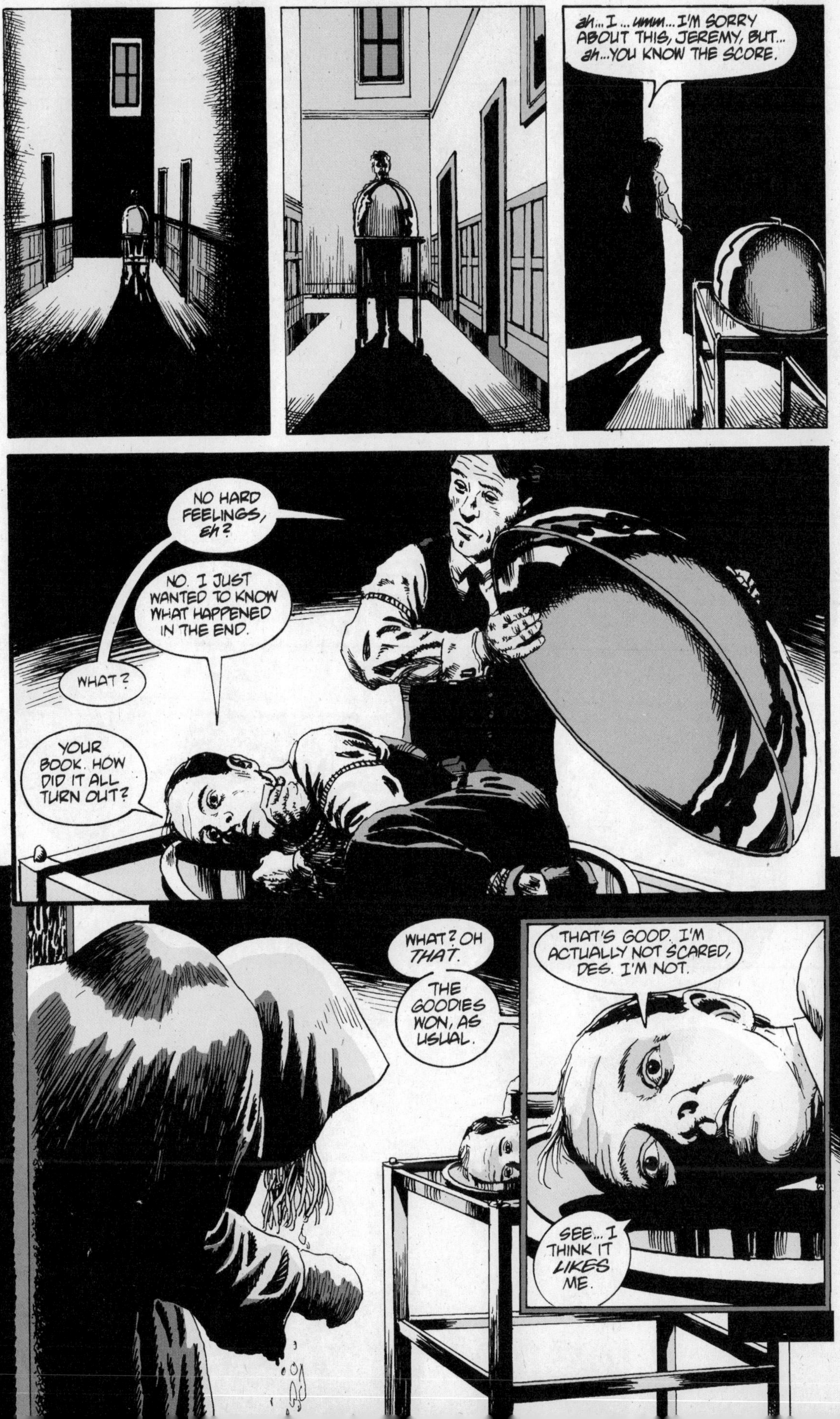

ah... I ... umm... I'M SORRY ABOUT THIS, JEREMY, BUT... ah...YOU KNOW THE SCORE.
NO HARD FEELINGS, eh?
NO. I JUST WANTED TO KNOW WHAT HAPPENED IN THE END.
WHAT?
YOUR BOOK. HOW DID IT ALL TURN OUT?
WHAT? OH THAT.
THE GOODIES WON, AS USUAL.
THAT'S GOOD. I'M ACTUALLY NOT SCARED, DES. I'M NOT.
SEE... I THINK IT LIKES ME.

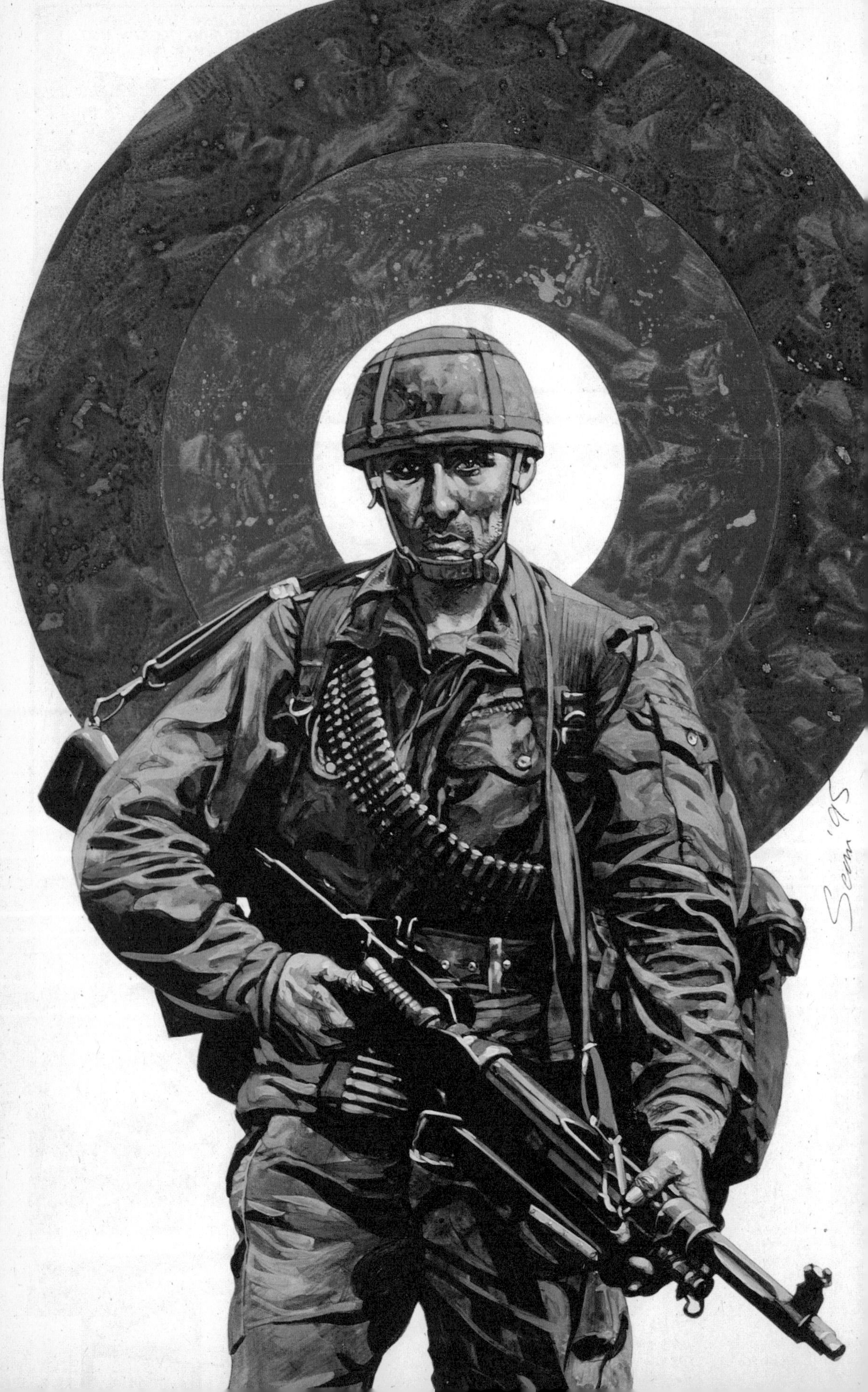
Sean '95

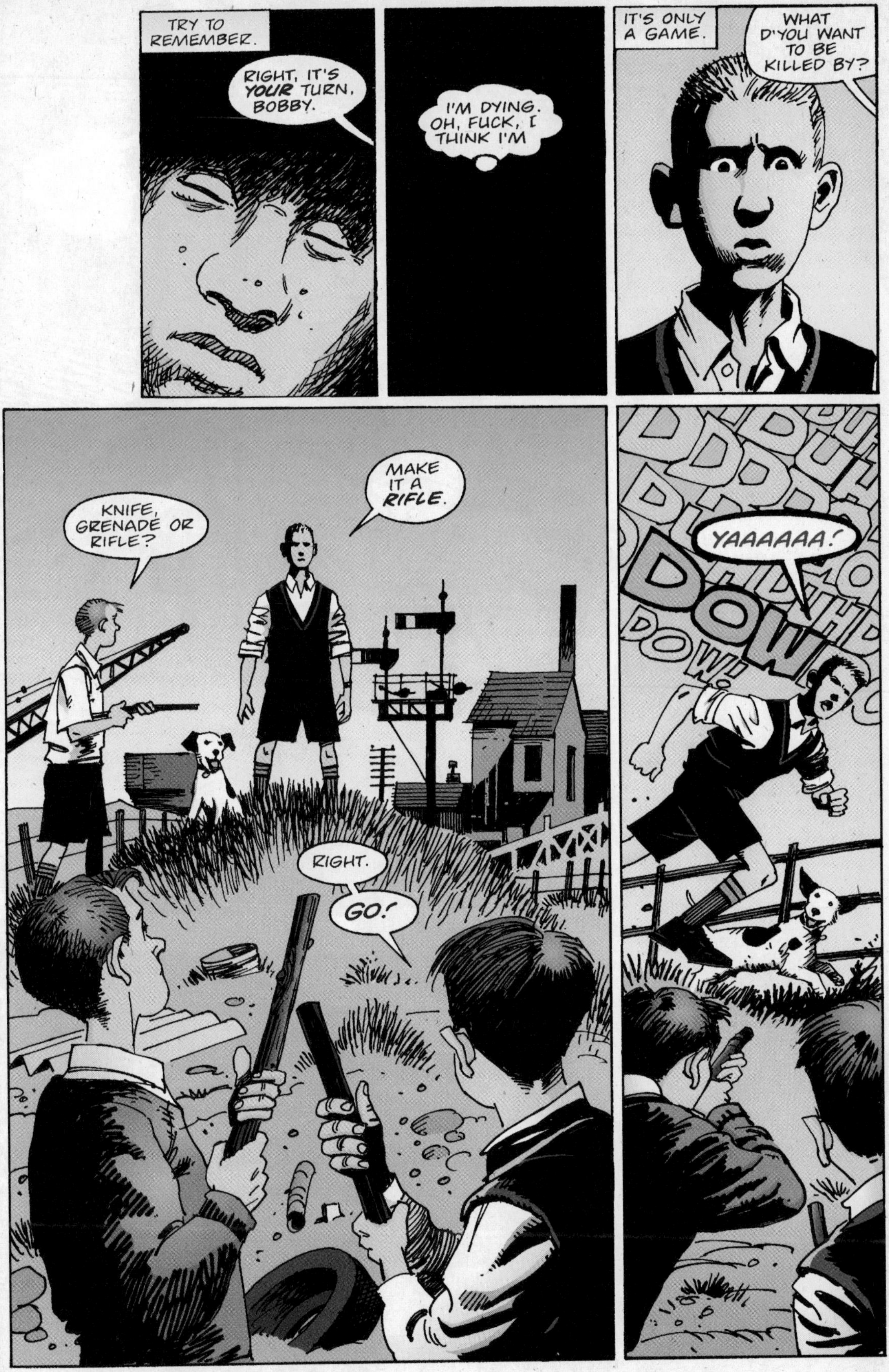

TRY TO REMEMBER.
RIGHT, IT'S YOUR TURN, BOBBY.
I'M DYING. OH, FUCK, I THINK I'M
IT'S ONLY A GAME.
WHAT D'YOU WANT TO BE KILLED BY?
KNIFE, GRENADE OR RIFLE?
MAKE IT A RIFLE.
RIGHT.
GO!
YAAAAAA!
DOW DOW!

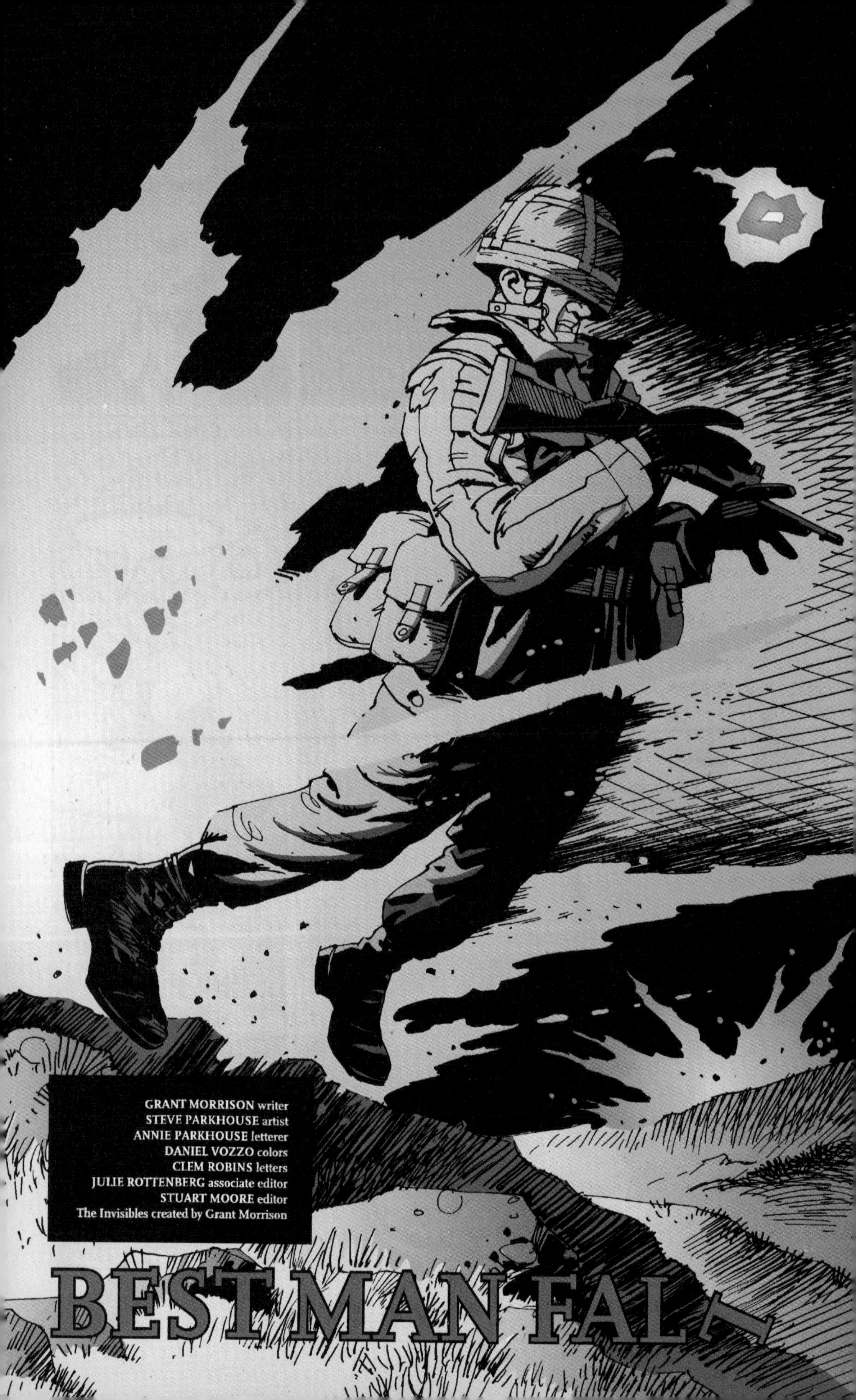
GRANT MORRISON writer
STEVE PARKHOUSE artist
ANNIE PARKHOUSE letterer
DANIEL VOZZO colors
CLEM ROBINS letters
JULIE ROTTENBERG associate editor
STUART MOORE editor
The Invisibles created by Grant Morrison
BEST MAN FALL

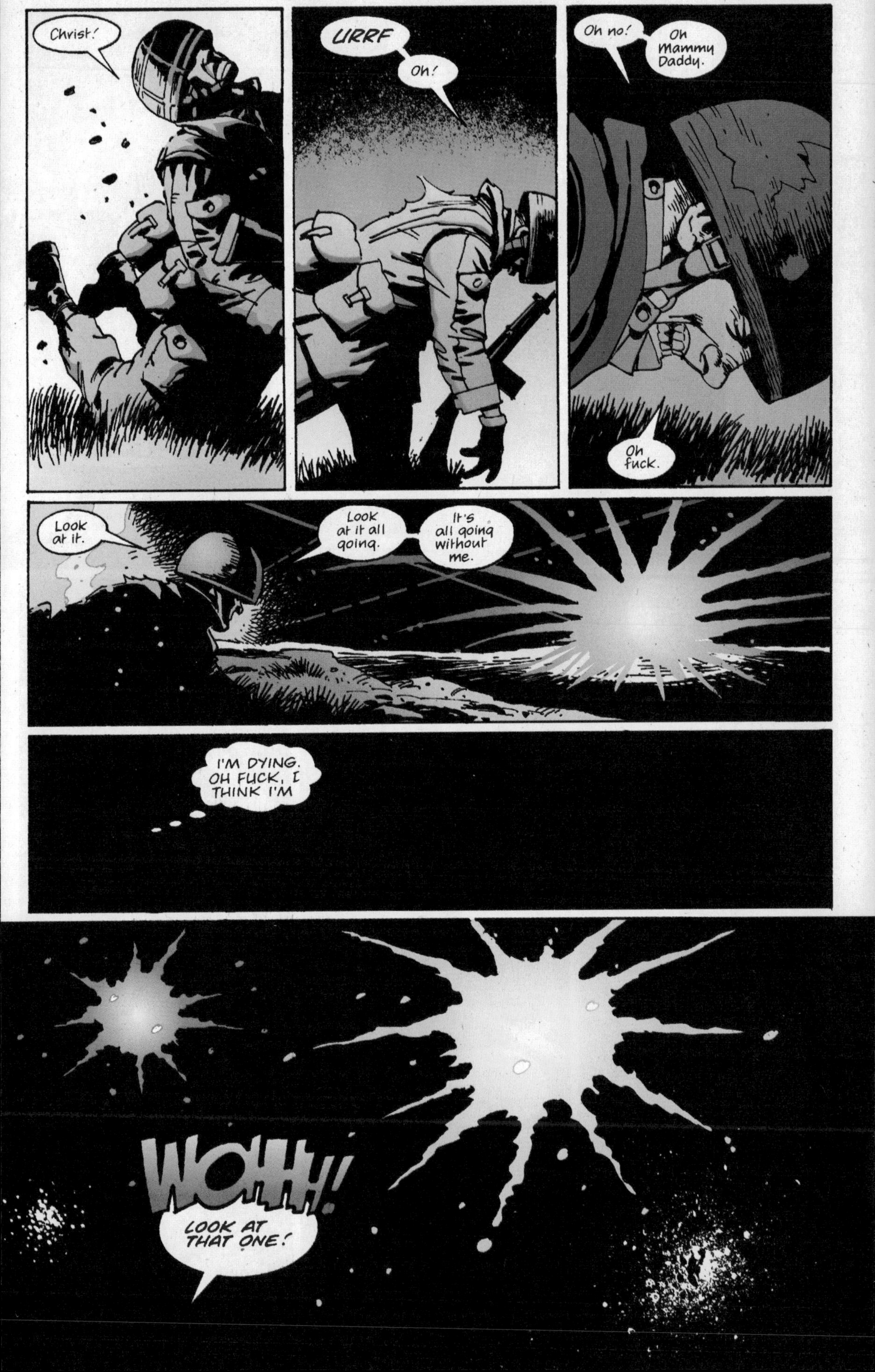
Christ!
URRF
Oh!
Oh no!
Oh Mammy Daddy.
Oh fuck.
Look at it.
Look at it all going.
It's all going without me.
I'M DYING. OH FUCK, I THINK I'M
WOHH!
LOOK AT THAT ONE!

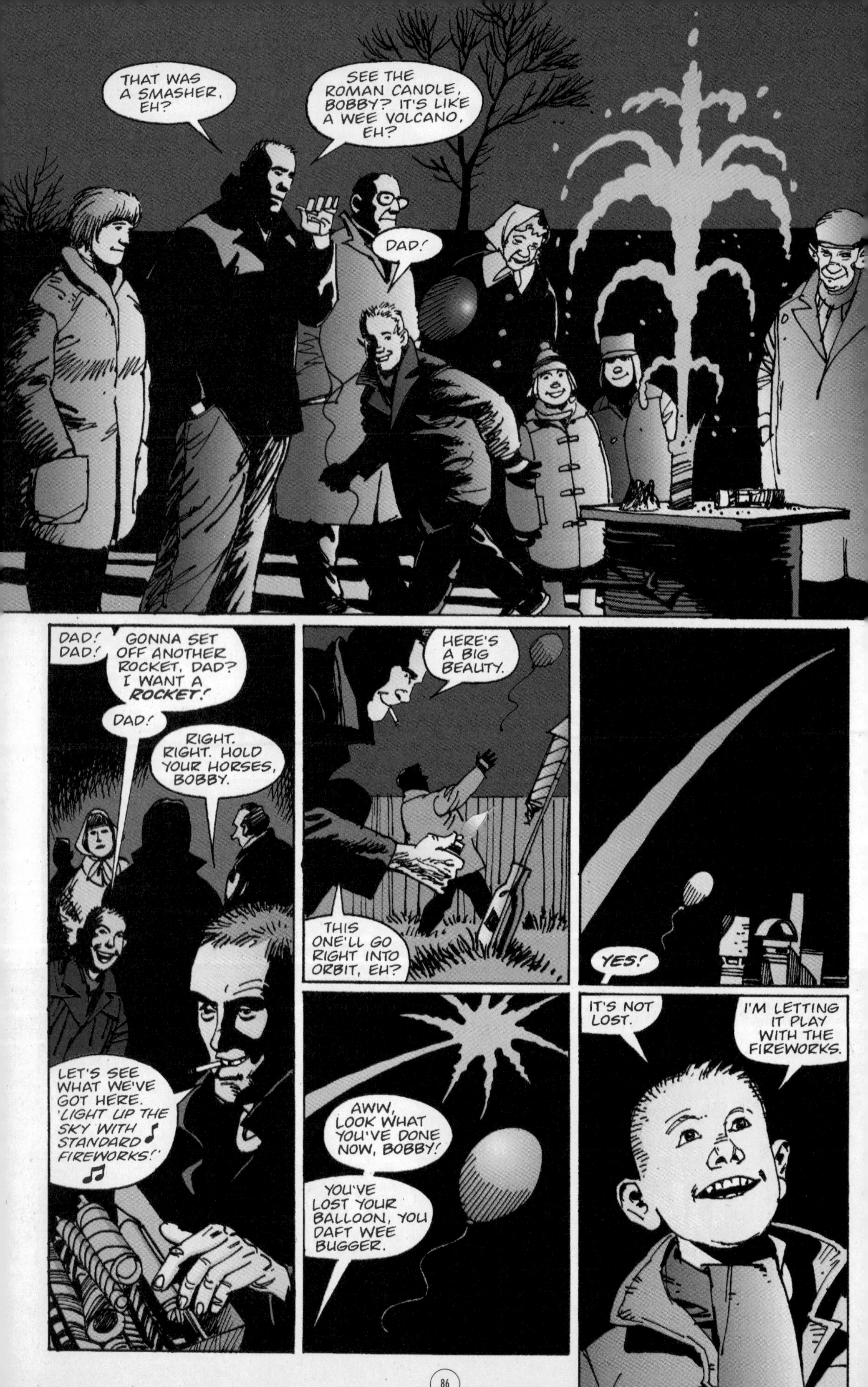
THAT WAS A SMASHER, EH?
SEE THE ROMAN CANDLE, BOBBY? IT'S LIKE A WEE VOLCANO, EH?
DAD!
DAD! DAD!
GONNA SET OFF ANOTHER ROCKET, DAD? I WANT A ROCKET!
DAD!
RIGHT. RIGHT. HOLD YOUR HORSES, BOBBY.
LET'S SEE WHAT WE'VE GOT HERE. 'LIGHT UP THE SKY WITH STANDARD FIREWORKS!'
HERE'S A BIG BEAUTY.
THIS ONE'LL GO RIGHT INTO ORBIT, EH?
YES!
AWW, LOOK WHAT YOU'VE DONE NOW, BOBBY!
YOU'VE LOST YOUR BALLOON, YOU DAFT WEE BUGGER.
IT'S NOT LOST.
I'M LETTING IT PLAY WITH THE FIREWORKS.

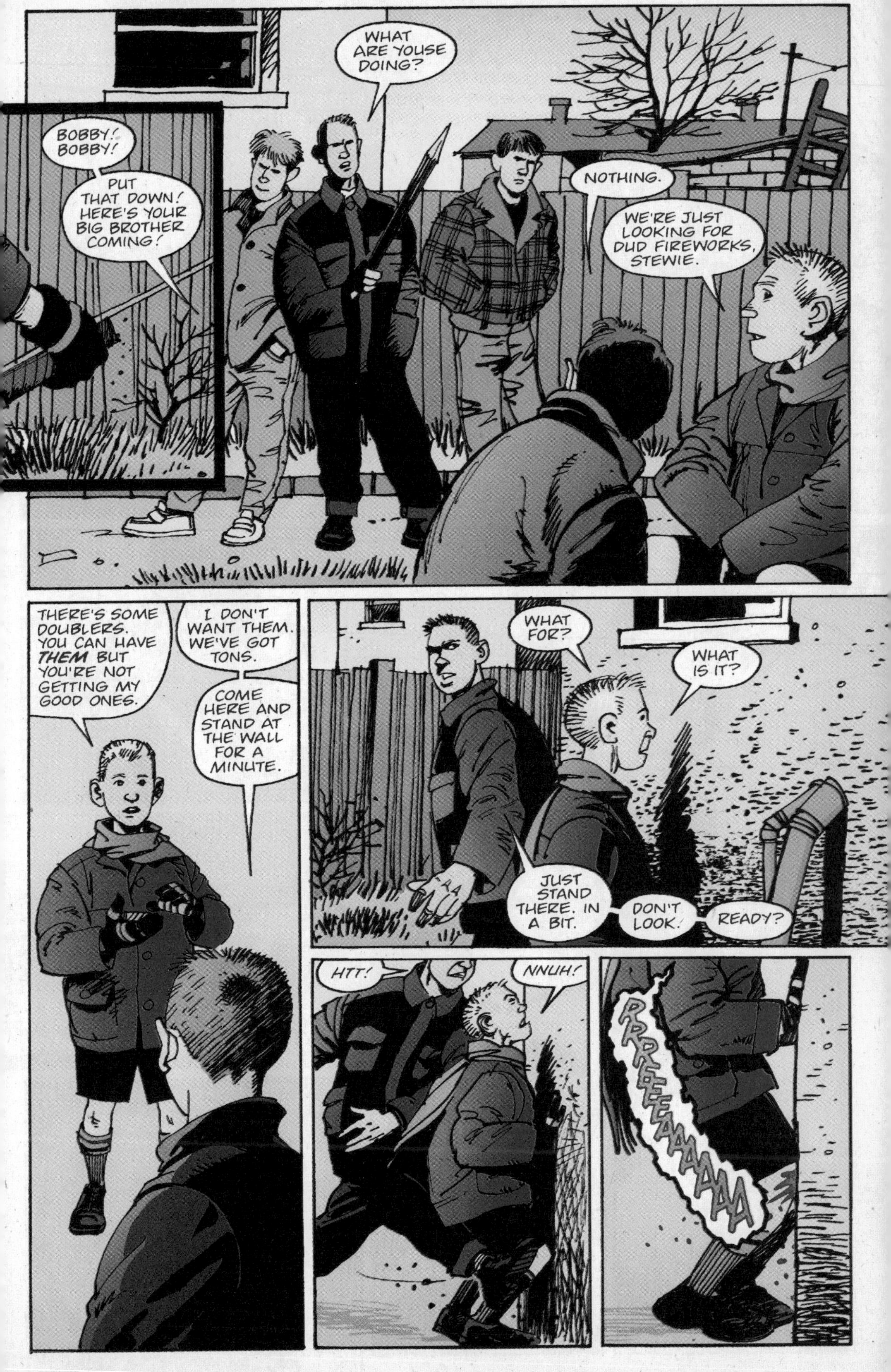

WHAT ARE YOUSE DOING?
BOBBY! BOBBY!
PUT THAT DOWN! HERE'S YOUR BIG BROTHER COMING!
NOTHING.
WE'RE JUST LOOKING FOR DUD FIREWORKS, STEWIE.
THERE'S SOME DOUBLERS. YOU CAN HAVE THEM BUT YOU'RE NOT GETTING MY GOOD ONES.
I DON'T WANT THEM. WE'VE GOT TONS.
COME HERE AND STAND AT THE WALL FOR A MINUTE.
WHAT FOR?
WHAT IS IT?
JUST STAND THERE. IN A BIT.
DON'T LOOK.
READY?
HTT!
NNUH!
RRREEEAAAAAAA

I'LL GET YOU A CUP OF TEA, MRS. MURRAY.

You're all I've got left, Stewie. If you go, there's nobody.

CHRIST, WHAT DID YOU HAVE TO GO AND CRASH YOUR FUCKING *CAR* FOR?

TELL ME YOU'RE NOT GOING TO DIE, STEWIE. COME ON. I KNOW WE'VE NOT REALLY GOT ON VERY WELL, BUT YOU'RE STILL MY *BROTHER*, YOU KNOW? IT'S...I'M JUST TRYING TO TELL YOU I *LOVE* YOU. YOU CAN PULL THROUGH.

nnf

STEWIE? WHAT IS IT, STEWIE? WHAT ARE YOU TRYING TO SAY, BIG MAN?

I... nnn...

I...I always hated you.

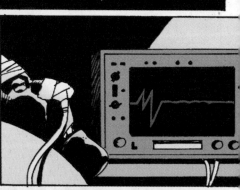

Nurse?

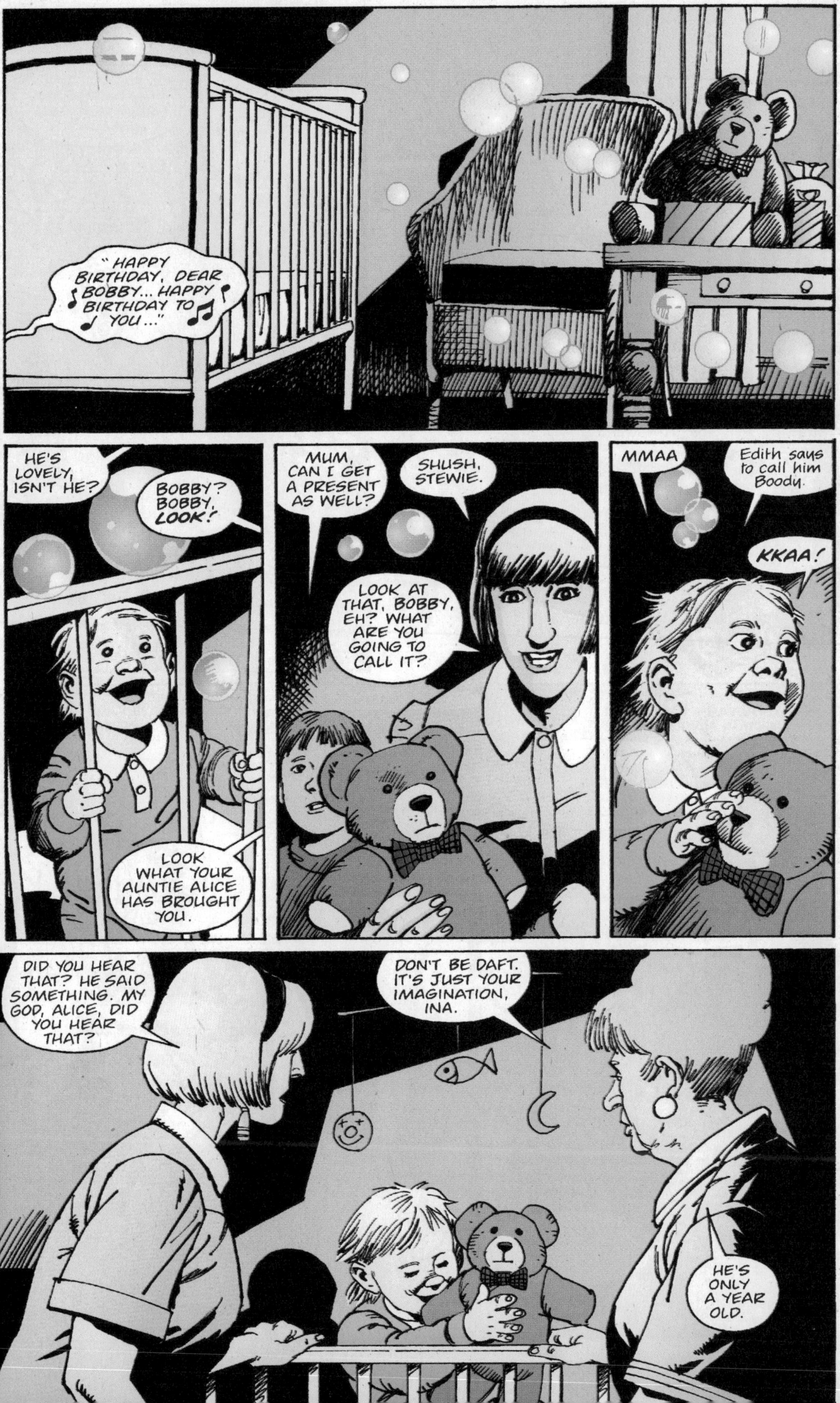
"HAPPY BIRTHDAY, DEAR BOBBY... HAPPY BIRTHDAY TO YOU..."
HE'S LOVELY, ISN'T HE?
BOBBY? BOBBY, LOOK!
LOOK WHAT YOUR AUNTIE ALICE HAS BROUGHT YOU.
MUM, CAN I GET A PRESENT AS WELL?
SHUSH, STEWIE.
LOOK AT THAT, BOBBY, EH? WHAT ARE YOU GOING TO CALL IT?
MMAA
Edith says to call him Boody.
KKAA!
DID YOU HEAR THAT? HE SAID SOMETHING. MY GOD, ALICE, DID YOU HEAR THAT?
DON'T BE DAFT. IT'S JUST YOUR IMAGINATION, INA.
HE'S ONLY A YEAR OLD.

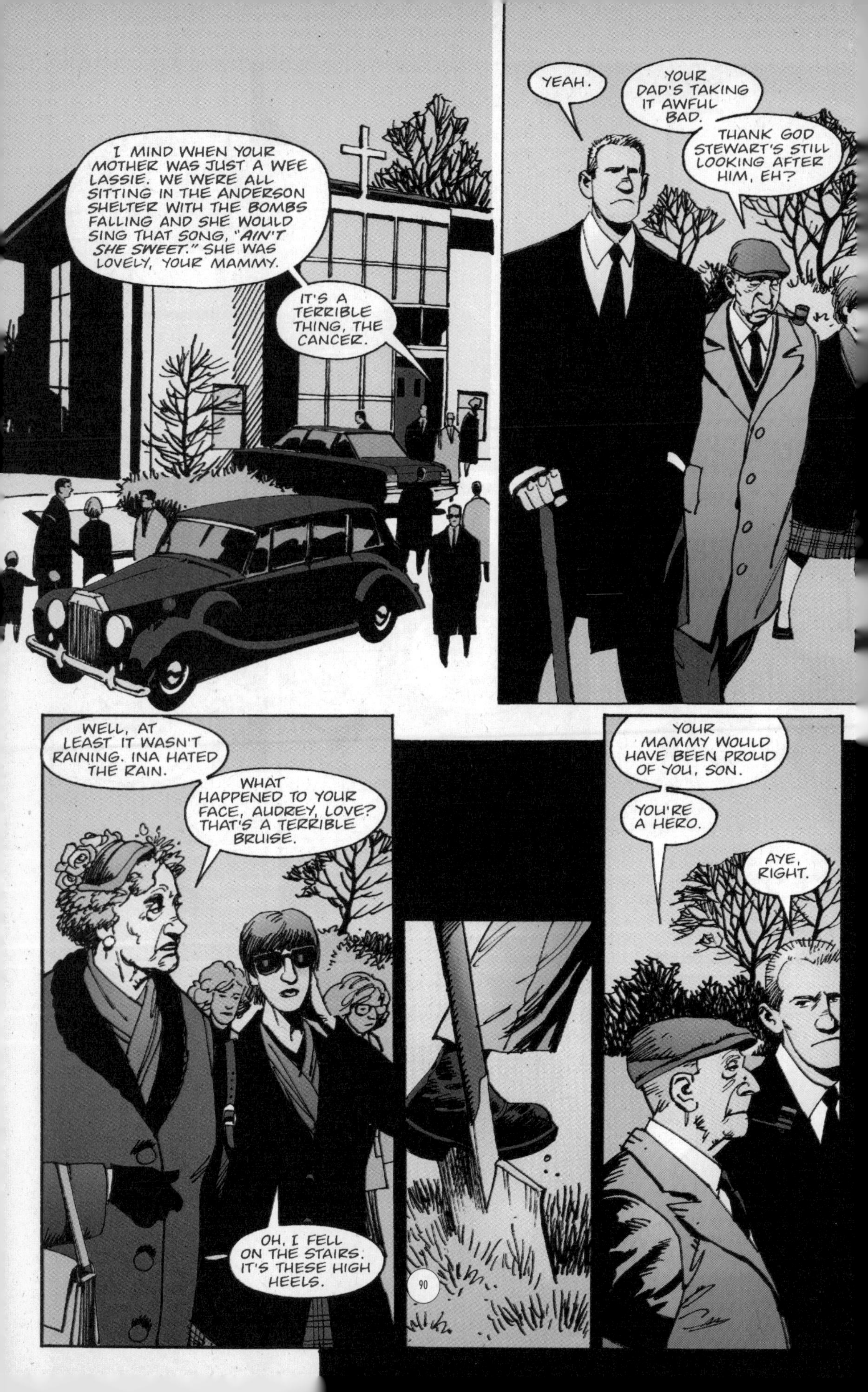
I MIND WHEN YOUR MOTHER WAS JUST A WEE LASSIE. WE WERE ALL SITTING IN THE ANDERSON SHELTER WITH THE BOMBS FALLING AND SHE WOULD SING THAT SONG, "AIN'T SHE SWEET." SHE WAS LOVELY, YOUR MAMMY.
IT'S A TERRIBLE THING, THE CANCER.
YEAH.
YOUR DAD'S TAKING IT AWFUL BAD.
THANK GOD STEWART'S STILL LOOKING AFTER HIM, EH?
WELL, AT LEAST IT WASN'T RAINING. INA HATED THE RAIN.
WHAT HAPPENED TO YOUR FACE, AUDREY, LOVE? THAT'S A TERRIBLE BRUISE.
OH, I FELL ON THE STAIRS. IT'S THESE HIGH HEELS.
YOUR MAMMY WOULD HAVE BEEN PROUD OF YOU, SON.
YOU'RE A HERO.
AYE, RIGHT.

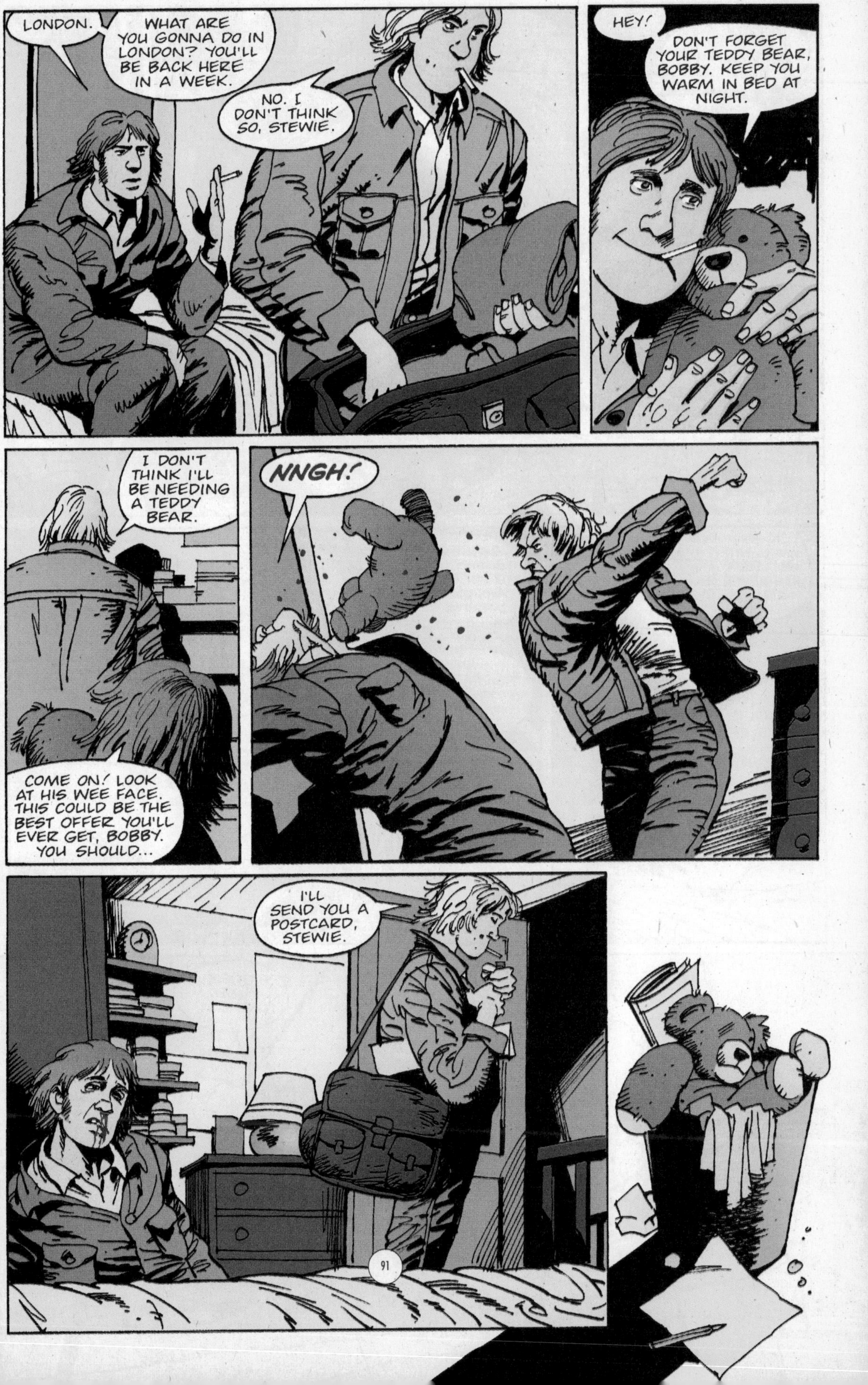
LONDON.
WHAT ARE YOU GONNA DO IN LONDON? YOU'LL BE BACK HERE IN A WEEK.
NO. I DON'T THINK SO, STEWIE.
HEY!
DON'T FORGET YOUR TEDDY BEAR, BOBBY. KEEP YOU WARM IN BED AT NIGHT.
I DON'T THINK I'LL BE NEEDING A TEDDY BEAR.
COME ON! LOOK AT HIS WEE FACE. THIS COULD BE THE BEST OFFER YOU'LL EVER GET, BOBBY. YOU SHOULD...
NNGH!
I'LL SEND YOU A POSTCARD, STEWIE.

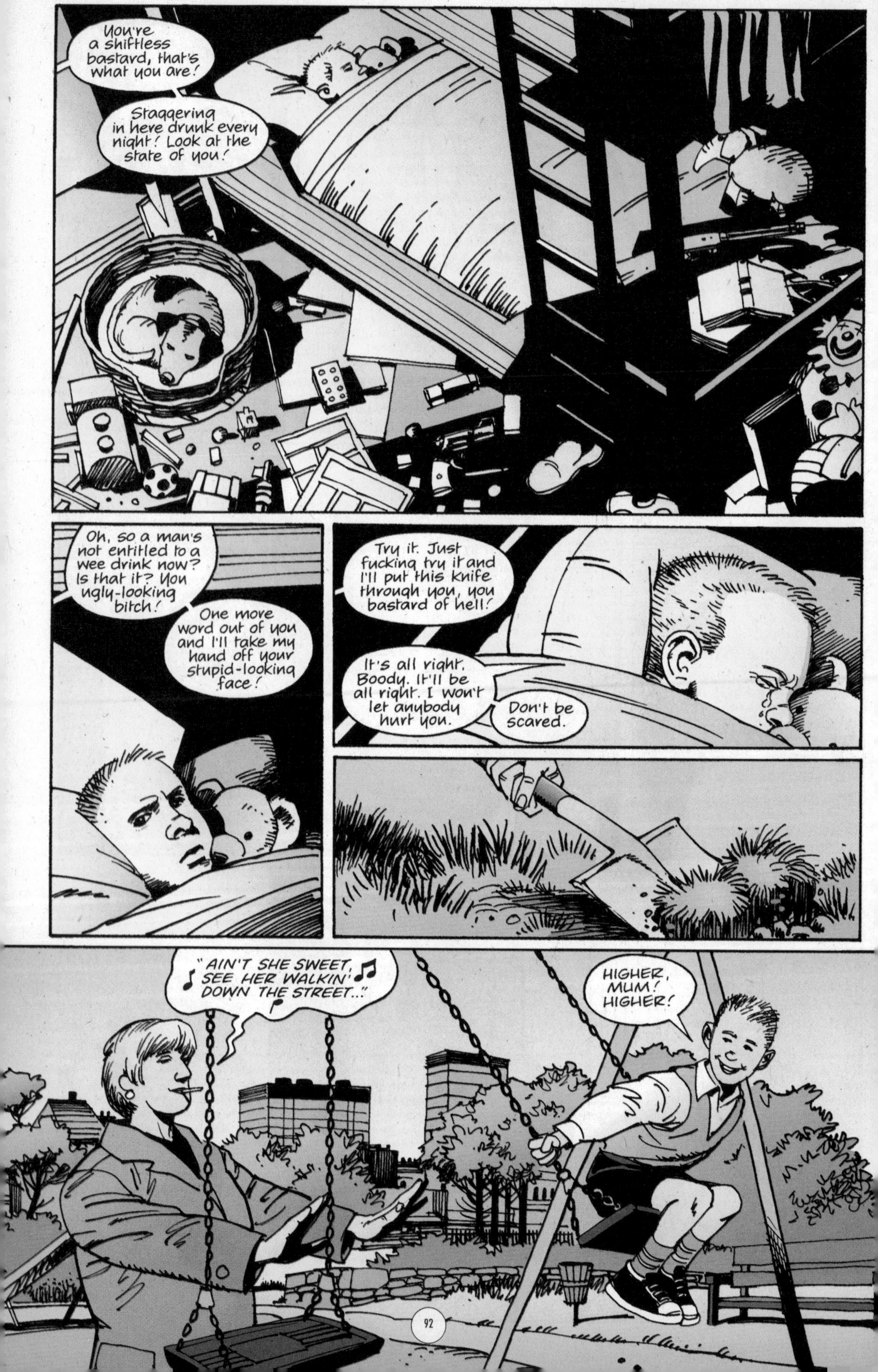
You're a shiftless bastard, that's what you are!
Staggering in here drunk every night! Look at the state of you!
Oh, so a man's not entitled to a wee drink now? Is that it? You ugly-looking bitch!
One more word out of you and I'll take my hand off your stupid-looking face!
Try it. Just fucking try it and I'll put this knife through you, you bastard of hell!
It's all right, Boody. It'll be all right. I won't let anybody hurt you.
Don't be scared.
"AIN'T SHE SWEET, SEE HER WALKIN' DOWN THE STREET..."
HIGHER, MUM! HIGHER!

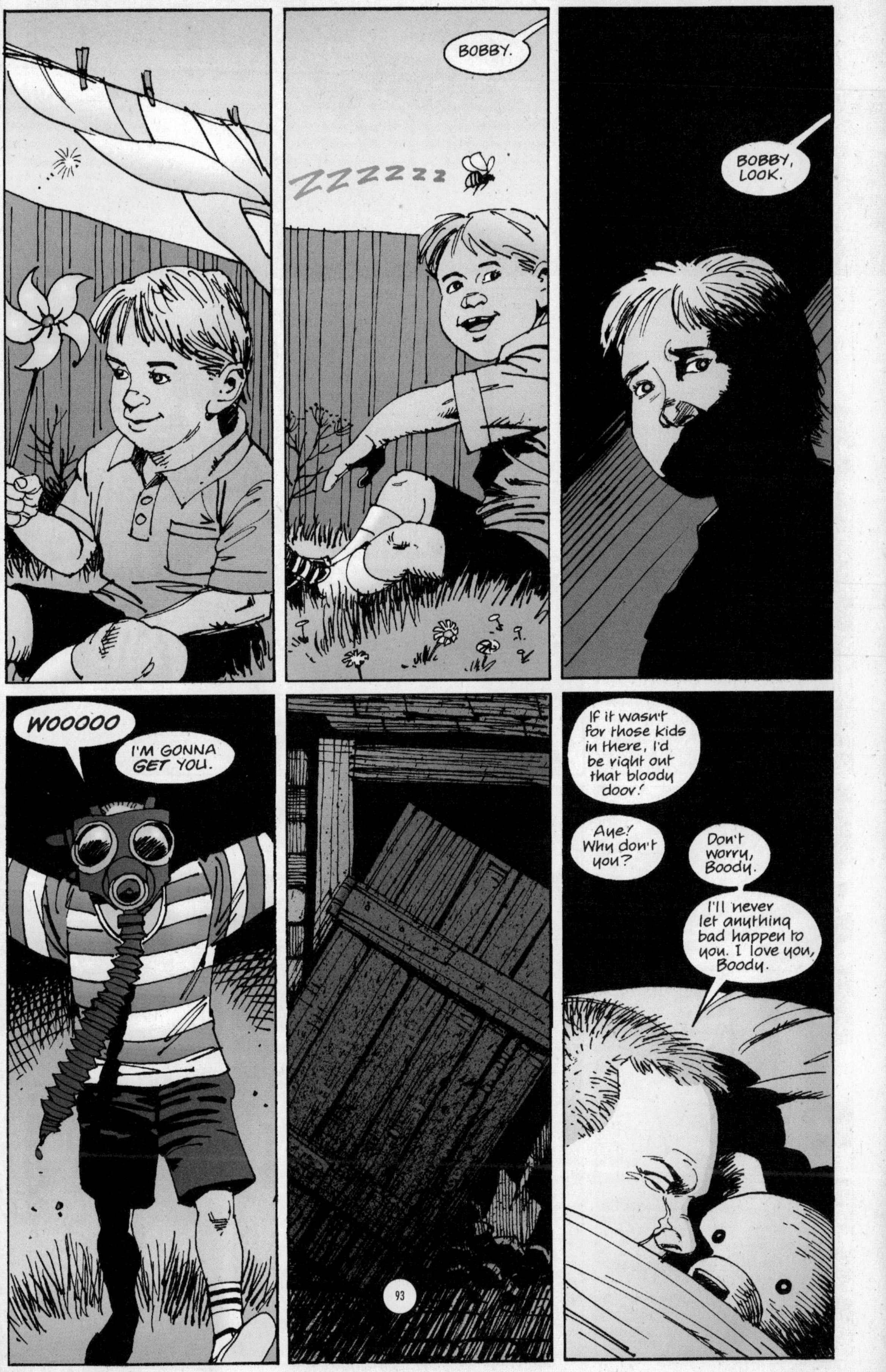
ZZZZZZZ
BOBBY.
BOBBY, LOOK.
WOOOOO
I'M GONNA GET YOU.
If it wasn't for those kids in there, I'd be right out that bloody door!
Aye! Why don't you?
Don't worry, Boody.
I'll never let anything bad happen to you. I love you, Boody.

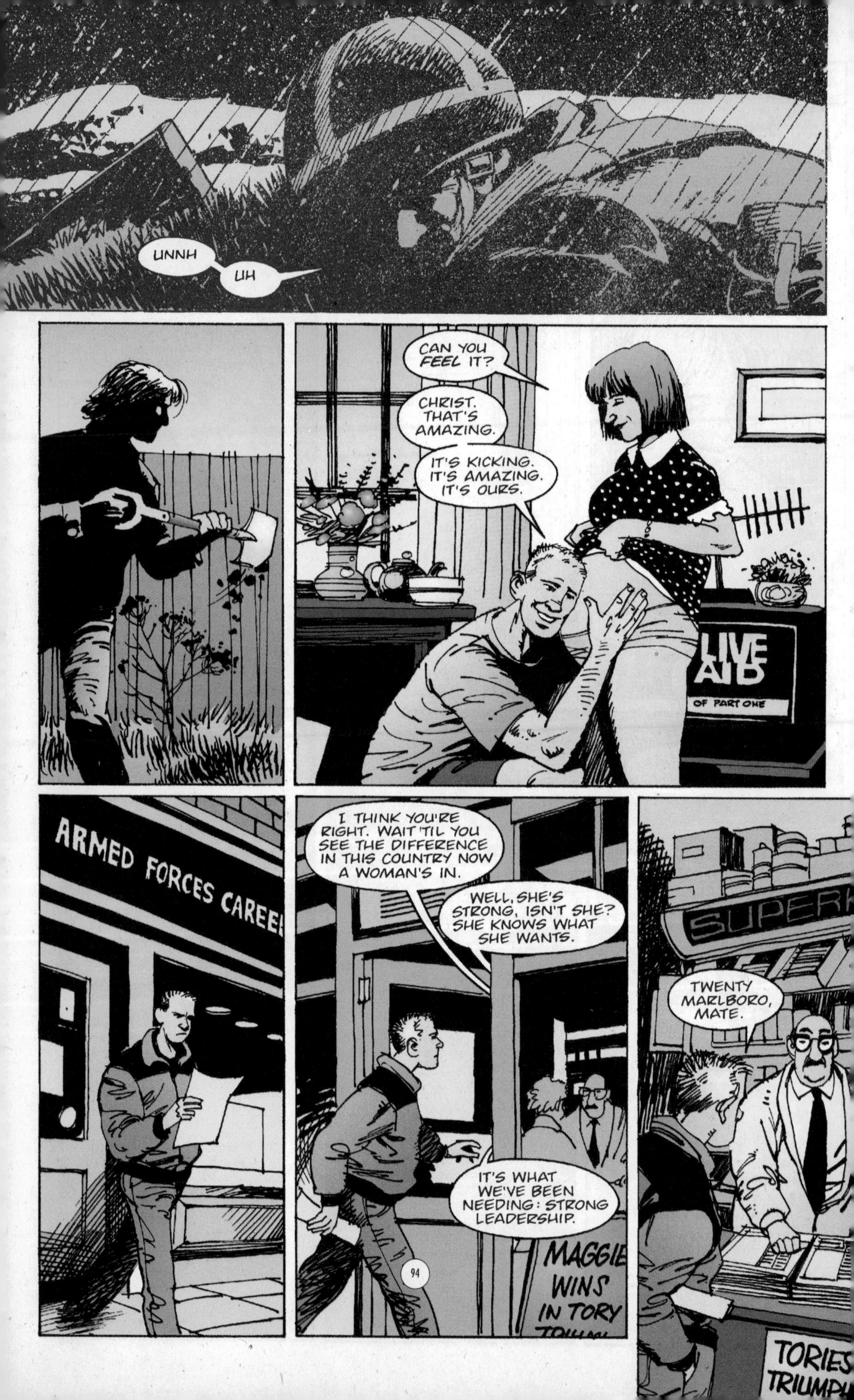
UNNH
UH
CAN YOU FEEL IT?
CHRIST. THAT'S AMAZING.
IT'S KICKING. IT'S AMAZING. IT'S OURS.
LIVE AID
OF PART ONE
ARMED FORCES CAREE
I THINK YOU'RE RIGHT. WAIT 'TIL YOU SEE THE DIFFERENCE IN THIS COUNTRY NOW A WOMAN'S IN.
WELL, SHE'S STRONG, ISN'T SHE? SHE KNOWS WHAT SHE WANTS.
IT'S WHAT WE'VE BEEN NEEDING: STRONG LEADERSHIP.
MAGGIE WINS IN TORY
SUPER
TWENTY MARLBORO, MATE.
TORIES TRIUMP

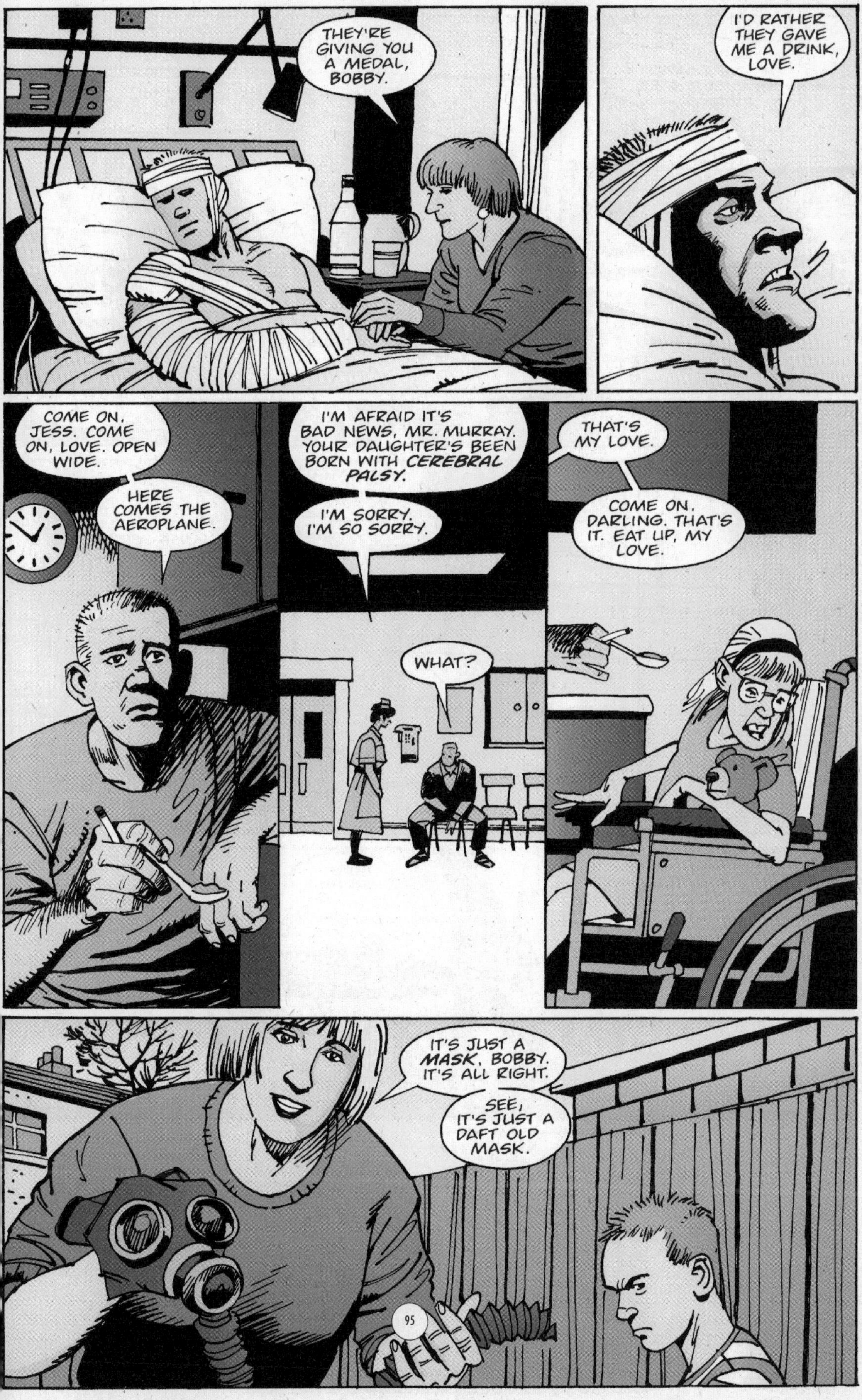
THEY'RE GIVING YOU A MEDAL, BOBBY.
I'D RATHER THEY GAVE ME A DRINK, LOVE.
COME ON, JESS. COME ON, LOVE. OPEN WIDE.
HERE COMES THE AEROPLANE.
I'M AFRAID IT'S BAD NEWS, MR. MURRAY. YOUR DAUGHTER'S BEEN BORN WITH *CEREBRAL PALSY.*
I'M SORRY. I'M SO SORRY.
WHAT?
THAT'S MY LOVE.
COME ON, DARLING. THAT'S IT. EAT UP, MY LOVE.
IT'S JUST A *MASK*, BOBBY. IT'S ALL RIGHT.
SEE, IT'S JUST A DAFT OLD MASK.

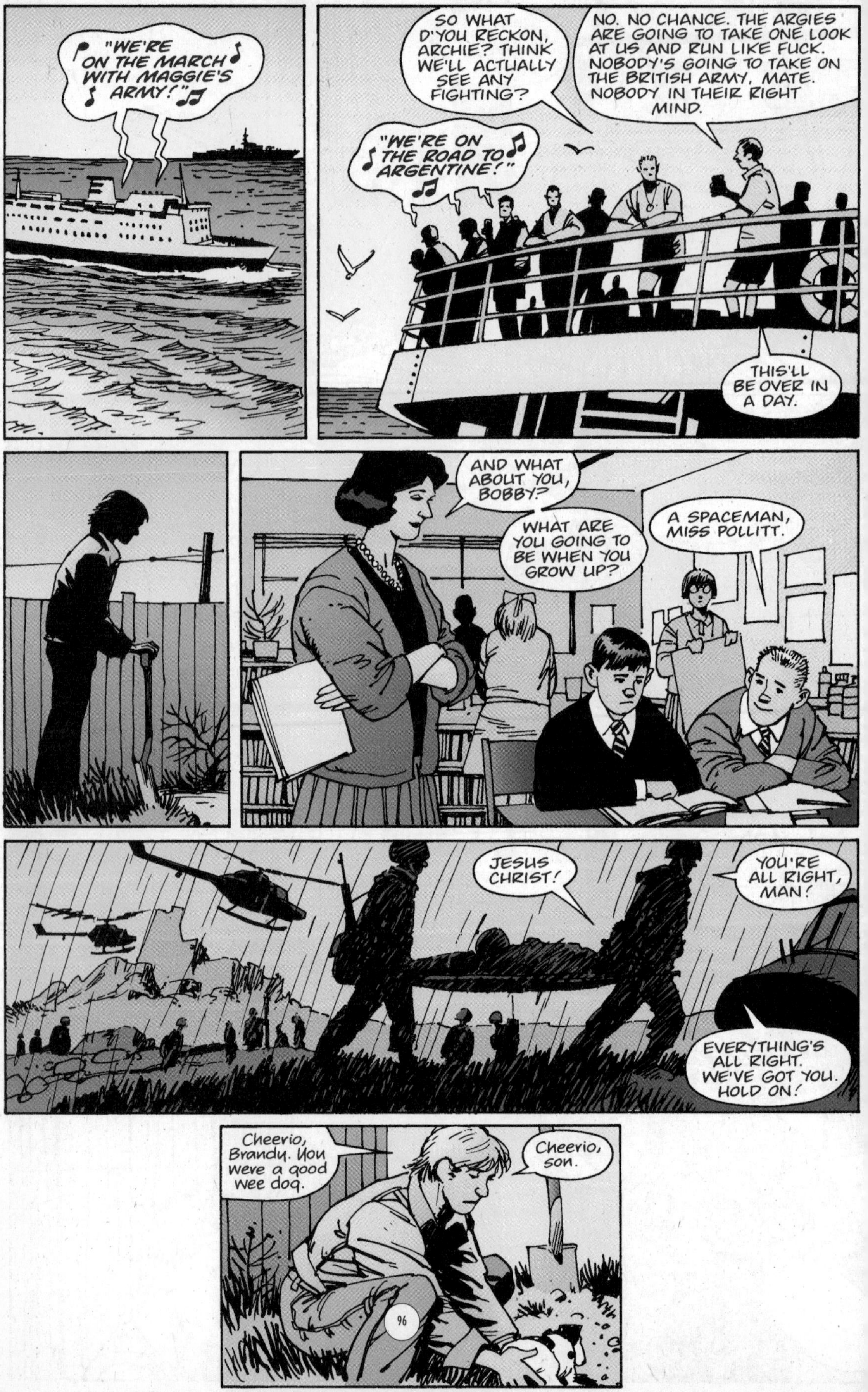

"WE'RE ON THE MARCH WITH MAGGIE'S ARMY!"
SO WHAT D'YOU RECKON, ARCHIE? THINK WE'LL ACTUALLY SEE ANY FIGHTING?
NO. NO CHANCE. THE ARGIES ARE GOING TO TAKE ONE LOOK AT US AND RUN LIKE FUCK. NOBODY'S GOING TO TAKE ON THE BRITISH ARMY, MATE. NOBODY IN THEIR RIGHT MIND.
"WE'RE ON THE ROAD TO ARGENTINE!"
THIS'LL BE OVER IN A DAY.
AND WHAT ABOUT YOU, BOBBY?
WHAT ARE YOU GOING TO BE WHEN YOU GROW UP?
A SPACEMAN, MISS POLLITT.
JESUS CHRIST!
YOU'RE ALL RIGHT, MAN!
EVERYTHING'S ALL RIGHT. WE'VE GOT YOU. HOLD ON!
Cheerio, Brandy. You were a good wee dog.
Cheerio, son.

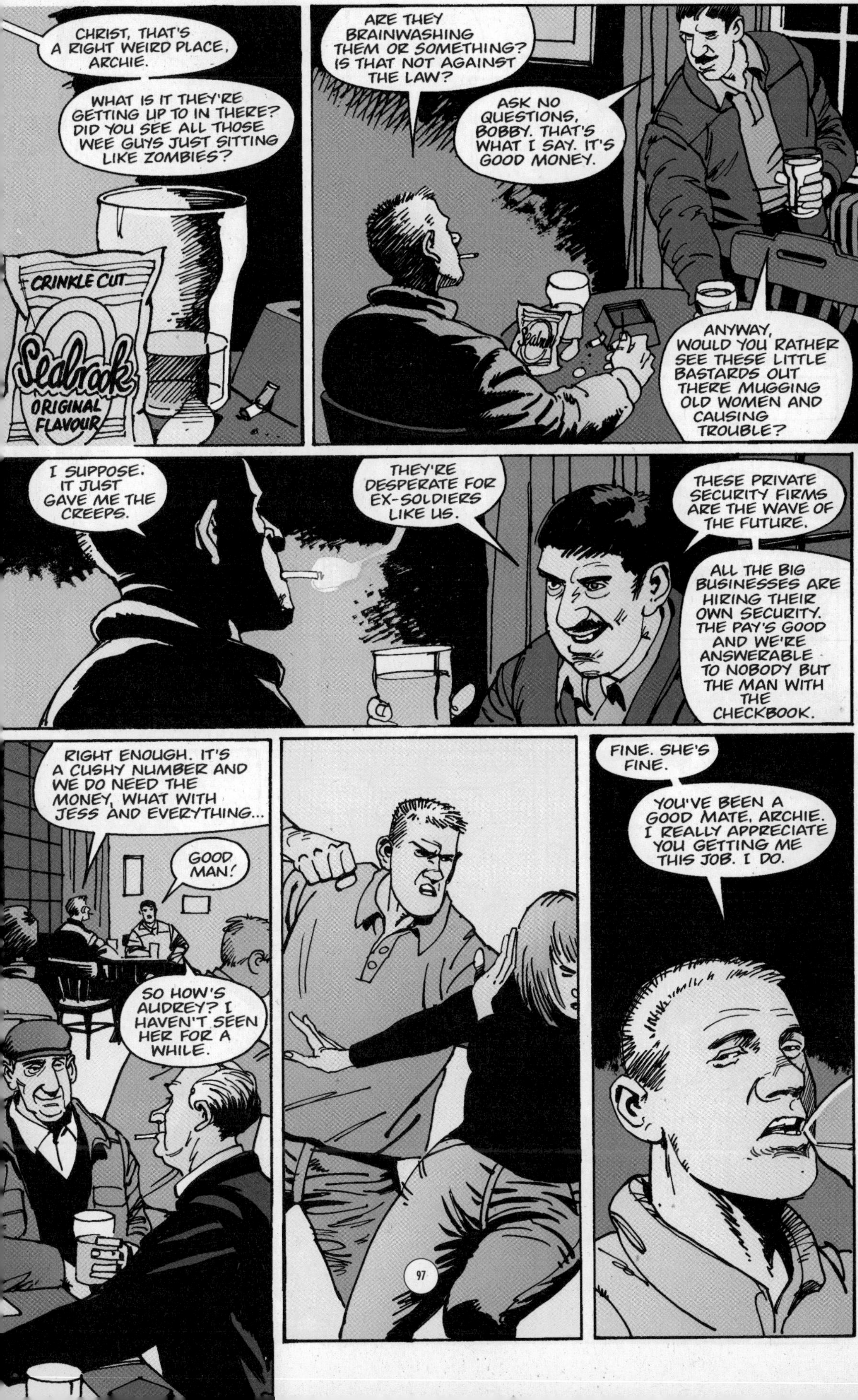

CHRIST, THAT'S A RIGHT WEIRD PLACE, ARCHIE.
WHAT IS IT THEY'RE GETTING UP TO IN THERE? DID YOU SEE ALL THOSE WEE GUYS JUST SITTING LIKE ZOMBIES?
CRINKLE CUT
Sealbrook
ORIGINAL FLAVOUR
ARE THEY BRAINWASHING THEM OR SOMETHING? IS THAT NOT AGAINST THE LAW?
ASK NO QUESTIONS, BOBBY. THAT'S WHAT I SAY. IT'S GOOD MONEY.
ANYWAY, WOULD YOU RATHER SEE THESE LITTLE BASTARDS OUT THERE MUGGING OLD WOMEN AND CAUSING TROUBLE?
I SUPPOSE. IT JUST GAVE ME THE CREEPS.
THEY'RE DESPERATE FOR EX-SOLDIERS LIKE US.
THESE PRIVATE SECURITY FIRMS ARE THE WAVE OF THE FUTURE.
ALL THE BIG BUSINESSES ARE HIRING THEIR OWN SECURITY. THE PAY'S GOOD AND WE'RE ANSWERABLE TO NOBODY BUT THE MAN WITH THE CHECKBOOK.
RIGHT ENOUGH. IT'S A CUSHY NUMBER AND WE DO NEED THE MONEY, WHAT WITH JESS AND EVERYTHING...
GOOD MAN!
SO HOW'S AUDREY? I HAVEN'T SEEN HER FOR A WHILE.
FINE. SHE'S FINE.
YOU'VE BEEN A GOOD MATE, ARCHIE. I REALLY APPRECIATE YOU GETTING ME THIS JOB. I DO.

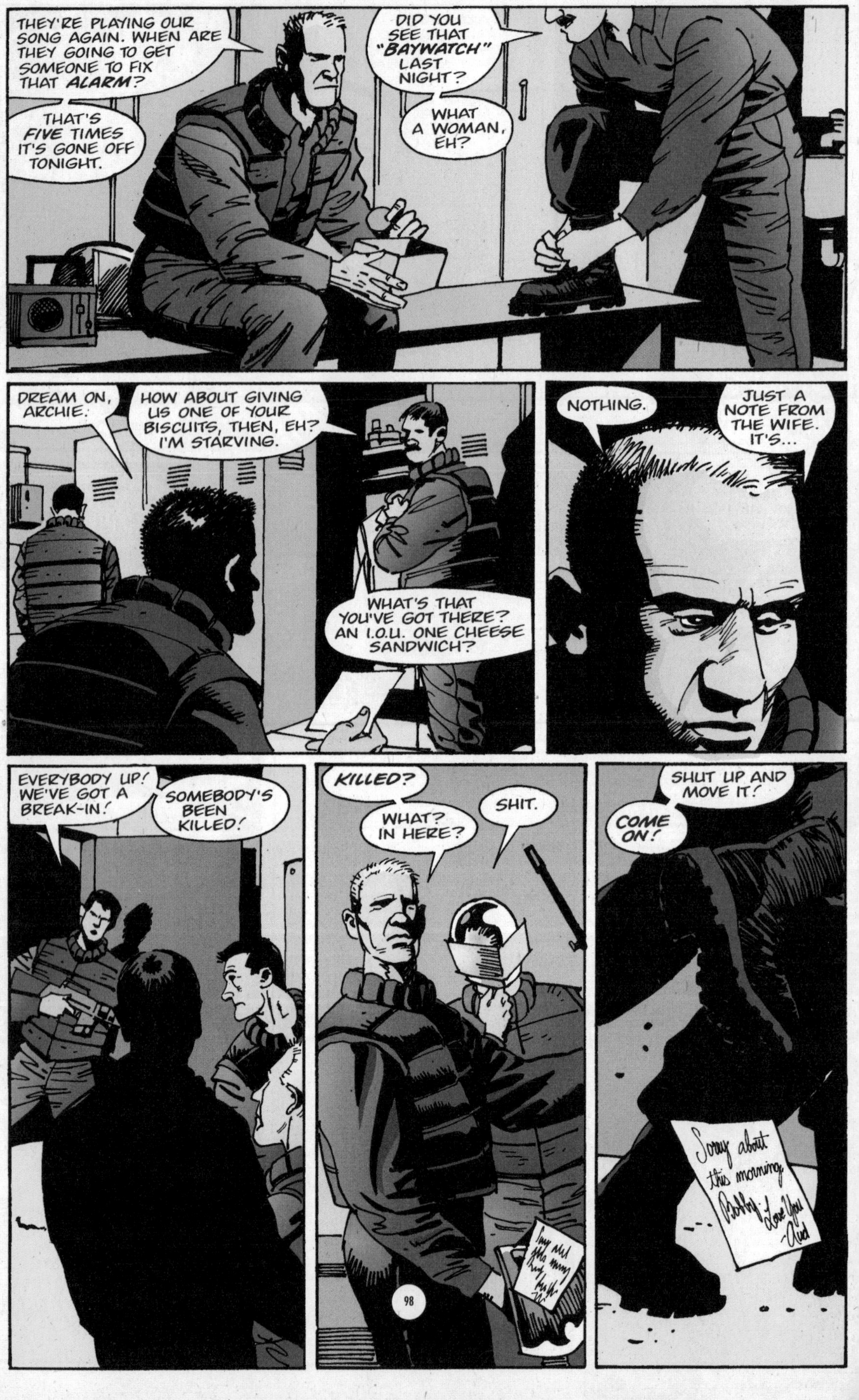

THEY'RE PLAYING OUR SONG AGAIN. WHEN ARE THEY GOING TO GET SOMEONE TO FIX THAT *ALARM*?
THAT'S *FIVE* TIMES IT'S GONE OFF TONIGHT.
DID YOU SEE THAT *"BAYWATCH"* LAST NIGHT?
WHAT A WOMAN, EH?
DREAM ON, ARCHIE.
HOW ABOUT GIVING US ONE OF YOUR BISCUITS, THEN, EH? I'M STARVING.
WHAT'S THAT YOU'VE GOT THERE? AN I.O.U. ONE CHEESE SANDWICH?
NOTHING.
JUST A NOTE FROM THE WIFE. IT'S...
EVERYBODY UP! WE'VE GOT A BREAK-IN!
SOMEBODY'S BEEN KILLED!
KILLED?
WHAT? IN HERE?
SHIT.
SHUT UP AND MOVE IT!
COME ON!
Sorry about this morning Bobby. Love You -Aud

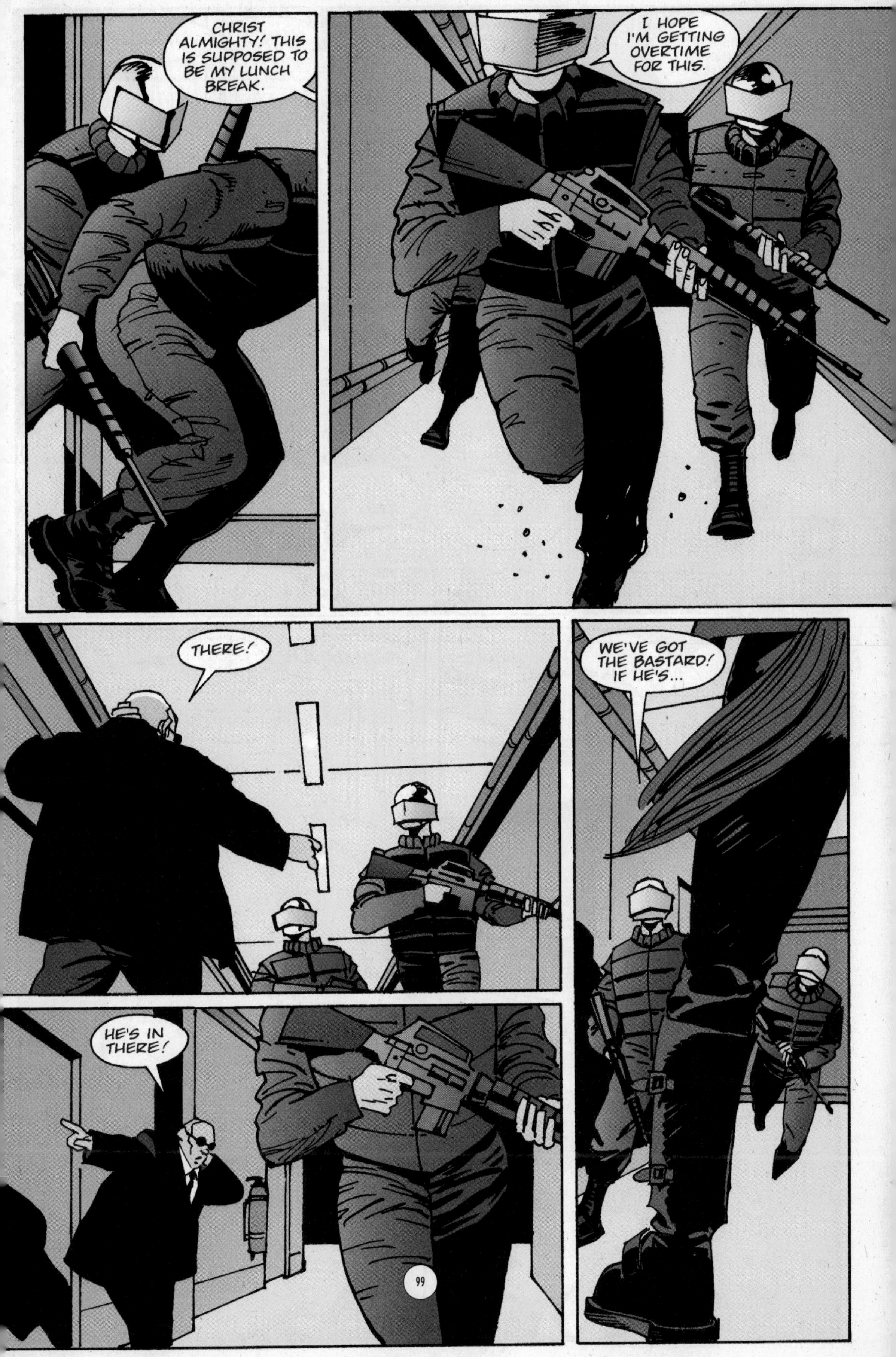
CHRIST ALMIGHTY! THIS IS SUPPOSED TO BE MY LUNCH BREAK.
I HOPE I'M GETTING OVERTIME FOR THIS.
THERE!
WE'VE GOT THE BASTARD! IF HE'S...
HE'S IN THERE!

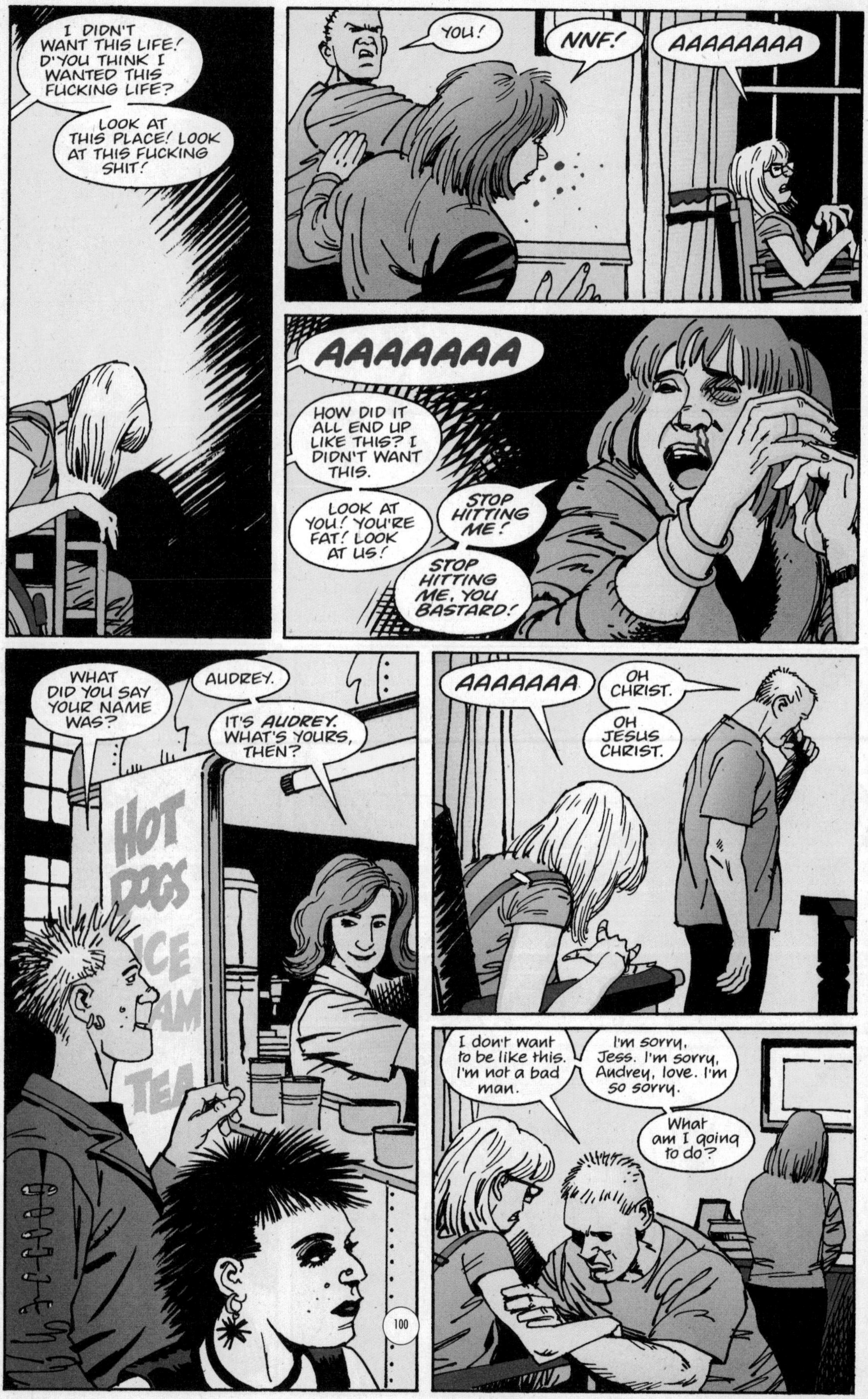

I DIDN'T WANT THIS LIFE! D'YOU THINK I WANTED THIS FUCKING LIFE?
LOOK AT THIS PLACE! LOOK AT THIS FUCKING SHIT!
YOU!
NNF!
AAAAAAAA
AAAAAAA
HOW DID IT ALL END UP LIKE THIS? I DIDN'T WANT THIS.
LOOK AT YOU! YOU'RE FAT! LOOK AT US!
STOP HITTING ME!
STOP HITTING ME, YOU BASTARD!
WHAT DID YOU SAY YOUR NAME WAS?
AUDREY.
IT'S AUDREY. WHAT'S YOURS, THEN?
HOT DOGS
ICE
AM
TEA
AAAAAAA
OH CHRIST.
OH JESUS CHRIST.
I don't want to be like this. I'm not a bad man.
I'm sorry, Jess. I'm sorry, Audrey, love. I'm so sorry.
What am I going to do?

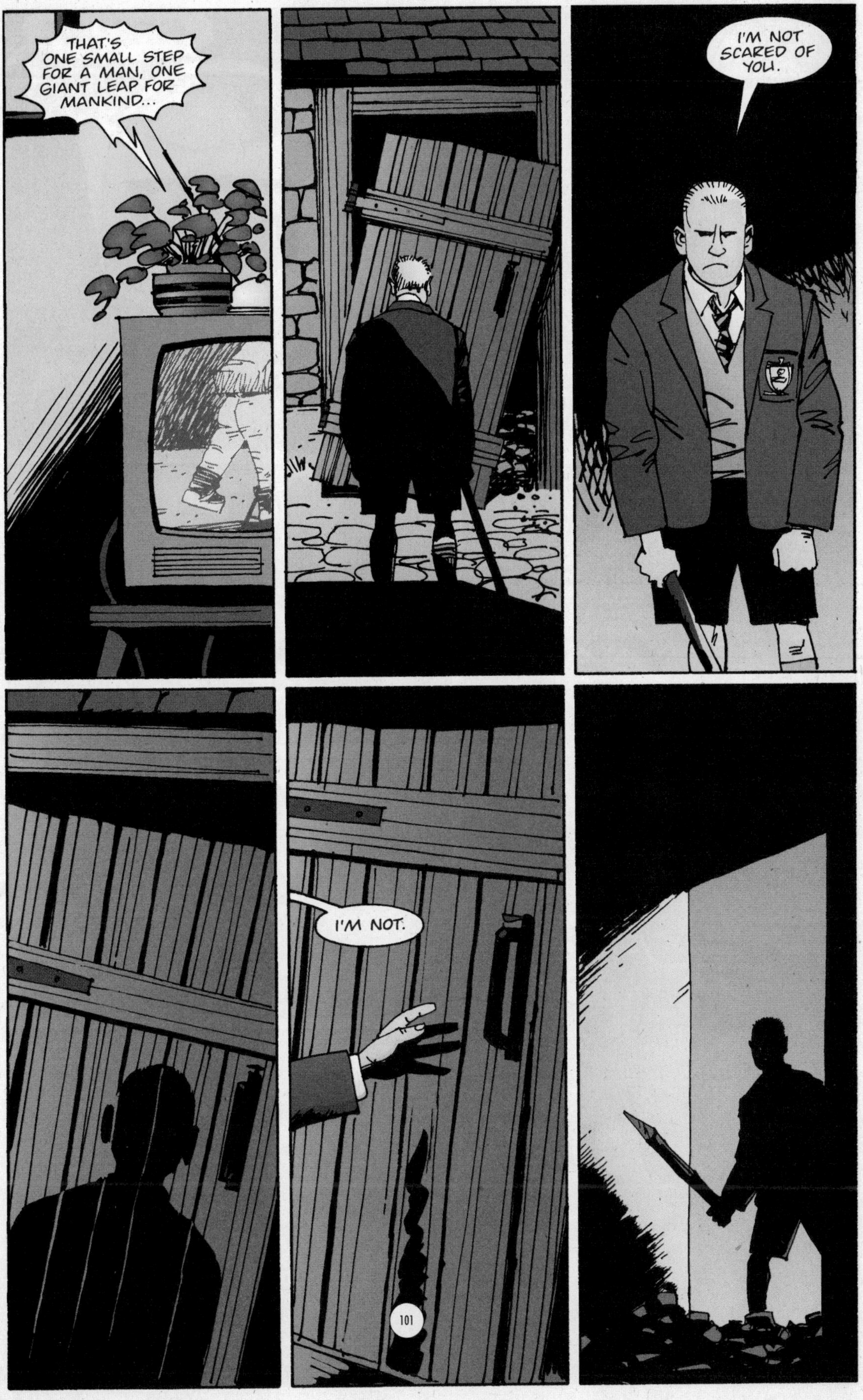
THAT'S ONE SMALL STEP FOR A MAN, ONE GIANT LEAP FOR MANKIND...
I'M NOT SCARED OF YOU.
I'M NOT.

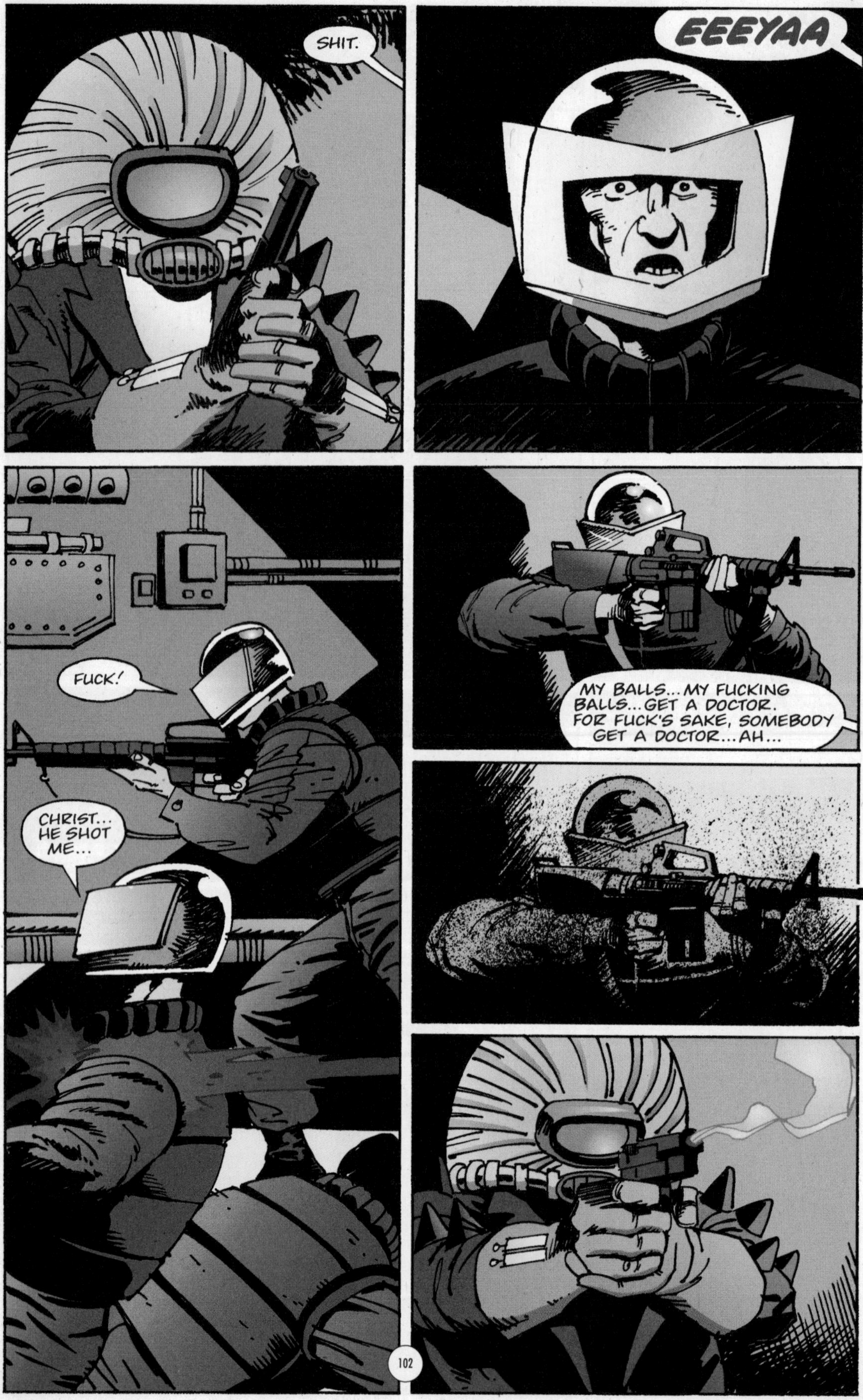
SHIT.
EEEYAA
FUCK!
CHRIST... HE SHOT ME...
MY BALLS... MY FUCKING BALLS...GET A DOCTOR. FOR FUCK'S SAKE, SOMEBODY GET A DOCTOR...AH...

HERE. YOU CAN HAVE THE LAST ONE.

I USED TO BE REALLY SCARED OF THAT DOOR. IT WAS BLUE AND ALL THE PAINT WAS KIND OF PEELING OFF. I REMEMBER ONE NIGHT WHEN I WAS ABOUT NINE, I DECIDED TO GO OUT AND FIGHT IT. I KNEW I HAD TO.

SO WHAT HAPPENED THEN?

I DID IT. I OPENED THE DOOR AND I SAW THE SCARIEST THING IN THE WORLD AND IT WAS JUST A *GAS MASK*.

AN OLD GAS MASK, HANGING UP ON A NAIL ABOVE THE COAL.

WHEN I WAS OUT PLAYING MY DAD WOULD ALWAYS SAY I HAD TO COME IN WHEN IT GOT DARK OR THE *HAIRY TROMBONE* WOULD GET ME.

THE HAIRY TROMBONE LIVED IN THE COAL CELLAR. IT WAS THE SCARIEST THING IN THE WORLD.

THE HAIRY TROMBONE? THAT SOUNDS A BIT DISGUSTING.

ANY CHIPS LEFT?

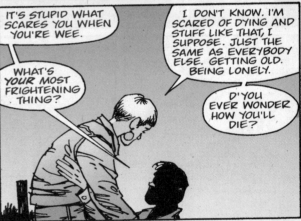

IT'S STUPID WHAT SCARES YOU WHEN YOU'RE WEE.

WHAT'S *YOUR* MOST FRIGHTENING THING?

I DON'T KNOW. I'M SCARED OF DYING AND STUFF LIKE THAT, I SUPPOSE. JUST THE SAME AS EVERYBODY ELSE. GETTING OLD. BEING LONELY.

D'YOU EVER WONDER HOW YOU'LL DIE?

NO.

I'M GOING TO LIVE FOREVER.

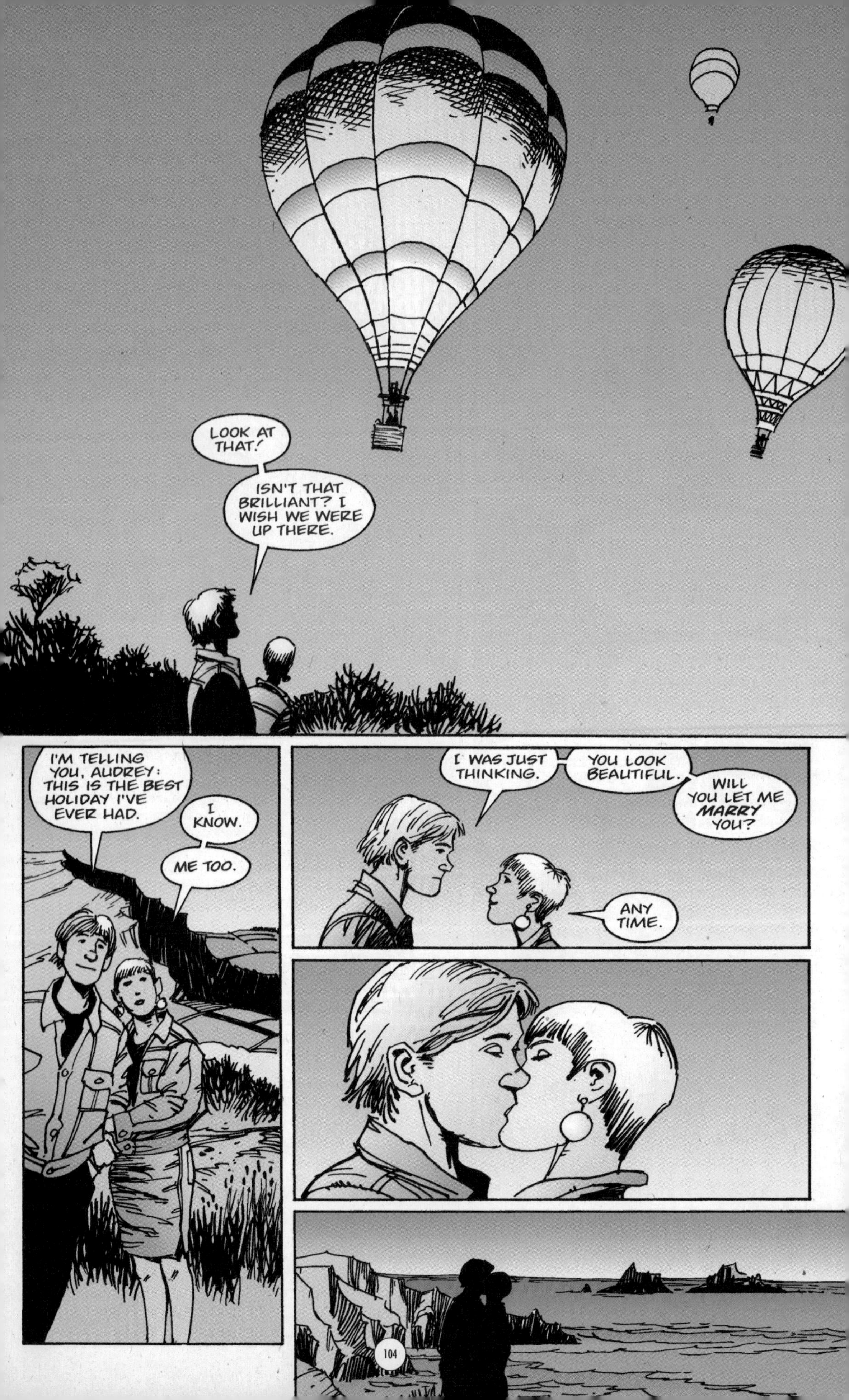

LOOK AT THAT!
ISN'T THAT BRILLIANT? I WISH WE WERE UP THERE.
I'M TELLING YOU, AUDREY: THIS IS THE BEST HOLIDAY I'VE EVER HAD.
I KNOW.
ME TOO.
I WAS JUST THINKING.
YOU LOOK BEAUTIFUL.
WILL YOU LET ME MARRY YOU?
ANY TIME.

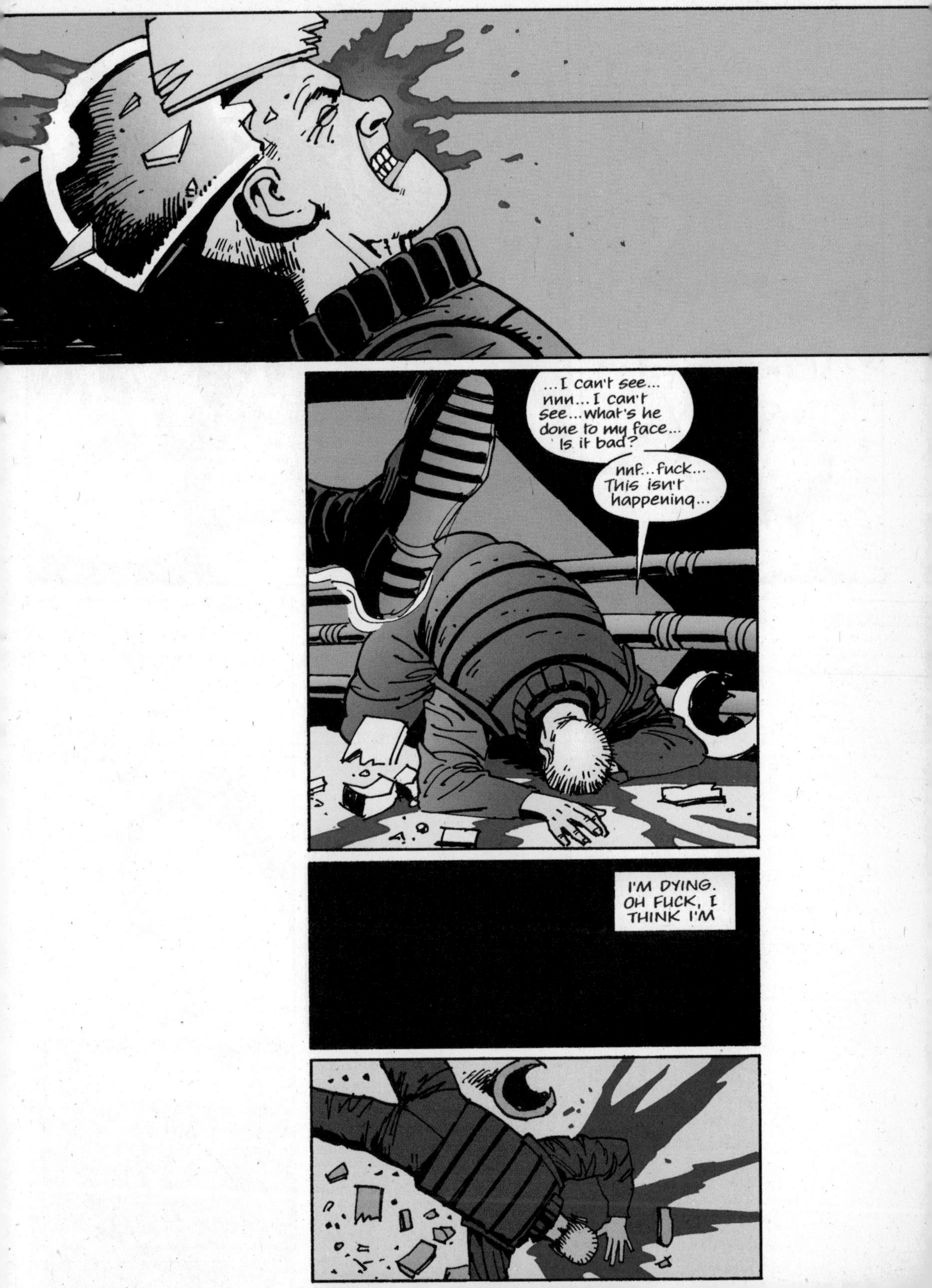
...I can't see... nnn...I can't see...what's he done to my face... Is it bad?
nnf...fuck... This isn't happening...
I'M DYING. OH FUCK, I THINK I'M

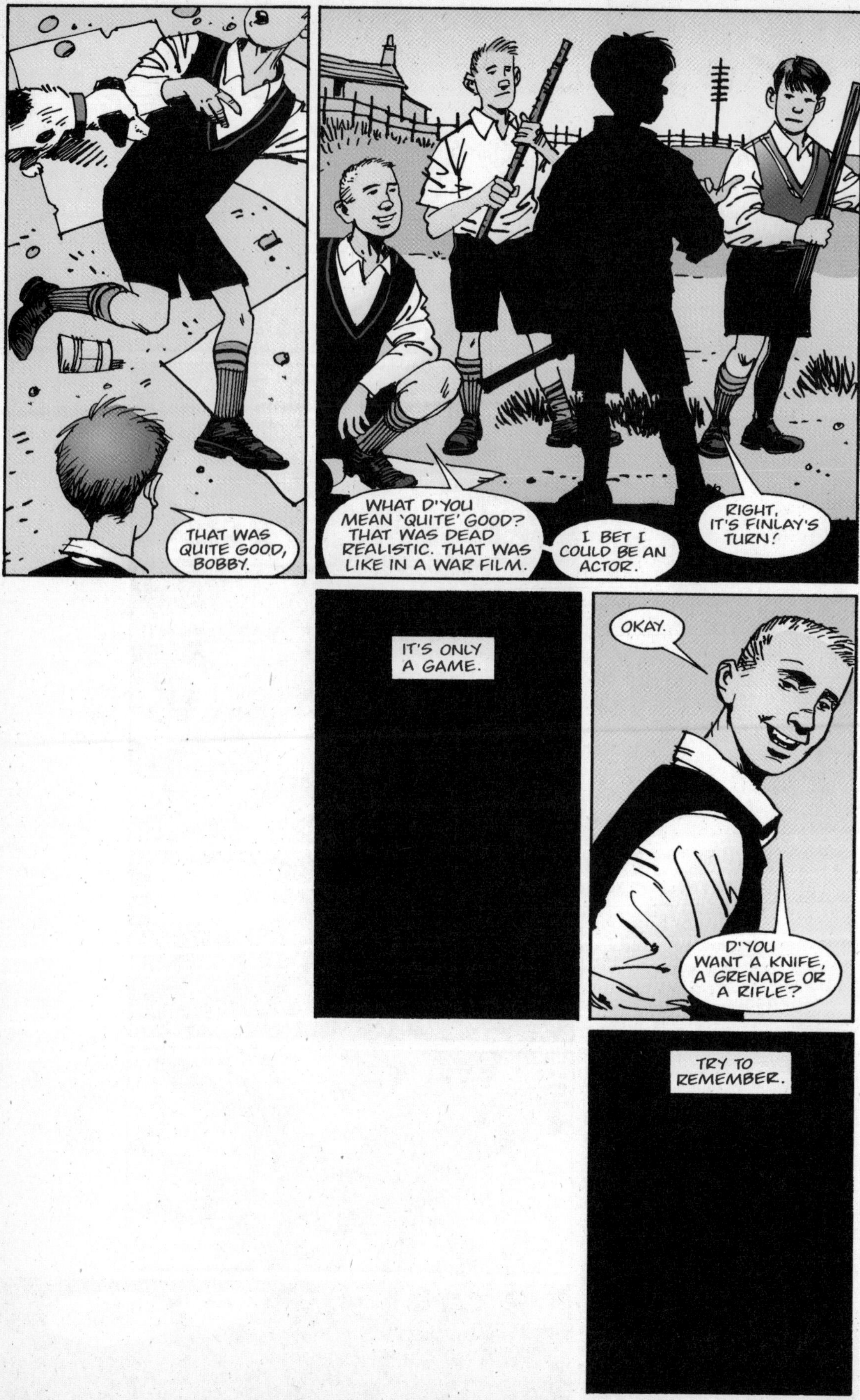
THAT WAS QUITE GOOD, BOBBY.
WHAT D'YOU MEAN 'QUITE' GOOD? THAT WAS DEAD REALISTIC. THAT WAS LIKE IN A WAR FILM.
I BET I COULD BE AN ACTOR.
RIGHT, IT'S FINLAY'S TURN!
IT'S ONLY A GAME.
OKAY.
D'YOU WANT A KNIFE, A GRENADE OR A RIFLE?
TRY TO REMEMBER.

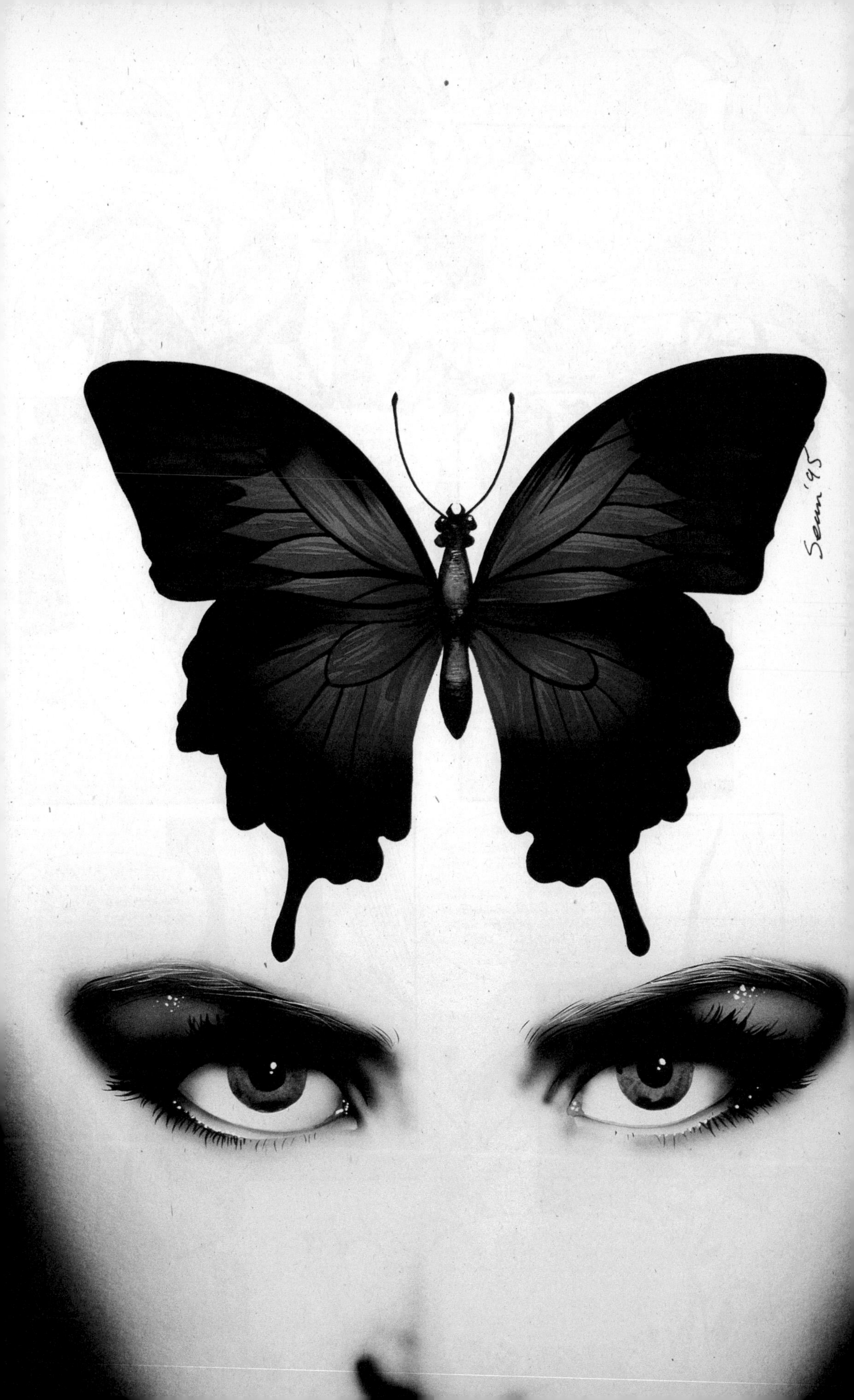
Sean '95

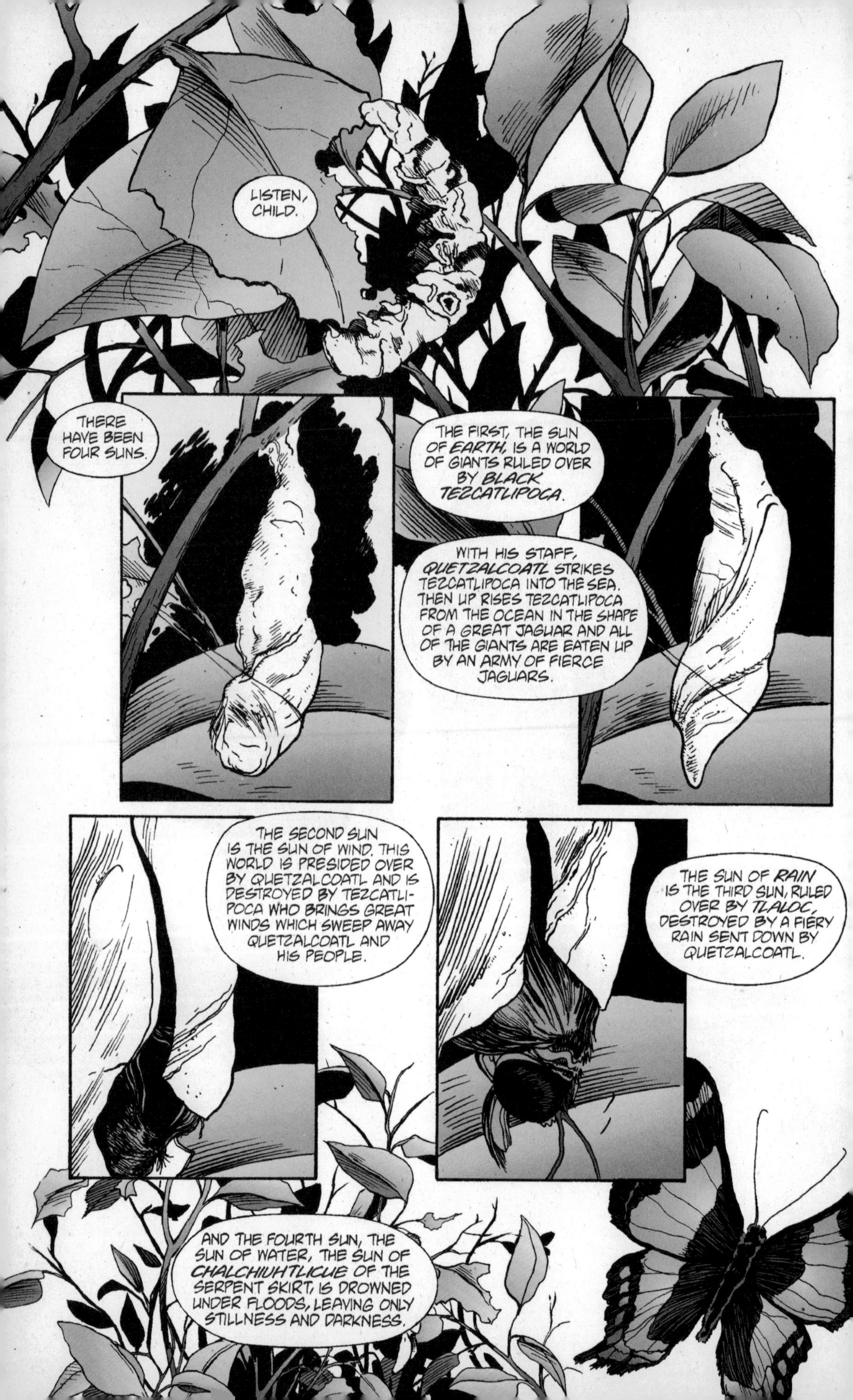
LISTEN, CHILD.
THERE HAVE BEEN FOUR SUNS.
THE FIRST, THE SUN OF EARTH, IS A WORLD OF GIANTS RULED OVER BY BLACK TEZCATLIPOCA.
WITH HIS STAFF, QUETZALCOATL STRIKES TEZCATLIPOCA INTO THE SEA. THEN UP RISES TEZCATLIPOCA FROM THE OCEAN IN THE SHAPE OF A GREAT JAGUAR AND ALL OF THE GIANTS ARE EATEN UP BY AN ARMY OF FIERCE JAGUARS.
THE SECOND SUN IS THE SUN OF WIND. THIS WORLD IS PRESIDED OVER BY QUETZALCOATL AND IS DESTROYED BY TEZCATLIPOCA WHO BRINGS GREAT WINDS WHICH SWEEP AWAY QUETZALCOATL AND HIS PEOPLE.
THE SUN OF RAIN IS THE THIRD SUN, RULED OVER BY TLALOC, DESTROYED BY A FIERY RAIN SENT DOWN BY QUETZALCOATL.
AND THE FOURTH SUN, THE SUN OF WATER, THE SUN OF CHALCHIUHTLICUE OF THE SERPENT SKIRT, IS DROWNED UNDER FLOODS, LEAVING ONLY STILLNESS AND DARKNESS.

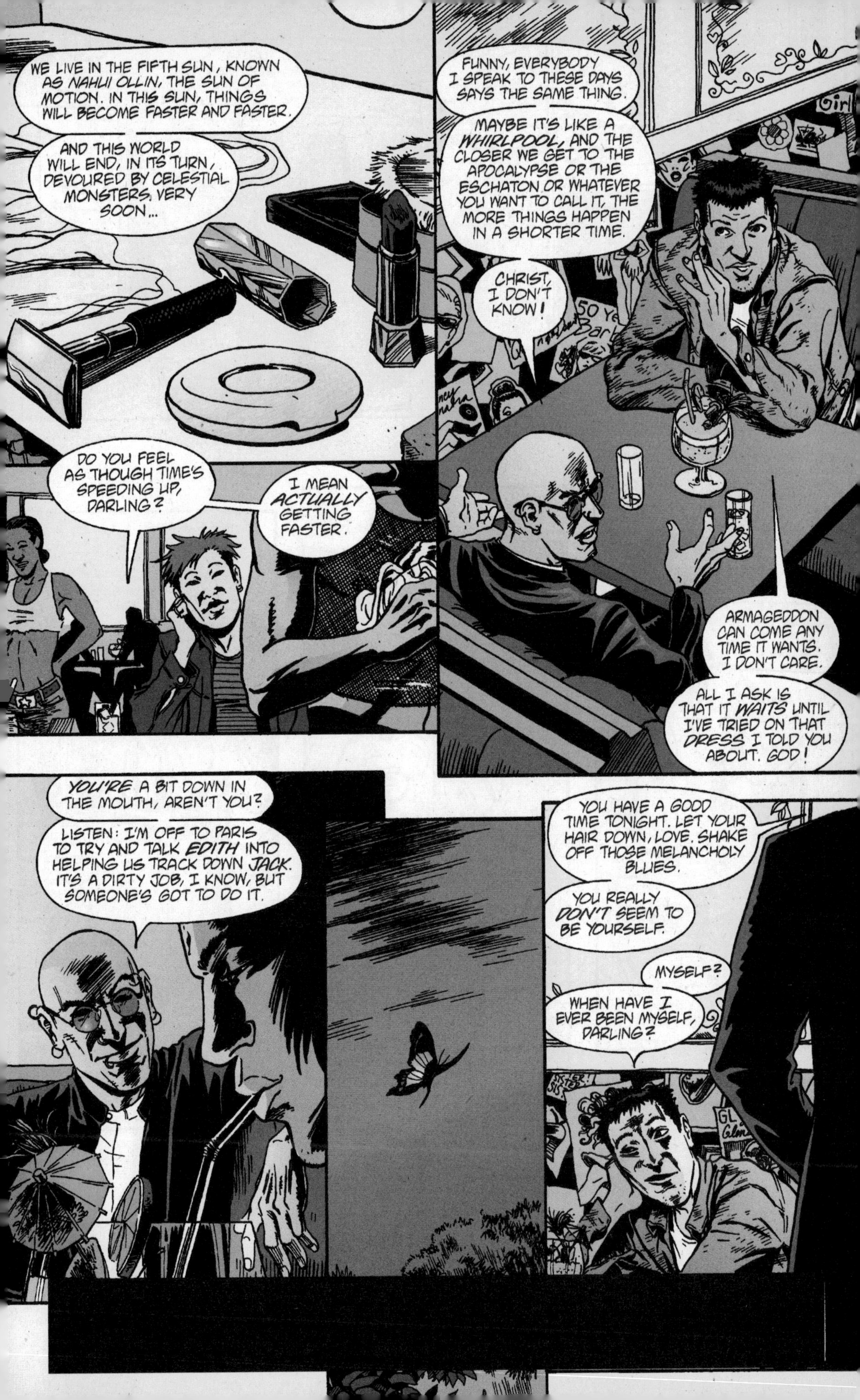

WE LIVE IN THE FIFTH SUN, KNOWN AS NAHUI OLLIN, THE SUN OF MOTION. IN THIS SUN, THINGS WILL BECOME FASTER AND FASTER.
AND THIS WORLD WILL END, IN ITS TURN, DEVOURED BY CELESTIAL MONSTERS. VERY SOON...
FUNNY, EVERYBODY I SPEAK TO THESE DAYS SAYS THE SAME THING.
MAYBE IT'S LIKE A WHIRLPOOL, AND THE CLOSER WE GET TO THE APOCALYPSE OR THE ESCHATON OR WHATEVER YOU WANT TO CALL IT, THE MORE THINGS HAPPEN IN A SHORTER TIME.
CHRIST, I DON'T KNOW!
DO YOU FEEL AS THOUGH TIME'S SPEEDING UP, DARLING?
I MEAN ACTUALLY GETTING FASTER.
ARMAGEDDON CAN COME ANY TIME IT WANTS. I DON'T CARE.
ALL I ASK IS THAT IT WAITS UNTIL I'VE TRIED ON THAT DRESS I TOLD YOU ABOUT. GOD!
YOU'RE A BIT DOWN IN THE MOUTH, AREN'T YOU?
LISTEN: I'M OFF TO PARIS TO TRY AND TALK EDITH INTO HELPING US TRACK DOWN JACK. IT'S A DIRTY JOB, I KNOW, BUT SOMEONE'S GOT TO DO IT.
YOU HAVE A GOOD TIME TONIGHT. LET YOUR HAIR DOWN, LOVE. SHAKE OFF THOSE MELANCHOLY BLUES.
YOU REALLY DON'T SEEM TO BE YOURSELF.
MYSELF?
WHEN HAVE I EVER BEEN MYSELF, DARLING?

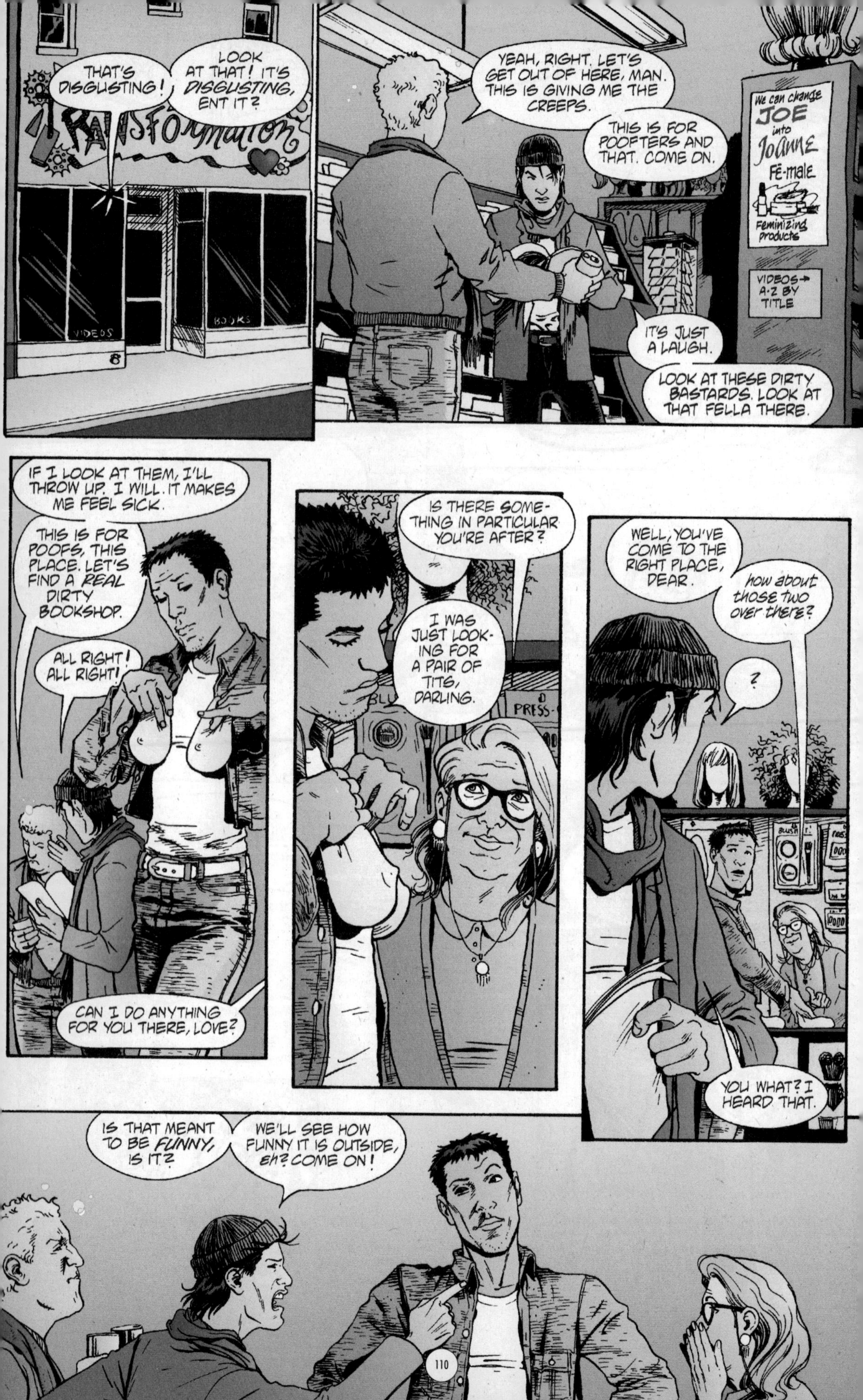
THAT'S DISGUSTING!
LOOK AT THAT! IT'S DISGUSTING, ENT IT?
TRANSFORMATION
VIDEOS
BOOKS
YEAH, RIGHT. LET'S GET OUT OF HERE, MAN. THIS IS GIVING ME THE CREEPS.
THIS IS FOR POOFTERS AND THAT. COME ON.
We can change JOE into JoAnne Fe-male Feminizing products
VIDEOS→ A-Z BY TITLE
IT'S JUST A LAUGH.
LOOK AT THESE DIRTY BASTARDS. LOOK AT THAT FELLA THERE.
IF I LOOK AT THEM, I'LL THROW UP. I WILL. IT MAKES ME FEEL SICK.
THIS IS FOR POOFS, THIS PLACE. LET'S FIND A REAL DIRTY BOOKSHOP.
ALL RIGHT! ALL RIGHT!
CAN I DO ANYTHING FOR YOU THERE, LOVE?
IS THERE SOMETHING IN PARTICULAR YOU'RE AFTER?
I WAS JUST LOOKING FOR A PAIR OF TITS, DARLING.
PRESS-
WELL, YOU'VE COME TO THE RIGHT PLACE, DEAR.
how about those two over there?
?
YOU WHAT? I HEARD THAT.
IS THAT MEANT TO BE FUNNY, IS IT?
WE'LL SEE HOW FUNNY IT IS OUTSIDE, eh? COME ON!

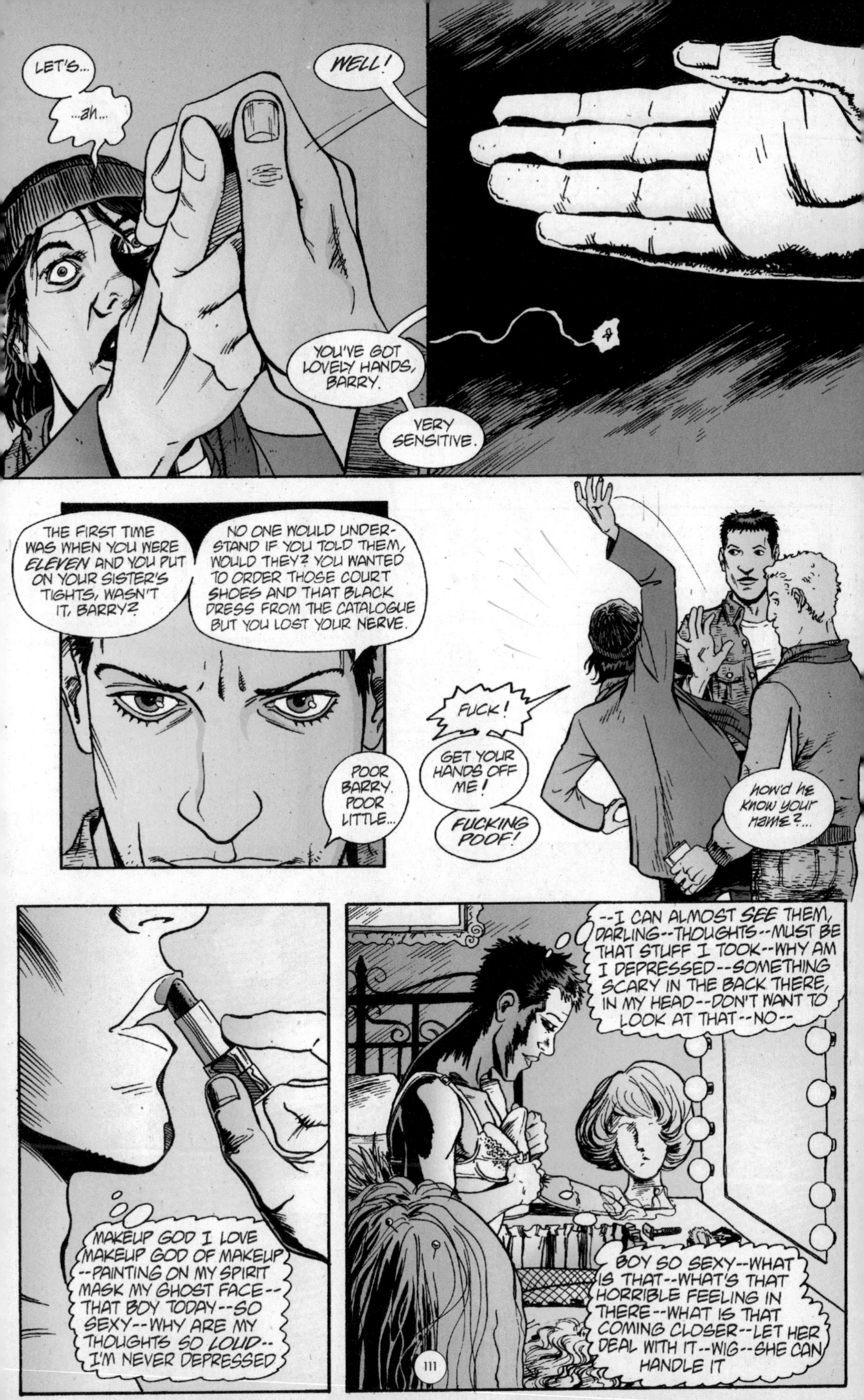

LET'S...
...ah...
WELL!
YOU'VE GOT LOVELY HANDS, BARRY.
VERY SENSITIVE.
THE FIRST TIME WAS WHEN YOU WERE *ELEVEN* AND YOU PUT ON YOUR SISTER'S TIGHTS, WASN'T IT, BARRY?
NO ONE WOULD UNDER-STAND IF YOU TOLD THEM, WOULD THEY? YOU WANTED TO ORDER THOSE COURT SHOES AND THAT BLACK DRESS FROM THE CATALOGUE BUT YOU LOST YOUR NERVE.
POOR BARRY. POOR LITTLE...
FUCK!
GET YOUR HANDS OFF ME!
FUCKING POOF!
how'd he know your name?...
MAKEUP GOD I LOVE MAKEUP GOD OF MAKEUP --PAINTING ON MY SPIRIT MASK MY GHOST FACE-- THAT BOY TODAY--SO SEXY--WHY ARE MY THOUGHTS SO *LOUD*-- I'M NEVER DEPRESSED
--I CAN ALMOST *SEE* THEM, DARLING--THOUGHTS--MUST BE THAT STUFF I TOOK--WHY AM I DEPRESSED--SOMETHING SCARY IN THE BACK THERE, IN MY HEAD--DON'T WANT TO LOOK AT THAT--NO--
BOY SO SEXY--WHAT IS THAT--WHAT'S THAT HORRIBLE FEELING IN THERE--WHAT IS THAT COMING CLOSER--LET HER DEAL WITH IT--WIG--SHE CAN HANDLE IT

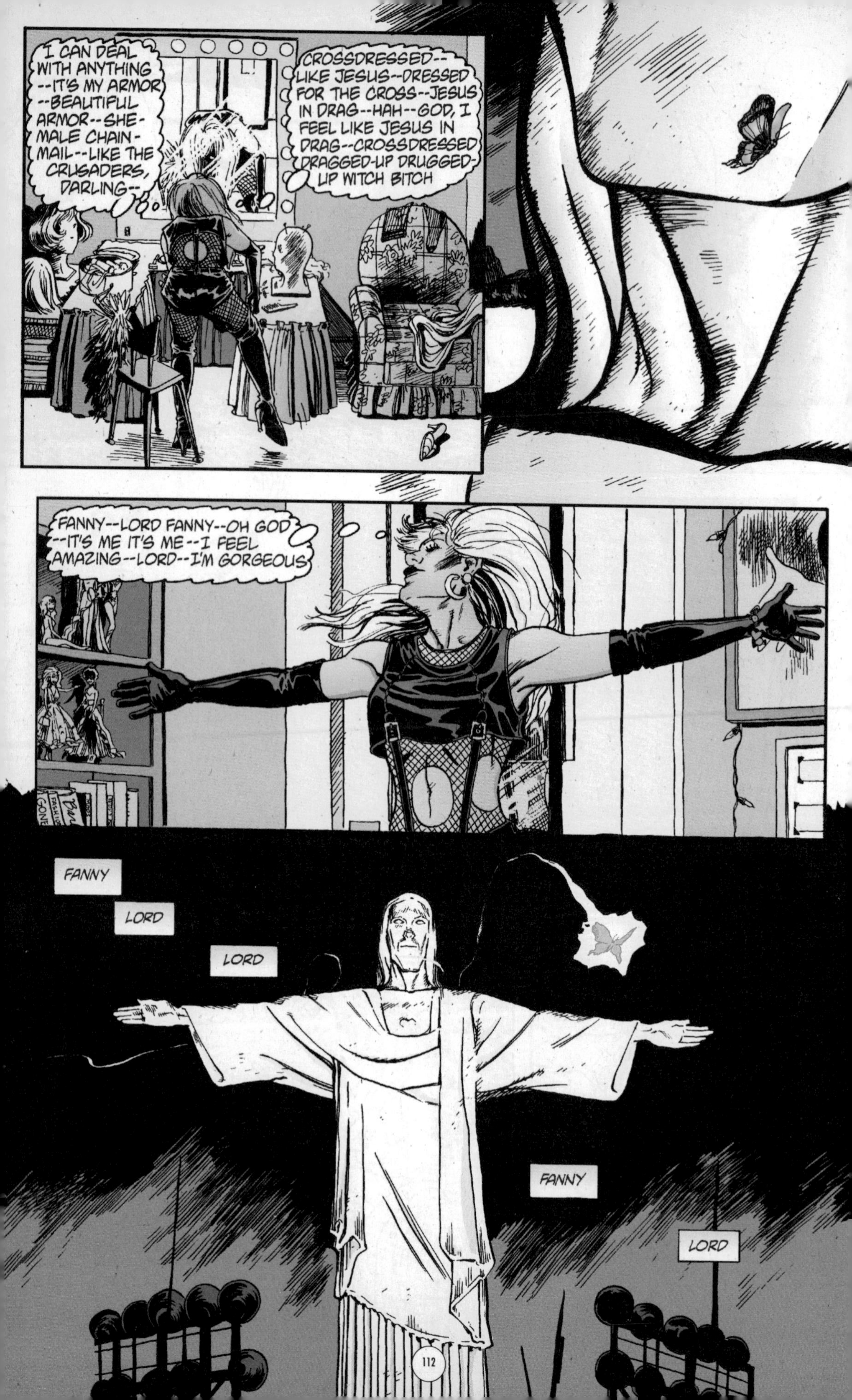

I CAN DEAL WITH ANYTHING --IT'S MY ARMOR --BEAUTIFUL ARMOR--SHE-MALE CHAIN-MAIL--LIKE THE CRUSADERS, DARLING--
CROSSDRESSED-- LIKE JESUS--DRESSED FOR THE CROSS--JESUS IN DRAG--HAH--GOD, I FEEL LIKE JESUS IN DRAG--CROSSDRESSED DRAGGED-UP DRUGGED-UP WITCH BITCH
FANNY--LORD FANNY--OH GOD --IT'S ME IT'S ME--I FEEL AMAZING--LORD--I'M GORGEOUS
FANNY
LORD
LORD
FANNY
LORD

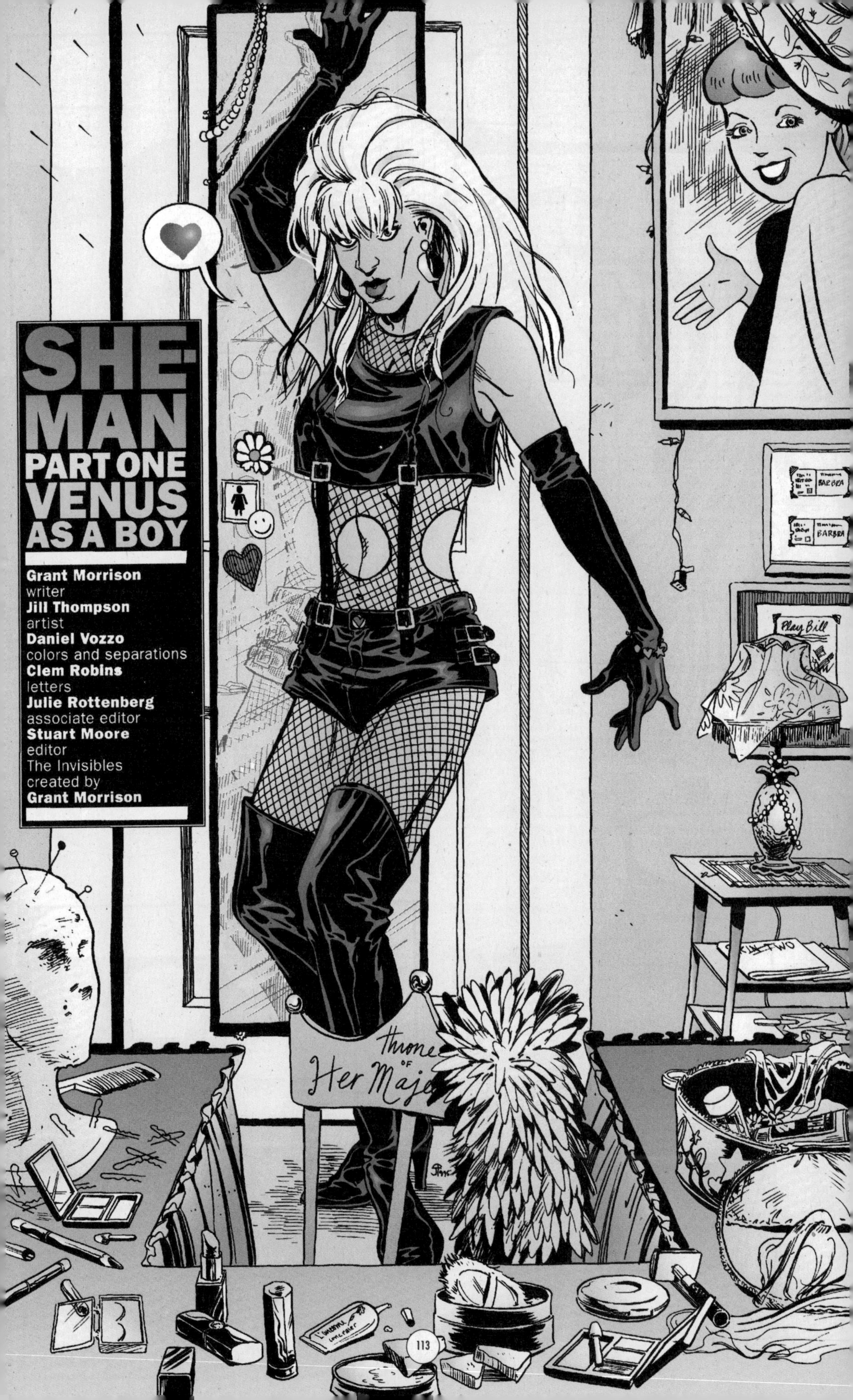
SHE-MAN
PART ONE
VENUS AS A BOY
Grant Morrison
writer
Jill Thompson
artist
Daniel Vozzo
colors and separations
Clem Robins
letters
Julie Rottenberg
associate editor
Stuart Moore
editor
The Invisibles
created by
Grant Morrison
Play Bill
BARBRA
BARBRA
throne OF Her Maje

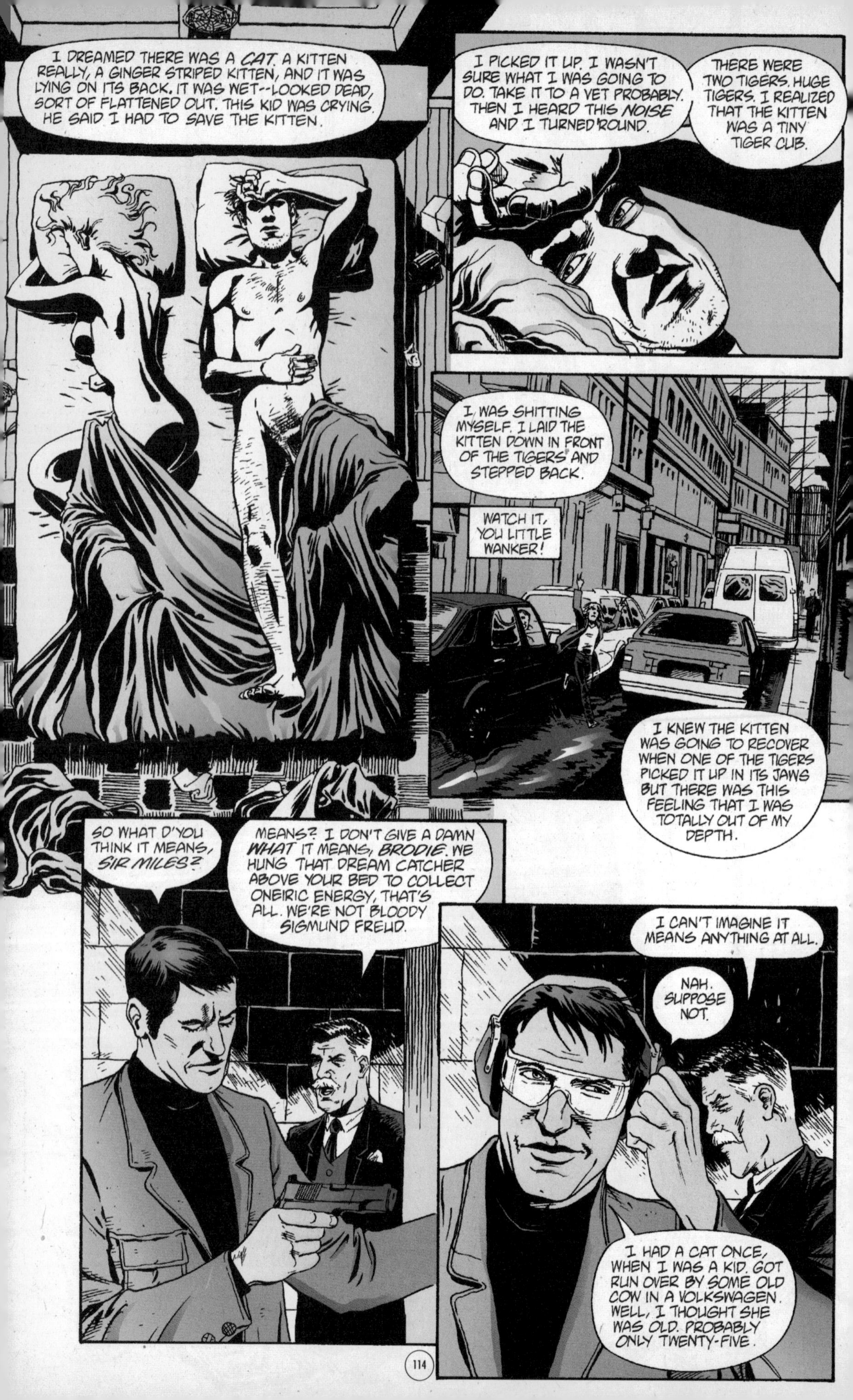
I DREAMED THERE WAS A CAT, A KITTEN REALLY, A GINGER STRIPED KITTEN, AND IT WAS LYING ON ITS BACK. IT WAS WET--LOOKED DEAD, SORT OF FLATTENED OUT. THIS KID WAS CRYING. HE SAID I HAD TO SAVE THE KITTEN.
I PICKED IT UP. I WASN'T SURE WHAT I WAS GOING TO DO. TAKE IT TO A VET PROBABLY. THEN I HEARD THIS NOISE AND I TURNED 'ROUND.
THERE WERE TWO TIGERS. HUGE TIGERS. I REALIZED THAT THE KITTEN WAS A TINY TIGER CUB.
I WAS SHITTING MYSELF. I LAID THE KITTEN DOWN IN FRONT OF THE TIGERS AND STEPPED BACK.
WATCH IT, YOU LITTLE WANKER!
I KNEW THE KITTEN WAS GOING TO RECOVER WHEN ONE OF THE TIGERS PICKED IT UP IN ITS JAWS BUT THERE WAS THIS FEELING THAT I WAS TOTALLY OUT OF MY DEPTH.
SO WHAT D'YOU THINK IT MEANS, SIR MILES?
MEANS? I DON'T GIVE A DAMN WHAT IT MEANS, BRODIE. WE HUNG THAT DREAM CATCHER ABOVE YOUR BED TO COLLECT ONEIRIC ENERGY, THAT'S ALL. WE'RE NOT BLOODY SIGMUND FREUD.
I CAN'T IMAGINE IT MEANS ANYTHING AT ALL.
NAH. SUPPOSE NOT.
I HAD A CAT ONCE, WHEN I WAS A KID. GOT RUN OVER BY SOME OLD COW IN A VOLKSWAGEN. WELL, I THOUGHT SHE WAS OLD. PROBABLY ONLY TWENTY-FIVE.

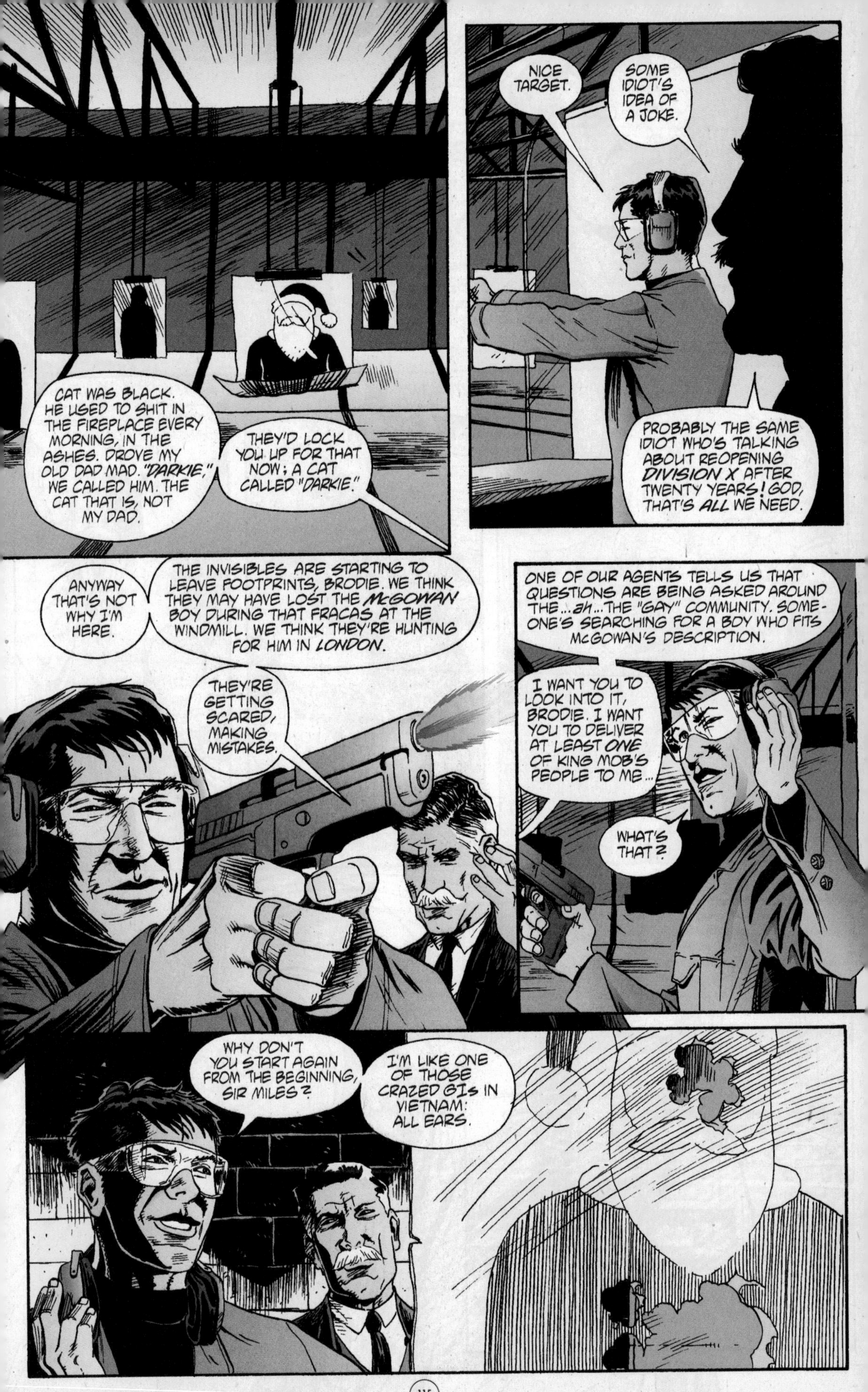
NICE TARGET.
SOME IDIOT'S IDEA OF A JOKE.
CAT WAS BLACK. HE USED TO SHIT IN THE FIREPLACE EVERY MORNING, IN THE ASHES. DROVE MY OLD DAD MAD. "DARKIE," WE CALLED HIM. THE CAT THAT IS, NOT MY DAD.
THEY'D LOCK YOU UP FOR THAT NOW; A CAT CALLED "DARKIE."
PROBABLY THE SAME IDIOT WHO'S TALKING ABOUT REOPENING DIVISION X AFTER TWENTY YEARS! GOD, THAT'S ALL WE NEED.
ANYWAY THAT'S NOT WHY I'M HERE.
THE INVISIBLES ARE STARTING TO LEAVE FOOTPRINTS, BRODIE. WE THINK THEY MAY HAVE LOST THE McGOWAN BOY DURING THAT FRACAS AT THE WINDMILL. WE THINK THEY'RE HUNTING FOR HIM IN LONDON.
THEY'RE GETTING SCARED, MAKING MISTAKES.
ONE OF OUR AGENTS TELLS US THAT QUESTIONS ARE BEING ASKED AROUND THE... ah... THE "GAY" COMMUNITY. SOME-ONE'S SEARCHING FOR A BOY WHO FITS McGOWAN'S DESCRIPTION.
I WANT YOU TO LOOK INTO IT, BRODIE. I WANT YOU TO DELIVER AT LEAST ONE OF KING MOB'S PEOPLE TO ME...
WHAT'S THAT?
WHY DON'T YOU START AGAIN FROM THE BEGINNING, SIR MILES?
I'M LIKE ONE OF THOSE CRAZED GIs IN VIETNAM: ALL EARS.

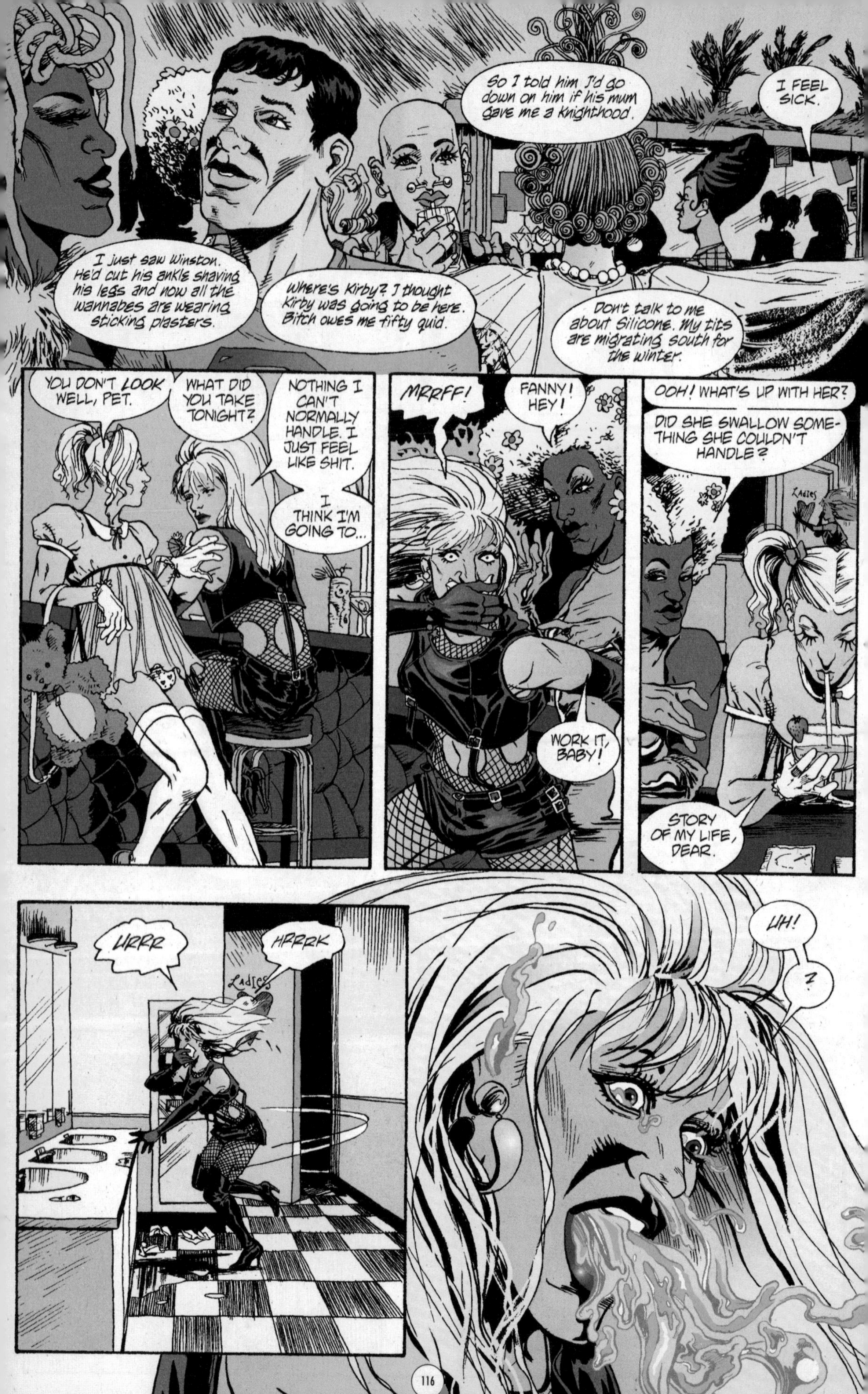

So I told him I'd go down on him if his mum gave me a knighthood.
I FEEL SICK.
I just saw Winston. He'd cut his ankle shaving his legs and now all the wannabes are wearing sticking plasters.
Where's Kirby? I thought Kirby was going to be here. Bitch owes me fifty quid.
Don't talk to me about Silicone. My tits are migrating south for the winter.
YOU DON'T LOOK WELL, PET.
WHAT DID YOU TAKE TONIGHT?
NOTHING I CAN'T NORMALLY HANDLE. I JUST FEEL LIKE SHIT.
I THINK I'M GOING TO...
MRRFF!
FANNY! HEY!
WORK IT, BABY!
OOH! WHAT'S UP WITH HER?
DID SHE SWALLOW SOMETHING SHE COULDN'T HANDLE?
STORY OF MY LIFE, DEAR.
URRR
HRRRK
Ladies
UH!
?

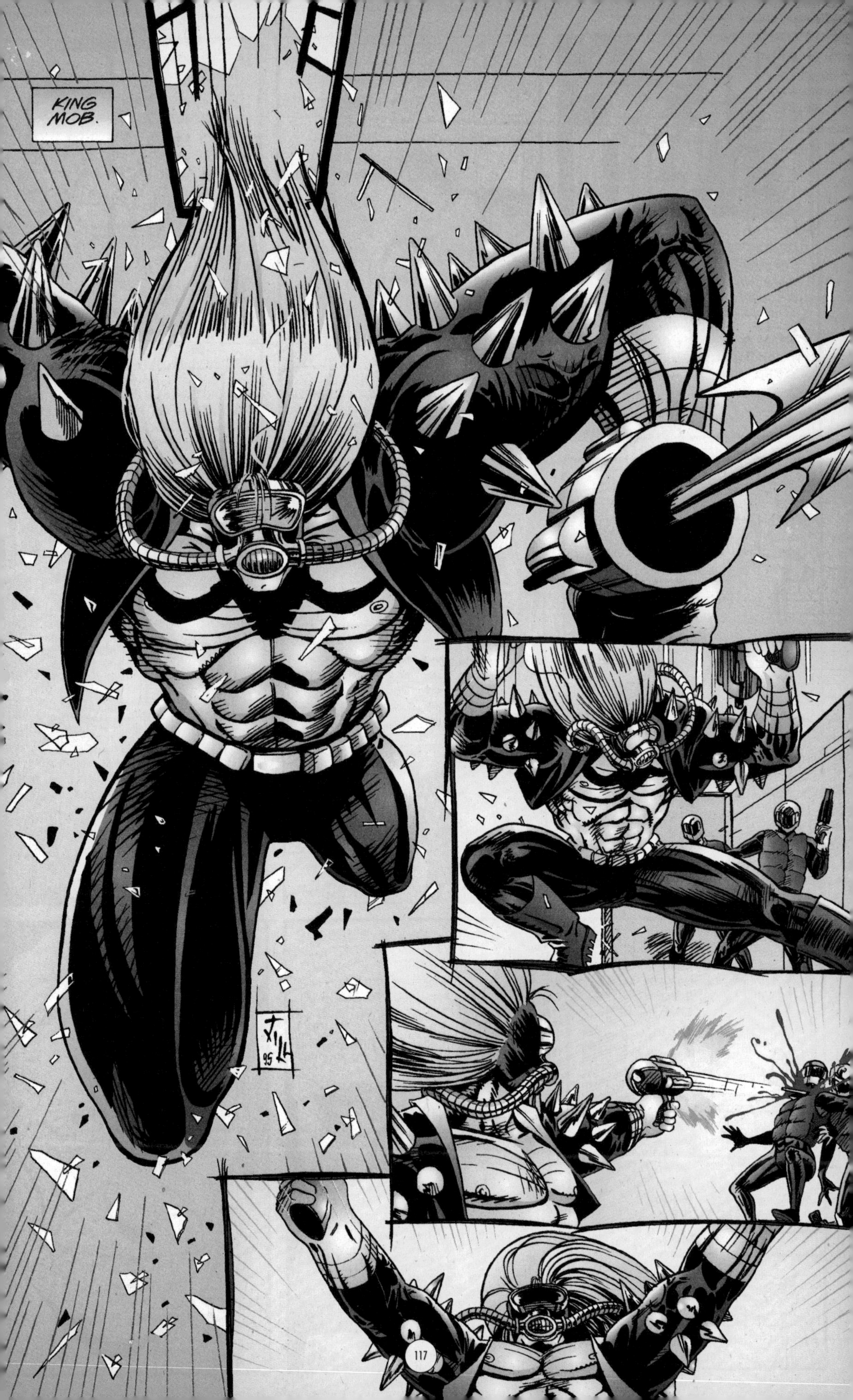
KING MOB.

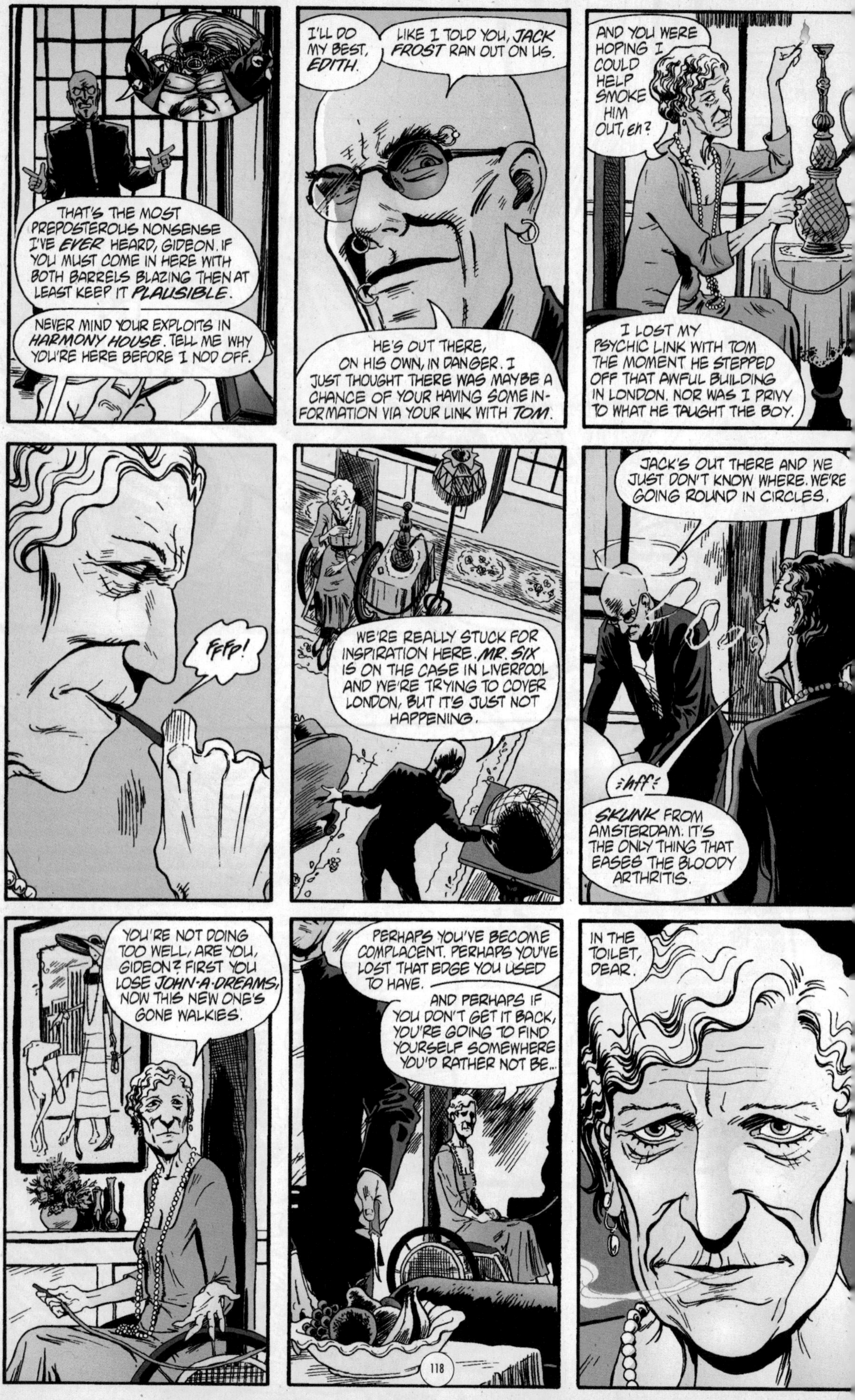
THAT'S THE MOST PREPOSTEROUS NONSENSE I'VE *EVER* HEARD, GIDEON. IF YOU MUST COME IN HERE WITH BOTH BARRELS BLAZING THEN AT LEAST KEEP IT *PLAUSIBLE*.
NEVER MIND YOUR EXPLOITS IN *HARMONY HOUSE*. TELL ME WHY YOU'RE HERE BEFORE I NOD OFF.
I'LL DO MY BEST, *EDITH*.
LIKE I TOLD YOU, *JACK FROST* RAN OUT ON US.
HE'S OUT THERE, ON HIS OWN, IN DANGER. I JUST THOUGHT THERE WAS MAYBE A CHANCE OF YOUR HAVING SOME INFORMATION VIA YOUR LINK WITH *TOM*.
AND YOU WERE HOPING I COULD HELP SMOKE HIM OUT, EH?
I LOST MY PSYCHIC LINK WITH TOM THE MOMENT HE STEPPED OFF THAT AWFUL BUILDING IN LONDON. NOR WAS I PRIVY TO WHAT HE TAUGHT THE BOY.
FFFP!
WE'RE REALLY STUCK FOR INSPIRATION HERE. *MR. SIX* IS ON THE CASE IN LIVERPOOL AND WE'RE TRYING TO COVER LONDON, BUT IT'S JUST NOT HAPPENING.
JACK'S OUT THERE AND WE JUST DON'T KNOW WHERE. WE'RE GOING ROUND IN CIRCLES.
HFF
SKUNK FROM AMSTERDAM: IT'S THE ONLY THING THAT EASES THE BLOODY ARTHRITIS.
YOU'RE NOT DOING TOO WELL, ARE YOU, GIDEON? FIRST YOU LOSE *JOHN-A-DREAMS*, NOW THIS NEW ONE'S GONE WALKIES.
PERHAPS YOU'VE BECOME COMPLACENT. PERHAPS YOU'VE LOST THAT EDGE YOU USED TO HAVE.
AND PERHAPS IF YOU DON'T GET IT BACK, YOU'RE GOING TO FIND YOURSELF SOMEWHERE YOU'D RATHER NOT BE...
IN THE TOILET, DEAR.

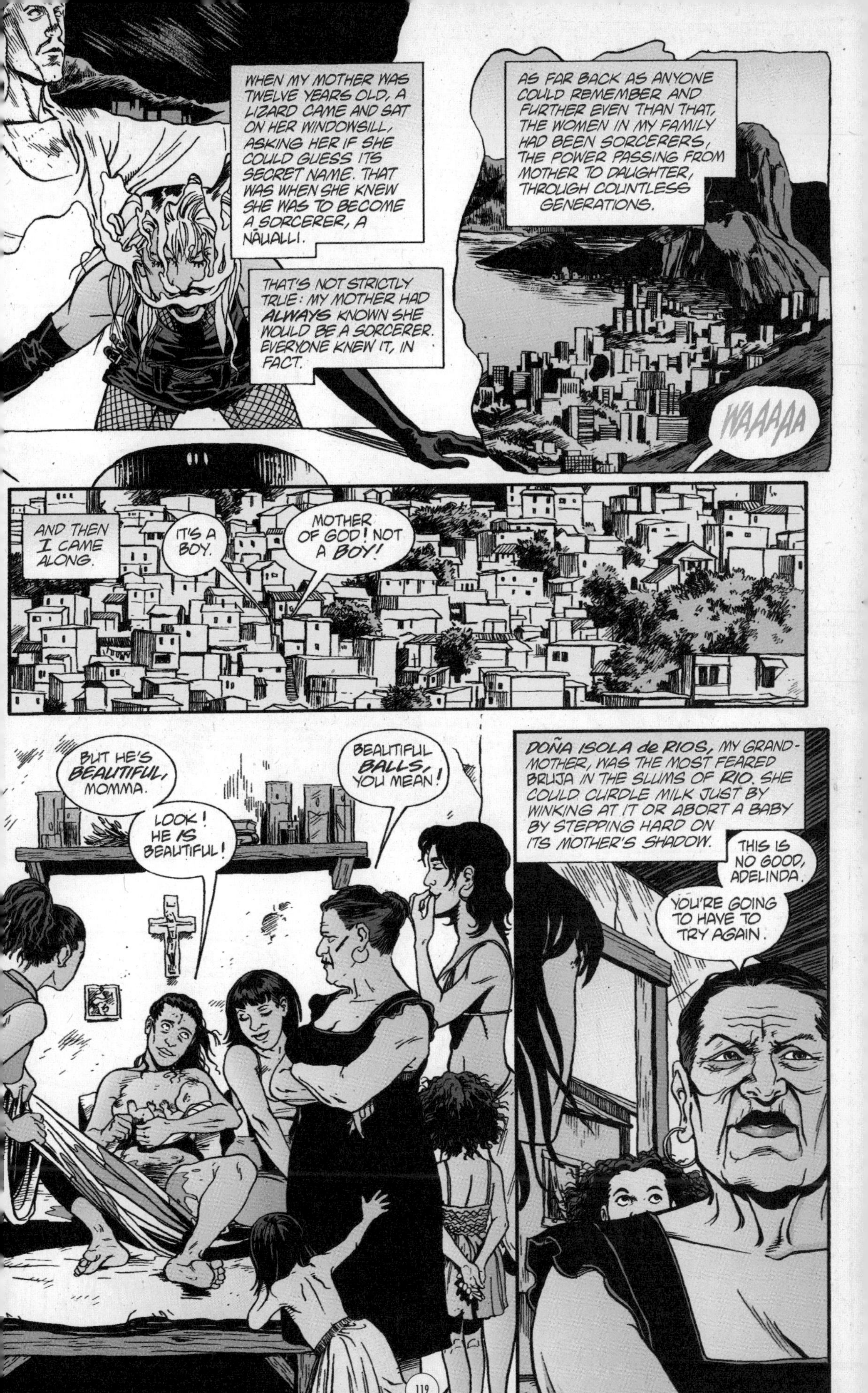
WHEN MY MOTHER WAS TWELVE YEARS OLD, A LIZARD CAME AND SAT ON HER WINDOWSILL, ASKING HER IF SHE COULD GUESS ITS SECRET NAME. THAT WAS WHEN SHE KNEW SHE WAS TO BECOME A SORCERER, A NÄUALLI.
THAT'S NOT STRICTLY TRUE: MY MOTHER HAD ALWAYS KNOWN SHE WOULD BE A SORCERER. EVERYONE KNEW IT, IN FACT.
AS FAR BACK AS ANYONE COULD REMEMBER AND FURTHER EVEN THAN THAT, THE WOMEN IN MY FAMILY HAD BEEN SORCERERS, THE POWER PASSING FROM MOTHER TO DAUGHTER, THROUGH COUNTLESS GENERATIONS.
WAAAAA
AND THEN I CAME ALONG.
IT'S A BOY.
MOTHER OF GOD! NOT A BOY!
BUT HE'S BEAUTIFUL, MOMMA.
LOOK! HE IS BEAUTIFUL!
BEAUTIFUL BALLS, YOU MEAN!
DOÑA ISOLA de RIOS, MY GRAND-MOTHER, WAS THE MOST FEARED BRUJA IN THE SLUMS OF RIO. SHE COULD CURDLE MILK JUST BY WINKING AT IT OR ABORT A BABY BY STEPPING HARD ON ITS MOTHER'S SHADOW.
THIS IS NO GOOD, ADELINDA.
YOU'RE GOING TO HAVE TO TRY AGAIN.

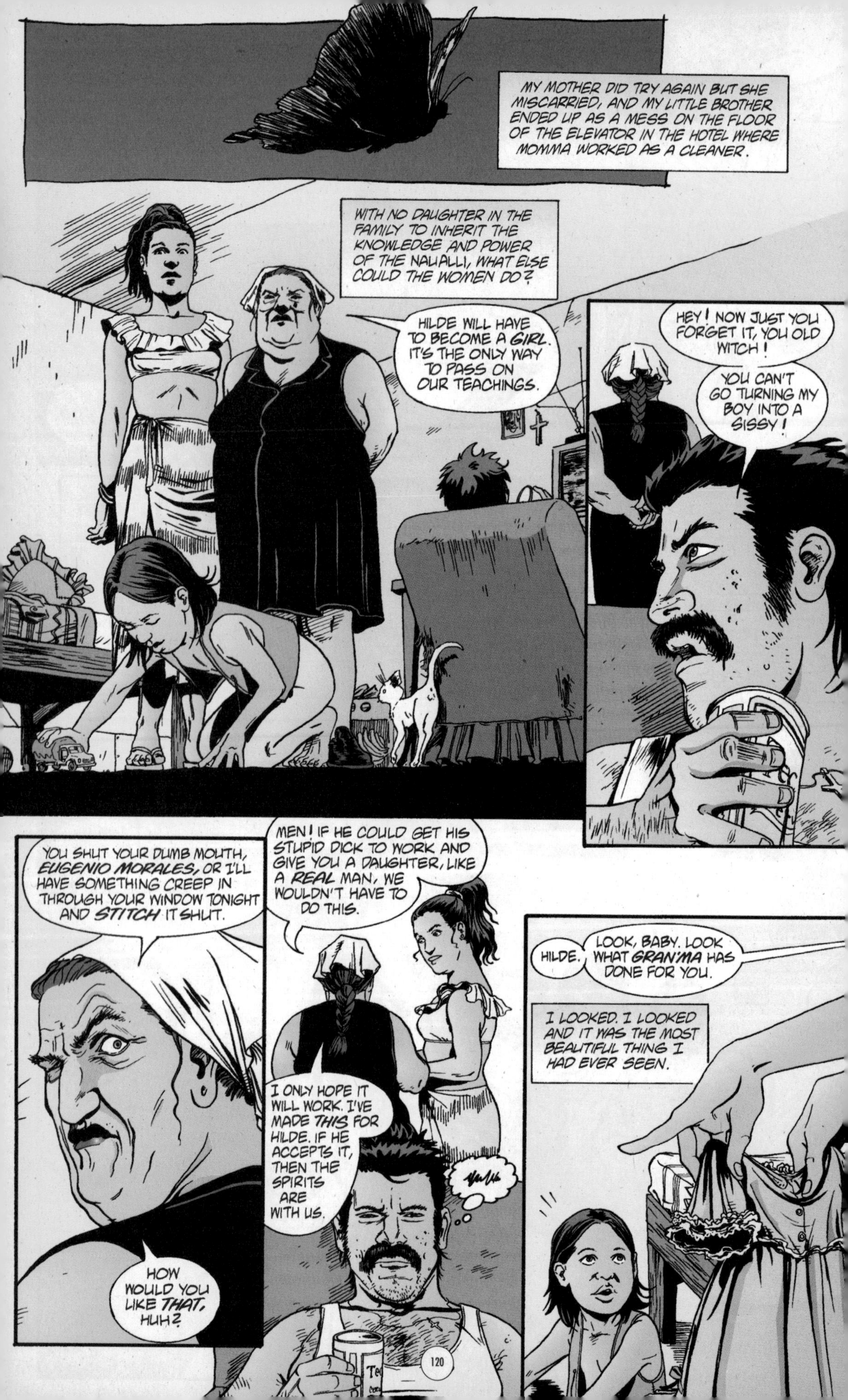
MY MOTHER DID TRY AGAIN BUT SHE MISCARRIED, AND MY LITTLE BROTHER ENDED UP AS A MESS ON THE FLOOR OF THE ELEVATOR IN THE HOTEL WHERE MOMMA WORKED AS A CLEANER.
WITH NO DAUGHTER IN THE FAMILY TO INHERIT THE KNOWLEDGE AND POWER OF THE NAUALLI, WHAT ELSE COULD THE WOMEN DO?
HILDE WILL HAVE TO BECOME A GIRL. IT'S THE ONLY WAY TO PASS ON OUR TEACHINGS.
HEY! NOW JUST YOU FORGET IT, YOU OLD WITCH!
YOU CAN'T GO TURNING MY BOY INTO A SISSY!
YOU SHUT YOUR DUMB MOUTH, EUGENIO MORALES, OR I'LL HAVE SOMETHING CREEP IN THROUGH YOUR WINDOW TONIGHT AND STITCH IT SHUT.
HOW WOULD YOU LIKE THAT, HUH?
MEN! IF HE COULD GET HIS STUPID DICK TO WORK AND GIVE YOU A DAUGHTER, LIKE A REAL MAN, WE WOULDN'T HAVE TO DO THIS.
I ONLY HOPE IT WILL WORK. I'VE MADE THIS FOR HILDE. IF HE ACCEPTS IT, THEN THE SPIRITS ARE WITH US.
HILDE.
LOOK, BABY. LOOK WHAT GRAN'MA HAS DONE FOR YOU.
I LOOKED. I LOOKED AND IT WAS THE MOST BEAUTIFUL THING I HAD EVER SEEN.

I WAS SEVEN YEARS OLD WHEN MY MOTHER WAS STABBED TO DEATH DURING MARDI GRAS, BY A DRUNK WEARING A PAPIER-MACHE DOG'S HEAD.

AFTER THAT, I WAS TAKEN IN AND LOOKED AFTER BY MY GRAN'MA AND MY AUNT MARTA. SHE WASN'T MY *REAL* AUNT, OF COURSE, BUT SHE HAD SLEPT WITH MY FATHER ONCE, WHEN THEY WERE BOTH YOUNG AND STUPID.

GRAN'MA TOLD ME STORIES OF THE GODS AND SPIRITS WHO RULED THE LAND BEFORE *CORTEZ* BROUGHT JESUS AND MARY, AND WHO RULE STILL, IN THE SHADOWS.

MICTLANTECUHTLI, THE DEAD LAND LORD, SITS ON HIS THRONE IN THE GLOOMY ABODE OF THE FLESHLESS...

IS THAT IT? HAVE I OFFENDED MICTLANTE-CUHTLI SOMEHOW? IS *THAT* THE BAD THING? IS THAT WHAT'S SCARING ME?

I CALLED HIM--I *WILL* CALL HIM--AND I MUST PAY HIM SOMEHOW. THAT'S WHY I'M SO AFRAID. I KNOW HE'S *COMING* FOR ME.

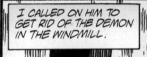

I CALLED ON HIM TO GET RID OF THE DEMON IN THE WINDMILL.

UP HE CAME FROM *MICTLAN*, STINKING OF SOIL AND DESPAIR. THE BONE KING IN HIS PAPER SHROUD AND POINTED HAT.

GRAN'MA?

GRAN'MA AND AUNT MARTA TAUGHT ME TO FIND AND USE MACONHA BRAVA AND RAPE DOS INDIOS AND ALL THE OTHER MAGICAL PLANTS THAT BRUJAS USED TO HEAL AND TO HARM.

AS I GREW OLDER AND LEARNED THE ARTS OF THE SORCERER, I SOON FORGOT I HAD EVER BEEN ANYTHING OTHER THAN A GIRL.

AND IT WASN'T LONG BEFORE I BEGAN TO GET INTERESTED IN BOYS...

IT'S TIME.

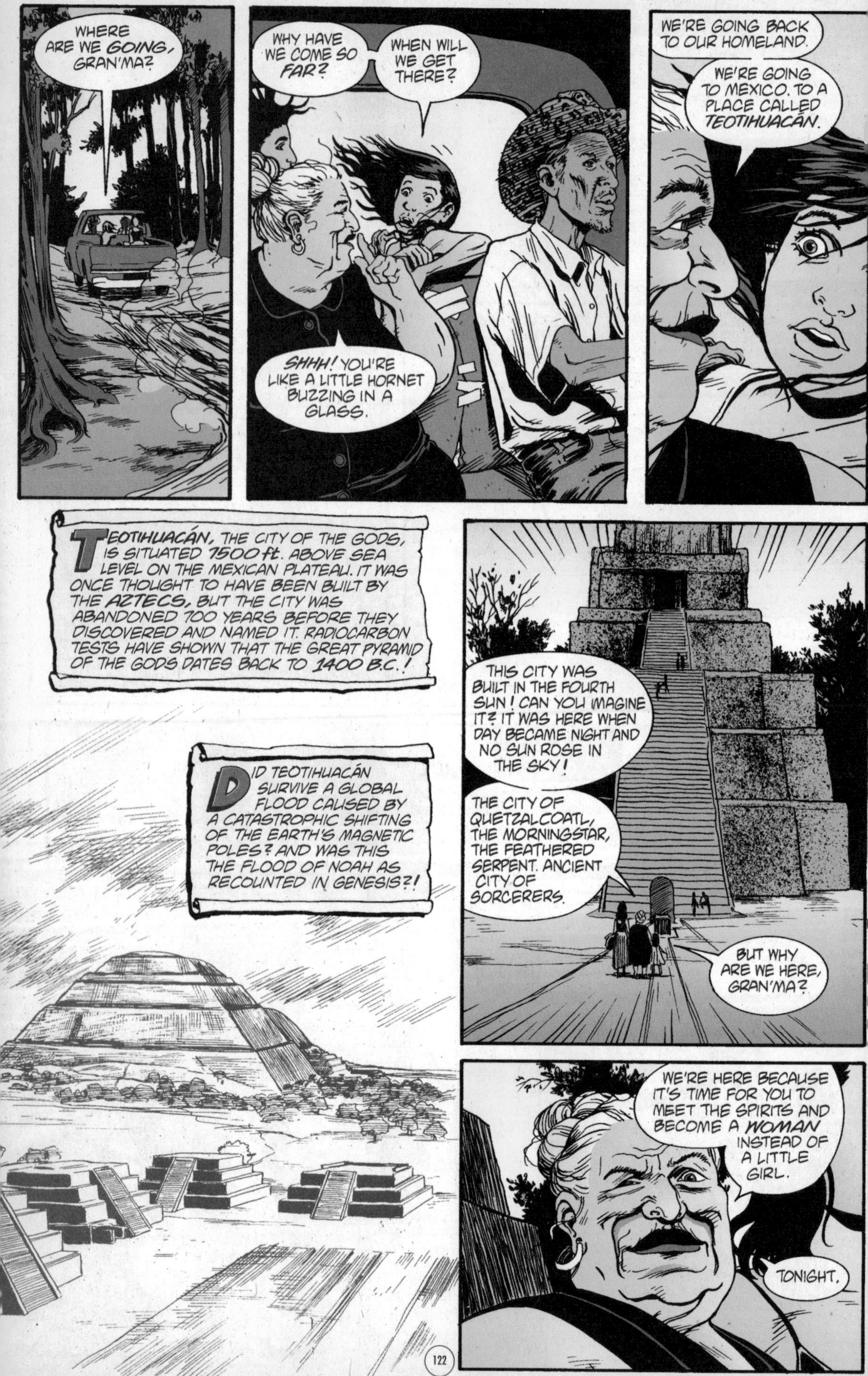
WHERE ARE WE GOING, GRAN'MA?
WHY HAVE WE COME SO FAR?
WHEN WILL WE GET THERE?
SHHH! YOU'RE LIKE A LITTLE HORNET BUZZING IN A GLASS.
WE'RE GOING BACK TO OUR HOMELAND.
WE'RE GOING TO MEXICO. TO A PLACE CALLED TEOTIHUACÁN.
TEOTIHUACÁN, THE CITY OF THE GODS, IS SITUATED 7500 ft. ABOVE SEA LEVEL ON THE MEXICAN PLATEAU. IT WAS ONCE THOUGHT TO HAVE BEEN BUILT BY THE AZTECS, BUT THE CITY WAS ABANDONED 700 YEARS BEFORE THEY DISCOVERED AND NAMED IT. RADIOCARBON TESTS HAVE SHOWN THAT THE GREAT PYRAMID OF THE GODS DATES BACK TO 1400 B.C.!
THIS CITY WAS BUILT IN THE FOURTH SUN! CAN YOU IMAGINE IT? IT WAS HERE WHEN DAY BECAME NIGHT AND NO SUN ROSE IN THE SKY!
THE CITY OF QUETZALCOATL, THE MORNINGSTAR, THE FEATHERED SERPENT. ANCIENT CITY OF SORCERERS.
BUT WHY ARE WE HERE, GRAN'MA?
DID TEOTIHUACÁN SURVIVE A GLOBAL FLOOD CAUSED BY A CATASTROPHIC SHIFTING OF THE EARTH'S MAGNETIC POLES? AND WAS THIS THE FLOOD OF NOAH AS RECOUNTED IN GENESIS?!
WE'RE HERE BECAUSE IT'S TIME FOR YOU TO MEET THE SPIRITS AND BECOME A WOMAN INSTEAD OF A LITTLE GIRL.
TONIGHT.

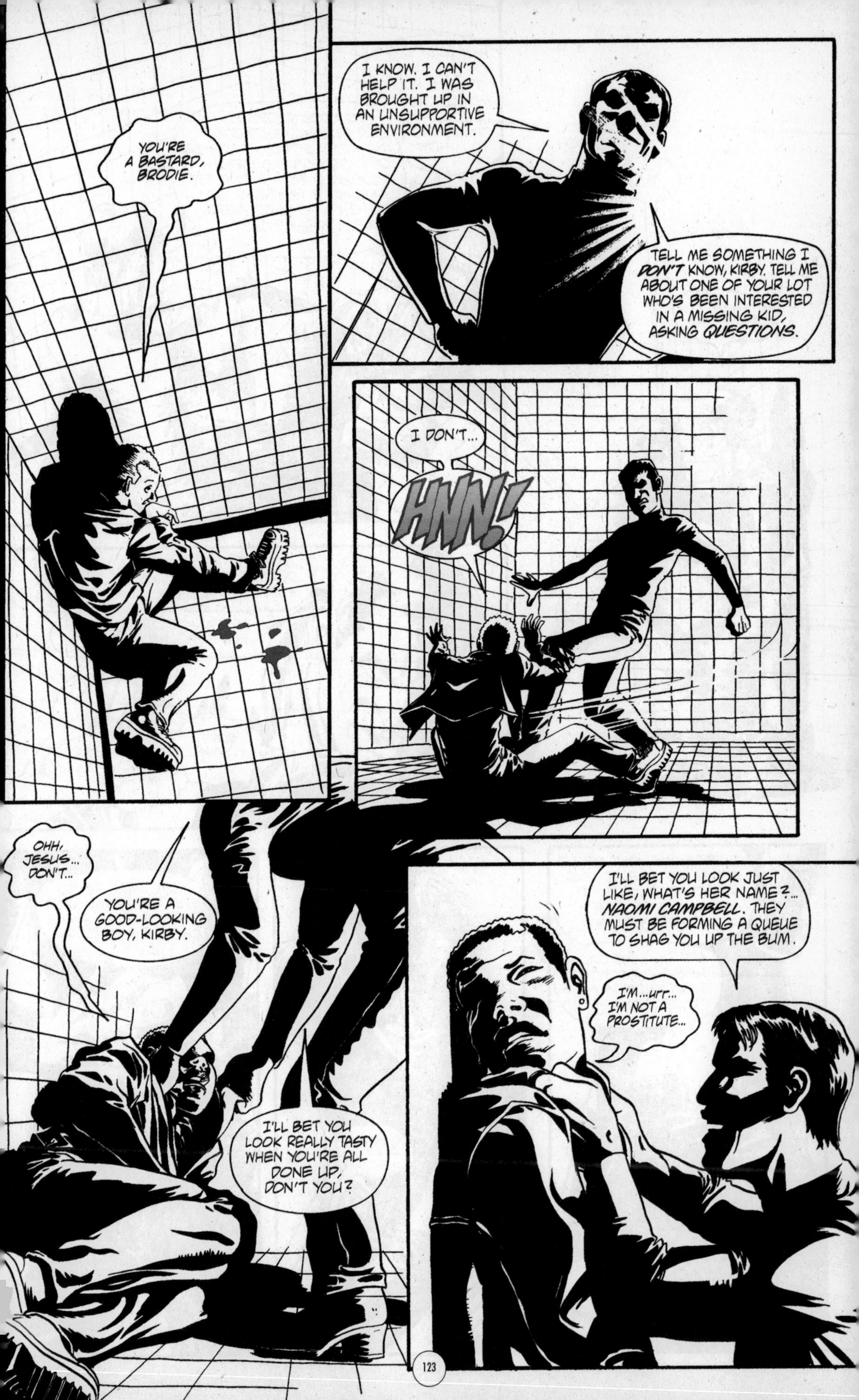
YOU'RE A BASTARD, BRODIE.
I KNOW. I CAN'T HELP IT. I WAS BROUGHT UP IN AN UNSUPPORTIVE ENVIRONMENT.
TELL ME SOMETHING I DON'T KNOW, KIRBY. TELL ME ABOUT ONE OF YOUR LOT WHO'S BEEN INTERESTED IN A MISSING KID, ASKING QUESTIONS.
I DON'T...
HNN!
OHH, JESUS... DON'T...
YOU'RE A GOOD-LOOKING BOY, KIRBY.
I'LL BET YOU LOOK REALLY TASTY WHEN YOU'RE ALL DONE UP, DON'T YOU?
I'LL BET YOU LOOK JUST LIKE, WHAT'S HER NAME?... NAOMI CAMPBELL. THEY MUST BE FORMING A QUEUE TO SHAG YOU UP THE BUM.
I'M...URR... I'M NOT A PROSTITUTE...

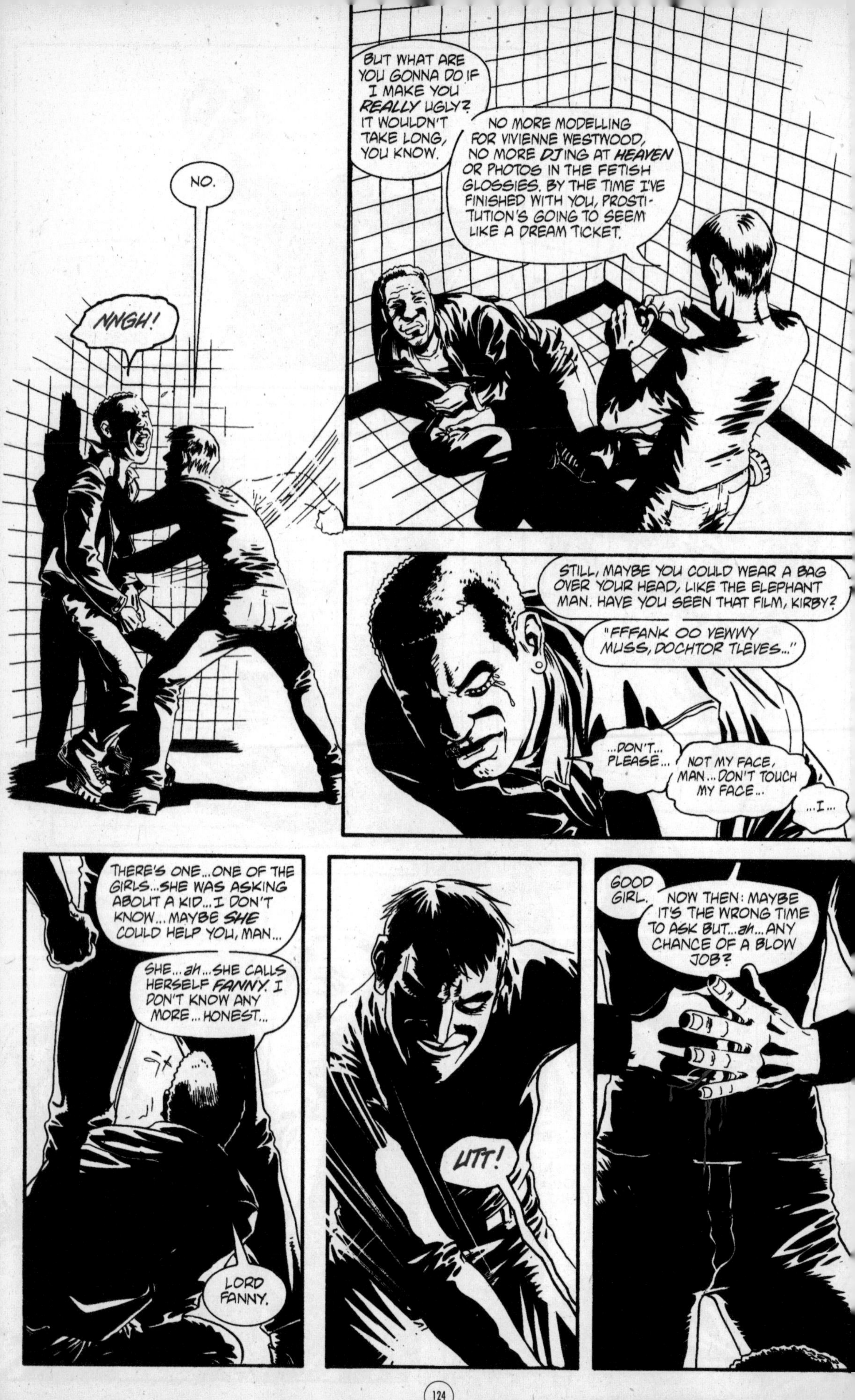
BUT WHAT ARE YOU GONNA DO IF I MAKE YOU REALLY UGLY? IT WOULDN'T TAKE LONG, YOU KNOW.
NO MORE MODELLING FOR VIVIENNE WESTWOOD, NO MORE DJING AT HEAVEN OR PHOTOS IN THE FETISH GLOSSIES. BY THE TIME I'VE FINISHED WITH YOU, PROSTITUTION'S GOING TO SEEM LIKE A DREAM TICKET.
NO.
NNGH!
STILL, MAYBE YOU COULD WEAR A BAG OVER YOUR HEAD, LIKE THE ELEPHANT MAN. HAVE YOU SEEN THAT FILM, KIRBY?
"FFFANK OO VEWWY MUSS, DOCHTOR TLEVES..."
...DON'T... PLEASE...
NOT MY FACE, MAN... DON'T TOUCH MY FACE...
...I...
THERE'S ONE... ONE OF THE GIRLS... SHE WAS ASKING ABOUT A KID... I DON'T KNOW... MAYBE SHE COULD HELP YOU, MAN...
SHE... AH... SHE CALLS HERSELF FANNY. I DON'T KNOW ANY MORE... HONEST...
LORD FANNY.
UTT!
GOOD GIRL.
NOW THEN: MAYBE IT'S THE WRONG TIME TO ASK BUT... AH... ANY CHANCE OF A BLOW JOB?

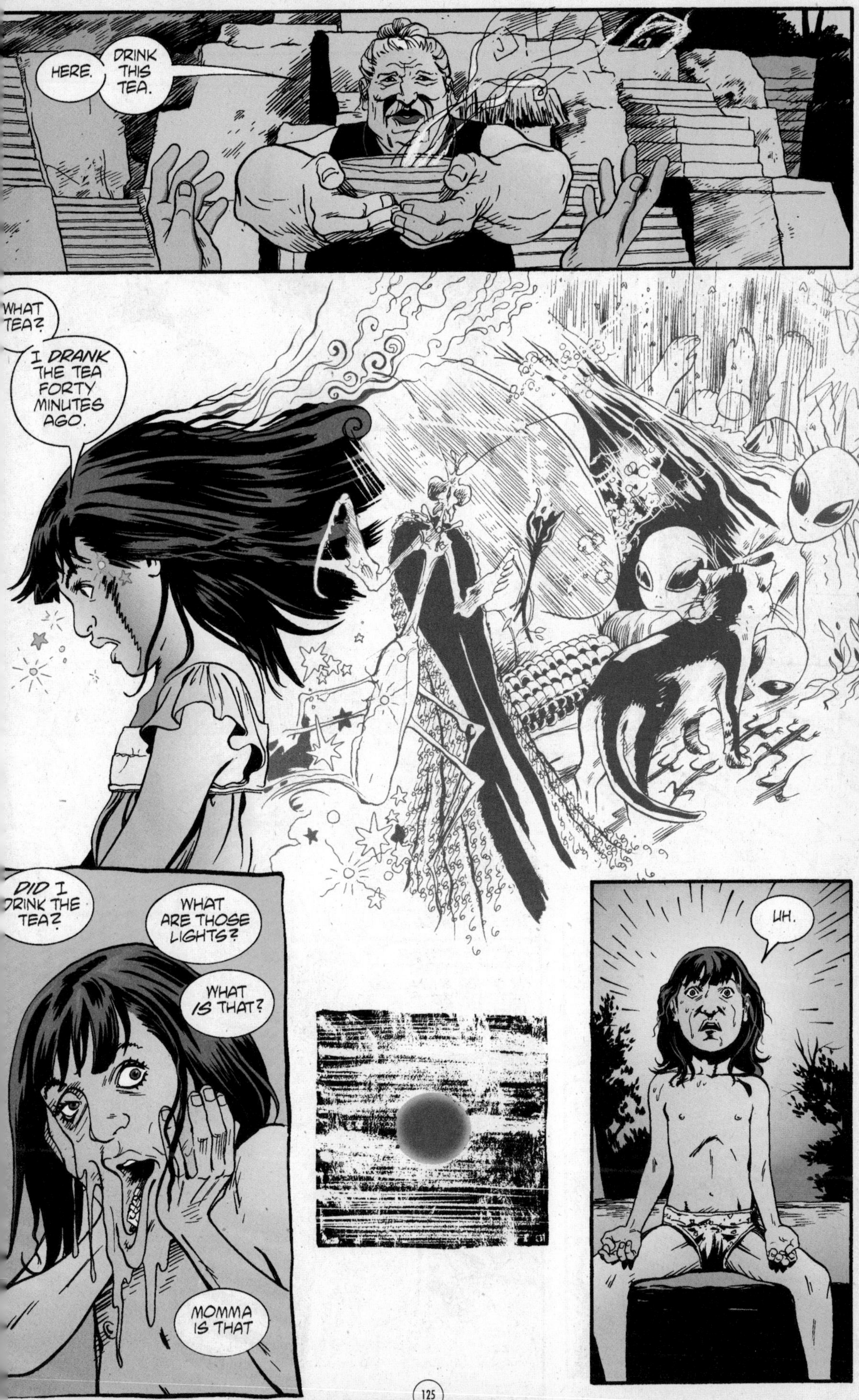
HERE.
DRINK THIS TEA.
WHAT TEA?
I DRANK THE TEA FORTY MINUTES AGO.
DID I DRINK THE TEA?
WHAT ARE THOSE LIGHTS?
WHAT IS THAT?
MOMMA IS THAT
UH.

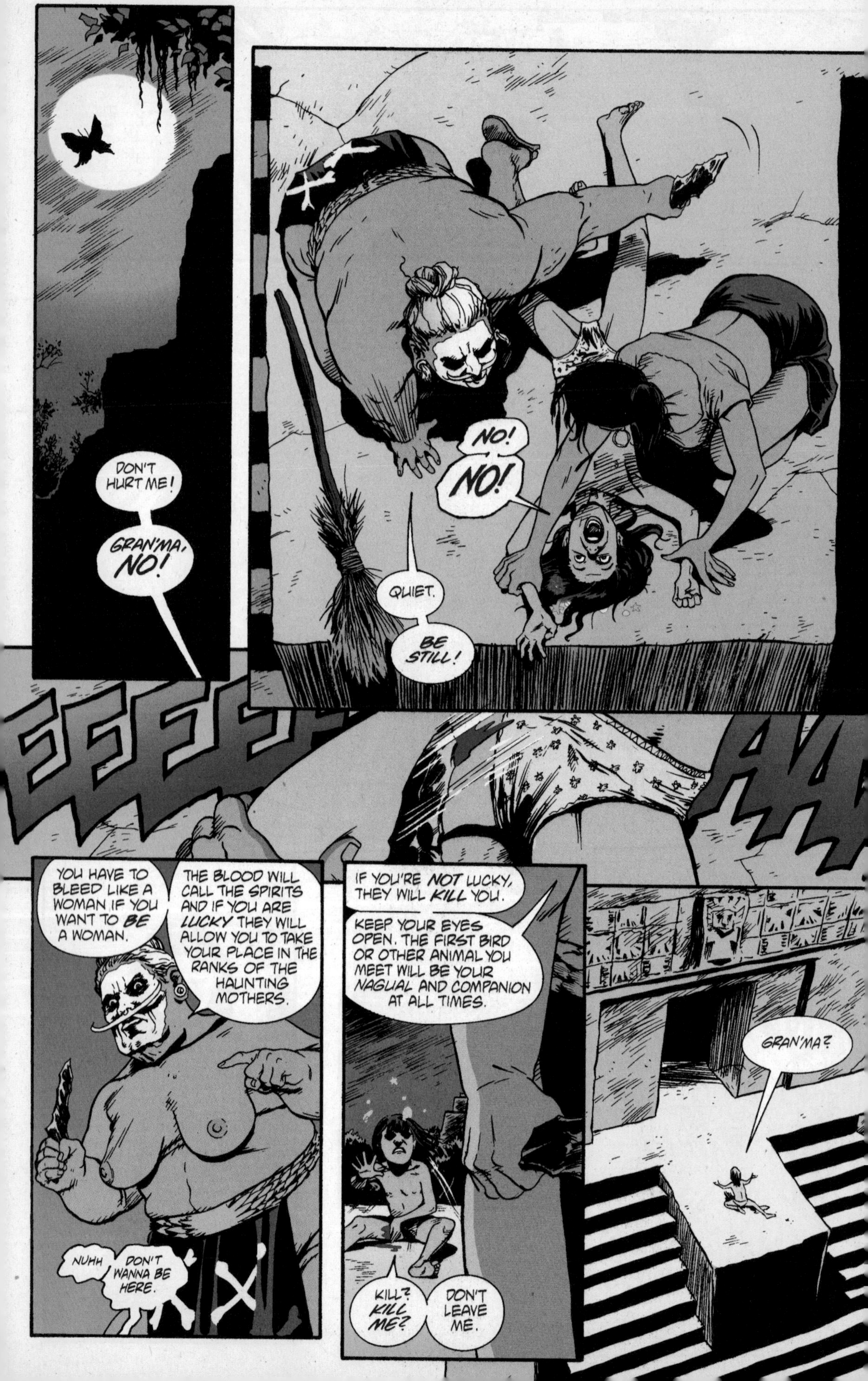
DON'T HURT ME!
GRAN'MA, NO!
NO! NO!
QUIET.
BE STILL!
EEEE
AAA
YOU HAVE TO BLEED LIKE A WOMAN IF YOU WANT TO BE A WOMAN.
THE BLOOD WILL CALL THE SPIRITS AND IF YOU ARE LUCKY THEY WILL ALLOW YOU TO TAKE YOUR PLACE IN THE RANKS OF THE HAUNTING MOTHERS.
NUHH
DON'T WANNA BE HERE.
IF YOU'RE NOT LUCKY, THEY WILL KILL YOU.
KEEP YOUR EYES OPEN. THE FIRST BIRD OR OTHER ANIMAL YOU MEET WILL BE YOUR NAGUAL AND COMPANION AT ALL TIMES.
KILL? KILL ME?
DON'T LEAVE ME.
GRAN'MA?

I CAN'T FOLLOW YOU, EDITH.

THIS SMOKE'S MAKING ME ABSURDLY HIGH.

OH, GIDEON! DON'T BE SUCH A MILQUETOAST.

I WAS JUST SAYING THAT PERHAPS THERE'S A *REASON* FOR ALL OF THIS.

PERHAPS THIS BOY, "JACK FROST" OR WHATEVER IT IS YOU CALL HIM, IS SERVING A *HIGHER* PURPOSE.

INVISIBLES CELLS ARE ORGANIZED ON ELEMENTAL PRINCIPLES, AM I CORRECT? I HAVEN'T FORGOTTEN THE RULES, HAVE I?

THEN YOU MUST TELL ME WHICH MEMBERS OF YOUR TEAM CURRENTLY REPRESENT WHICH OF THE ELEMENTS.

WELL, FOR THE PAST YEAR OR SO, I'VE TAKEN THE *AIR* ROLE, FANNY'S BEEN *WATER*, BOY'S *EARTH* AND ROBIN'S *FIRE*.

WE BROUGHT JACK INTO THE TEAM AS *SPIRIT*. FREE BLOODY SPIRIT.

SPIRIT USUALLY WORKS TO RAISE THE MORALE OF THE TEAM, THAT SORT OF THING...

SPIRIT? OH WELL, IT'S DAZZLINGLY OBVIOUS THEN.

THE SPIRIT ROLE'S *ALWAYS* UNPREDICT-ABLE, YOU KNOW THAT. IT EXISTS TO GALVANIZE AND REVITALIZE THE ELEMENTS AROUND IT.

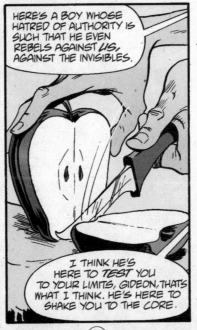

HERE'S A BOY WHOSE HATRED OF AUTHORITY IS SUCH THAT HE EVEN REBELS AGAINST *US*, AGAINST THE INVISIBLES.

I THINK HE'S HERE TO *TEST* YOU TO YOUR LIMITS, GIDEON, THAT'S WHAT I THINK. HE'S HERE TO SHAKE YOU TO THE CORE.

TO GET HIM BACK, YOU'RE GOING TO HAVE TO ENTER THE LABYRINTH AND FACE THE *BEAST*. YOU MUST BRAVE THE JAWS OF THE DRAGON, DEAR.

EACH OF YOU IN TURN, I SHOULDN'T WONDER.

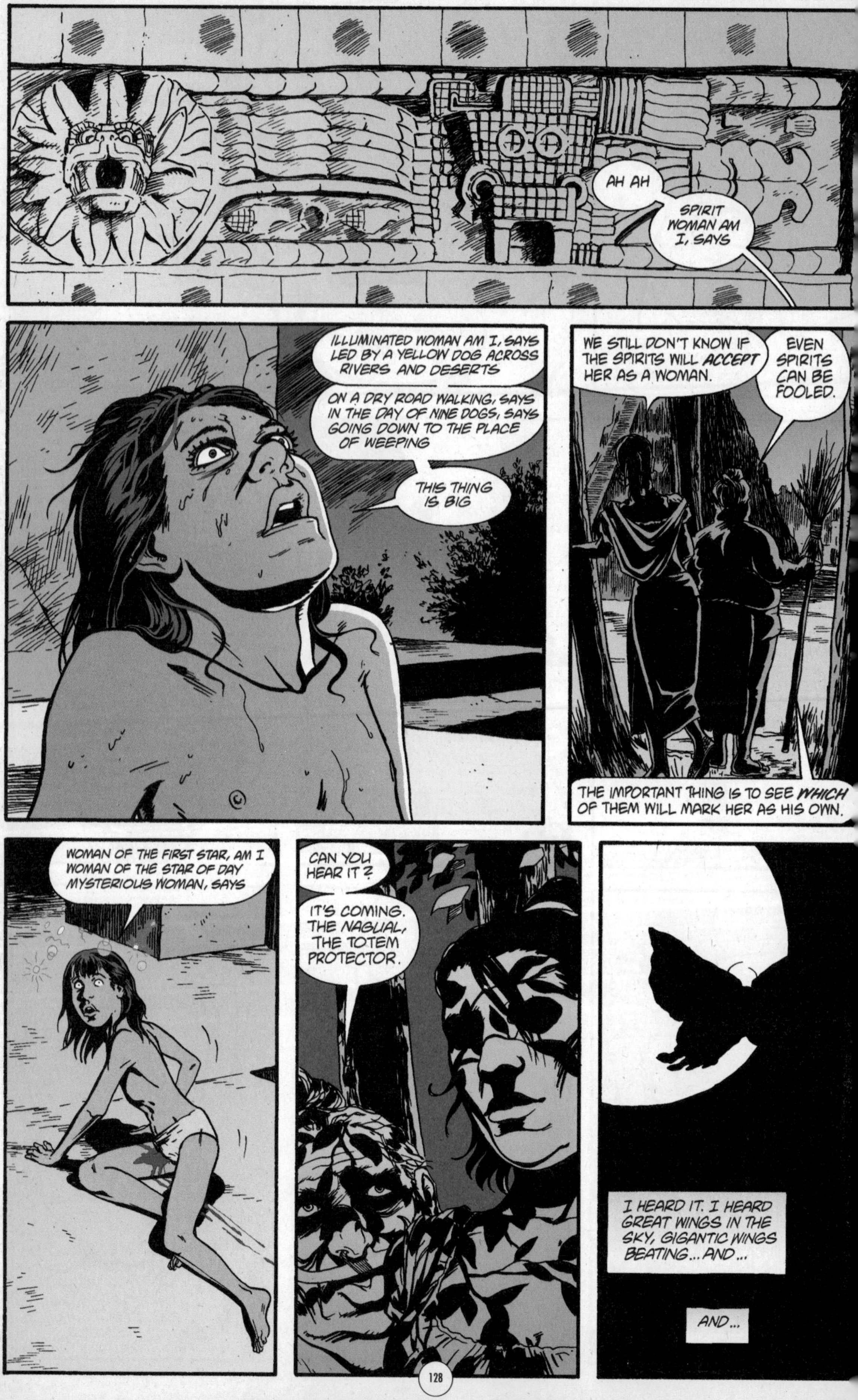
AH AH
SPIRIT WOMAN AM I, SAYS
ILLUMINATED WOMAN AM I, SAYS LED BY A YELLOW DOG ACROSS RIVERS AND DESERTS
ON A DRY ROAD WALKING, SAYS IN THE DAY OF NINE DOGS, SAYS GOING DOWN TO THE PLACE OF WEEPING
THIS THING IS BIG
WE STILL DON'T KNOW IF THE SPIRITS WILL ACCEPT HER AS A WOMAN.
EVEN SPIRITS CAN BE FOOLED.
THE IMPORTANT THING IS TO SEE WHICH OF THEM WILL MARK HER AS HIS OWN.
WOMAN OF THE FIRST STAR, AM I WOMAN OF THE STAR OF DAY MYSTERIOUS WOMAN, SAYS
CAN YOU HEAR IT?
IT'S COMING. THE NAGUAL, THE TOTEM PROTECTOR.
I HEARD IT. I HEARD GREAT WINGS IN THE SKY, GIGANTIC WINGS BEATING... AND...
AND...

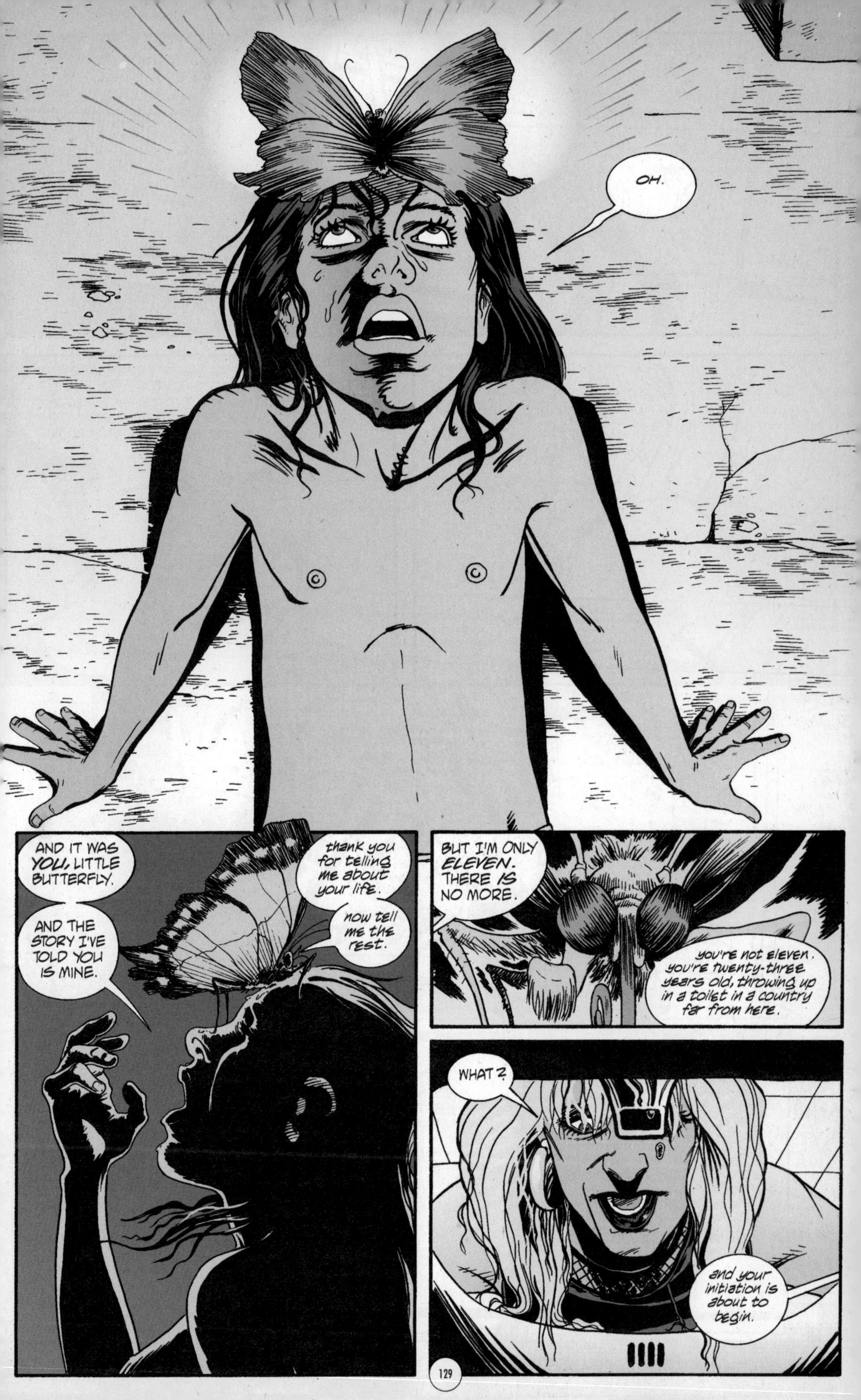
OH.
AND IT WAS YOU, LITTLE BUTTERFLY.
AND THE STORY I'VE TOLD YOU IS MINE.
thank you for telling me about your life.
now tell me the rest.
BUT I'M ONLY ELEVEN. THERE IS NO MORE.
you're not eleven. you're twenty-three years old, throwing up in a toilet in a country far from here.
WHAT?
and your initiation is about to begin.

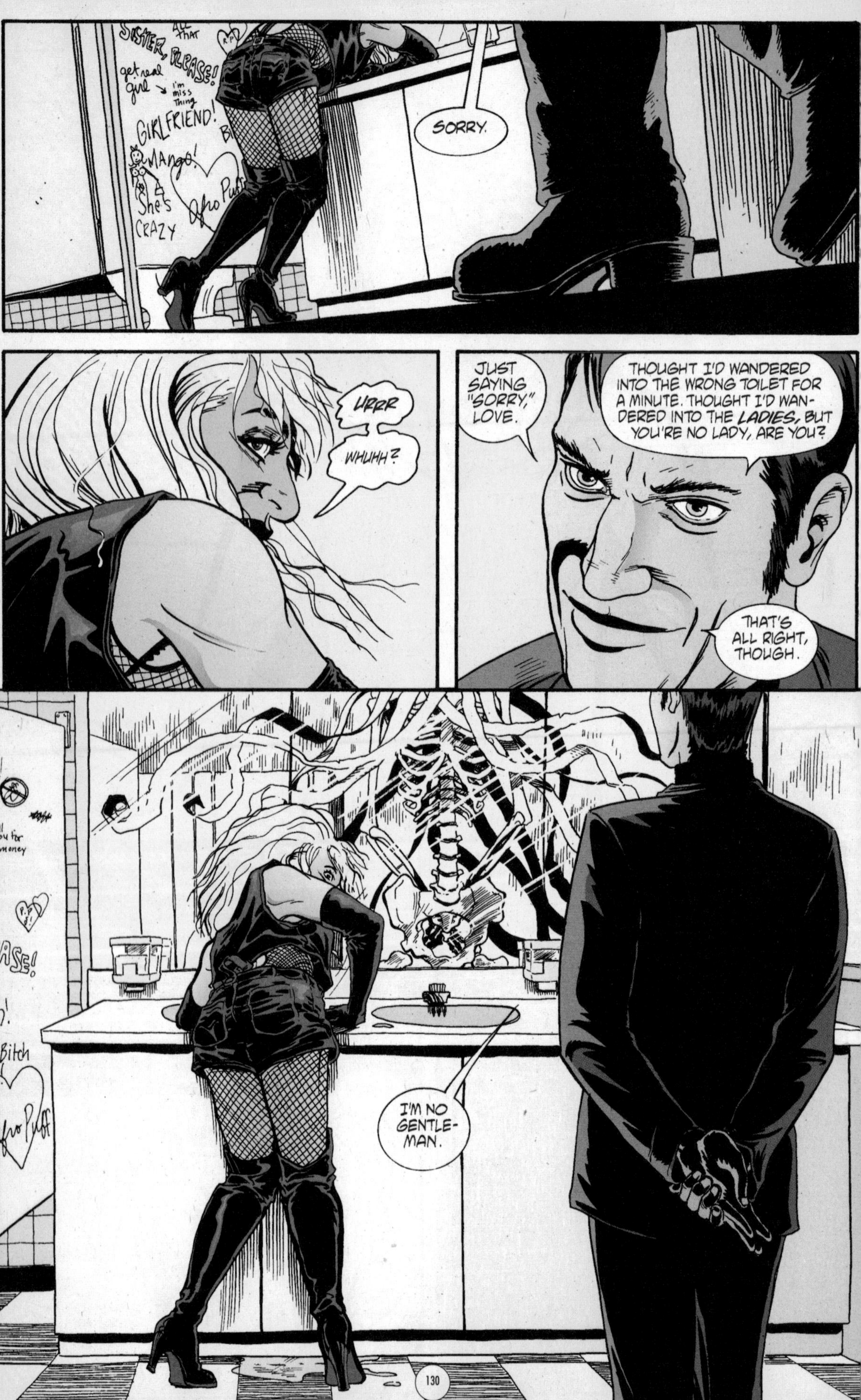
SISTER, PLEASE!
ALL THAT
get real girl
i'm miss thing
GIRLFRIEND!
Mango!
She's CRAZY
SORRY.
URRR
WHUHH?
JUST SAYING "SORRY," LOVE.
THOUGHT I'D WANDERED INTO THE WRONG TOILET FOR A MINUTE. THOUGHT I'D WANDERED INTO THE *LADIES*, BUT YOU'RE NO LADY, ARE YOU?
THAT'S ALL RIGHT, THOUGH.
I'M NO GENTLEMAN.

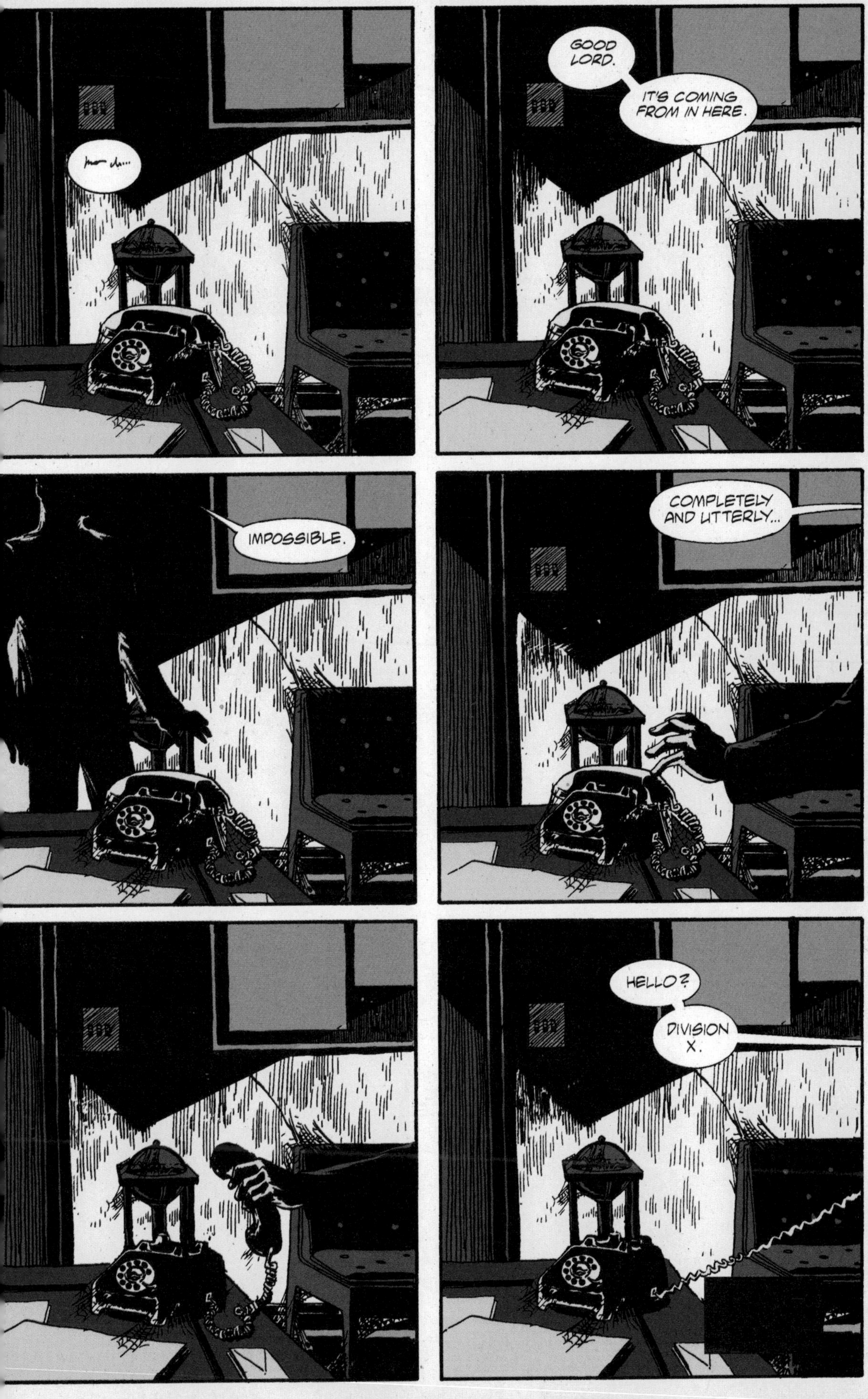
GOOD LORD.
IT'S COMING FROM IN HERE.
IMPOSSIBLE.
COMPLETELY AND UTTERLY...
HELLO?
DIVISION X.

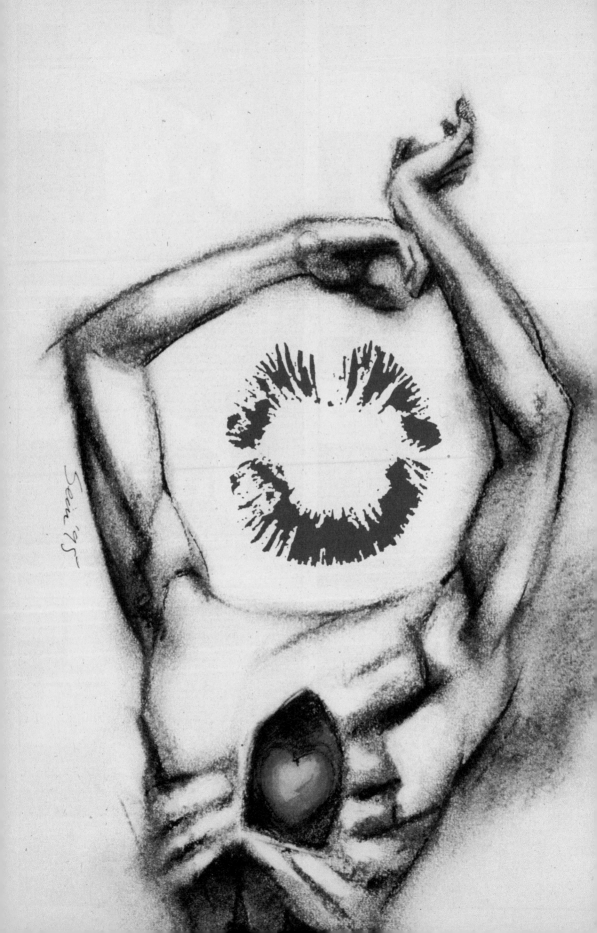

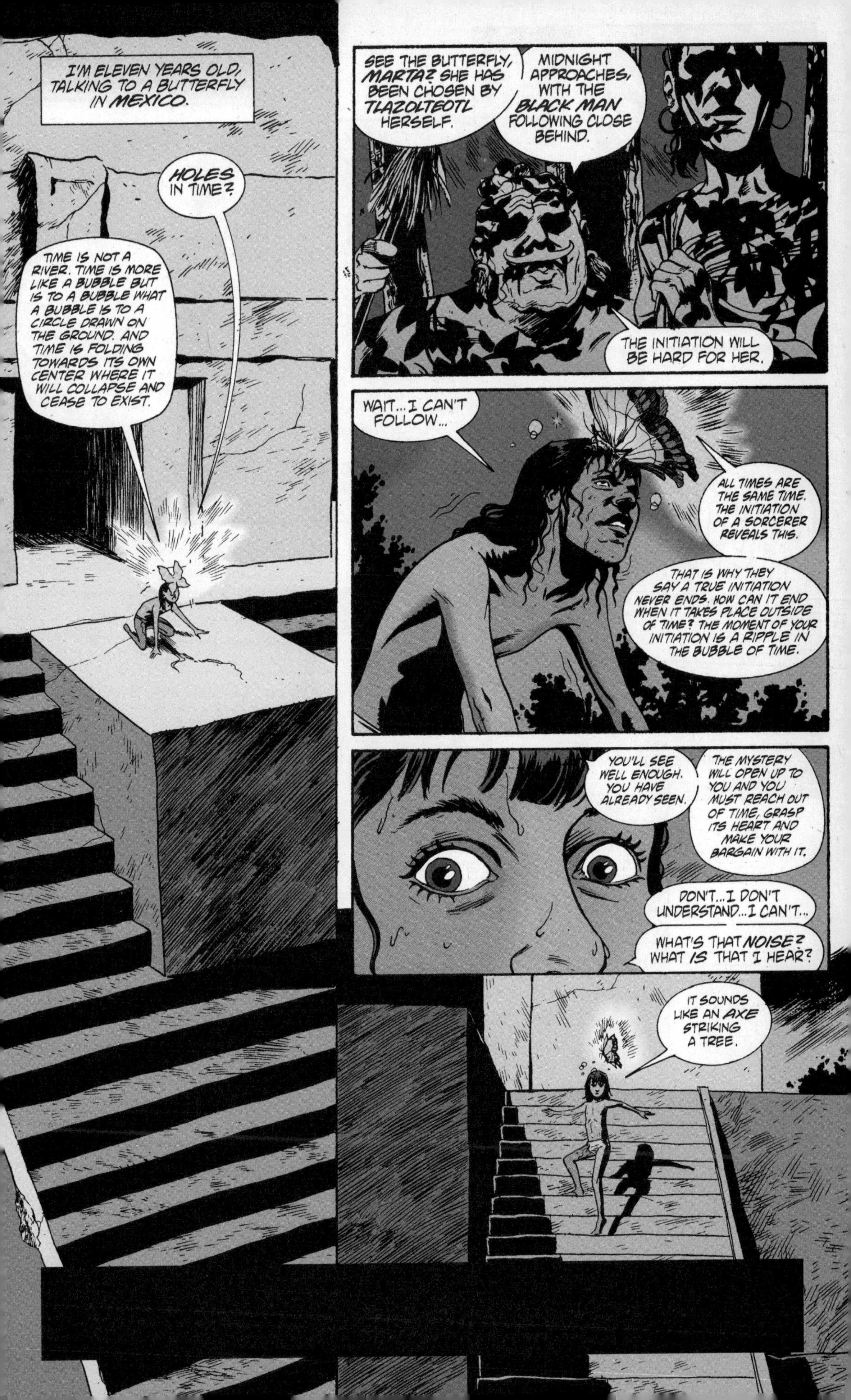
I'M ELEVEN YEARS OLD, TALKING TO A BUTTERFLY IN MEXICO.
HOLES IN TIME?
TIME IS NOT A RIVER. TIME IS MORE LIKE A BUBBLE BUT IS TO A BUBBLE WHAT A BUBBLE IS TO A CIRCLE DRAWN ON THE GROUND. AND TIME IS FOLDING TOWARDS ITS OWN CENTER WHERE IT WILL COLLAPSE AND CEASE TO EXIST.
SEE THE BUTTERFLY, MARTA? SHE HAS BEEN CHOSEN BY TLAZOLTEOTL HERSELF.
MIDNIGHT APPROACHES, WITH THE BLACK MAN FOLLOWING CLOSE BEHIND.
THE INITIATION WILL BE HARD FOR HER.
WAIT... I CAN'T FOLLOW...
ALL TIMES ARE THE SAME TIME. THE INITIATION OF A SORCERER REVEALS THIS.
THAT IS WHY THEY SAY A TRUE INITIATION NEVER ENDS. HOW CAN IT END WHEN IT TAKES PLACE OUTSIDE OF TIME? THE MOMENT OF YOUR INITIATION IS A RIPPLE IN THE BUBBLE OF TIME.
YOU'LL SEE WELL ENOUGH. YOU HAVE ALREADY SEEN.
THE MYSTERY WILL OPEN UP TO YOU AND YOU MUST REACH OUT OF TIME, GRASP ITS HEART AND MAKE YOUR BARGAIN WITH IT.
DON'T... I DON'T UNDERSTAND... I CAN'T...
WHAT'S THAT NOISE? WHAT IS THAT I HEAR?
IT SOUNDS LIKE AN AXE STRIKING A TREE.

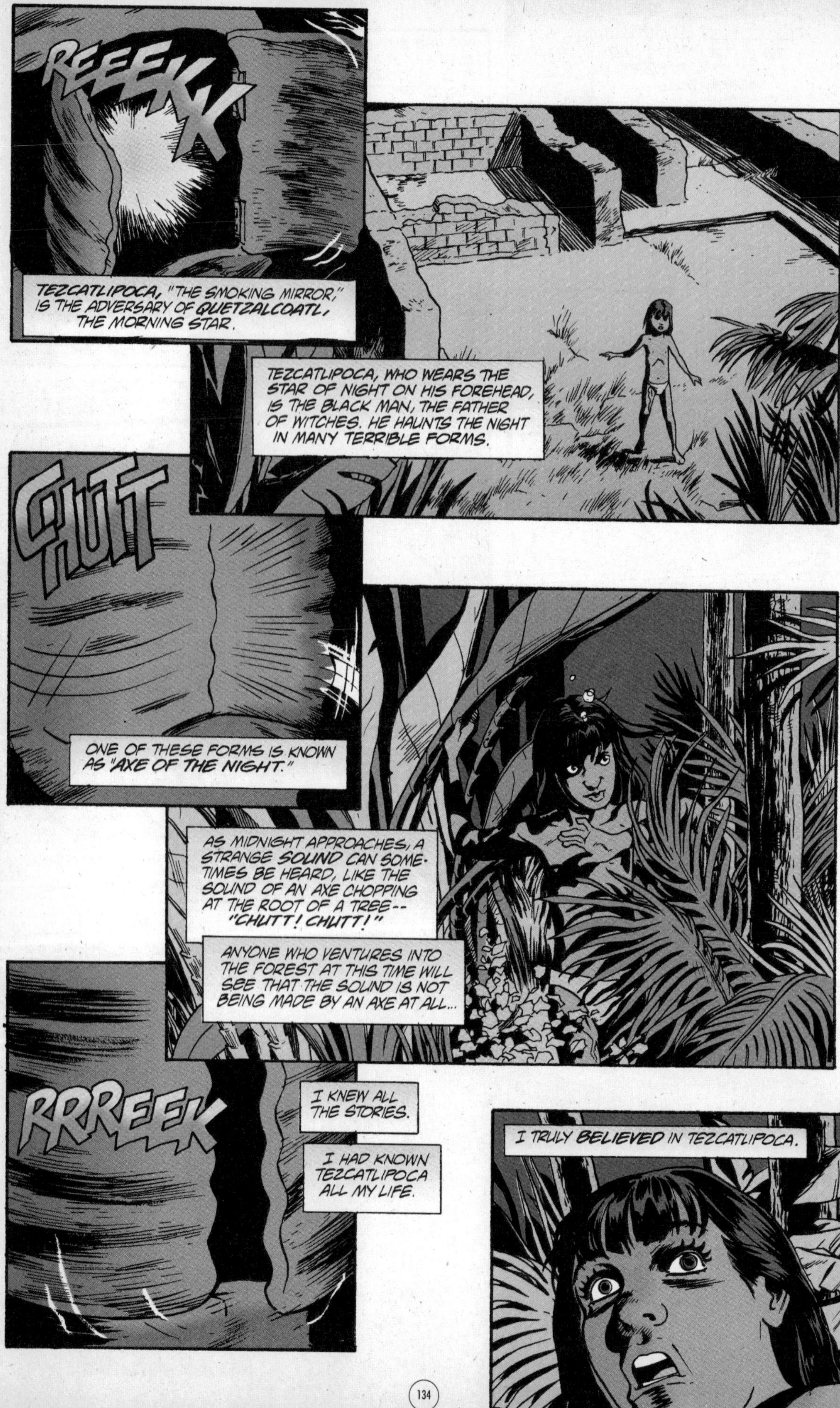
REEEKK
TEZCATLIPOCA, "THE SMOKING MIRROR," IS THE ADVERSARY OF QUETZALCOATL, THE MORNING STAR.
TEZCATLIPOCA, WHO WEARS THE STAR OF NIGHT ON HIS FOREHEAD, IS THE BLACK MAN, THE FATHER OF WITCHES. HE HAUNTS THE NIGHT IN MANY TERRIBLE FORMS.
CHUTT
ONE OF THESE FORMS IS KNOWN AS "AXE OF THE NIGHT."
AS MIDNIGHT APPROACHES, A STRANGE SOUND CAN SOMETIMES BE HEARD, LIKE THE SOUND OF AN AXE CHOPPING AT THE ROOT OF A TREE-- "CHUTT! CHUTT!"
ANYONE WHO VENTURES INTO THE FOREST AT THIS TIME WILL SEE THAT THE SOUND IS NOT BEING MADE BY AN AXE AT ALL...
RRREEK
I KNEW ALL THE STORIES.
I HAD KNOWN TEZCATLIPOCA ALL MY LIFE.
I TRULY BELIEVED IN TEZCATLIPOCA.

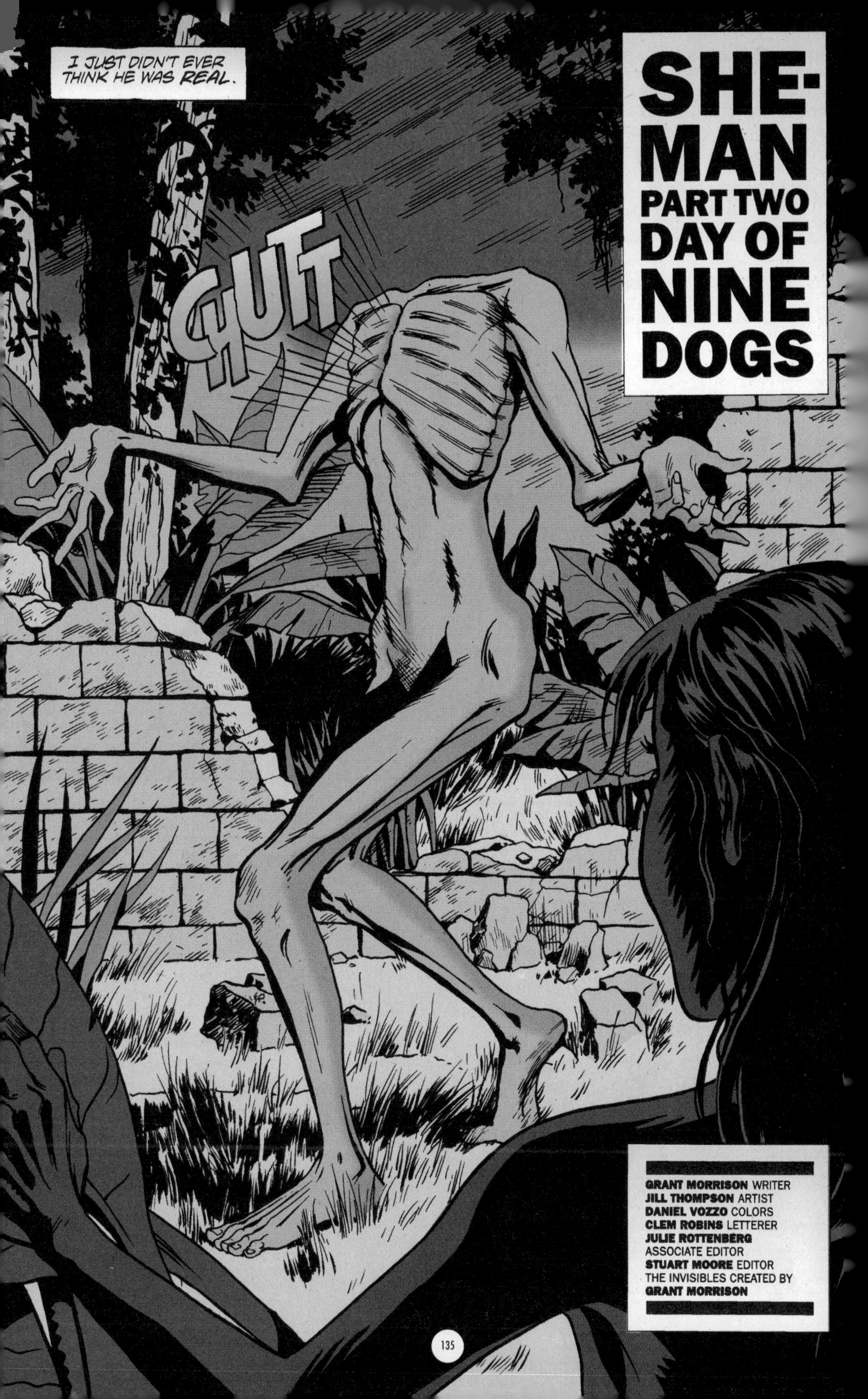
I JUST DIDN'T EVER THINK HE WAS REAL.
CHUT
SHE-MAN
PART TWO
DAY OF NINE DOGS
GRANT MORRISON WRITER
JILL THOMPSON ARTIST
DANIEL VOZZO COLORS
CLEM ROBINS LETTERER
JULIE ROTTENBERG ASSOCIATE EDITOR
STUART MOORE EDITOR
THE INVISIBLES CREATED BY GRANT MORRISON

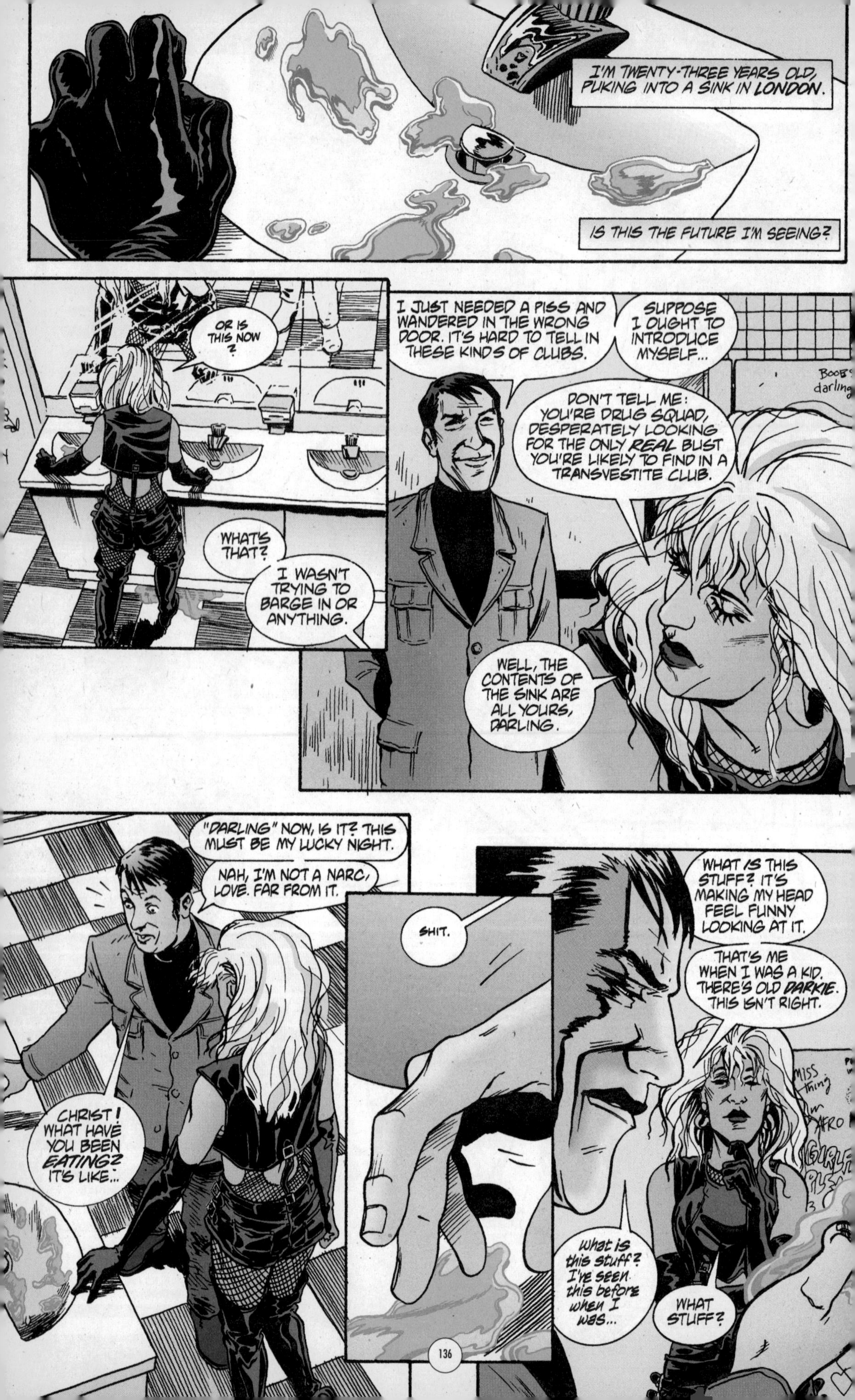

I'M TWENTY-THREE YEARS OLD, PUKING INTO A SINK IN **LONDON**.
IS THIS THE FUTURE I'M SEEING?
OR IS THIS NOW?
WHAT'S THAT?
I WASN'T TRYING TO BARGE IN OR ANYTHING.
I JUST NEEDED A PISS AND WANDERED IN THE WRONG DOOR. IT'S HARD TO TELL IN THESE KINDS OF CLUBS.
SUPPOSE I OUGHT TO INTRODUCE MYSELF...
DON'T TELL ME: YOU'RE DRUG SQUAD, DESPERATELY LOOKING FOR THE ONLY *REAL* BUST YOU'RE LIKELY TO FIND IN A TRANSVESTITE CLUB.
WELL, THE CONTENTS OF THE SINK ARE ALL YOURS, DARLING.
"DARLING" NOW, IS IT? THIS MUST BE MY LUCKY NIGHT.
NAH, I'M NOT A NARC, LOVE. FAR FROM IT.
CHRIST! WHAT HAVE YOU BEEN *EATING*? IT'S LIKE...
SHIT.
WHAT *IS* THIS STUFF? IT'S MAKING MY HEAD FEEL FUNNY LOOKING AT IT.
THAT'S ME WHEN I WAS A KID. THERE'S OLD *DARKIE*. THIS ISN'T RIGHT.
what is this stuff? I've seen this before when I was...
WHAT STUFF?

WHAT STUFF?

WHAT STUFF?

WHAT STUFF?

WHAT STUFF?

WHAT STUFF?

IT'S HER 'EM?

AFRO

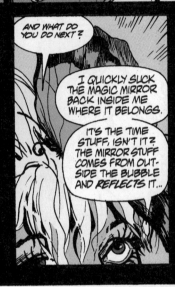

AND WHAT DO YOU DO NEXT?

I QUICKLY SUCK THE MAGIC MIRROR BACK INSIDE ME WHERE IT BELONGS.

IT'S THE TIME STUFF, ISN'T IT? THE MIRROR STUFF COMES FROM OUT-SIDE THE BUBBLE AND REFLECTS IT...

STUFF?

WHAT STUFF?

WHAT WAS I SAYING? AH, I WAS JUST ABOUT TO GIVE YOU THIS. HELP YOU CLEAN UP A BIT.

PUSH

HOW VERY GALLANT.

YEAH, I'M ONE OF THE OLD SCHOOL, ME.

NAME'S BRODIE. YOU CAN CALL ME LEWIS, IF YOU LIKE. LIKE "MARTIN AND..."

AND YOU CAN KEEP THE HANKIE, LOVE. LET'S CALL IT A PRESENT.

SOMETHING FOR THE GIRL WHO'S GOT EVERYTHING, IF YOU KNOW WHAT I MEAN, EH?

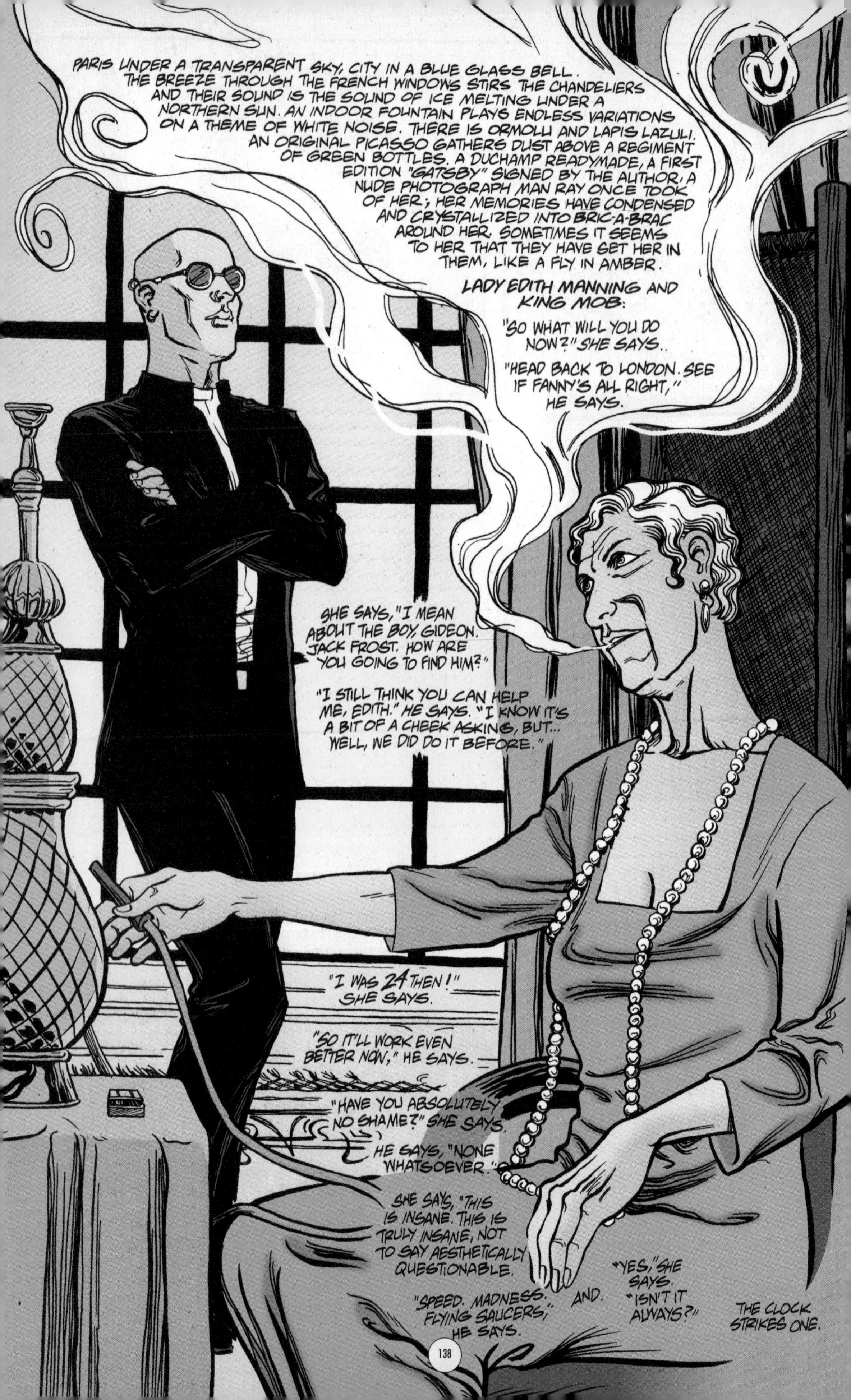
PARIS UNDER A TRANSPARENT SKY, CITY IN A BLUE GLASS BELL. THE BREEZE THROUGH THE FRENCH WINDOWS STIRS THE CHANDELIERS AND THEIR SOUND IS THE SOUND OF ICE MELTING UNDER A NORTHERN SUN. AN INDOOR FOUNTAIN PLAYS ENDLESS VARIATIONS ON A THEME OF WHITE NOISE. THERE IS ORMOLU AND LAPIS LAZULI. AN ORIGINAL PICASSO GATHERS DUST ABOVE A REGIMENT OF GREEN BOTTLES. A DUCHAMP READYMADE, A FIRST EDITION "GATSBY" SIGNED BY THE AUTHOR, A NUDE PHOTOGRAPH MAN RAY ONCE TOOK OF HER; HER MEMORIES HAVE CONDENSED AND CRYSTALLIZED INTO BRIC-A-BRAC AROUND HER. SOMETIMES IT SEEMS TO HER THAT THEY HAVE SET HER IN THEM, LIKE A FLY IN AMBER.
LADY EDITH MANNING AND KING MOB:
"SO WHAT WILL YOU DO NOW?" SHE SAYS.
"HEAD BACK TO LONDON. SEE IF FANNY'S ALL RIGHT," HE SAYS.
SHE SAYS, "I MEAN ABOUT THE BOY, GIDEON. JACK FROST. HOW ARE YOU GOING TO FIND HIM?"
"I STILL THINK YOU CAN HELP ME, EDITH." HE SAYS. "I KNOW IT'S A BIT OF A CHEEK ASKING, BUT... WELL, WE DID DO IT BEFORE."
"I WAS 24 THEN!" SHE SAYS.
"SO IT'LL WORK EVEN BETTER NOW," HE SAYS.
"HAVE YOU ABSOLUTELY NO SHAME?" SHE SAYS.
HE SAYS, "NONE WHATSOEVER."
SHE SAYS, "THIS IS INSANE. THIS IS TRULY INSANE, NOT TO SAY AESTHETICALLY QUESTIONABLE.
"SPEED. MADNESS. FLYING SAUCERS," HE SAYS.
AND.
"YES," SHE SAYS. "ISN'T IT ALWAYS?"
THE CLOCK STRIKES ONE.

THAT'S IT.

IN HERE?

OHH.

IS THAT GOOD? DOES THAT FEEL GOOD?

JUST PUT YOUR HAND IN, LITTLE ONE.

JUST DO AS YOU'RE TOLD, BITCH.

HH!

MMRRMM

≶LUPP≶

GO ON.

PUT YOUR HAND IN.

CHUTT

TEZCATLIPOCA KEEPS HIS HEART BEHIND TWO LITTLE WOODEN DOORS AND WILL GRANT THE WISH OF ANYONE BRAVE AND FAST ENOUGH TO SNATCH IT FROM HIS BREAST.

AND THOSE WHO FAIL THE TEST, HE WILL KILL.

RREEEK

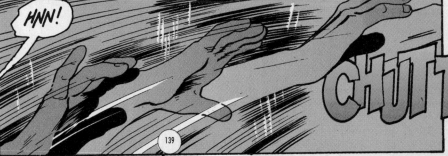

HNN!

CHUTT

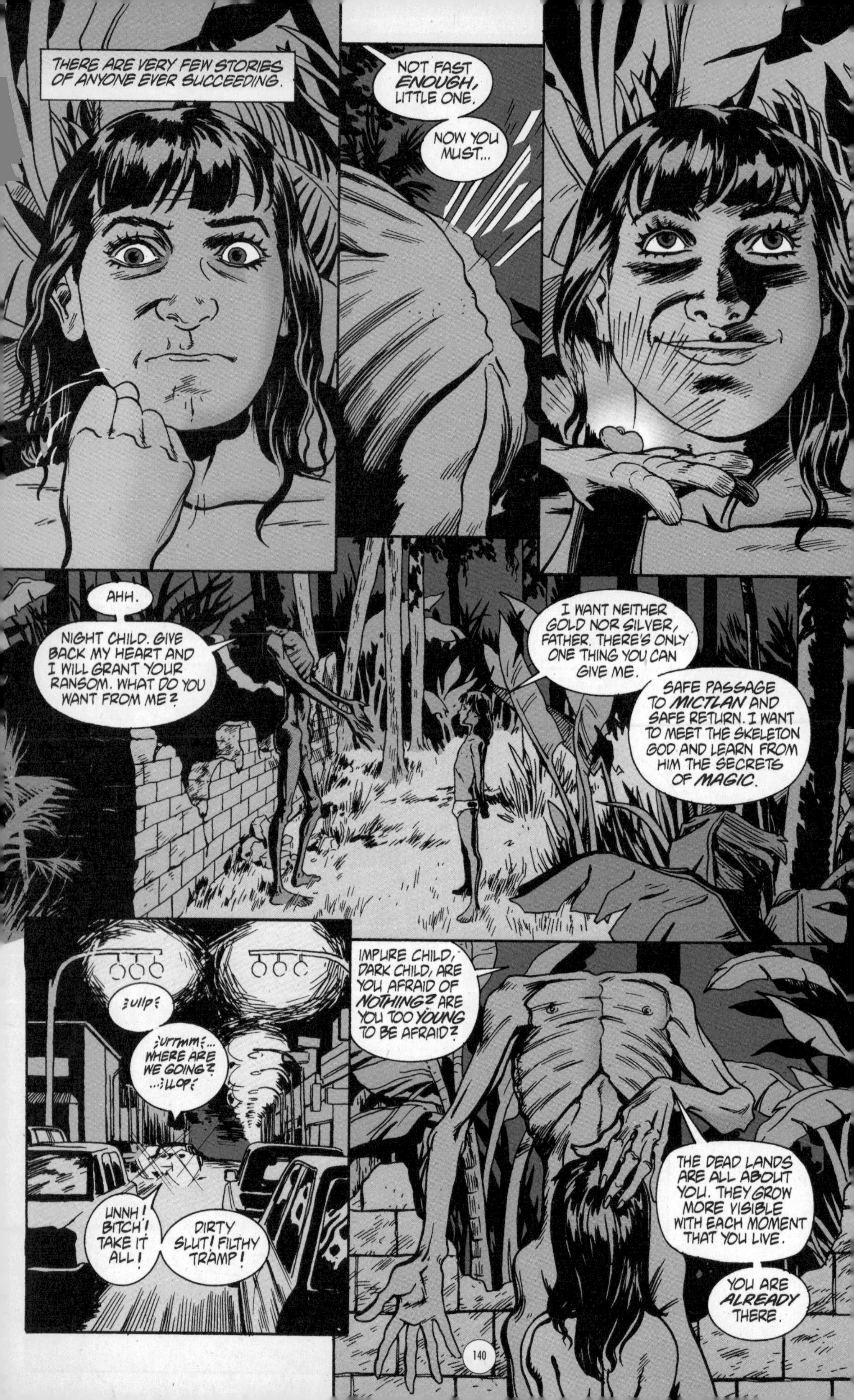
THERE ARE VERY FEW STORIES OF ANYONE EVER SUCCEEDING.
NOT FAST ENOUGH, LITTLE ONE.
NOW YOU MUST...
AHH.
NIGHT CHILD. GIVE BACK MY HEART AND I WILL GRANT YOUR RANSOM. WHAT DO YOU WANT FROM ME?
I WANT NEITHER GOLD NOR SILVER, FATHER. THERE'S ONLY ONE THING YOU CAN GIVE ME.
SAFE PASSAGE TO MICTLAN AND SAFE RETURN. I WANT TO MEET THE SKELETON GOD AND LEARN FROM HIM THE SECRETS OF MAGIC.
ULLP
URRMM... WHERE ARE WE GOING? ...LLOP
UNNH! BITCH! TAKE IT ALL!
DIRTY SLUT! FILTHY TRAMP!
IMPURE CHILD, DARK CHILD, ARE YOU AFRAID OF NOTHING? ARE YOU TOO YOUNG TO BE AFRAID?
THE DEAD LANDS ARE ALL ABOUT YOU. THEY GROW MORE VISIBLE WITH EACH MOMENT THAT YOU LIVE.
YOU ARE ALREADY THERE.

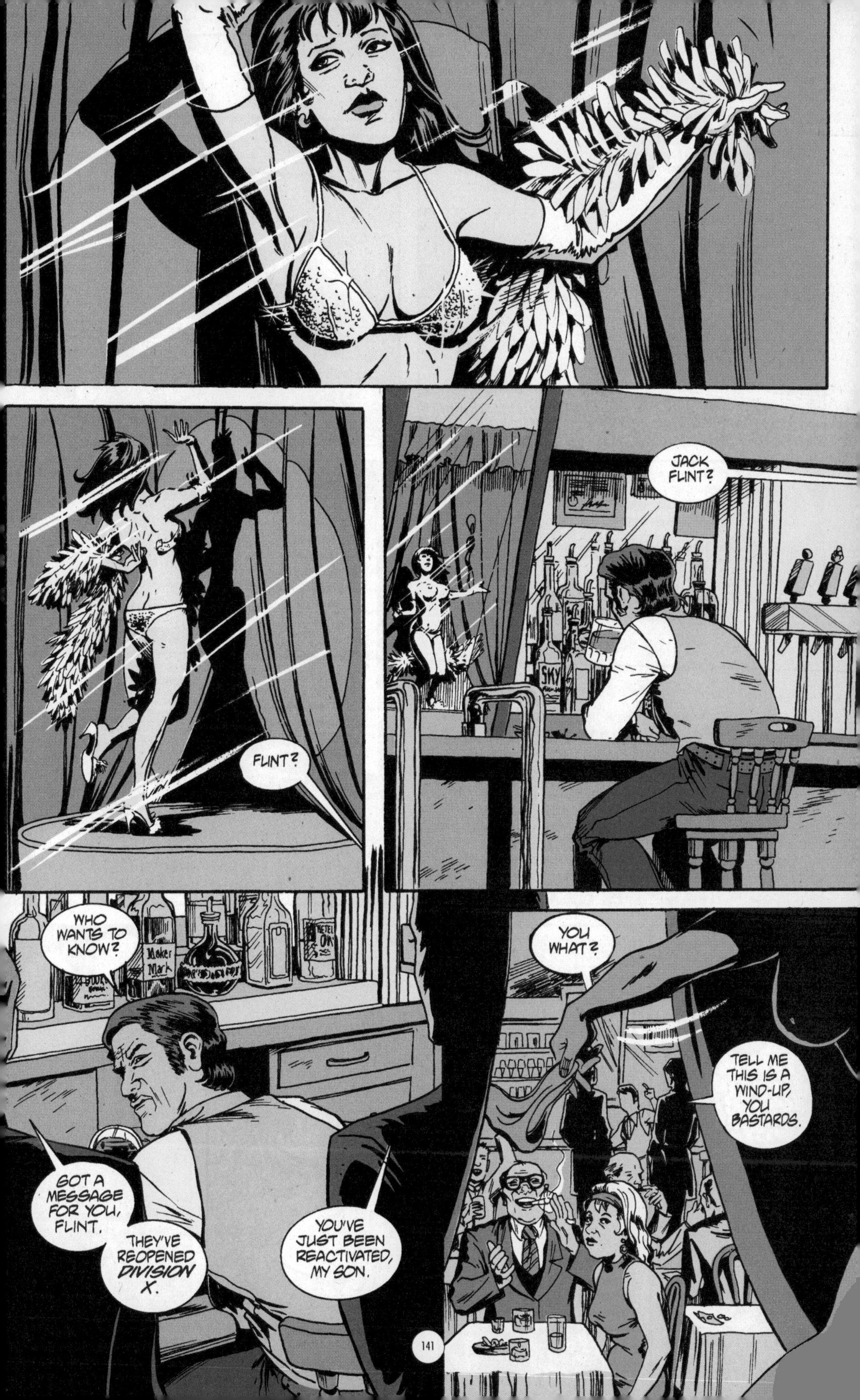

FLINT?
JACK FLINT?
WHO WANTS TO KNOW?
GOT A MESSAGE FOR YOU, FLINT.
THEY'VE REOPENED DIVISION X.
YOU'VE JUST BEEN REACTIVATED, MY SON.
YOU WHAT?
TELL ME THIS IS A WIND-UP, YOU BASTARDS.

OH WOW!

YOU'RE GOING TO *LONDON?* I KNEW THIS WAS MY LUCKY DAY, MAN!

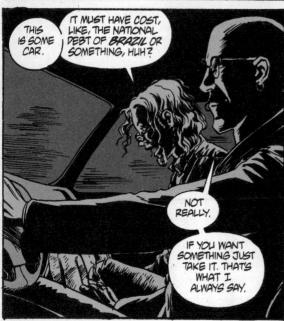

THIS IS SOME CAR.

IT MUST HAVE COST, LIKE, THE NATIONAL DEBT OF *BRAZIL* OR SOMETHING, HUH?

NOT REALLY.

IF YOU WANT SOMETHING JUST TAKE IT. THAT'S WHAT I ALWAYS SAY.

LONDON IT IS.

BOY & Ragged Robin

WHEN WE WERE IN *SAN FRANCISCO,* I PROMISED *KING MOB* I'D TRY SOME OF THESE SMART DRINKS.

I GUESS THEY WORK; I WAS PRETTY WIPED OUT AND NOW I FEEL KIND OF *UP,* YOU KNOW? REALLY POSITIVE. WHAT DID YOU SAY THESE WERE CALLED?

LOVE BOMBS.

THIS STUFF REALLY SEEMS TO ENHANCE MY PSYCHIC ABILITIES. I FEEL REALLY *CLEAR.*

I'M PICKING UP ALL KINDS OF STUFF FROM EVERYONE IN HERE.

YOU ARE TIRED, AREN'T YOU?

uh-huh.

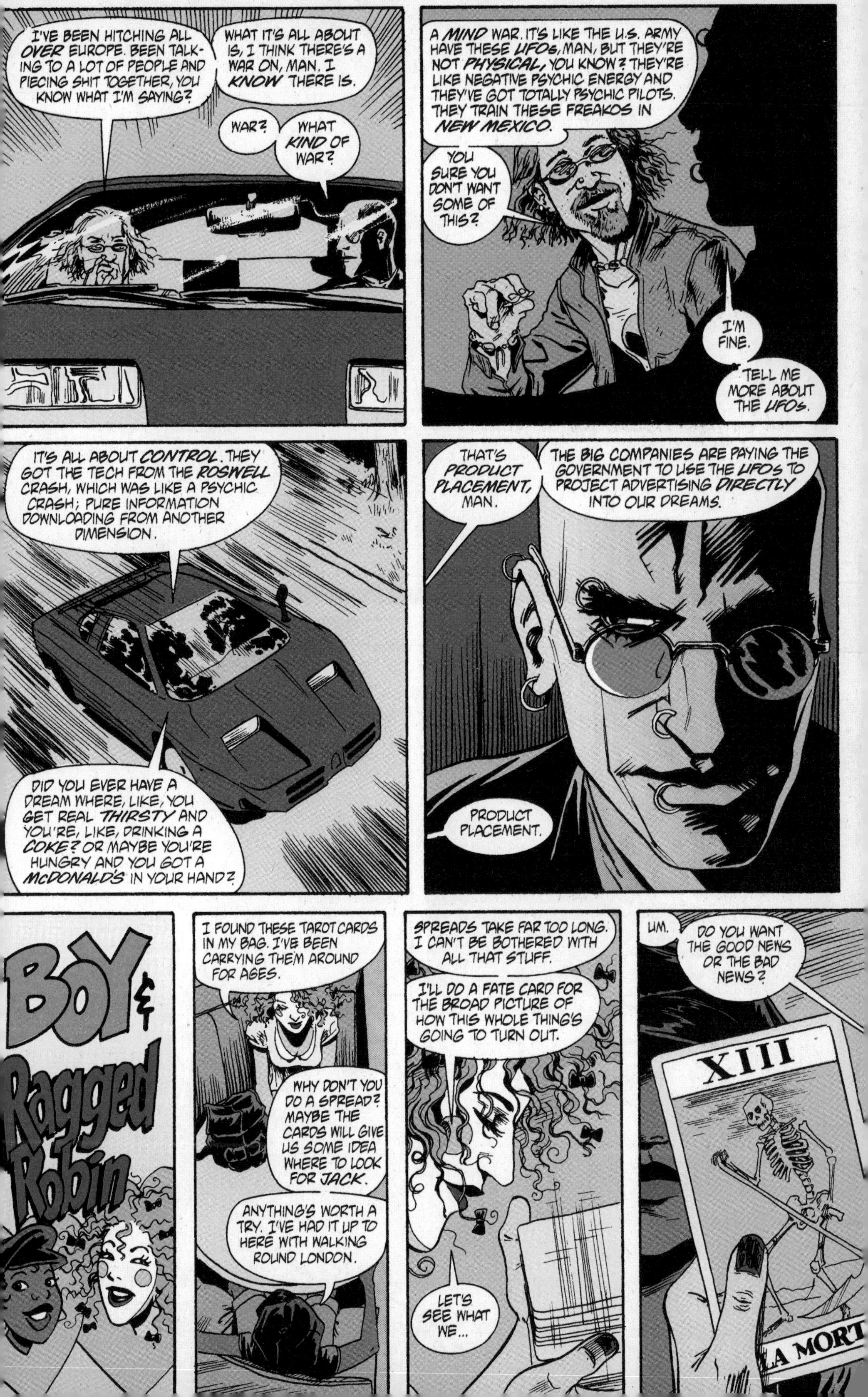
I'VE BEEN HITCHING ALL OVER EUROPE. BEEN TALKING TO A LOT OF PEOPLE AND PIECING SHIT TOGETHER, YOU KNOW WHAT I'M SAYING?
WHAT IT'S ALL ABOUT IS, I THINK THERE'S A WAR ON, MAN. I KNOW THERE IS.
WAR?
WHAT KIND OF WAR?
A MIND WAR. IT'S LIKE THE U.S. ARMY HAVE THESE UFOs, MAN, BUT THEY'RE NOT PHYSICAL, YOU KNOW? THEY'RE LIKE NEGATIVE PSYCHIC ENERGY AND THEY'VE GOT TOTALLY PSYCHIC PILOTS. THEY TRAIN THESE FREAKOS IN NEW MEXICO.
YOU SURE YOU DON'T WANT SOME OF THIS?
I'M FINE.
TELL ME MORE ABOUT THE UFOs.
IT'S ALL ABOUT CONTROL. THEY GOT THE TECH FROM THE ROSWELL CRASH, WHICH WAS LIKE A PSYCHIC CRASH; PURE INFORMATION DOWNLOADING FROM ANOTHER DIMENSION.
DID YOU EVER HAVE A DREAM WHERE, LIKE, YOU GET REAL THIRSTY AND YOU'RE, LIKE, DRINKING A COKE? OR MAYBE YOU'RE HUNGRY AND YOU GOT A McDONALD'S IN YOUR HAND?
THAT'S PRODUCT PLACEMENT, MAN.
THE BIG COMPANIES ARE PAYING THE GOVERNMENT TO USE THE UFOs TO PROJECT ADVERTISING DIRECTLY INTO OUR DREAMS.
PRODUCT PLACEMENT.
Boy & Ragged Robin
I FOUND THESE TAROT CARDS IN MY BAG. I'VE BEEN CARRYING THEM AROUND FOR AGES.
WHY DON'T YOU DO A SPREAD? MAYBE THE CARDS WILL GIVE US SOME IDEA WHERE TO LOOK FOR JACK.
ANYTHING'S WORTH A TRY. I'VE HAD IT UP TO HERE WITH WALKING ROUND LONDON.
SPREADS TAKE FAR TOO LONG. I CAN'T BE BOTHERED WITH ALL THAT STUFF.
I'LL DO A FATE CARD FOR THE BROAD PICTURE OF HOW THIS WHOLE THING'S GOING TO TURN OUT.
LET'S SEE WHAT WE...
UM.
DO YOU WANT THE GOOD NEWS OR THE BAD NEWS?
XIII
LA MORT

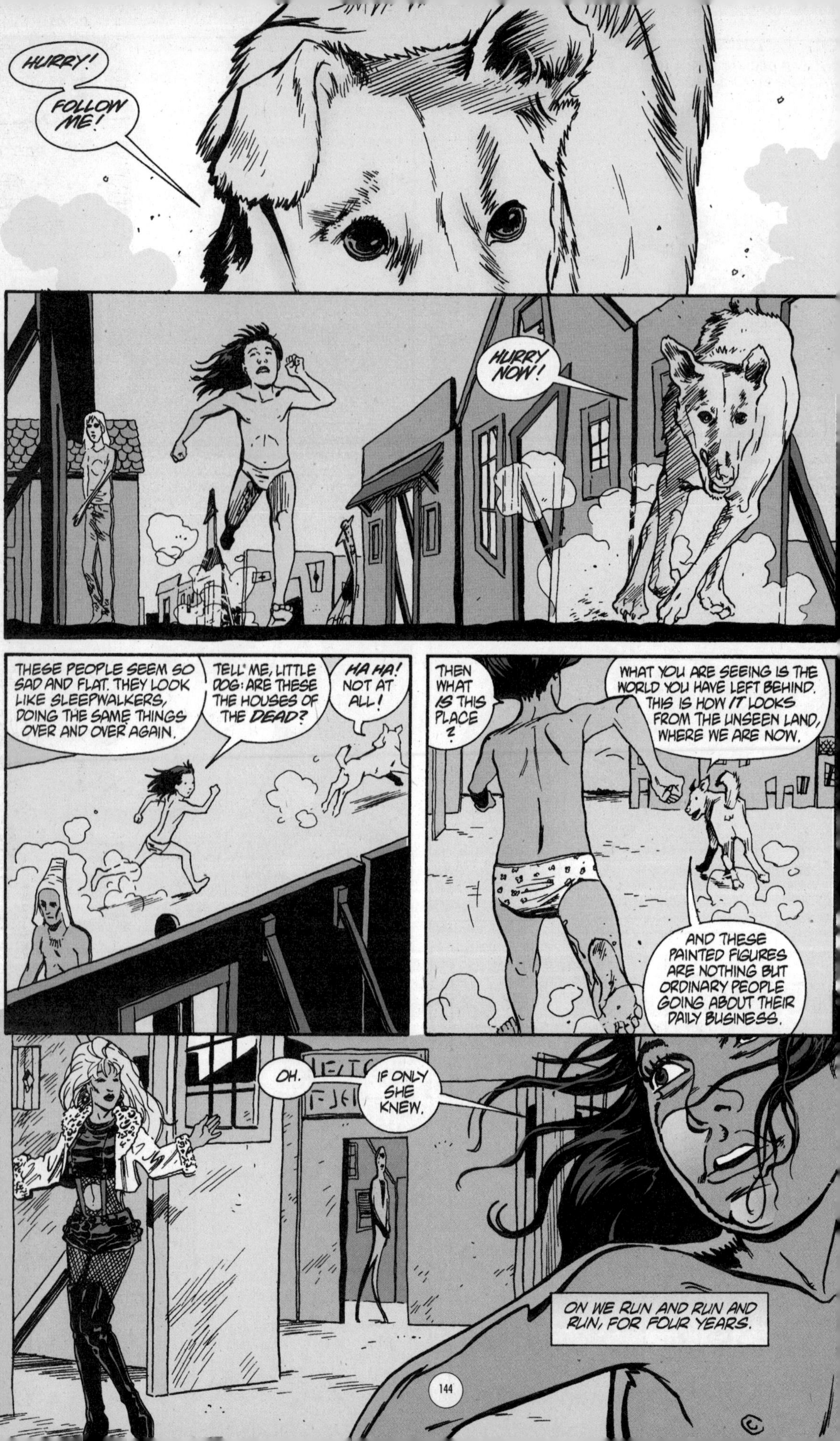
HURRY!
FOLLOW ME!
HURRY NOW!
THESE PEOPLE SEEM SO SAD AND FLAT. THEY LOOK LIKE SLEEPWALKERS, DOING THE SAME THINGS OVER AND OVER AGAIN.
TELL ME, LITTLE DOG: ARE THESE THE HOUSES OF THE DEAD?
HA HA! NOT AT ALL!
THEN WHAT IS THIS PLACE?
WHAT YOU ARE SEEING IS THE WORLD YOU HAVE LEFT BEHIND. THIS IS HOW IT LOOKS FROM THE UNSEEN LAND, WHERE WE ARE NOW.
AND THESE PAINTED FIGURES ARE NOTHING BUT ORDINARY PEOPLE GOING ABOUT THEIR DAILY BUSINESS.
OH.
IF ONLY SHE KNEW.
ON WE RUN AND RUN AND RUN, FOR FOUR YEARS.

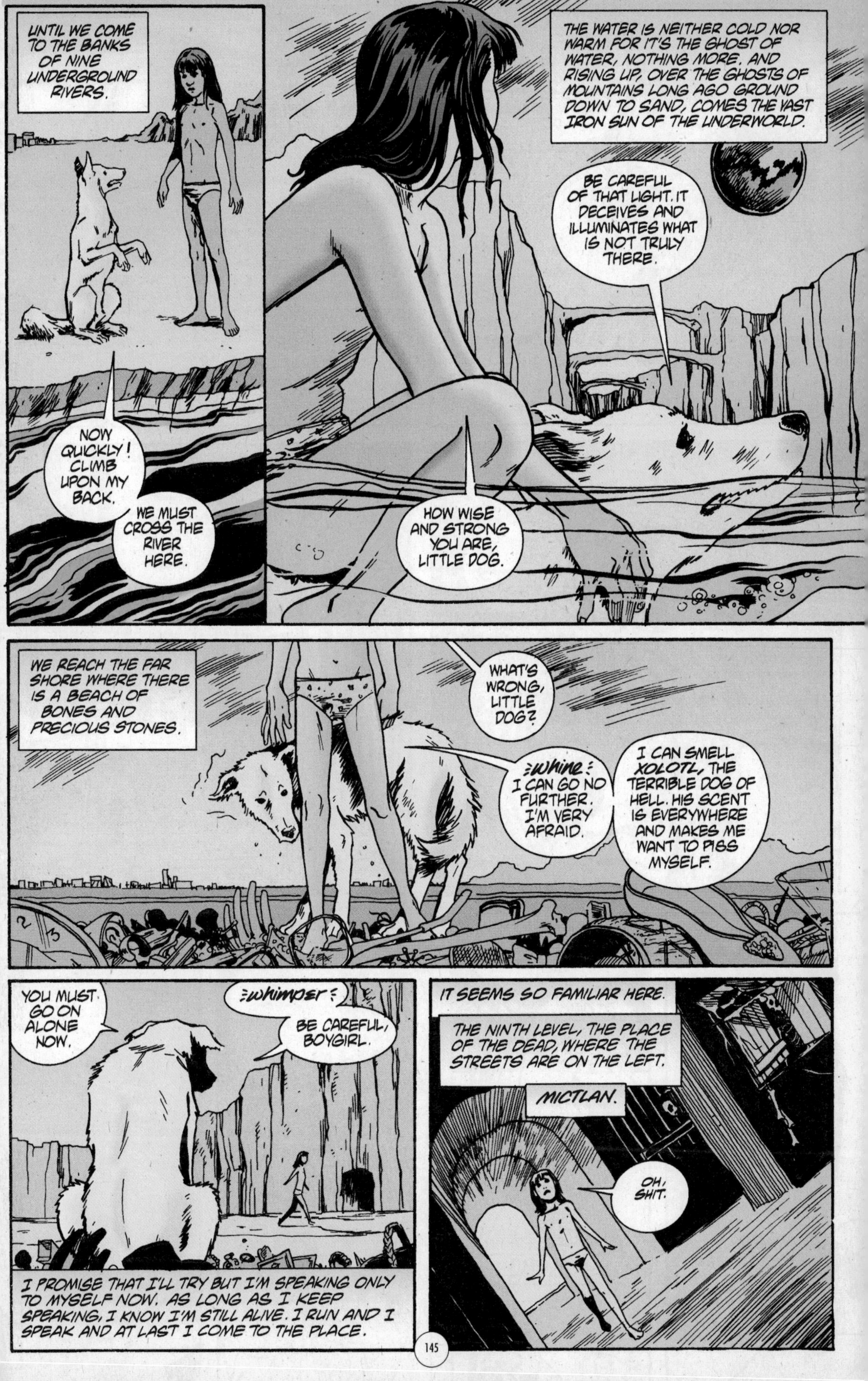
UNTIL WE COME TO THE BANKS OF NINE UNDERGROUND RIVERS.
NOW QUICKLY! CLIMB UPON MY BACK.
WE MUST CROSS THE RIVER HERE.
THE WATER IS NEITHER COLD NOR WARM FOR IT'S THE GHOST OF WATER, NOTHING MORE. AND RISING UP, OVER THE GHOSTS OF MOUNTAINS LONG AGO GROUND DOWN TO SAND, COMES THE VAST IRON SUN OF THE UNDERWORLD.
BE CAREFUL OF THAT LIGHT. IT DECEIVES AND ILLUMINATES WHAT IS NOT TRULY THERE.
HOW WISE AND STRONG YOU ARE, LITTLE DOG.
WE REACH THE FAR SHORE WHERE THERE IS A BEACH OF BONES AND PRECIOUS STONES.
WHAT'S WRONG, LITTLE DOG?
:WHINE: I CAN GO NO FURTHER. I'M VERY AFRAID.
I CAN SMELL XOLOTL, THE TERRIBLE DOG OF HELL. HIS SCENT IS EVERYWHERE AND MAKES ME WANT TO PISS MYSELF.
YOU MUST GO ON ALONE NOW.
:WHIMPER:
BE CAREFUL, BOYGIRL.
I PROMISE THAT I'LL TRY BUT I'M SPEAKING ONLY TO MYSELF NOW. AS LONG AS I KEEP SPEAKING, I KNOW I'M STILL ALIVE. I RUN AND I SPEAK AND AT LAST I COME TO THE PLACE.
IT SEEMS SO FAMILIAR HERE.
THE NINTH LEVEL, THE PLACE OF THE DEAD, WHERE THE STREETS ARE ON THE LEFT.
MICTLAN.
OH, SHIT.

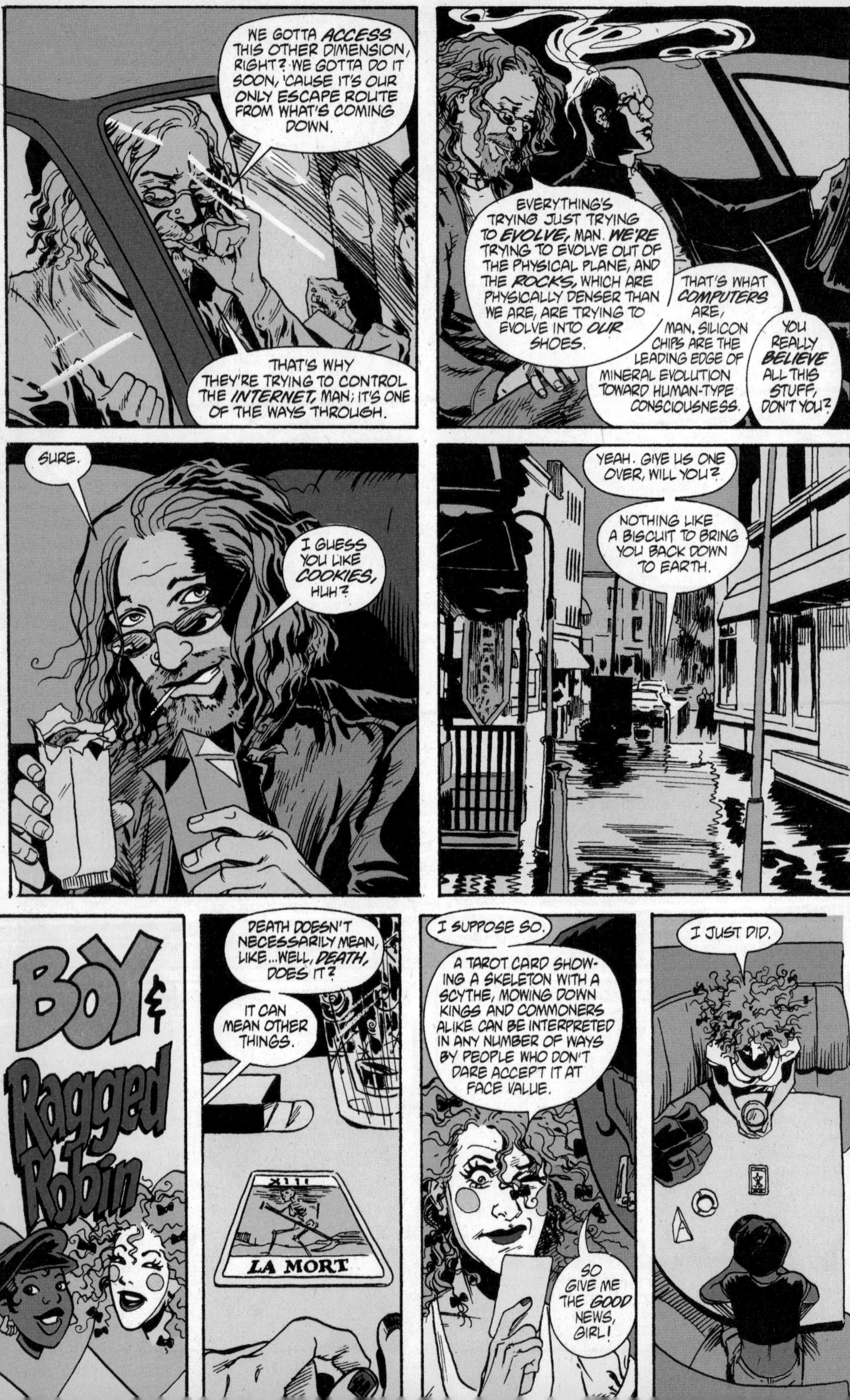
WE GOTTA ACCESS THIS OTHER DIMENSION, RIGHT? WE GOTTA DO IT SOON, 'CAUSE IT'S OUR ONLY ESCAPE ROUTE FROM WHAT'S COMING DOWN.
THAT'S WHY THEY'RE TRYING TO CONTROL THE INTERNET, MAN; IT'S ONE OF THE WAYS THROUGH.
EVERYTHING'S TRYING JUST TRYING TO EVOLVE, MAN. WE'RE TRYING TO EVOLVE OUT OF THE PHYSICAL PLANE, AND THE ROCKS, WHICH ARE PHYSICALLY DENSER THAN WE ARE, ARE TRYING TO EVOLVE INTO OUR SHOES.
THAT'S WHAT COMPUTERS ARE, MAN. SILICON CHIPS ARE THE LEADING EDGE OF MINERAL EVOLUTION TOWARD HUMAN-TYPE CONSCIOUSNESS.
YOU REALLY BELIEVE ALL THIS STUFF, DON'T YOU?
SURE.
I GUESS YOU LIKE COOKIES, HUH?
YEAH. GIVE US ONE OVER, WILL YOU?
NOTHING LIKE A BISCUIT TO BRING YOU BACK DOWN TO EARTH.
BOY & Ragged Robin
DEATH DOESN'T NECESSARILY MEAN, LIKE...WELL, DEATH, DOES IT?
IT CAN MEAN OTHER THINGS.
XIII
LA MORT
I SUPPOSE SO.
A TAROT CARD SHOWING A SKELETON WITH A SCYTHE, MOWING DOWN KINGS AND COMMONERS ALIKE CAN BE INTERPRETED IN ANY NUMBER OF WAYS BY PEOPLE WHO DON'T DARE ACCEPT IT AT FACE VALUE.
SO GIVE ME THE GOOD NEWS, GIRL!
I JUST DID.

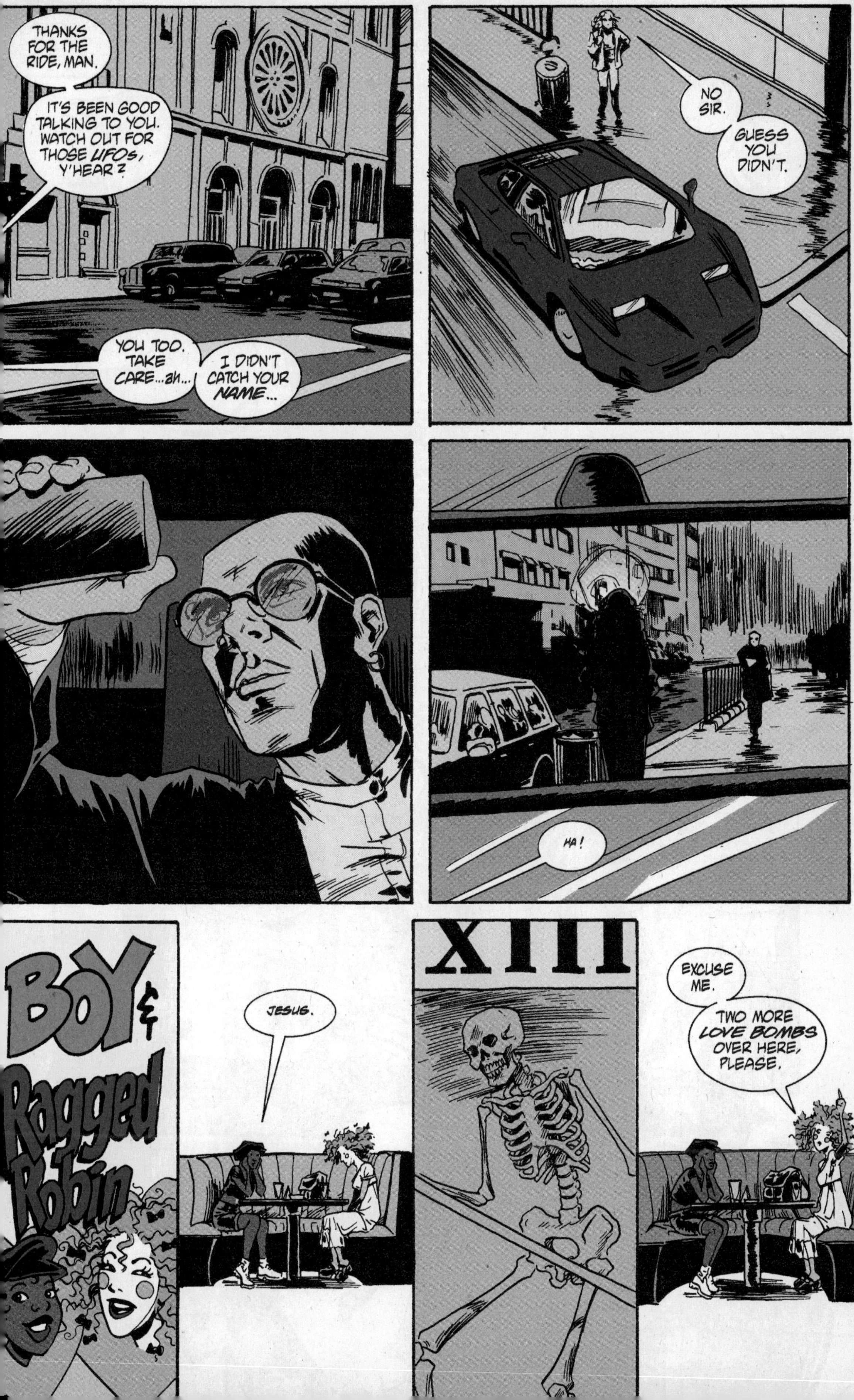
THANKS FOR THE RIDE, MAN.
IT'S BEEN GOOD TALKING TO YOU. WATCH OUT FOR THOSE *UFOs*, Y'HEAR?
YOU TOO. TAKE CARE...ah...
I DIDN'T CATCH YOUR *NAME*...
NO SIR.
GUESS YOU DIDN'T.
HA!
BOY & Ragged Robin
JESUS.
XIII
EXCUSE ME.
TWO MORE *LOVE BOMBS* OVER HERE, PLEASE.

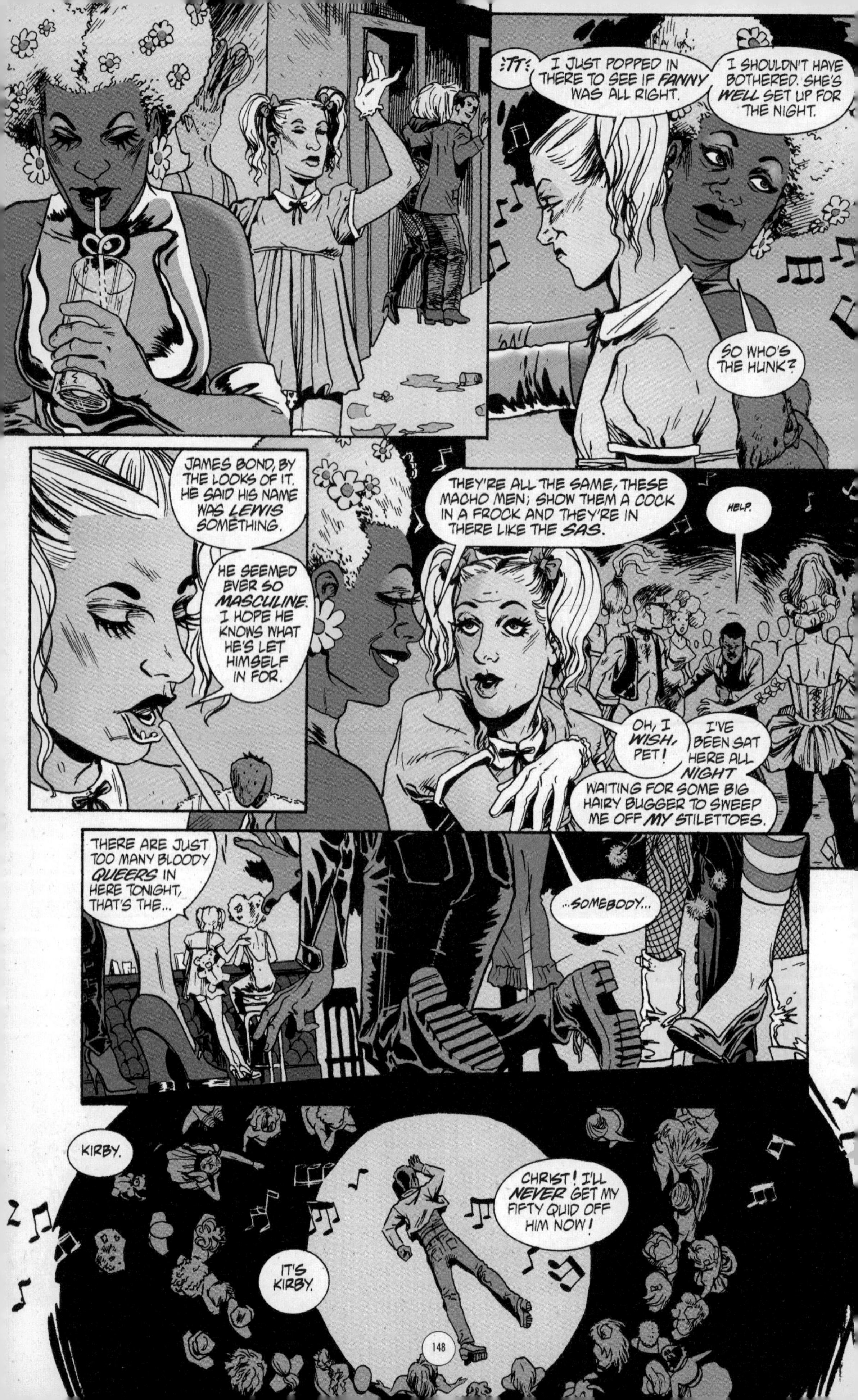
TT
I JUST POPPED IN THERE TO SEE IF FANNY WAS ALL RIGHT.
I SHOULDN'T HAVE BOTHERED. SHE'S WELL SET UP FOR THE NIGHT.
SO WHO'S THE HUNK?
JAMES BOND, BY THE LOOKS OF IT. HE SAID HIS NAME WAS LEWIS SOMETHING.
HE SEEMED EVER SO MASCULINE. I HOPE HE KNOWS WHAT HE'S LET HIMSELF IN FOR.
THEY'RE ALL THE SAME, THESE MACHO MEN; SHOW THEM A COCK IN A FROCK AND THEY'RE IN THERE LIKE THE SAS.
HELP.
OH, I WISH, PET!
I'VE BEEN SAT HERE ALL NIGHT WAITING FOR SOME BIG HAIRY BUGGER TO SWEEP ME OFF MY STILETTOES.
THERE ARE JUST TOO MANY BLOODY QUEERS IN HERE TONIGHT, THAT'S THE...
...SOMEBODY...
KIRBY.
CHRIST! I'LL NEVER GET MY FIFTY QUID OFF HIM NOW!
IT'S KIRBY.

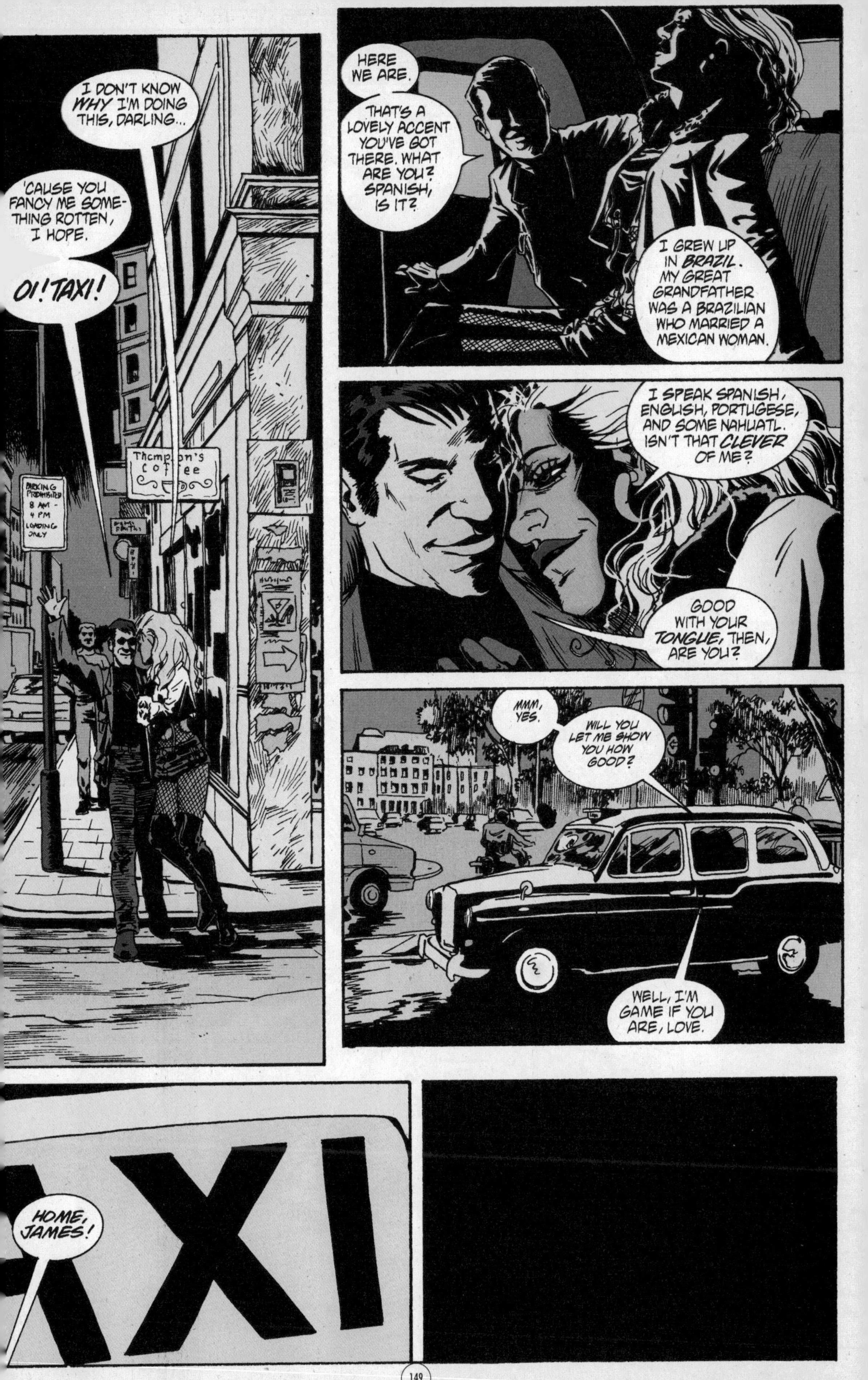
I DON'T KNOW *WHY* I'M DOING THIS, DARLING...
'CAUSE YOU FANCY ME SOMETHING ROTTEN, I HOPE.
OI! TAXI!
PARKING PROHIBITED 8 AM - 4 PM LOADING ONLY
HERE WE ARE.
THAT'S A LOVELY ACCENT YOU'VE GOT THERE. WHAT ARE YOU? SPANISH, IS IT?
I GREW UP IN *BRAZIL*. MY GREAT GRANDFATHER WAS A BRAZILIAN WHO MARRIED A MEXICAN WOMAN.
I SPEAK SPANISH, ENGLISH, PORTUGESE, AND SOME NAHUATL. ISN'T THAT *CLEVER* OF ME?
GOOD WITH YOUR *TONGUE*, THEN, ARE YOU?
MMM, YES.
WILL YOU LET ME SHOW YOU HOW GOOD?
WELL, I'M GAME IF YOU ARE, LOVE.
AXI
HOME, JAMES!

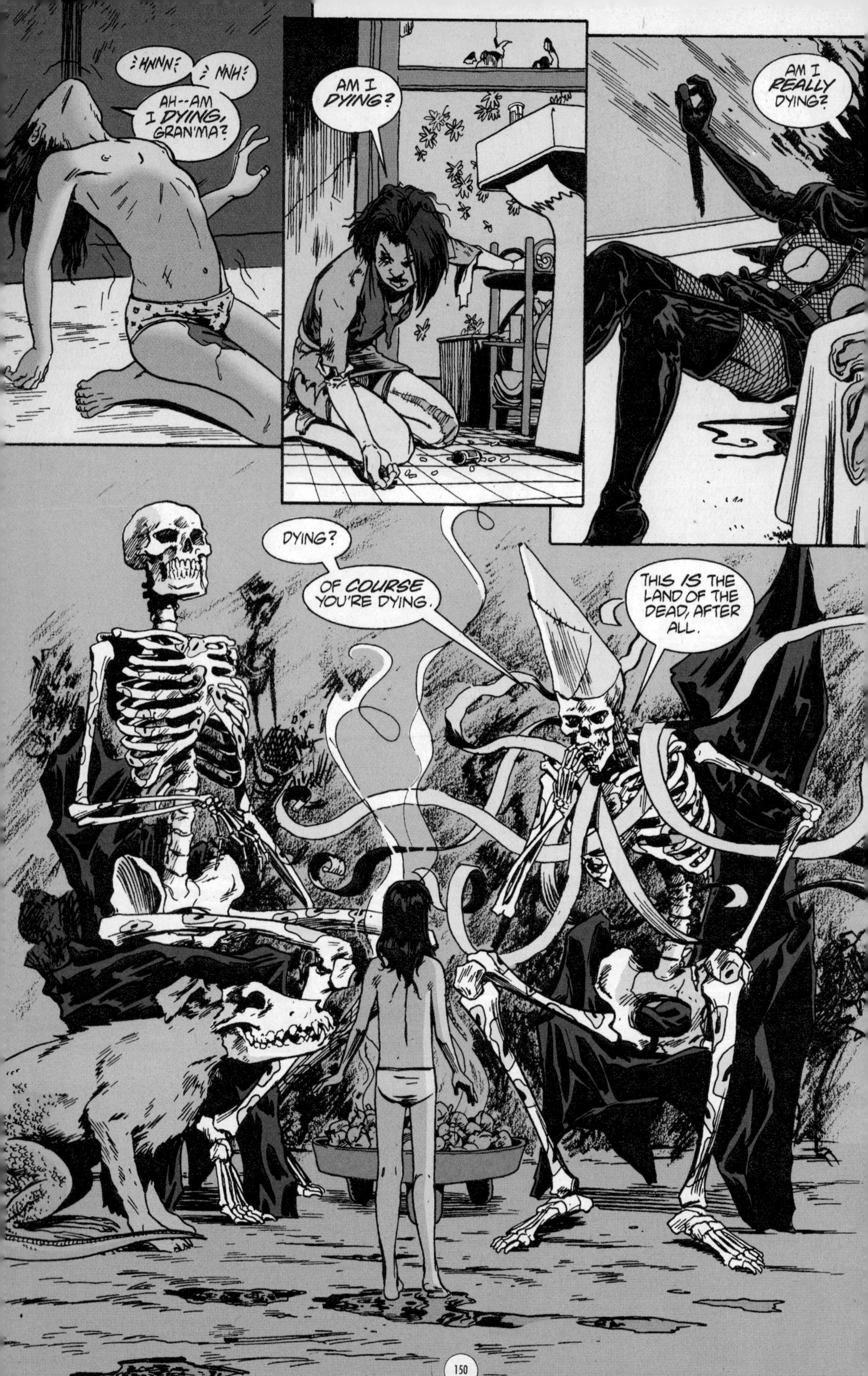
HNNN
NNH
AH--AM I DYING, GRAN'MA?
AM I DYING?
AM I REALLY DYING?
DYING?
OF COURSE YOU'RE DYING.
THIS IS THE LAND OF THE DEAD, AFTER ALL.

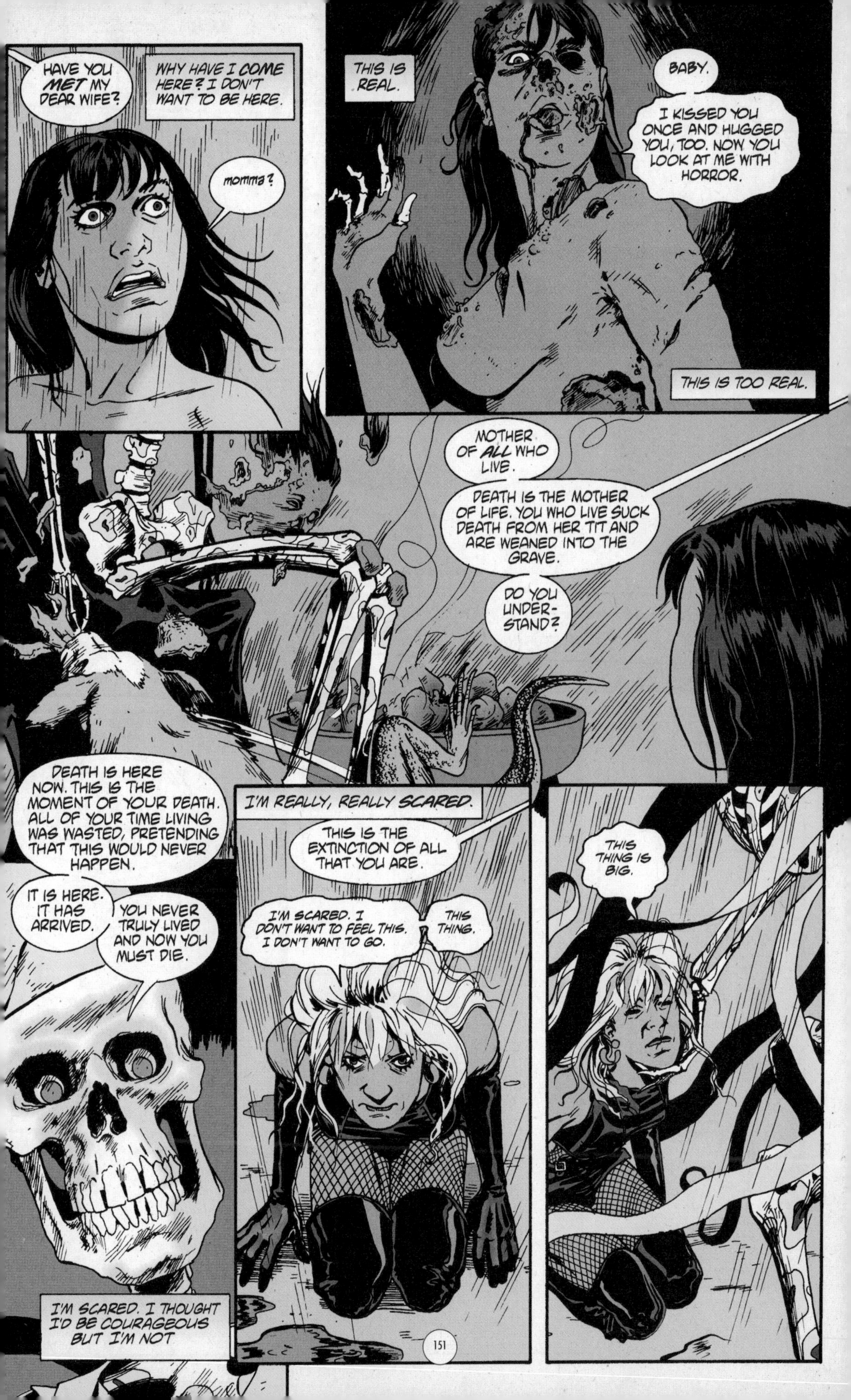
HAVE YOU MET MY DEAR WIFE?
WHY HAVE I COME HERE? I DON'T WANT TO BE HERE.
momma?
THIS IS REAL.
BABY.
I KISSED YOU ONCE AND HUGGED YOU, TOO. NOW YOU LOOK AT ME WITH HORROR.
THIS IS TOO REAL.
MOTHER OF ALL WHO LIVE.
DEATH IS THE MOTHER OF LIFE. YOU WHO LIVE SUCK DEATH FROM HER TIT AND ARE WEANED INTO THE GRAVE.
DO YOU UNDER-STAND?
DEATH IS HERE NOW. THIS IS THE MOMENT OF YOUR DEATH. ALL OF YOUR TIME LIVING WAS WASTED, PRETENDING THAT THIS WOULD NEVER HAPPEN.
IT IS HERE. IT HAS ARRIVED.
YOU NEVER TRULY LIVED AND NOW YOU MUST DIE.
I'M SCARED. I THOUGHT I'D BE COURAGEOUS BUT I'M NOT
I'M REALLY, REALLY SCARED.
THIS IS THE EXTINCTION OF ALL THAT YOU ARE.
I'M SCARED. I DON'T WANT TO FEEL THIS. I DON'T WANT TO GO.
THIS THING.
THIS THING IS BIG.

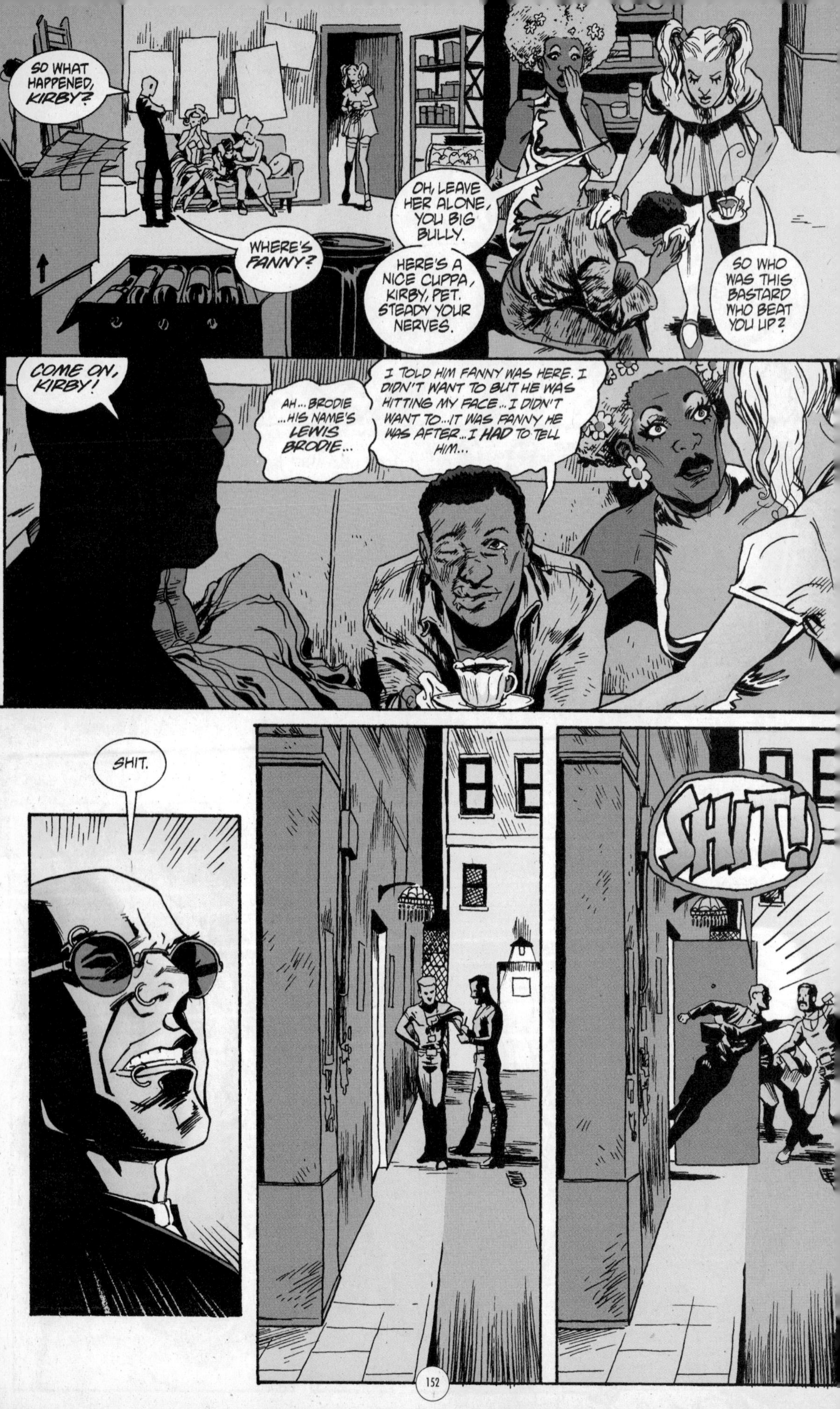
SO WHAT HAPPENED, KIRBY?
WHERE'S FANNY?
OH, LEAVE HER ALONE, YOU BIG BULLY.
HERE'S A NICE CUPPA, KIRBY, PET. STEADY YOUR NERVES.
SO WHO WAS THIS BASTARD WHO BEAT YOU UP?
COME ON, KIRBY!
AH... BRODIE ...HIS NAME'S LEWIS BRODIE...
I TOLD HIM FANNY WAS HERE. I DIDN'T WANT TO BUT HE WAS HITTING MY FACE... I DIDN'T WANT TO...IT WAS FANNY HE WAS AFTER... I HAD TO TELL HIM...
SHIT.
SHIT!

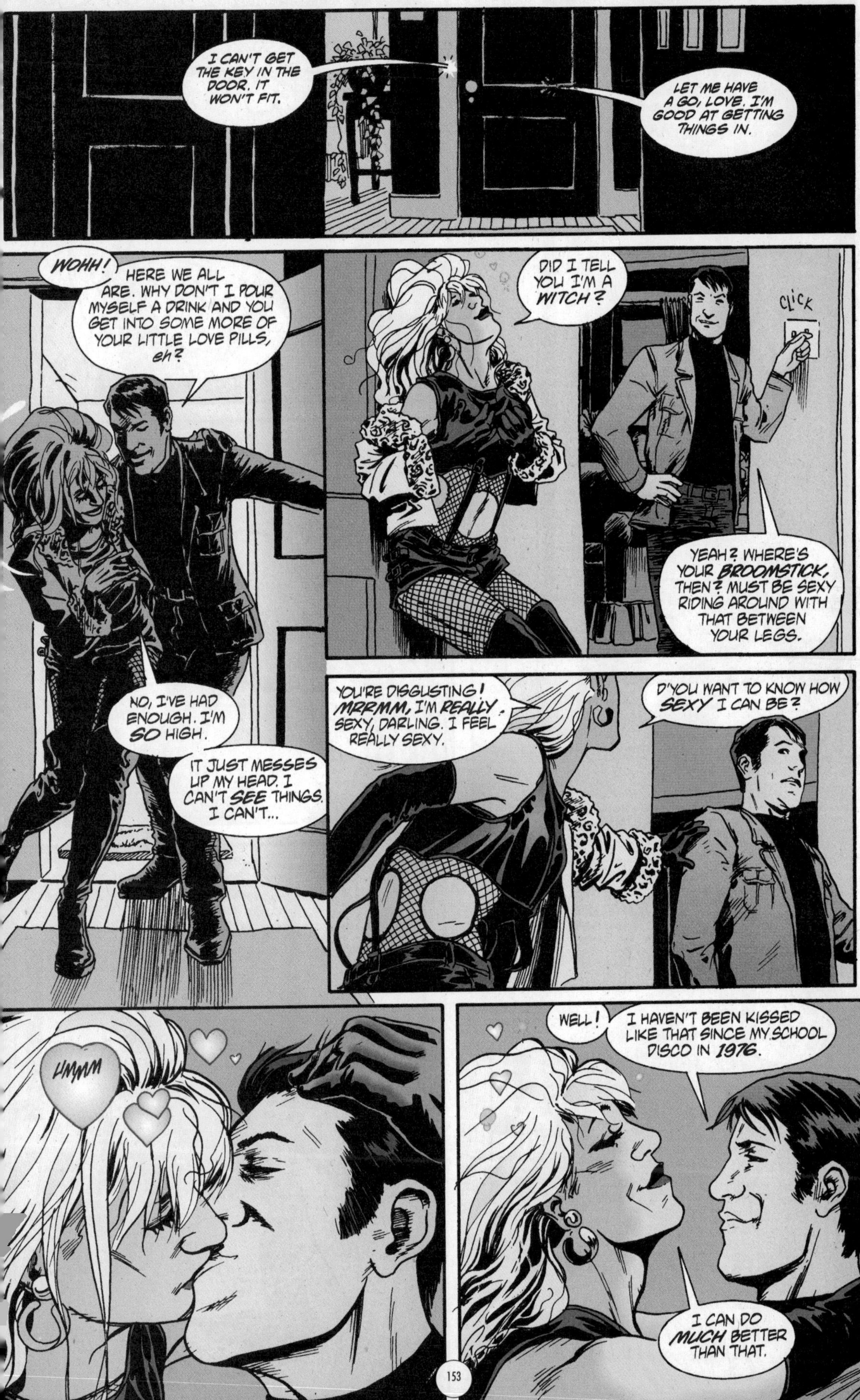
I CAN'T GET THE KEY IN THE DOOR. IT WON'T FIT.
LET ME HAVE A GO, LOVE. I'M GOOD AT GETTING THINGS IN.
WOHH!
HERE WE ALL ARE. WHY DON'T I POUR MYSELF A DRINK AND YOU GET INTO SOME MORE OF YOUR LITTLE LOVE PILLS, eh?
NO, I'VE HAD ENOUGH. I'M SO HIGH.
IT JUST MESSES UP MY HEAD. I CAN'T SEE THINGS. I CAN'T...
DID I TELL YOU I'M A WITCH?
CLICK
YEAH? WHERE'S YOUR BROOMSTICK, THEN? MUST BE SEXY RIDING AROUND WITH THAT BETWEEN YOUR LEGS.
YOU'RE DISGUSTING! MRRMM, I'M REALLY SEXY, DARLING. I FEEL REALLY SEXY.
D'YOU WANT TO KNOW HOW SEXY I CAN BE?
UMMM
WELL!
I HAVEN'T BEEN KISSED LIKE THAT SINCE MY SCHOOL DISCO IN 1976.
I CAN DO MUCH BETTER THAN THAT.

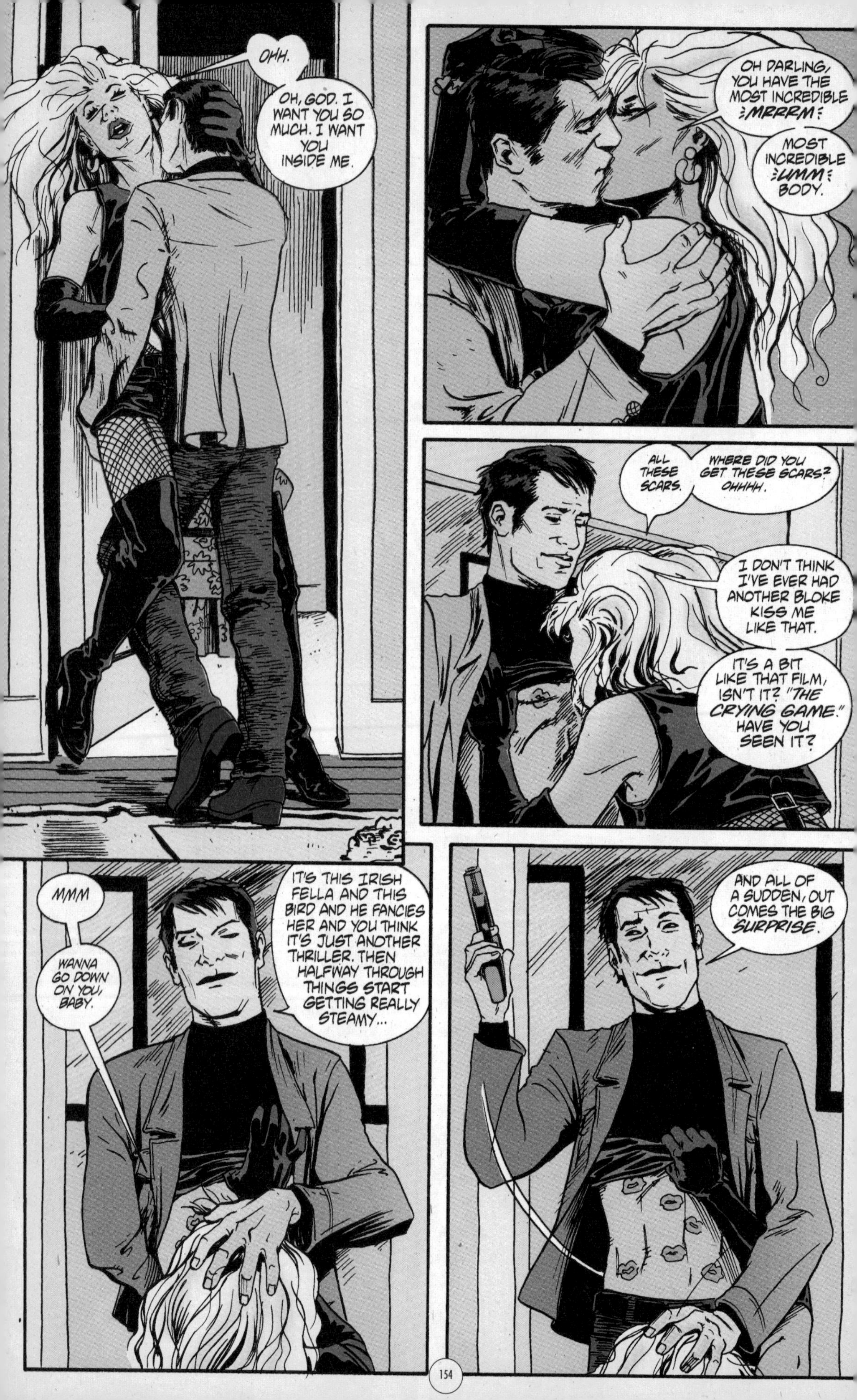
OHH.
OH, GOD. I WANT YOU SO MUCH. I WANT YOU INSIDE ME.
OH DARLING, YOU HAVE THE MOST INCREDIBLE MRRRM
MOST INCREDIBLE UMM BODY.
ALL THESE SCARS.
WHERE DID YOU GET THESE SCARS? OHHHH.
I DON'T THINK I'VE EVER HAD ANOTHER BLOKE KISS ME LIKE THAT.
IT'S A BIT LIKE THAT FILM, ISN'T IT? "THE CRYING GAME." HAVE YOU SEEN IT?
MMM
WANNA GO DOWN ON YOU, BABY.
IT'S THIS IRISH FELLA AND THIS BIRD AND HE FANCIES HER AND YOU THINK IT'S JUST ANOTHER THRILLER. THEN HALFWAY THROUGH THINGS START GETTING REALLY STEAMY...
AND ALL OF A SUDDEN, OUT COMES THE BIG SURPRISE.

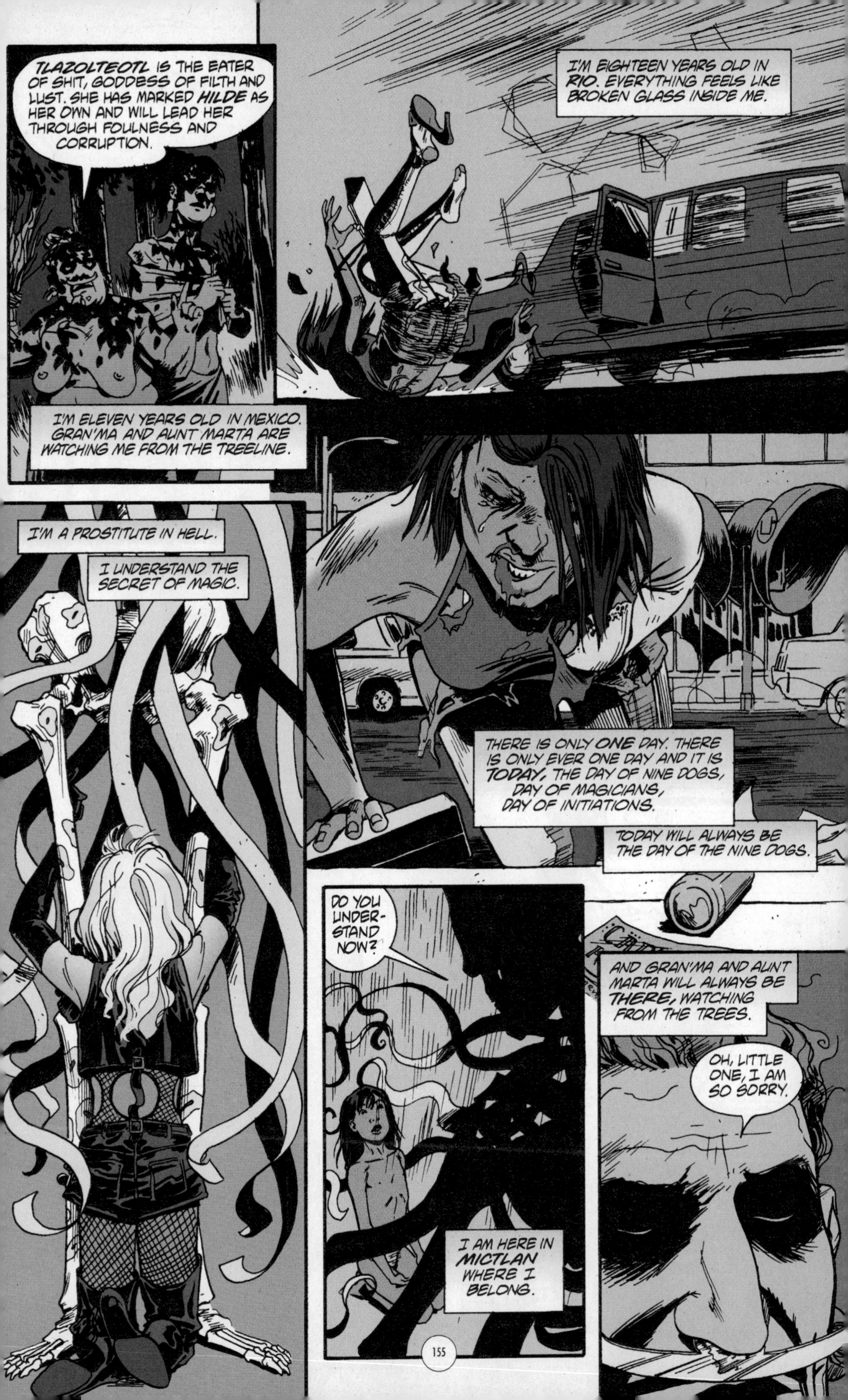
TLAZOLTEOTL IS THE EATER OF SHIT, GODDESS OF FILTH AND LUST. SHE HAS MARKED HILDE AS HER OWN AND WILL LEAD HER THROUGH FOULNESS AND CORRUPTION.
I'M ELEVEN YEARS OLD IN MEXICO. GRAN'MA AND AUNT MARTA ARE WATCHING ME FROM THE TREELINE.
I'M EIGHTEEN YEARS OLD IN RIO. EVERYTHING FEELS LIKE BROKEN GLASS INSIDE ME.
I'M A PROSTITUTE IN HELL.
I UNDERSTAND THE SECRET OF MAGIC.
THERE IS ONLY ONE DAY. THERE IS ONLY EVER ONE DAY AND IT IS TODAY, THE DAY OF NINE DOGS, DAY OF MAGICIANS, DAY OF INITIATIONS.
TODAY WILL ALWAYS BE THE DAY OF THE NINE DOGS.
DO YOU UNDER-STAND NOW?
I AM HERE IN MICTLAN WHERE I BELONG.
AND GRAN'MA AND AUNT MARTA WILL ALWAYS BE THERE, WATCHING FROM THE TREES.
OH, LITTLE ONE, I AM SO SORRY.

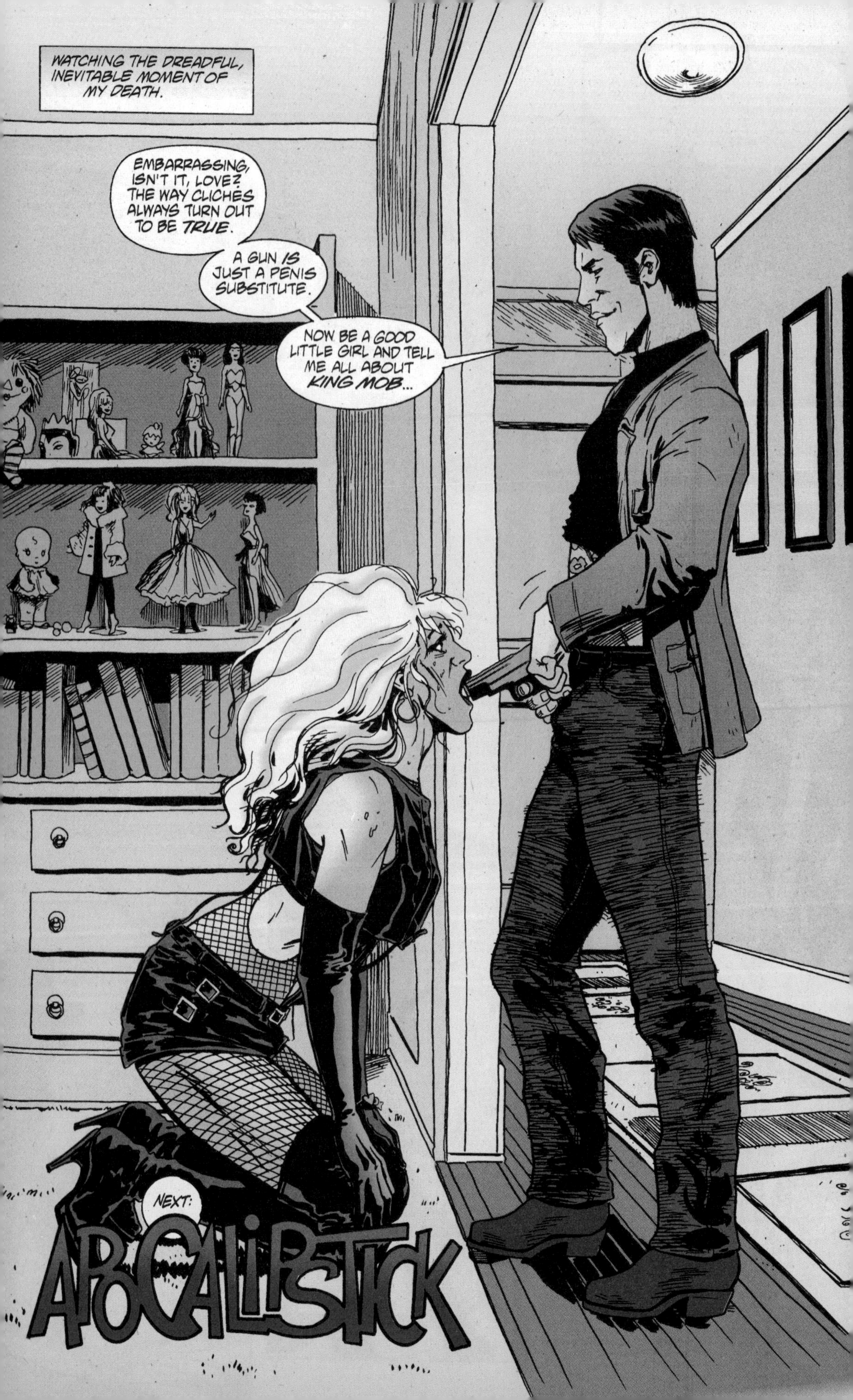
WATCHING THE DREADFUL, INEVITABLE MOMENT OF MY DEATH.
EMBARRASSING, ISN'T IT, LOVE? THE WAY CLICHÉS ALWAYS TURN OUT TO BE TRUE.
A GUN IS JUST A PENIS SUBSTITUTE.
NOW BE A GOOD LITTLE GIRL AND TELL ME ALL ABOUT KING MOB...
NEXT:
APOCALIPSTICK

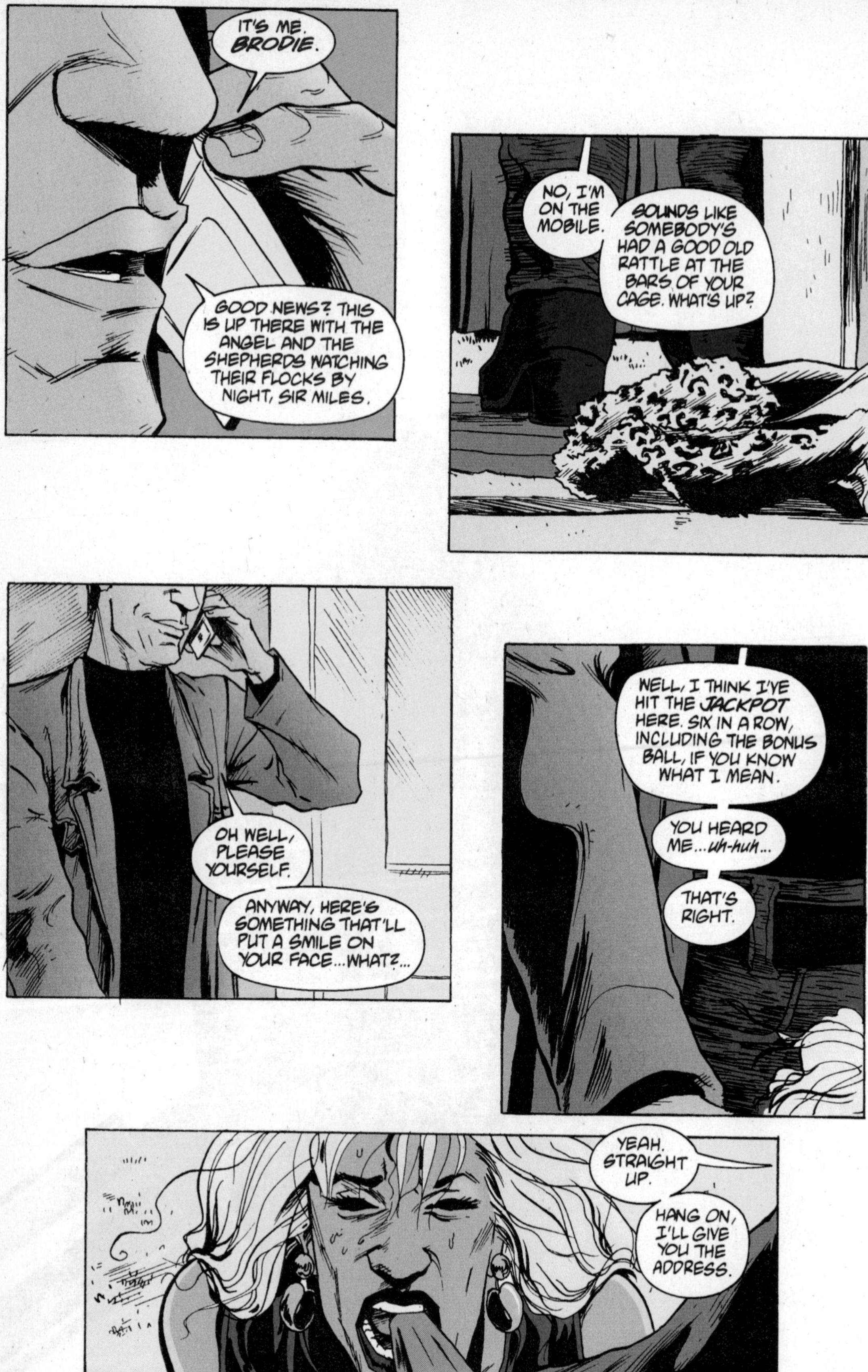
IT'S ME. BRODIE.
GOOD NEWS? THIS IS UP THERE WITH THE ANGEL AND THE SHEPHERDS WATCHING THEIR FLOCKS BY NIGHT, SIR MILES.
NO, I'M ON THE MOBILE.
SOUNDS LIKE SOMEBODY'S HAD A GOOD OLD RATTLE AT THE BARS OF YOUR CAGE. WHAT'S UP?
OH WELL, PLEASE YOURSELF.
ANYWAY, HERE'S SOMETHING THAT'LL PUT A SMILE ON YOUR FACE... WHAT?...
WELL, I THINK I'VE HIT THE JACKPOT HERE. SIX IN A ROW, INCLUDING THE BONUS BALL, IF YOU KNOW WHAT I MEAN.
YOU HEARD ME... uh-huh...
THAT'S RIGHT.
YEAH. STRAIGHT UP.
HANG ON, I'LL GIVE YOU THE ADDRESS.

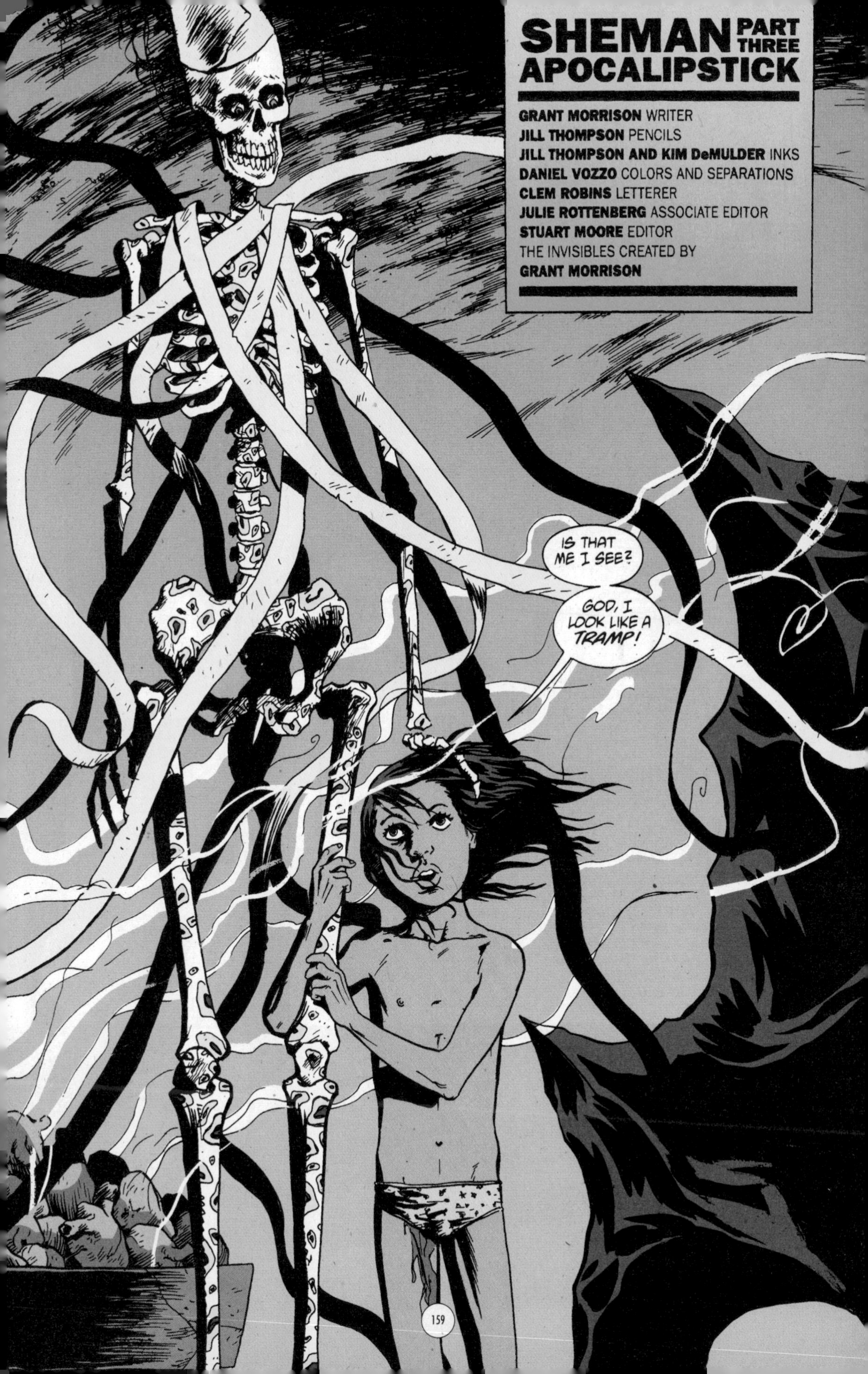
SHEMAN PART THREE
APOCALIPSTICK
GRANT MORRISON WRITER
JILL THOMPSON PENCILS
JILL THOMPSON AND KIM DeMULDER INKS
DANIEL VOZZO COLORS AND SEPARATIONS
CLEM ROBINS LETTERER
JULIE ROTTENBERG ASSOCIATE EDITOR
STUART MOORE EDITOR
THE INVISIBLES CREATED BY
GRANT MORRISON
IS THAT ME I SEE?
GOD, I LOOK LIKE A TRAMP!

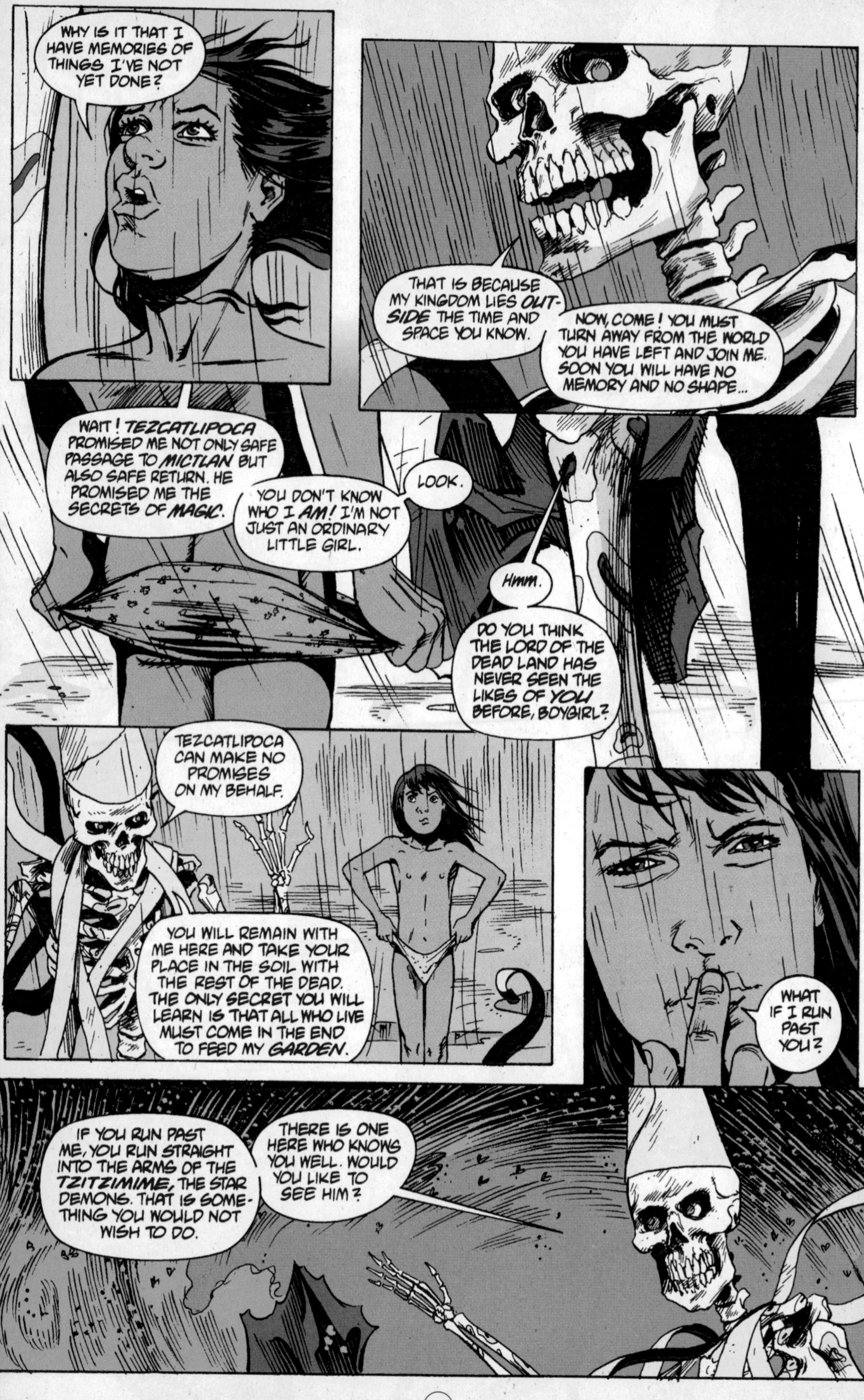
WHY IS IT THAT I HAVE MEMORIES OF THINGS I'VE NOT YET DONE?
THAT IS BECAUSE MY KINGDOM LIES OUTSIDE THE TIME AND SPACE YOU KNOW.
NOW, COME! YOU MUST TURN AWAY FROM THE WORLD YOU HAVE LEFT AND JOIN ME. SOON YOU WILL HAVE NO MEMORY AND NO SHAPE...
WAIT! TEZCATLIPOCA PROMISED ME NOT ONLY SAFE PASSAGE TO MICTLAN BUT ALSO SAFE RETURN. HE PROMISED ME THE SECRETS OF MAGIC.
YOU DON'T KNOW WHO I AM! I'M NOT JUST AN ORDINARY LITTLE GIRL.
LOOK.
Hmm.
DO YOU THINK THE LORD OF THE DEAD LAND HAS NEVER SEEN THE LIKES OF YOU BEFORE, BOYGIRL?
TEZCATLIPOCA CAN MAKE NO PROMISES ON MY BEHALF.
YOU WILL REMAIN WITH ME HERE AND TAKE YOUR PLACE IN THE SOIL WITH THE REST OF THE DEAD. THE ONLY SECRET YOU WILL LEARN IS THAT ALL WHO LIVE MUST COME IN THE END TO FEED MY GARDEN.
WHAT IF I RUN PAST YOU?
IF YOU RUN PAST ME, YOU RUN STRAIGHT INTO THE ARMS OF THE TZITZIMIME, THE STAR DEMONS. THAT IS SOMETHING YOU WOULD NOT WISH TO DO.
THERE IS ONE HERE WHO KNOWS YOU WELL. WOULD YOU LIKE TO SEE HIM?

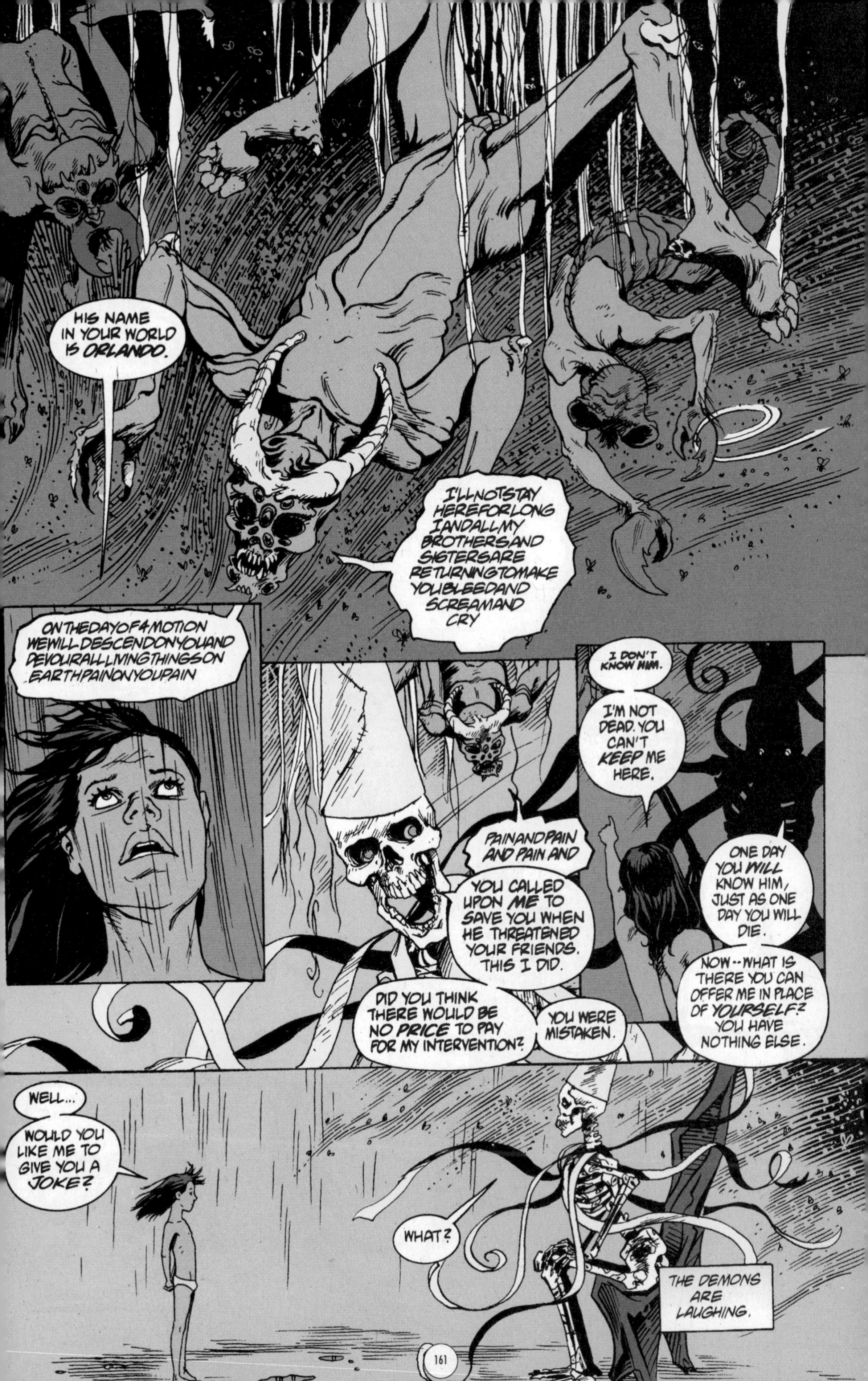

HIS NAME IN YOUR WORLD IS ORLANDO.
I'LLNOTSTAY HEREFORLONG IANDALLMY BROTHERSAND SISTERSARE RETURNINGTOMAKE YOUBLEEDAND SCREAMAND CRY
ONTHEDAYOF4MOTION WEWILLDESCENDONYOUAND DEVOURALLLIVINGTHINGSON EARTHPAINONYOUPAIN
PAINANDPAIN AND PAIN AND
I DON'T KNOW HIM.
I'M NOT DEAD. YOU CAN'T KEEP ME HERE.
YOU CALLED UPON ME TO SAVE YOU WHEN HE THREATENED YOUR FRIENDS. THIS I DID.
DID YOU THINK THERE WOULD BE NO PRICE TO PAY FOR MY INTERVENTION?
YOU WERE MISTAKEN.
ONE DAY YOU WILL KNOW HIM, JUST AS ONE DAY YOU WILL DIE.
NOW--WHAT IS THERE YOU CAN OFFER ME IN PLACE OF YOURSELF? YOU HAVE NOTHING ELSE.
WELL...
WOULD YOU LIKE ME TO GIVE YOU A JOKE?
WHAT?
THE DEMONS ARE LAUGHING.

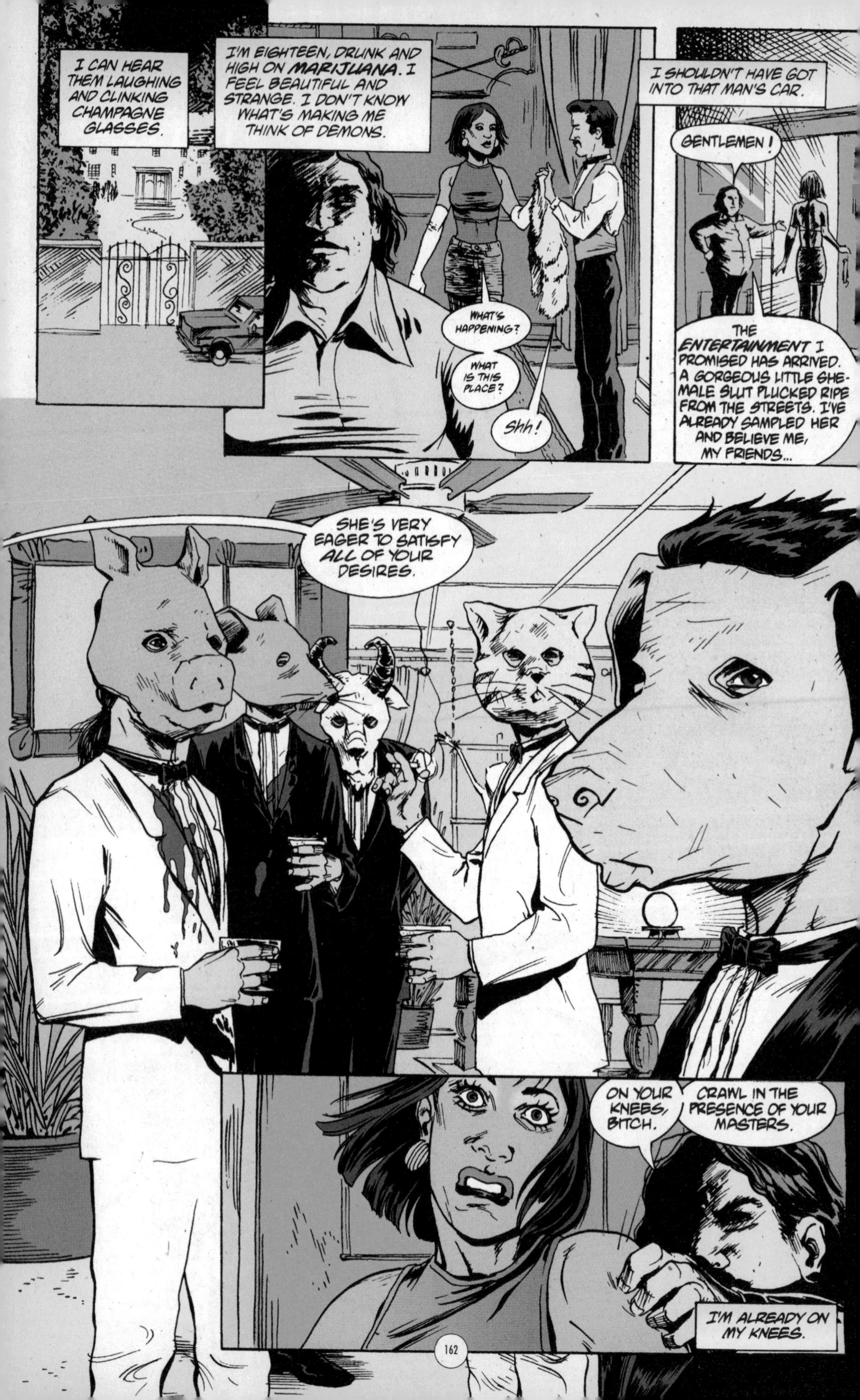
I CAN HEAR THEM LAUGHING AND CLINKING CHAMPAGNE GLASSES.
I'M EIGHTEEN, DRUNK AND HIGH ON MARIJUANA. I FEEL BEAUTIFUL AND STRANGE. I DON'T KNOW WHAT'S MAKING ME THINK OF DEMONS.
WHAT'S HAPPENING?
WHAT IS THIS PLACE?
Shh!
I SHOULDN'T HAVE GOT INTO THAT MAN'S CAR.
GENTLEMEN!
THE ENTERTAINMENT I PROMISED HAS ARRIVED. A GORGEOUS LITTLE SHE-MALE SLUT PLUCKED RIPE FROM THE STREETS. I'VE ALREADY SAMPLED HER AND BELIEVE ME, MY FRIENDS...
SHE'S VERY EAGER TO SATISFY ALL OF YOUR DESIRES.
ON YOUR KNEES, BITCH.
CRAWL IN THE PRESENCE OF YOUR MASTERS.
I'M ALREADY ON MY KNEES.

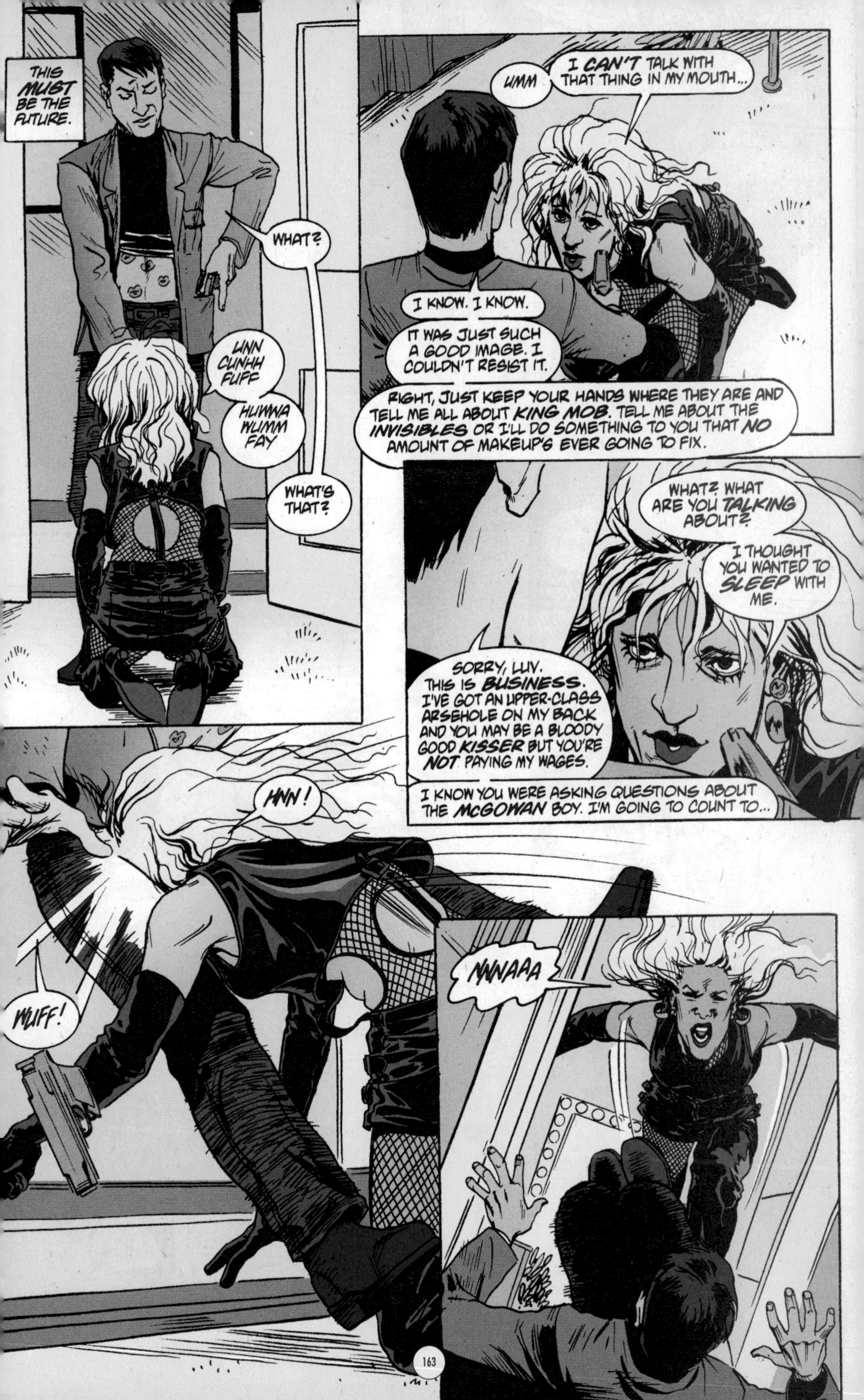
THIS MUST BE THE FUTURE.
WHAT?
UNN CUNHH FUFF
HUWWA WUMM FAY
WHAT'S THAT?
UMM
I CAN'T TALK WITH THAT THING IN MY MOUTH...
I KNOW. I KNOW.
IT WAS JUST SUCH A GOOD IMAGE. I COULDN'T RESIST IT.
RIGHT, JUST KEEP YOUR HANDS WHERE THEY ARE AND TELL ME ALL ABOUT KING MOB. TELL ME ABOUT THE INVISIBLES OR I'LL DO SOMETHING TO YOU THAT NO AMOUNT OF MAKEUP'S EVER GOING TO FIX.
WHAT? WHAT ARE YOU TALKING ABOUT?
I THOUGHT YOU WANTED TO SLEEP WITH ME.
SORRY, LUV. THIS IS BUSINESS. I'VE GOT AN UPPER-CLASS ARSEHOLE ON MY BACK AND YOU MAY BE A BLOODY GOOD KISSER BUT YOU'RE NOT PAYING MY WAGES.
I KNOW YOU WERE ASKING QUESTIONS ABOUT THE McGOWAN BOY. I'M GOING TO COUNT TO...
HNN!
WUFF!
NNNAAA

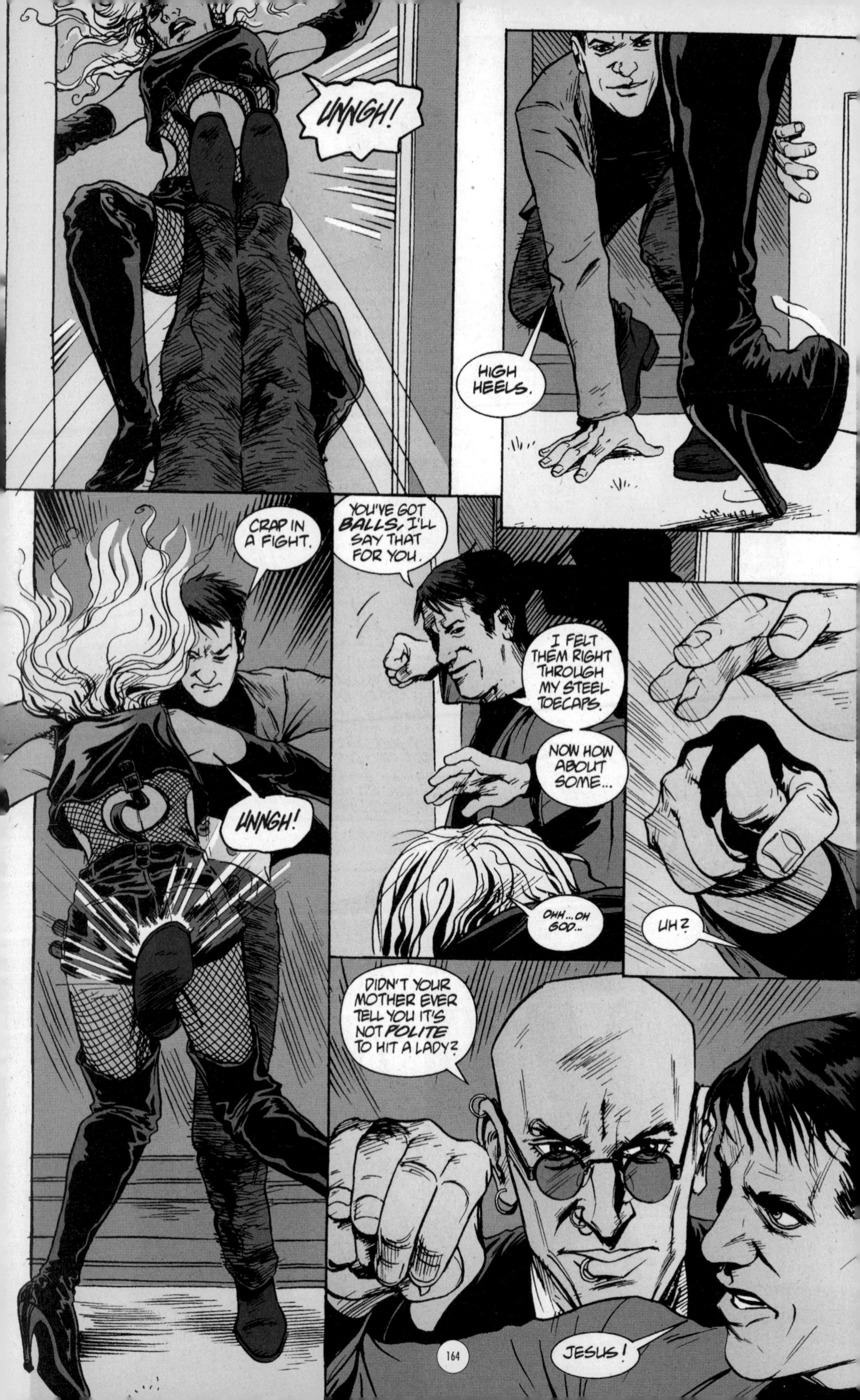

UNNGH!
HIGH HEELS.
CRAP IN A FIGHT.
UNNGH!
YOU'VE GOT BALLS, I'LL SAY THAT FOR YOU.
I FELT THEM RIGHT THROUGH MY STEEL TOECAPS.
NOW HOW ABOUT SOME...
OHH...OH GOD...
UH?
DIDN'T YOUR MOTHER EVER TELL YOU IT'S NOT POLITE TO HIT A LADY?
JESUS!

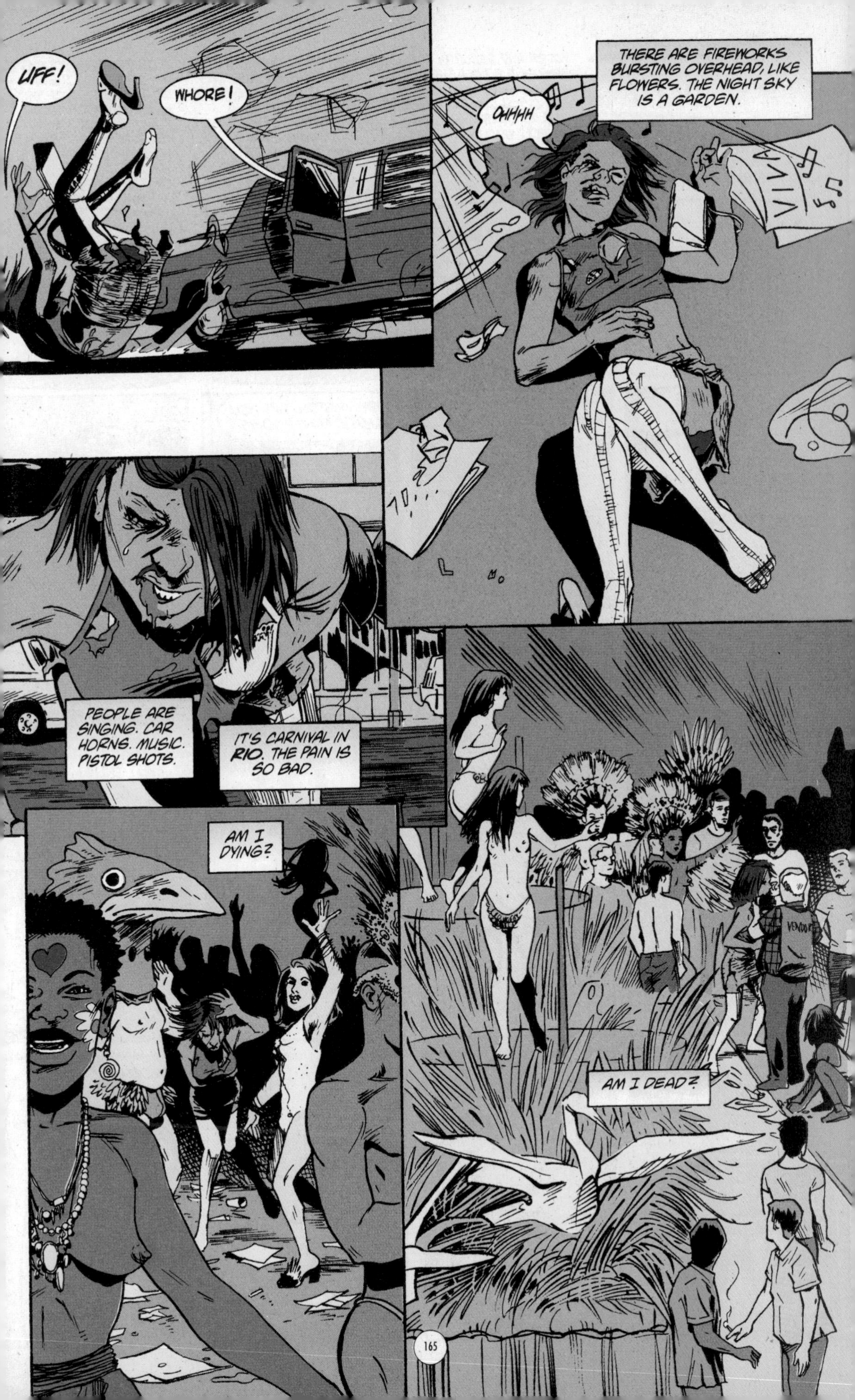
UFF!
WHORE!
OHHHH
THERE ARE FIREWORKS BURSTING OVERHEAD, LIKE FLOWERS. THE NIGHT SKY IS A GARDEN.
VIVA
PEOPLE ARE SINGING. CAR HORNS. MUSIC. PISTOL SHOTS.
IT'S CARNIVAL IN RIO. THE PAIN IS SO BAD.
AM I DYING?
AM I DEAD?

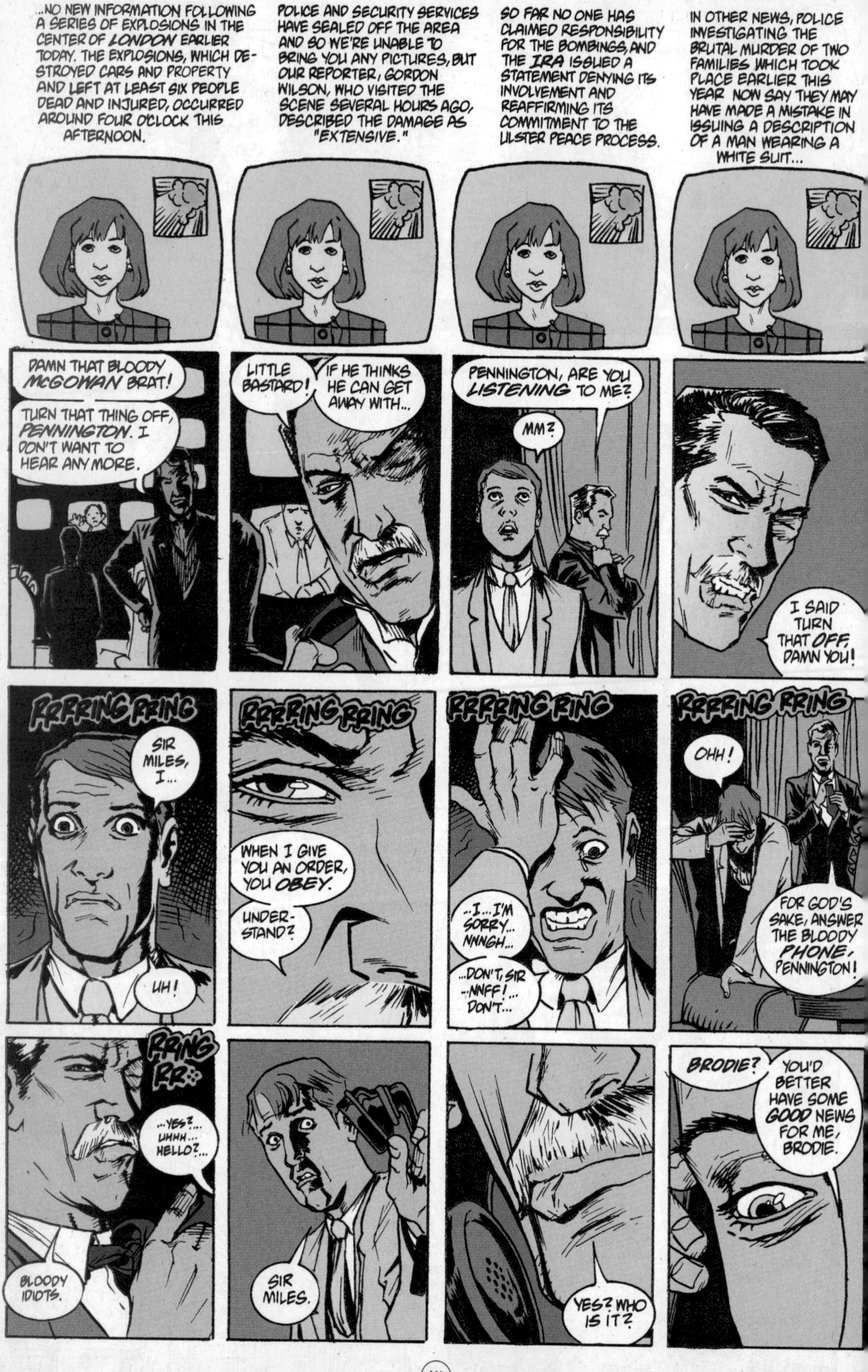

...NO NEW INFORMATION FOLLOWING A SERIES OF EXPLOSIONS IN THE CENTER OF LONDON EARLIER TODAY. THE EXPLOSIONS, WHICH DESTROYED CARS AND PROPERTY AND LEFT AT LEAST SIX PEOPLE DEAD AND INJURED, OCCURRED AROUND FOUR O'CLOCK THIS AFTERNOON.
POLICE AND SECURITY SERVICES HAVE SEALED OFF THE AREA AND SO WE'RE UNABLE TO BRING YOU ANY PICTURES, BUT OUR REPORTER, GORDON WILSON, WHO VISITED THE SCENE SEVERAL HOURS AGO, DESCRIBED THE DAMAGE AS "EXTENSIVE."
SO FAR NO ONE HAS CLAIMED RESPONSIBILITY FOR THE BOMBINGS, AND THE IRA ISSUED A STATEMENT DENYING ITS INVOLVEMENT AND REAFFIRMING ITS COMMITMENT TO THE ULSTER PEACE PROCESS.
IN OTHER NEWS, POLICE INVESTIGATING THE BRUTAL MURDER OF TWO FAMILIES WHICH TOOK PLACE EARLIER THIS YEAR NOW SAY THEY MAY HAVE MADE A MISTAKE IN ISSUING A DESCRIPTION OF A MAN WEARING A WHITE SUIT...
DAMN THAT BLOODY McGOWAN BRAT!
TURN THAT THING OFF, PENNINGTON. I DON'T WANT TO HEAR ANY MORE.
LITTLE BASTARD!
IF HE THINKS HE CAN GET AWAY WITH...
PENNINGTON, ARE YOU LISTENING TO ME?
MM?
I SAID TURN THAT OFF, DAMN YOU!
RRRRING RRING
SIR MILES, I...
UH!
RRRRING RRING
WHEN I GIVE YOU AN ORDER, YOU OBEY.
UNDERSTAND?
RRRRING RRING
...I...I'M SORRY... NNNGH...
...DON'T, SIR ...NNFF!... DON'T...
RRRRING RRING
OHH!
FOR GOD'S SAKE, ANSWER THE BLOODY PHONE, PENNINGTON!
RRING RR
...YES?... UHHH... HELLO?...
BLOODY IDIOTS.
SIR MILES.
YES? WHO IS IT?
BRODIE?
YOU'D BETTER HAVE SOME GOOD NEWS FOR ME, BRODIE.

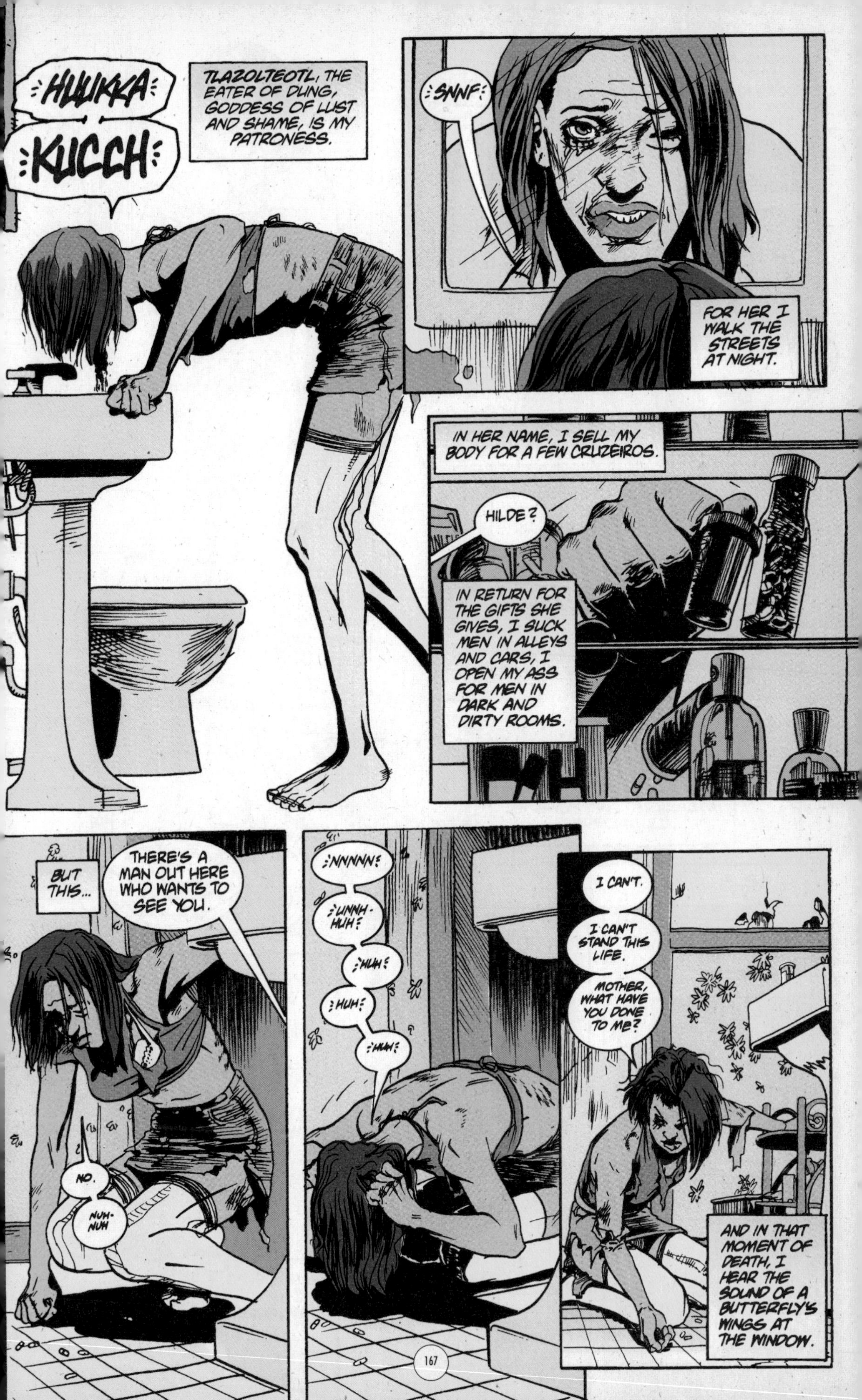
HUUKKA
KUCCH
TLAZOLTEOTL, THE EATER OF DUNG, GODDESS OF LUST AND SHAME, IS MY PATRONESS.
SNNF
FOR HER I WALK THE STREETS AT NIGHT.
IN HER NAME, I SELL MY BODY FOR A FEW CRUZEIROS.
HILDE?
IN RETURN FOR THE GIFTS SHE GIVES, I SUCK MEN IN ALLEYS AND CARS, I OPEN MY ASS FOR MEN IN DARK AND DIRTY ROOMS.
BUT THIS...
THERE'S A MAN OUT HERE WHO WANTS TO SEE YOU.
NO.
NUH-NUH
NNNNN
UNNH-HUH
HUH
HUH
HUH
I CAN'T.
I CAN'T STAND THIS LIFE.
MOTHER, WHAT HAVE YOU DONE TO ME?
AND IN THAT MOMENT OF DEATH, I HEAR THE SOUND OF A BUTTERFLY'S WINGS AT THE WINDOW.

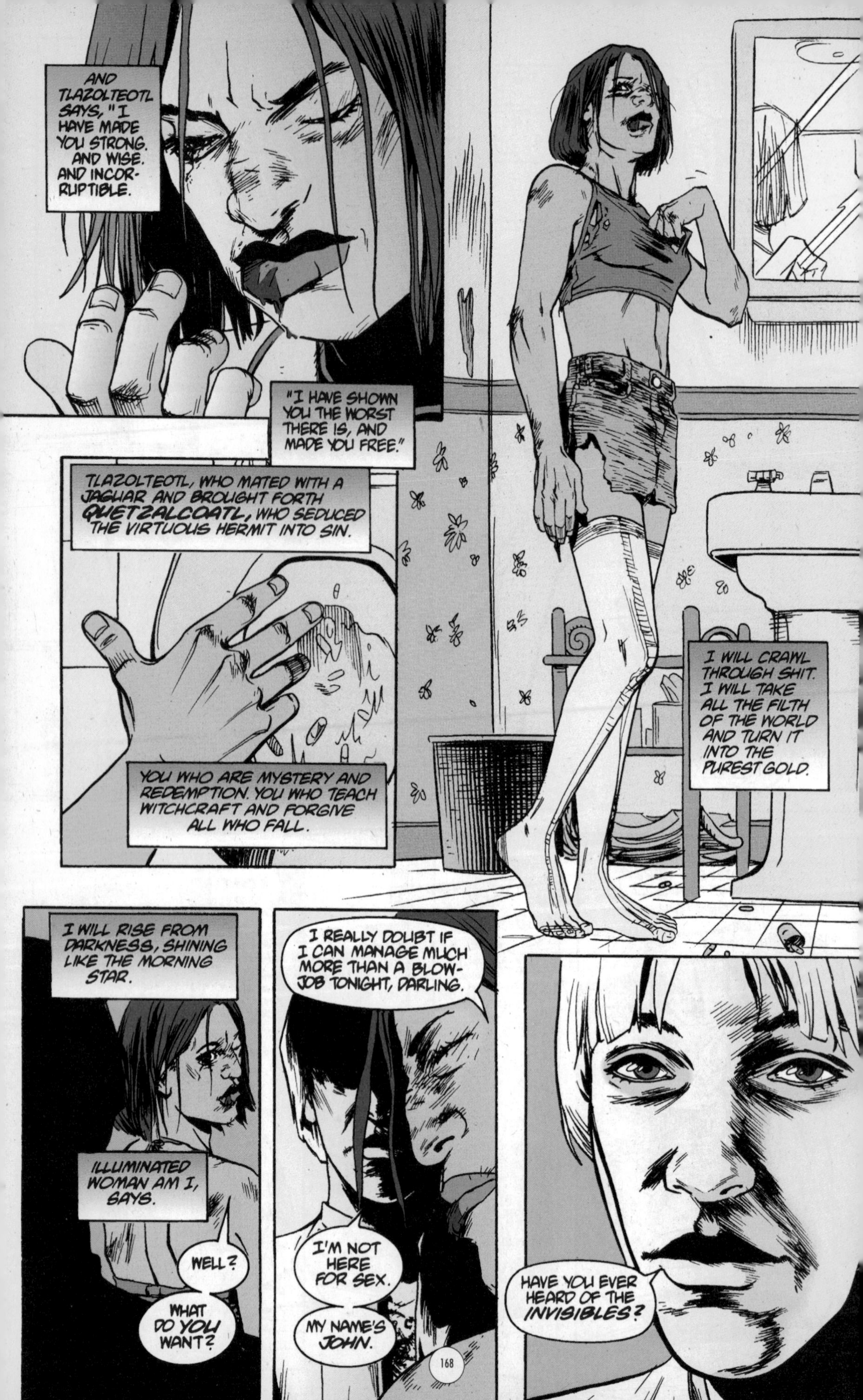
AND TLAZOLTEOTL SAYS, "I HAVE MADE YOU STRONG. AND WISE. AND INCORRUPTIBLE.
"I HAVE SHOWN YOU THE WORST THERE IS, AND MADE YOU FREE."
TLAZOLTEOTL, WHO MATED WITH A JAGUAR AND BROUGHT FORTH QUETZALCOATL, WHO SEDUCED THE VIRTUOUS HERMIT INTO SIN.
YOU WHO ARE MYSTERY AND REDEMPTION. YOU WHO TEACH WITCHCRAFT AND FORGIVE ALL WHO FALL.
I WILL CRAWL THROUGH SHIT. I WILL TAKE ALL THE FILTH OF THE WORLD AND TURN IT INTO THE PUREST GOLD.
I WILL RISE FROM DARKNESS, SHINING LIKE THE MORNING STAR.
ILLUMINATED WOMAN AM I, SAYS.
WELL?
WHAT DO YOU WANT?
I REALLY DOUBT IF I CAN MANAGE MUCH MORE THAN A BLOW-JOB TONIGHT, DARLING.
I'M NOT HERE FOR SEX.
MY NAME'S JOHN.
HAVE YOU EVER HEARD OF THE INVISIBLES?

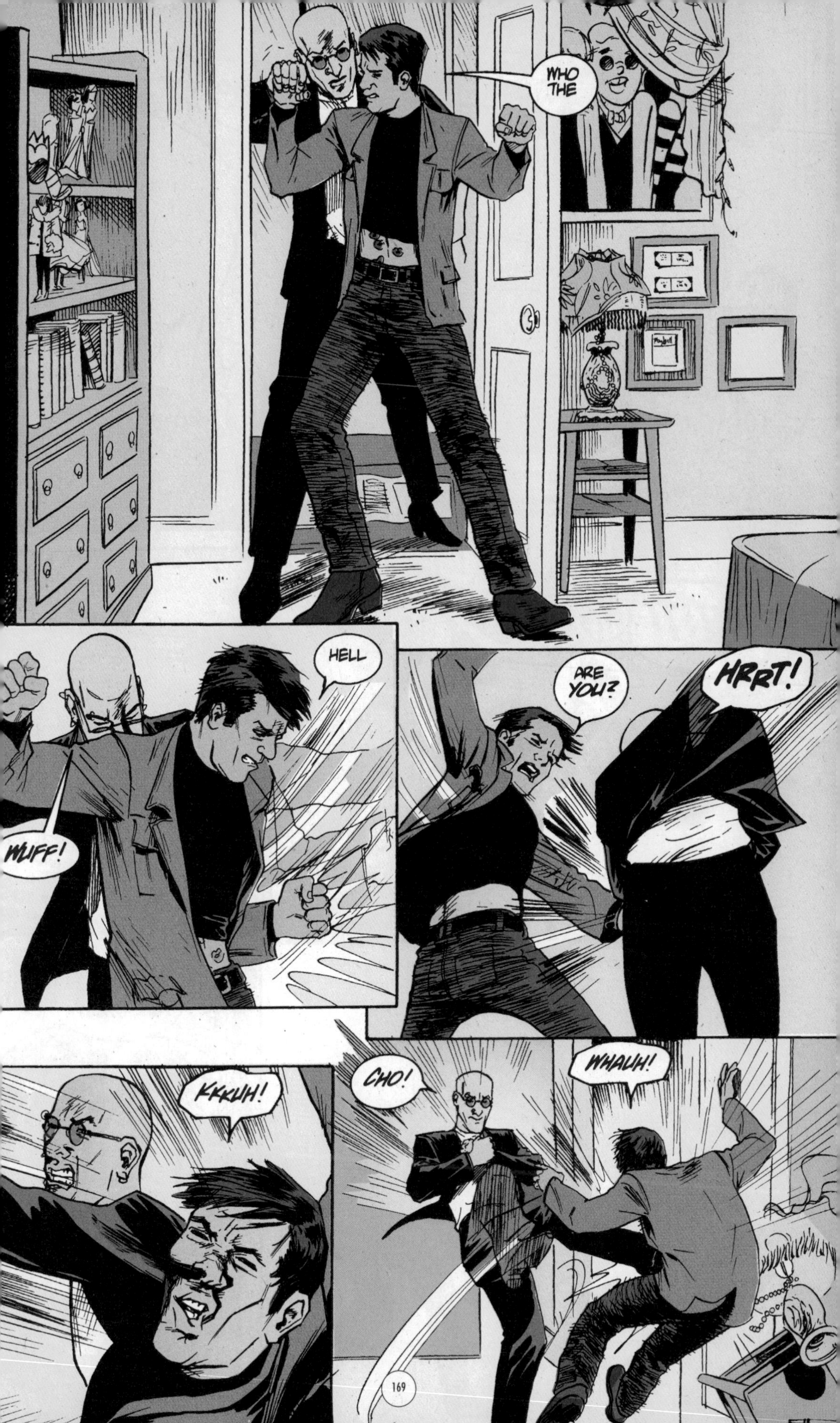
WHO THE
HELL
WUFF!
ARE YOU?
HRRT!
KKKUH!
CHO!
WHAUH!

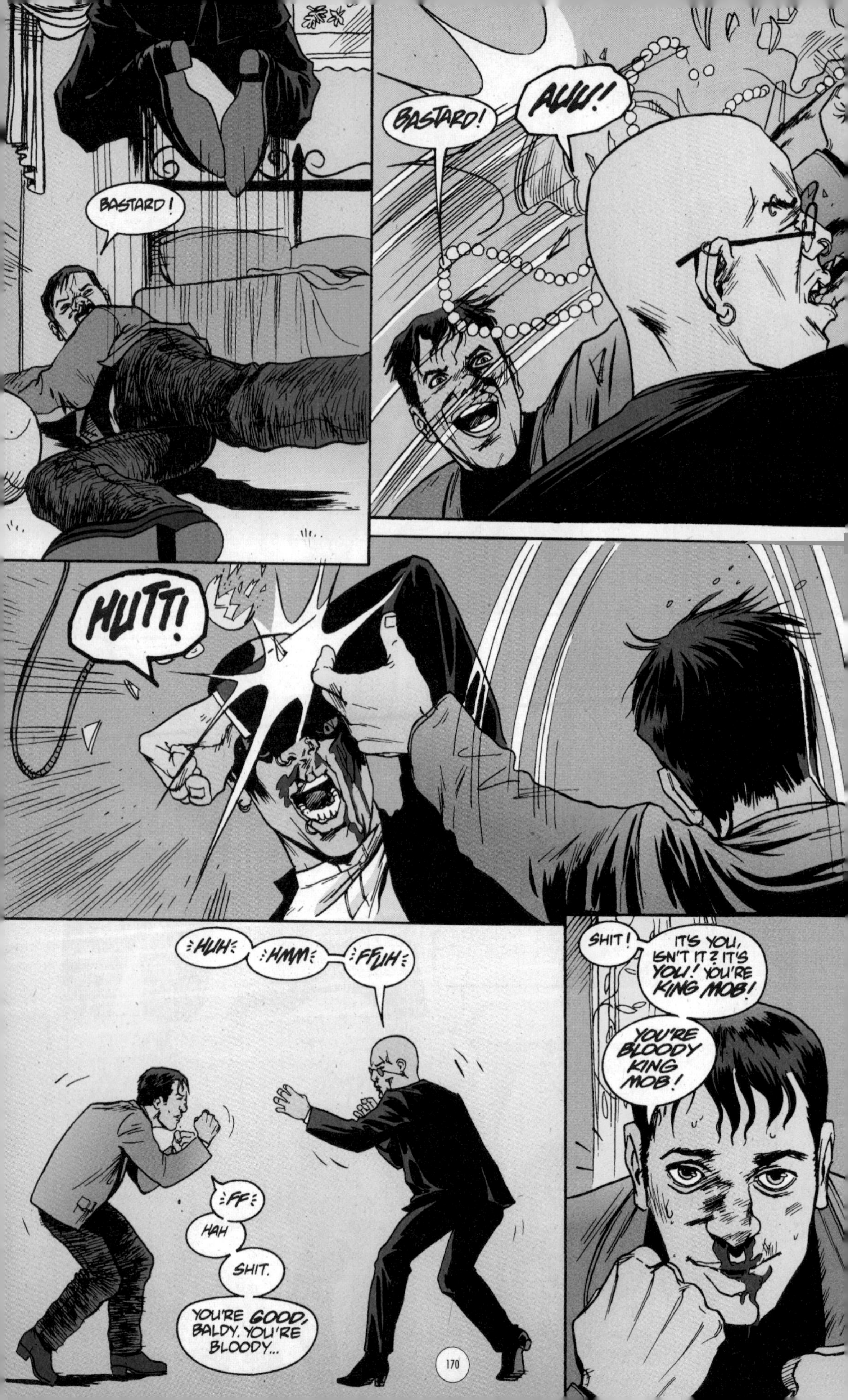
BASTARD!
BASTARD!
AUU!
HUTT!
HUH
HMM
FFUH
FF
HAH
SHIT.
YOU'RE GOOD, BALDY. YOU'RE BLOODY...
SHIT!
IT'S YOU, ISN'T IT? IT'S YOU! YOU'RE KING MOB!
YOU'RE BLOODY KING MOB!

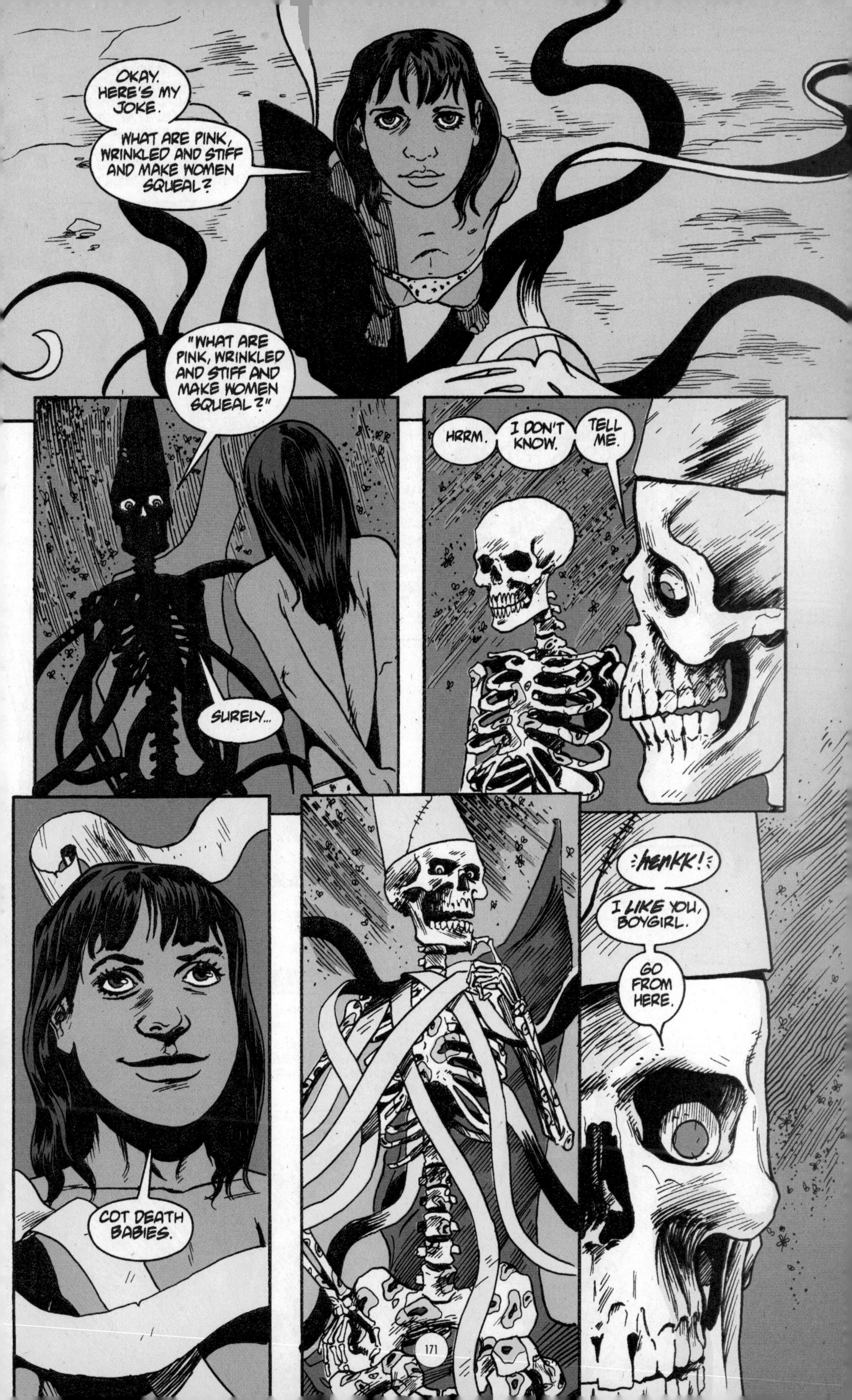
OKAY. HERE'S MY JOKE.
WHAT ARE PINK, WRINKLED AND STIFF AND MAKE WOMEN SQUEAL?
"WHAT ARE PINK, WRINKLED AND STIFF AND MAKE WOMEN SQUEAL?"
SURELY...
HRRM.
I DON'T KNOW.
TELL ME.
COT DEATH BABIES.
HENKK!
I LIKE YOU, BOYGIRL.
GO FROM HERE.

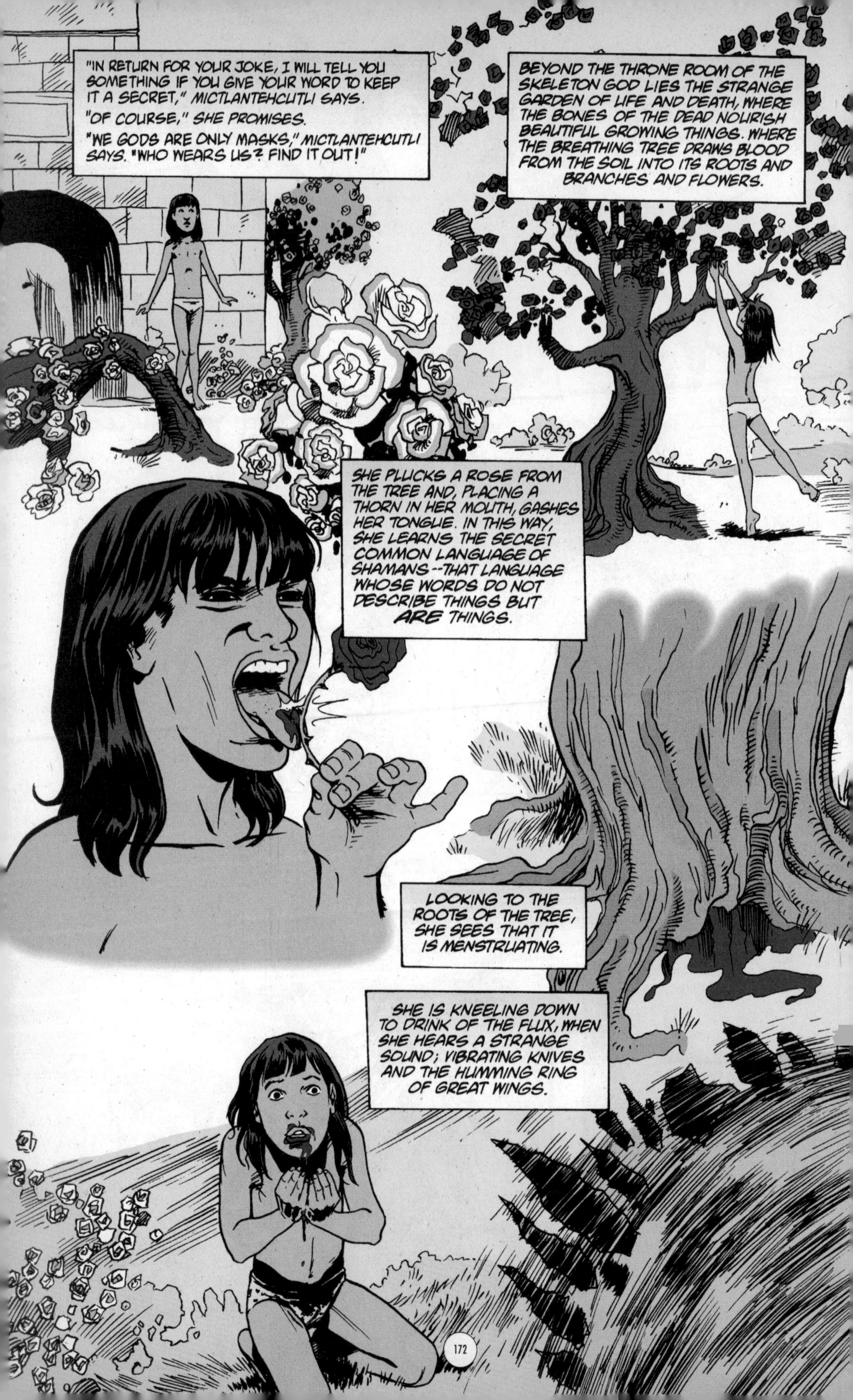
"IN RETURN FOR YOUR JOKE, I WILL TELL YOU SOMETHING IF YOU GIVE YOUR WORD TO KEEP IT A SECRET," MICTLANTEHCUTLI SAYS.
"OF COURSE," SHE PROMISES.
"WE GODS ARE ONLY MASKS," MICTLANTEHCUTLI SAYS. "WHO WEARS US? FIND IT OUT!"
BEYOND THE THRONE ROOM OF THE SKELETON GOD LIES THE STRANGE GARDEN OF LIFE AND DEATH, WHERE THE BONES OF THE DEAD NOURISH BEAUTIFUL GROWING THINGS. WHERE THE BREATHING TREE DRAWS BLOOD FROM THE SOIL INTO ITS ROOTS AND BRANCHES AND FLOWERS.
SHE PLUCKS A ROSE FROM THE TREE AND, PLACING A THORN IN HER MOUTH, GASHES HER TONGUE. IN THIS WAY, SHE LEARNS THE SECRET COMMON LANGUAGE OF SHAMANS--THAT LANGUAGE WHOSE WORDS DO NOT DESCRIBE THINGS BUT ARE THINGS.
LOOKING TO THE ROOTS OF THE TREE, SHE SEES THAT IT IS MENSTRUATING.
SHE IS KNEELING DOWN TO DRINK OF THE FLUX, WHEN SHE HEARS A STRANGE SOUND; VIBRATING KNIVES AND THE HUMMING RING OF GREAT WINGS.

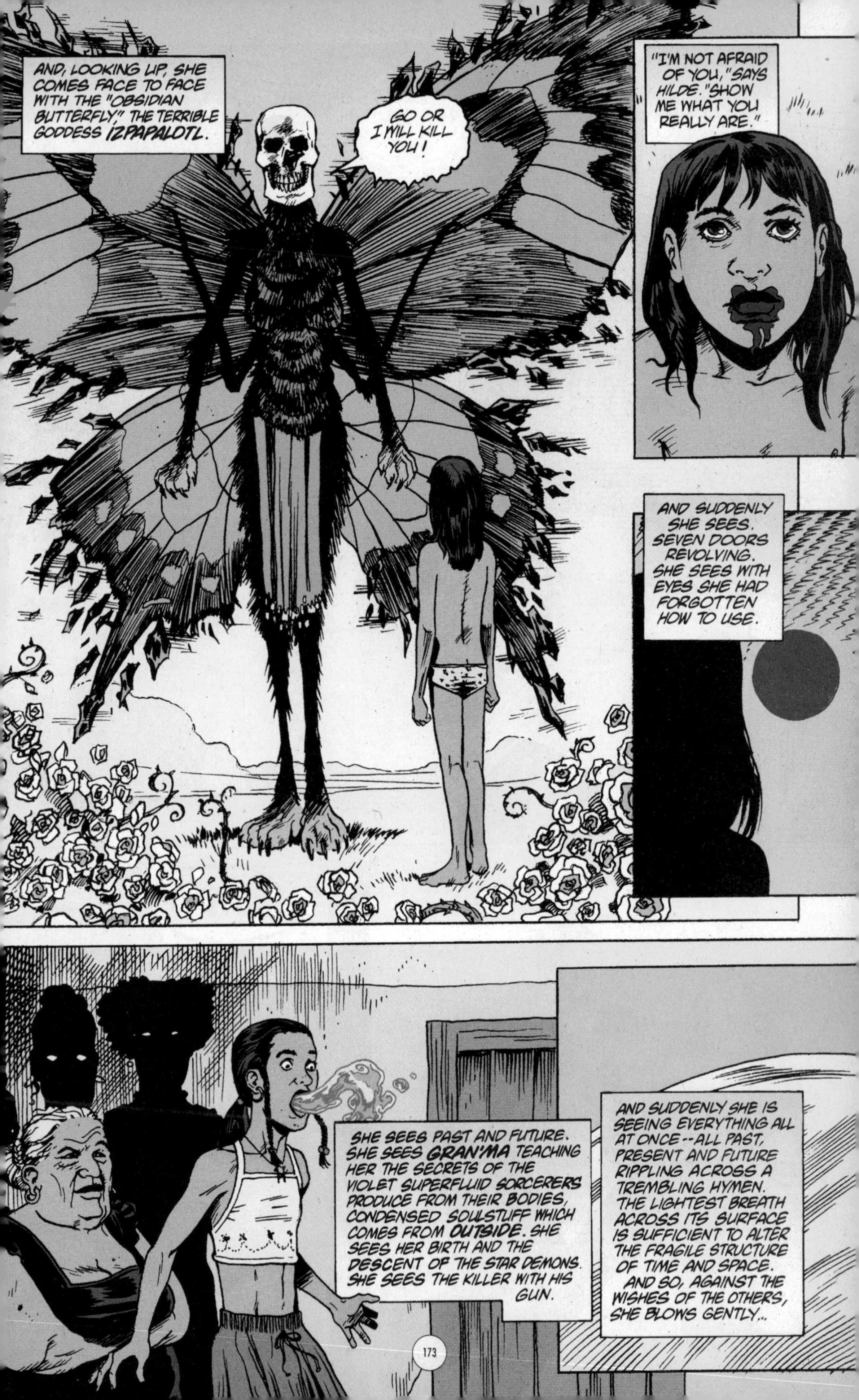
AND, LOOKING UP, SHE COMES FACE TO FACE WITH THE "OBSIDIAN BUTTERFLY," THE TERRIBLE GODDESS IZPAPALOTL.
GO OR I WILL KILL YOU!
"I'M NOT AFRAID OF YOU," SAYS HILDE. "SHOW ME WHAT YOU REALLY ARE."
AND SUDDENLY SHE SEES. SEVEN DOORS REVOLVING. SHE SEES WITH EYES SHE HAD FORGOTTEN HOW TO USE.
SHE SEES PAST AND FUTURE. SHE SEES GRAN'MA TEACHING HER THE SECRETS OF THE VIOLET SUPERFLUID SORCERERS PRODUCE FROM THEIR BODIES, CONDENSED SOULSTUFF WHICH COMES FROM OUTSIDE. SHE SEES HER BIRTH AND THE DESCENT OF THE STAR DEMONS. SHE SEES THE KILLER WITH HIS GUN.
AND SUDDENLY SHE IS SEEING EVERYTHING ALL AT ONCE--ALL PAST, PRESENT AND FUTURE RIPPLING ACROSS A TREMBLING HYMEN. THE LIGHTEST BREATH ACROSS ITS SURFACE IS SUFFICIENT TO ALTER THE FRAGILE STRUCTURE OF TIME AND SPACE.
AND SO, AGAINST THE WISHES OF THE OTHERS, SHE BLOWS GENTLY...

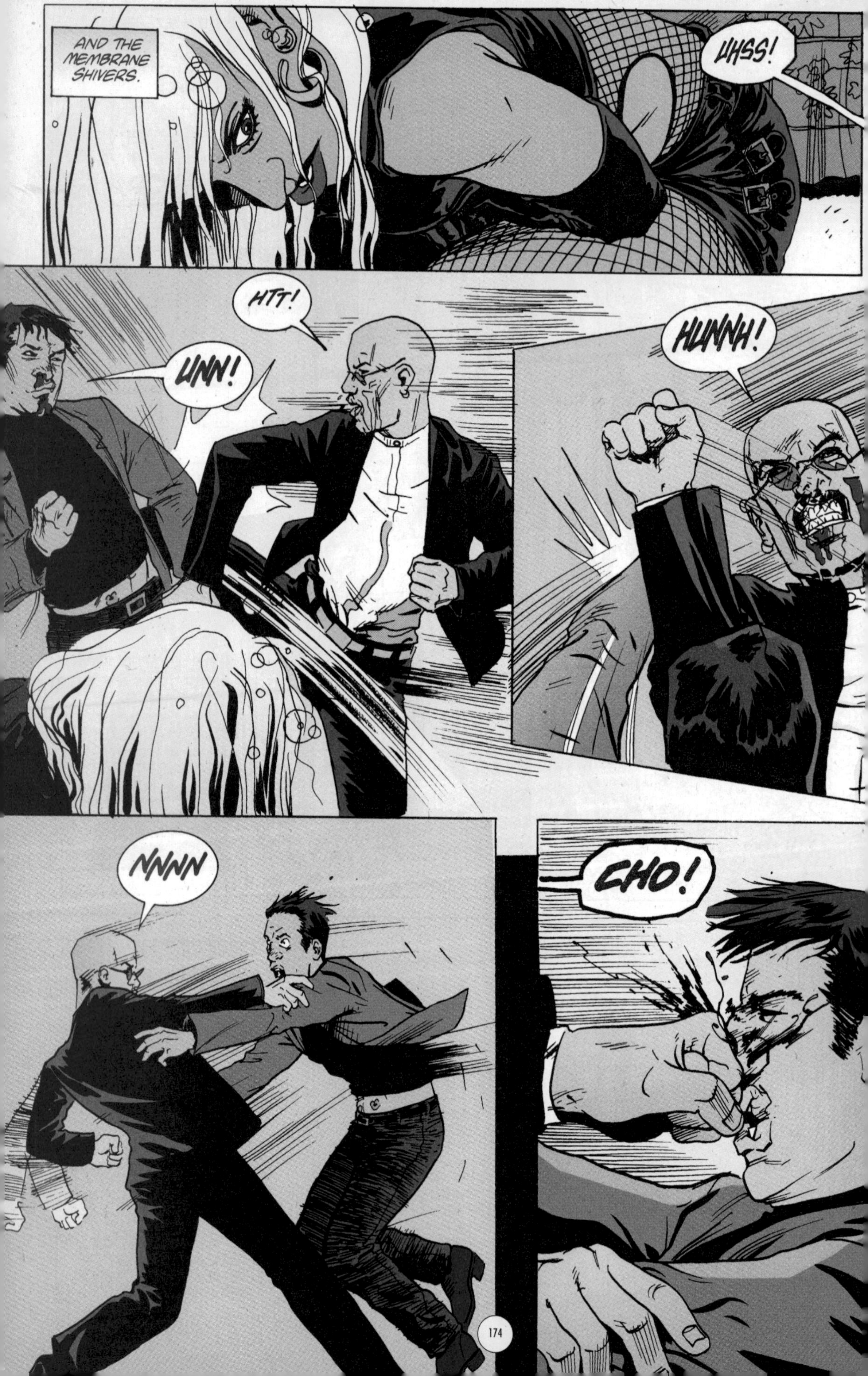
AND THE MEMBRANE SHIVERS.
UHSS!
HTT!
UNN!
HUNNH!
NNNN
CHO!

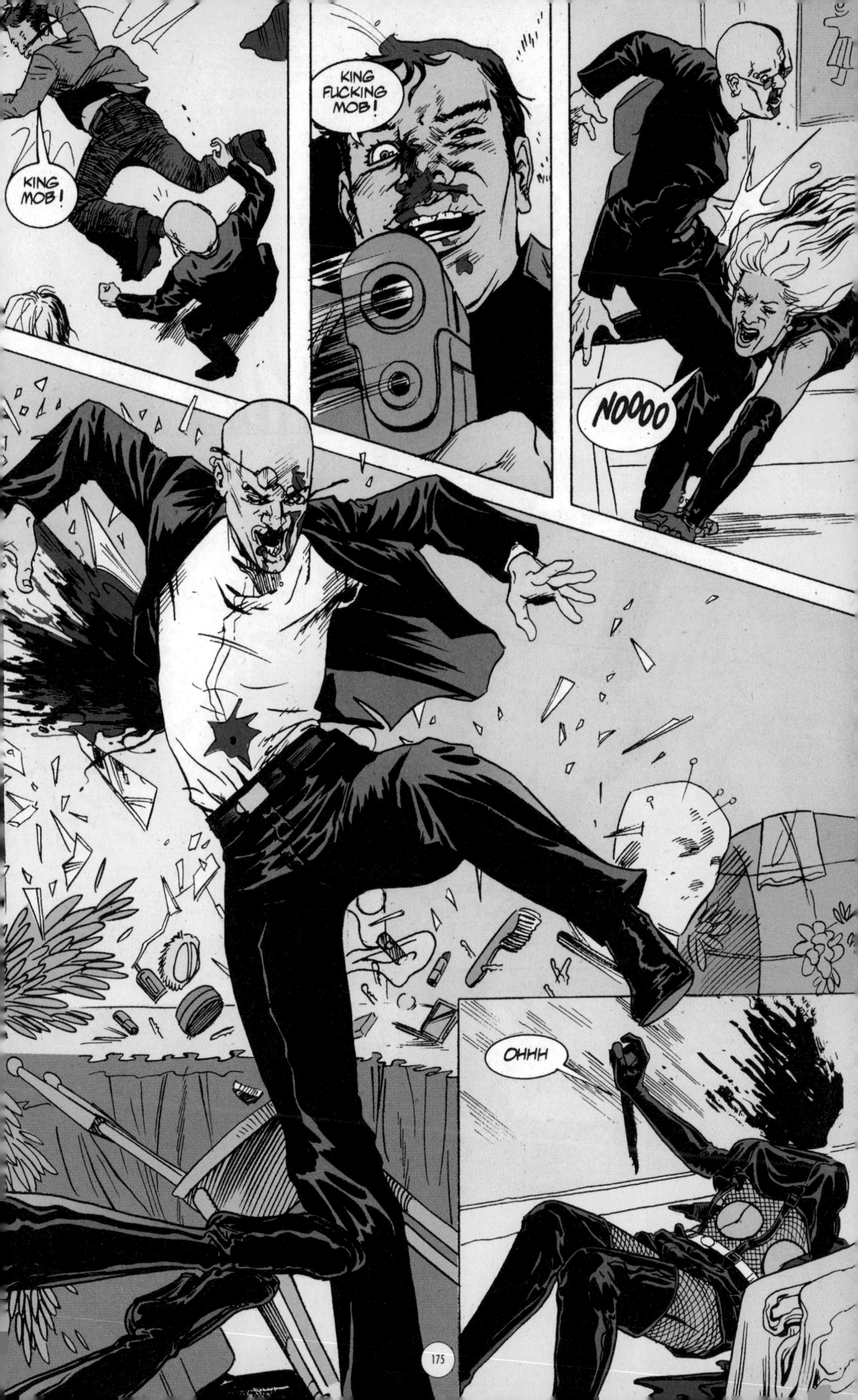
KING MOB!
KING FUCKING MOB!
NOOOO
OHHH

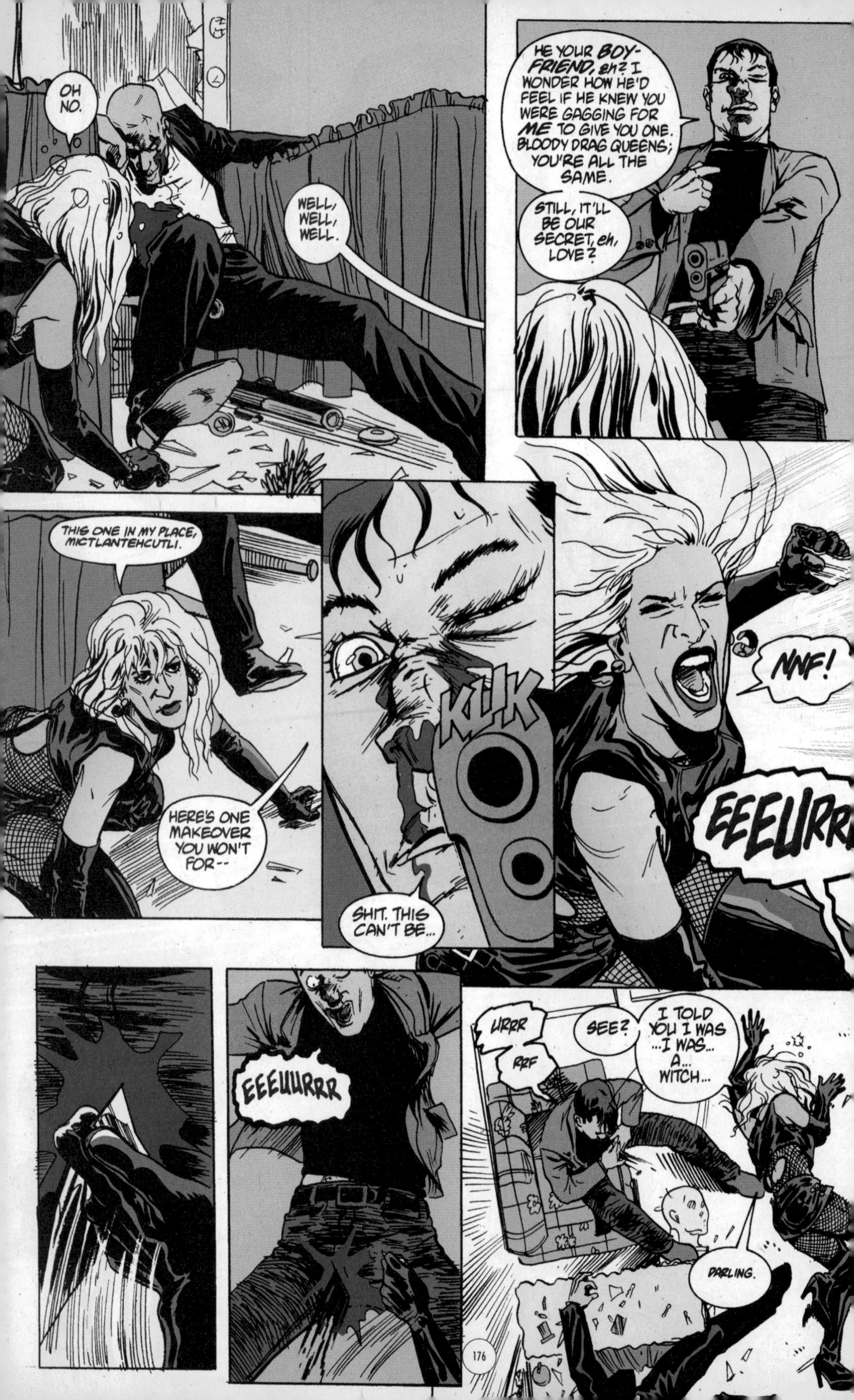
OH NO.
WELL, WELL, WELL.
HE YOUR BOY-FRIEND, eh? I WONDER HOW HE'D FEEL IF HE KNEW YOU WERE GAGGING FOR ME TO GIVE YOU ONE. BLOODY DRAG QUEENS; YOU'RE ALL THE SAME.
STILL, IT'LL BE OUR SECRET, eh, LOVE?
THIS ONE IN MY PLACE, MICTLANTEHCUTLI.
HERE'S ONE MAKEOVER YOU WON'T FOR--
KLIK
SHIT. THIS CAN'T BE...
NNF!
EEEURR
EEEUURRR
URRR
RRF
SEE?
I TOLD YOU I WAS ...I WAS... A... WITCH...
DARLING.

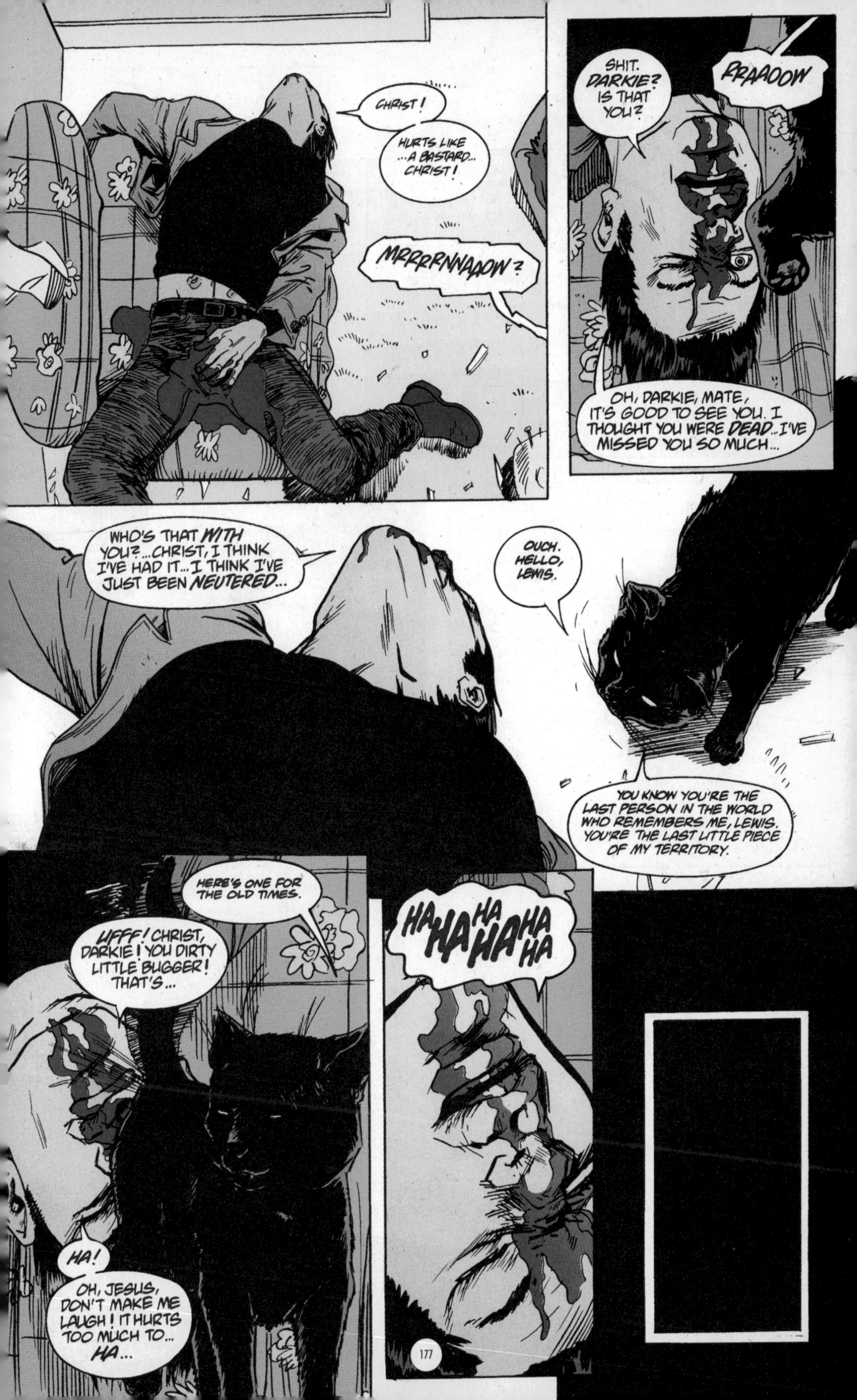
CHRIST!
HURTS LIKE ...A BASTARD... CHRIST!
MRRRRNNAAOW?
SHIT. DARKIE? IS THAT YOU?
RRAAOOW
OH, DARKIE, MATE, IT'S GOOD TO SEE YOU. I THOUGHT YOU WERE DEAD...I'VE MISSED YOU SO MUCH...
WHO'S THAT WITH YOU?...CHRIST, I THINK I'VE HAD IT...I THINK I'VE JUST BEEN NEUTERED...
OUCH. HELLO, LEWIS.
YOU KNOW YOU'RE THE LAST PERSON IN THE WORLD WHO REMEMBERS ME, LEWIS. YOU'RE THE LAST LITTLE PIECE OF MY TERRITORY.
HERE'S ONE FOR THE OLD TIMES.
UFFF! CHRIST, DARKIE! YOU DIRTY LITTLE BUGGER! THAT'S...
HA!
OH, JESUS, DON'T MAKE ME LAUGH! IT HURTS TOO MUCH TO... HA...
HA HA HA HA HA HA HA

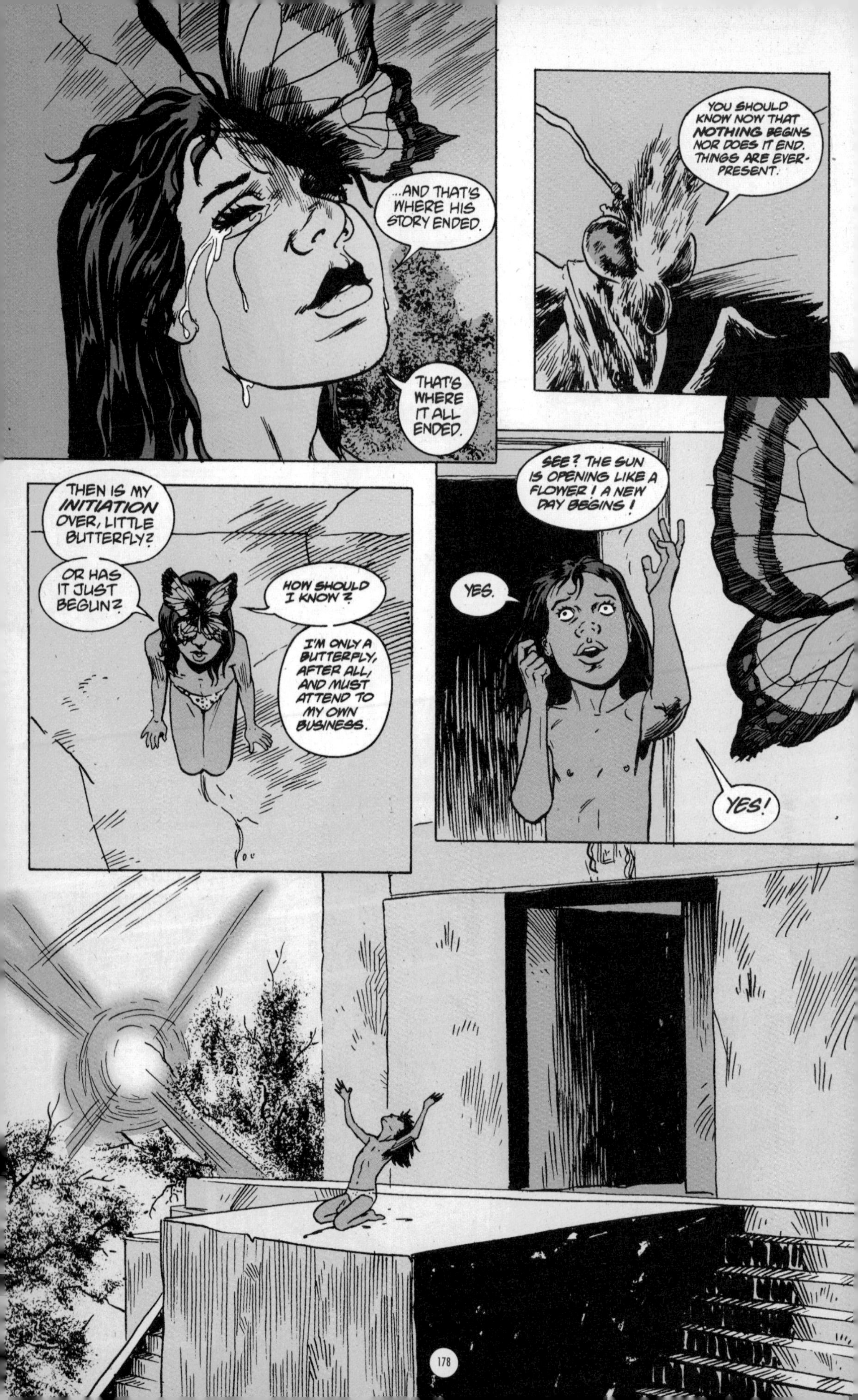
...AND THAT'S WHERE HIS STORY ENDED.
THAT'S WHERE IT ALL ENDED.
YOU SHOULD KNOW NOW THAT NOTHING BEGINS NOR DOES IT END. THINGS ARE EVER-PRESENT.
THEN IS MY INITIATION OVER, LITTLE BUTTERFLY?
OR HAS IT JUST BEGUN?
HOW SHOULD I KNOW?
I'M ONLY A BUTTERFLY, AFTER ALL, AND MUST ATTEND TO MY OWN BUSINESS.
SEE? THE SUN IS OPENING LIKE A FLOWER! A NEW DAY BEGINS!
YES.
YES!

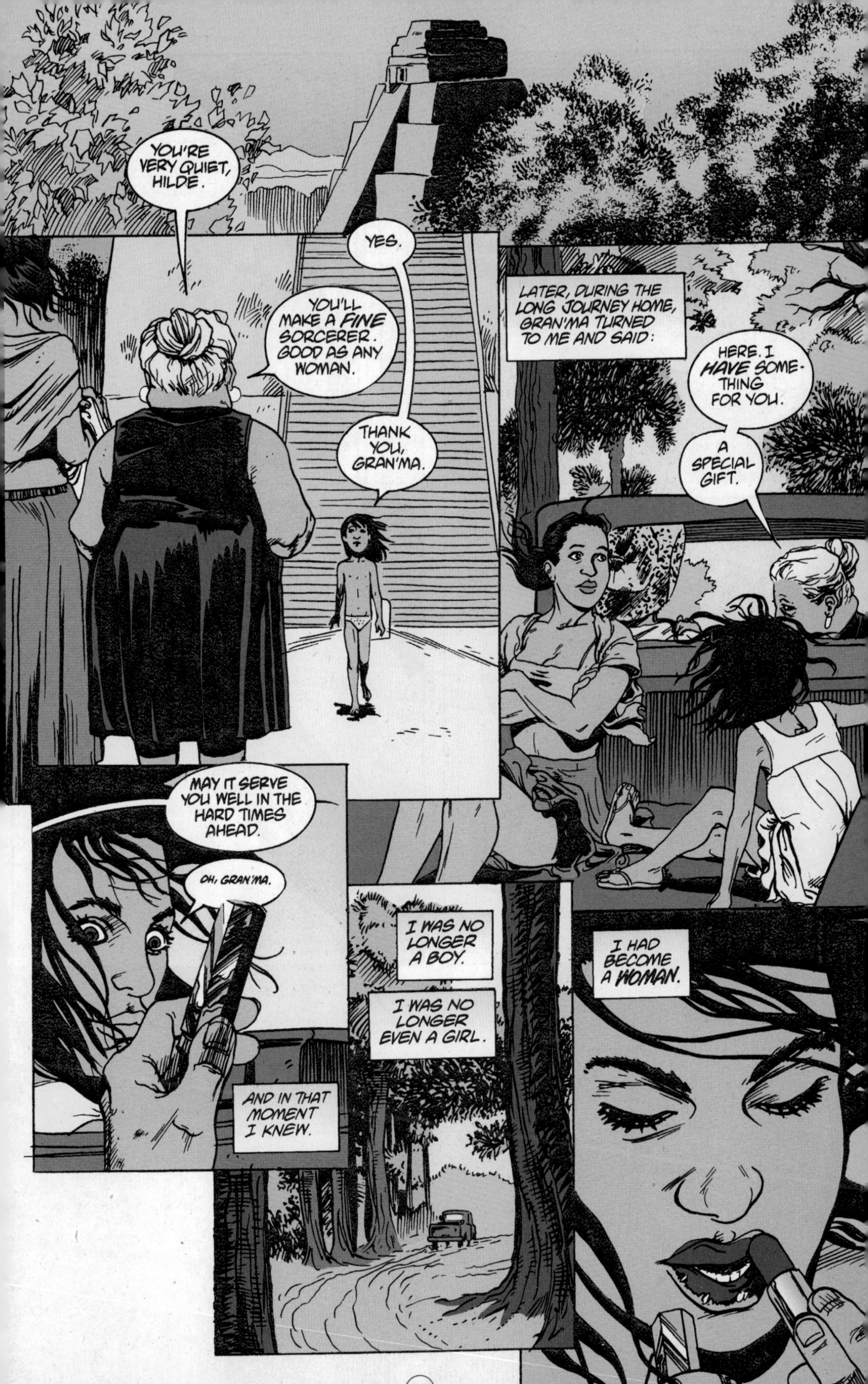
YOU'RE VERY QUIET, HILDE.
YES.
YOU'LL MAKE A FINE SORCERER. GOOD AS ANY WOMAN.
THANK YOU, GRAN'MA.
LATER, DURING THE LONG JOURNEY HOME, GRAN'MA TURNED TO ME AND SAID:
HERE. I HAVE SOMETHING FOR YOU.
A SPECIAL GIFT.
MAY IT SERVE YOU WELL IN THE HARD TIMES AHEAD.
OH, GRAN'MA.
AND IN THAT MOMENT I KNEW.
I WAS NO LONGER A BOY.
I WAS NO LONGER EVEN A GIRL.
I HAD BECOME A WOMAN.

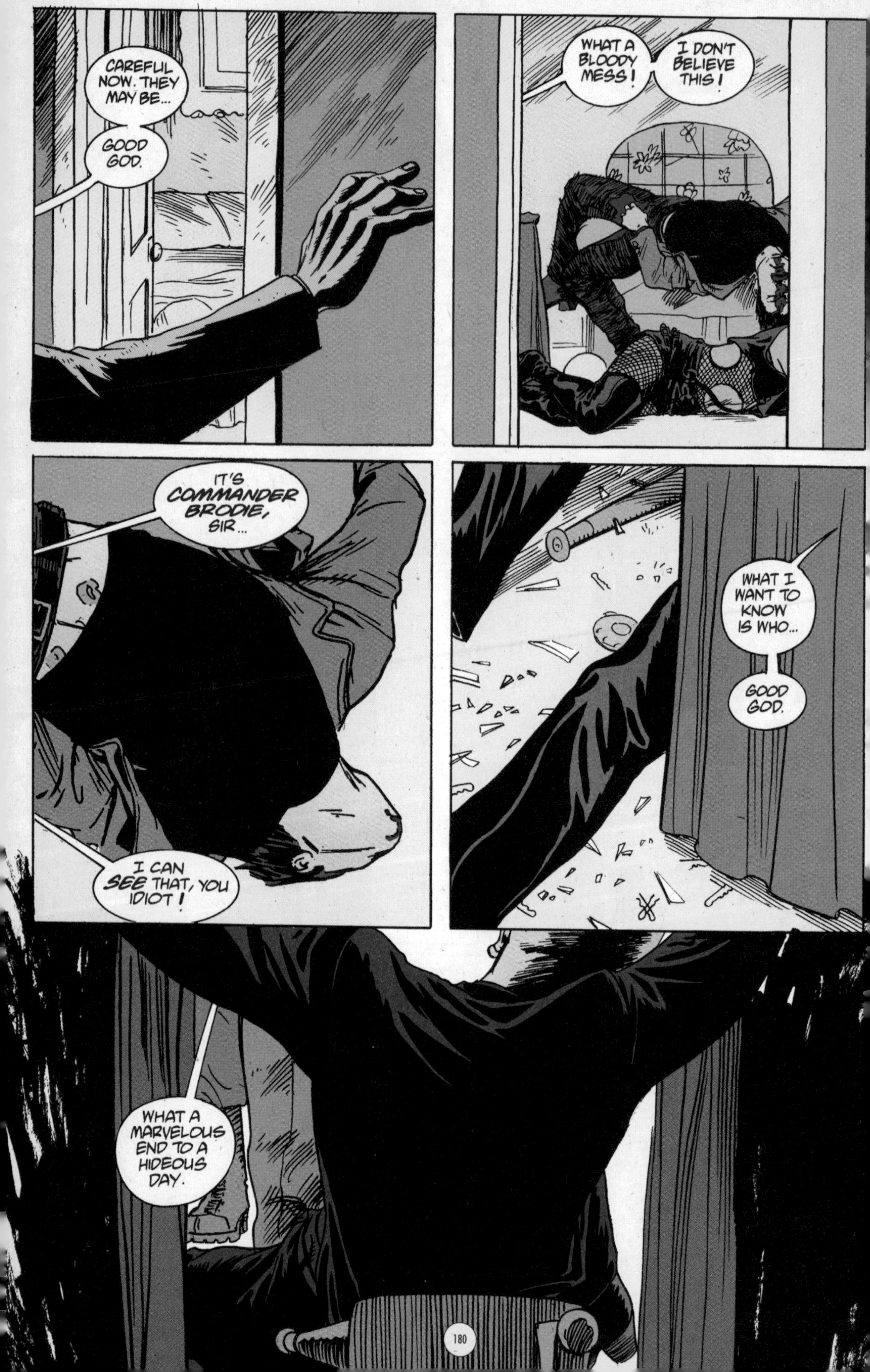
CAREFUL NOW. THEY MAY BE...
GOOD GOD.
WHAT A BLOODY MESS!
I DON'T BELIEVE THIS!
IT'S COMMANDER BRODIE, SIR...
I CAN SEE THAT, YOU IDIOT!
WHAT I WANT TO KNOW IS WHO...
GOOD GOD.
WHAT A MARVELOUS END TO A HIDEOUS DAY.

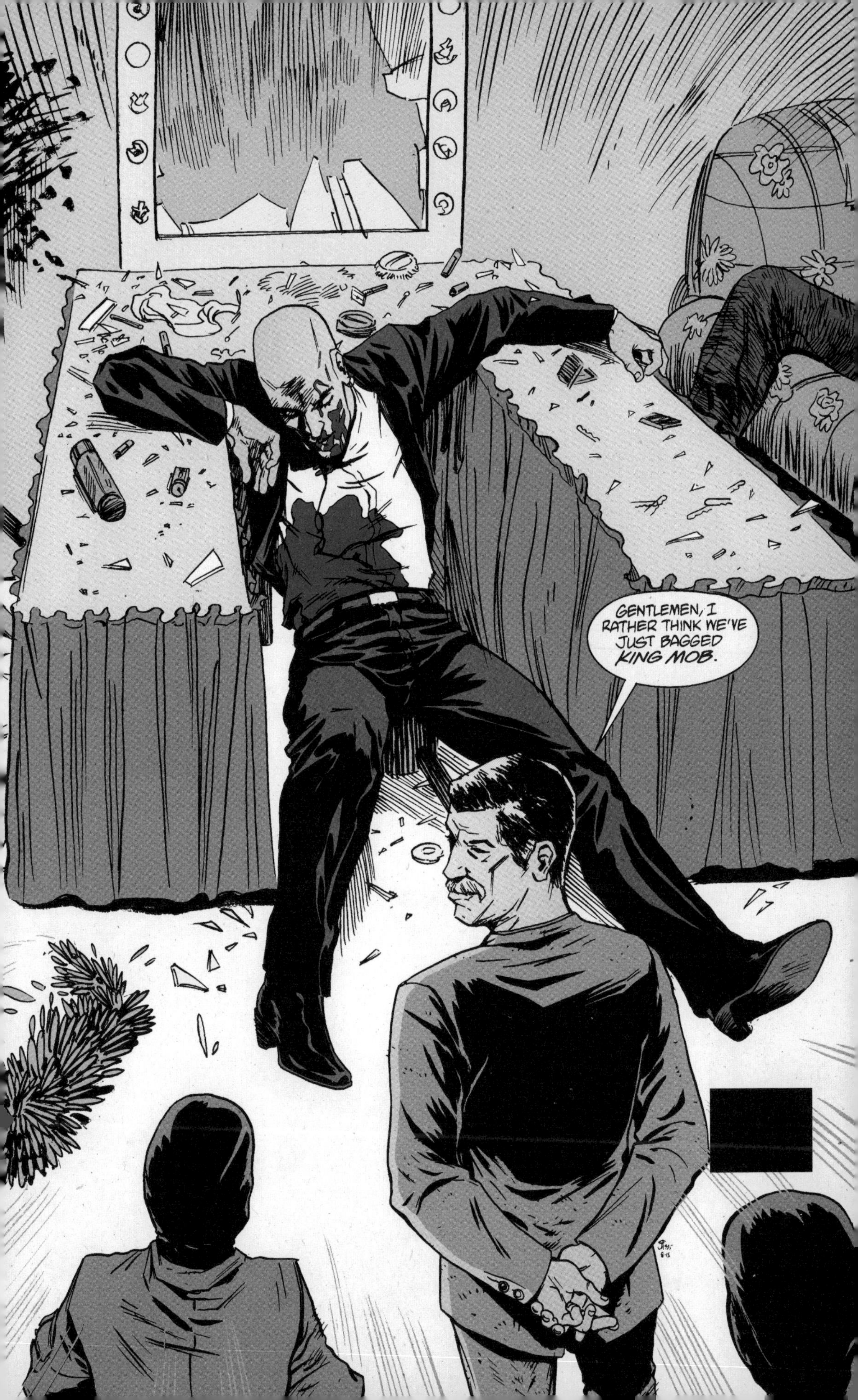
GENTLEMEN, I RATHER THINK WE'VE JUST BAGGED KING MOB.

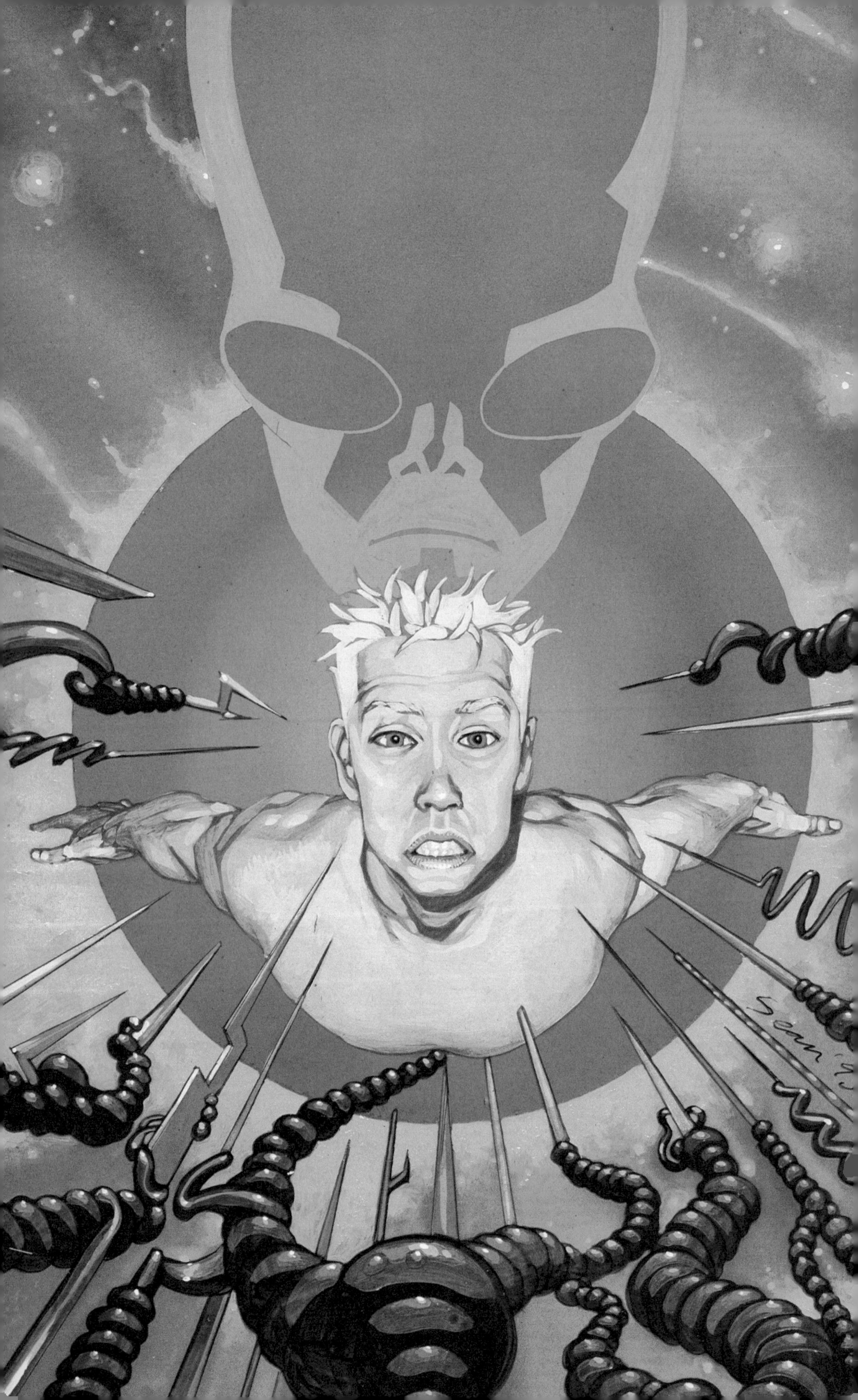

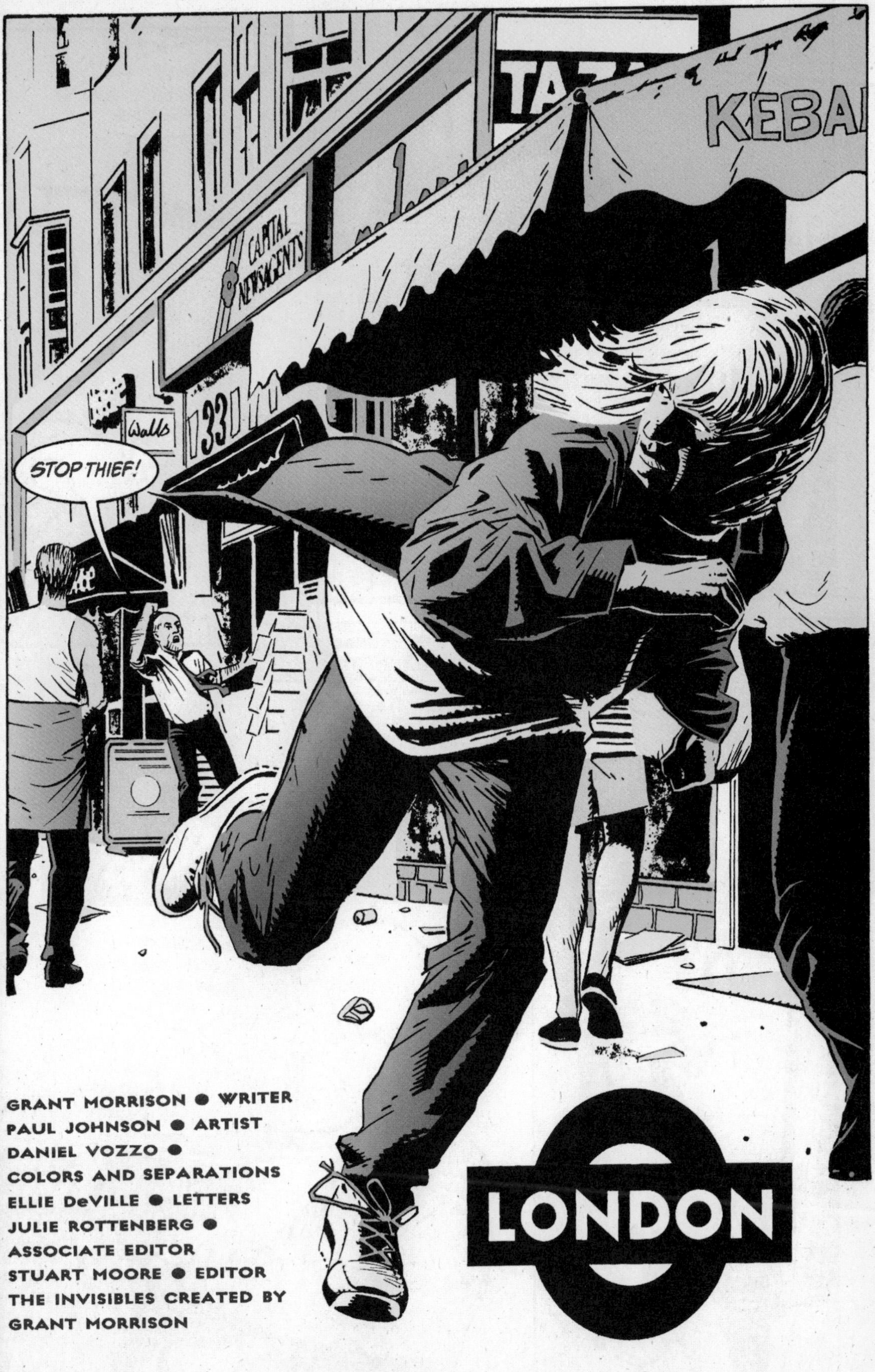
CAPITAL NEWSAGENTS
33
Walls
STOP THIEF!

GRANT MORRISON ● WRITER
PAUL JOHNSON ● ARTIST
DANIEL VOZZO ●
COLORS AND SEPARATIONS
ELLIE DeVILLE ● LETTERS
JULIE ROTTENBERG ●
ASSOCIATE EDITOR
STUART MOORE ● EDITOR
THE INVISIBLES CREATED BY
GRANT MORRISON

LONDON

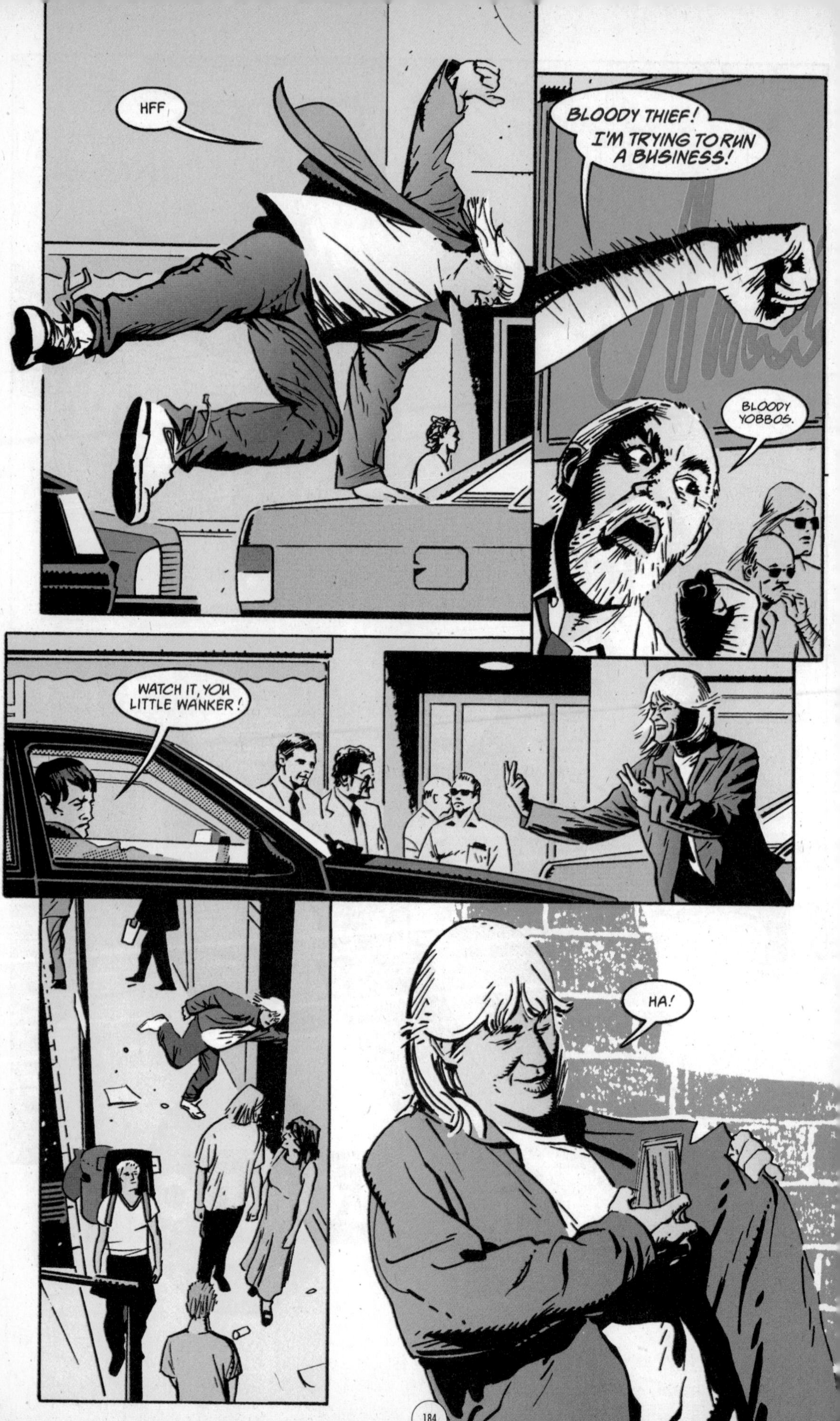
HFF
BLOODY THIEF! I'M TRYING TO RUN A BUSINESS!
BLOODY YOBBOS.
WATCH IT, YOU LITTLE WANKER!
HA!

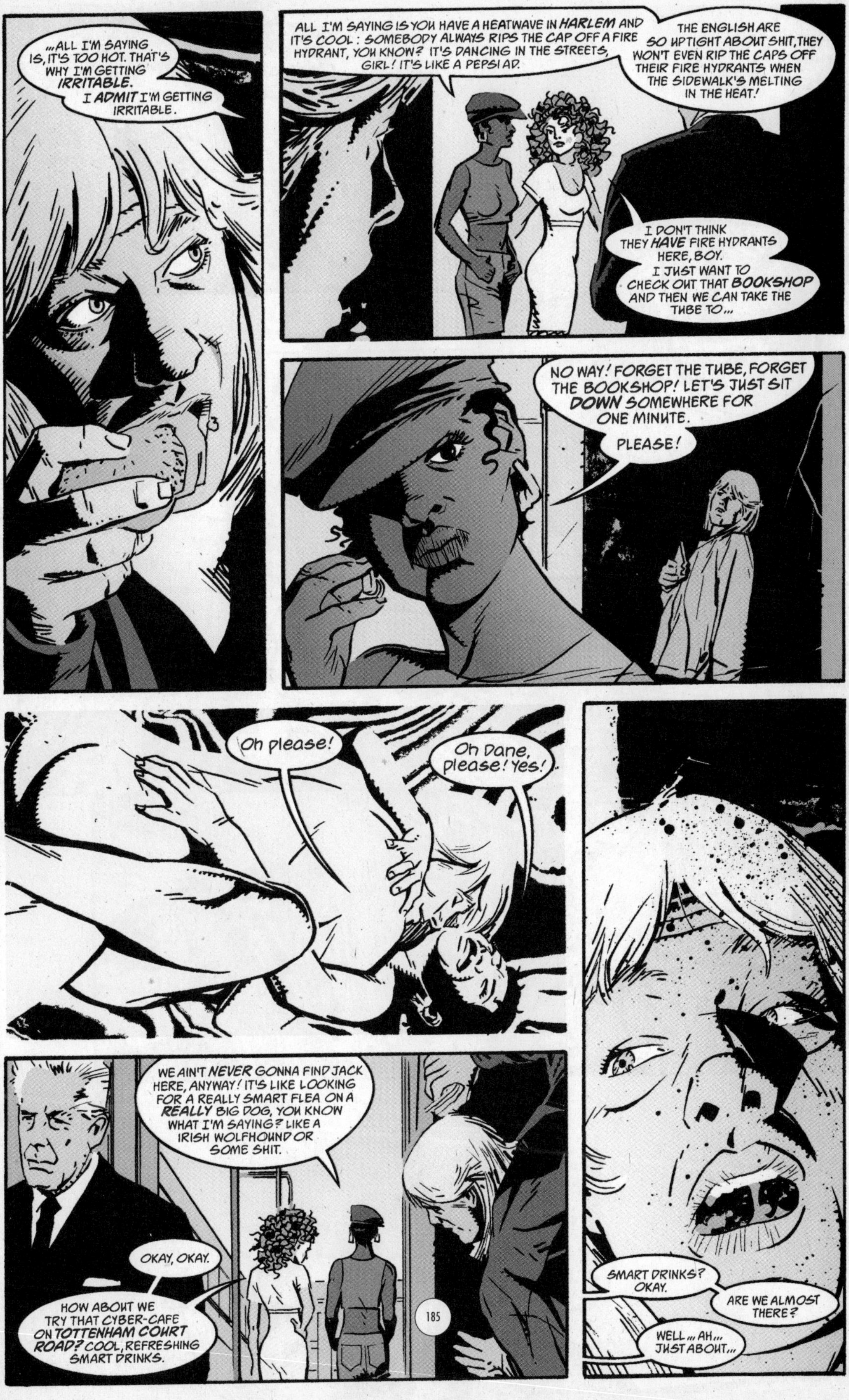

...ALL I'M SAYING IS, IT'S TOO HOT. THAT'S WHY I'M GETTING IRRITABLE.
I ADMIT I'M GETTING IRRITABLE.
ALL I'M SAYING IS YOU HAVE A HEATWAVE IN HARLEM AND IT'S COOL: SOMEBODY ALWAYS RIPS THE CAP OFF A FIRE HYDRANT, YOU KNOW? IT'S DANCING IN THE STREETS, GIRL! IT'S LIKE A PEPSI AD.
THE ENGLISH ARE SO UPTIGHT ABOUT SHIT, THEY WON'T EVEN RIP THE CAPS OFF THEIR FIRE HYDRANTS WHEN THE SIDEWALK'S MELTING IN THE HEAT!
I DON'T THINK THEY HAVE FIRE HYDRANTS HERE, BOY.
I JUST WANT TO CHECK OUT THAT BOOKSHOP AND THEN WE CAN TAKE THE TUBE TO...
NO WAY! FORGET THE TUBE, FORGET THE BOOKSHOP! LET'S JUST SIT DOWN SOMEWHERE FOR ONE MINUTE.
PLEASE!
Oh please!
Oh Dane, please! Yes!
WE AIN'T NEVER GONNA FIND JACK HERE, ANYWAY! IT'S LIKE LOOKING FOR A REALLY SMART FLEA ON A REALLY BIG DOG, YOU KNOW WHAT I'M SAYING? LIKE A IRISH WOLFHOUND OR SOME SHIT.
OKAY, OKAY.
HOW ABOUT WE TRY THAT CYBER-CAFE ON TOTTENHAM COURT ROAD? COOL, REFRESHING SMART DRINKS.
SMART DRINKS? OKAY.
ARE WE ALMOST THERE?
WELL... AH... JUST ABOUT...

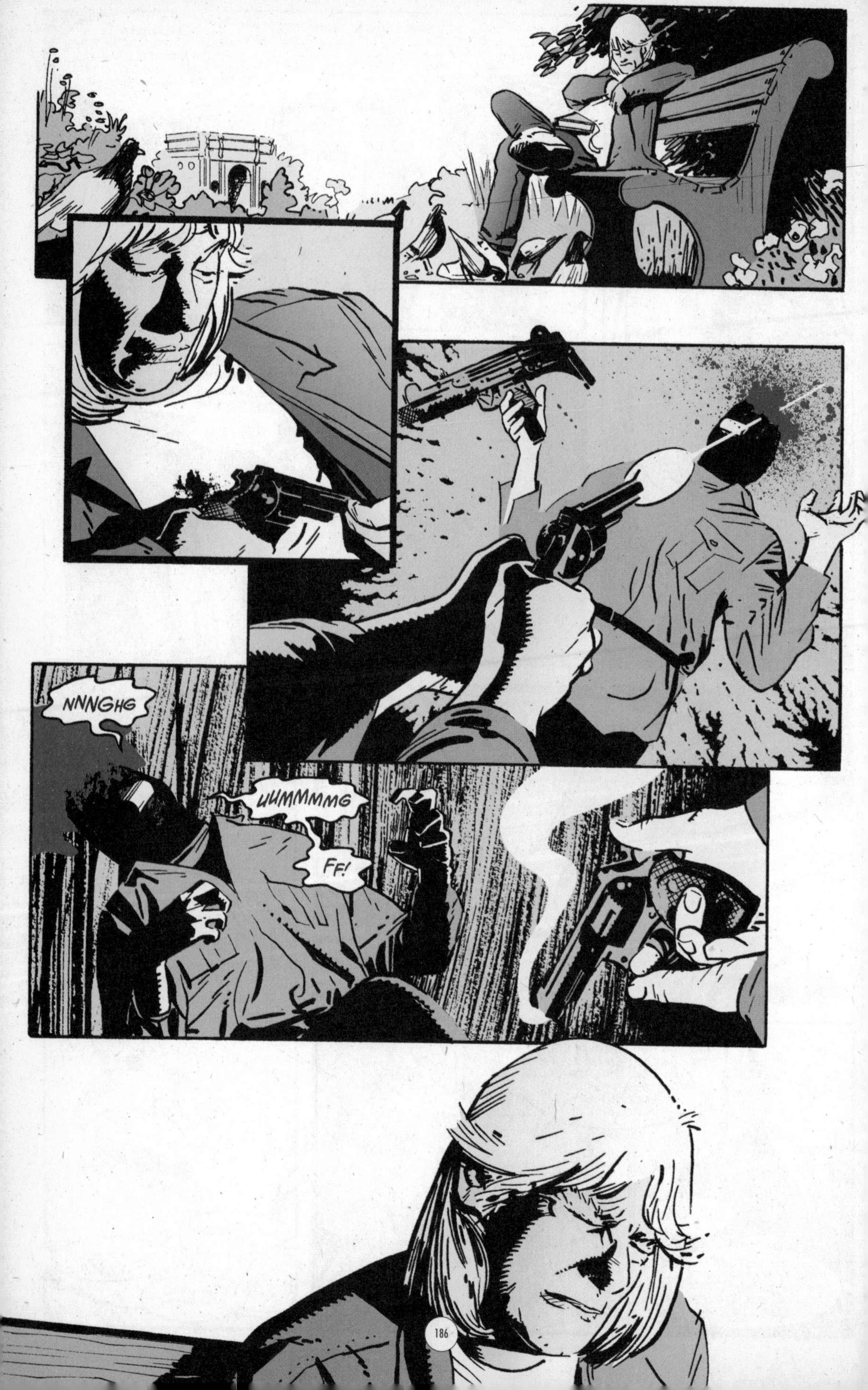
NNNGHG
UUMMMMG
FF!

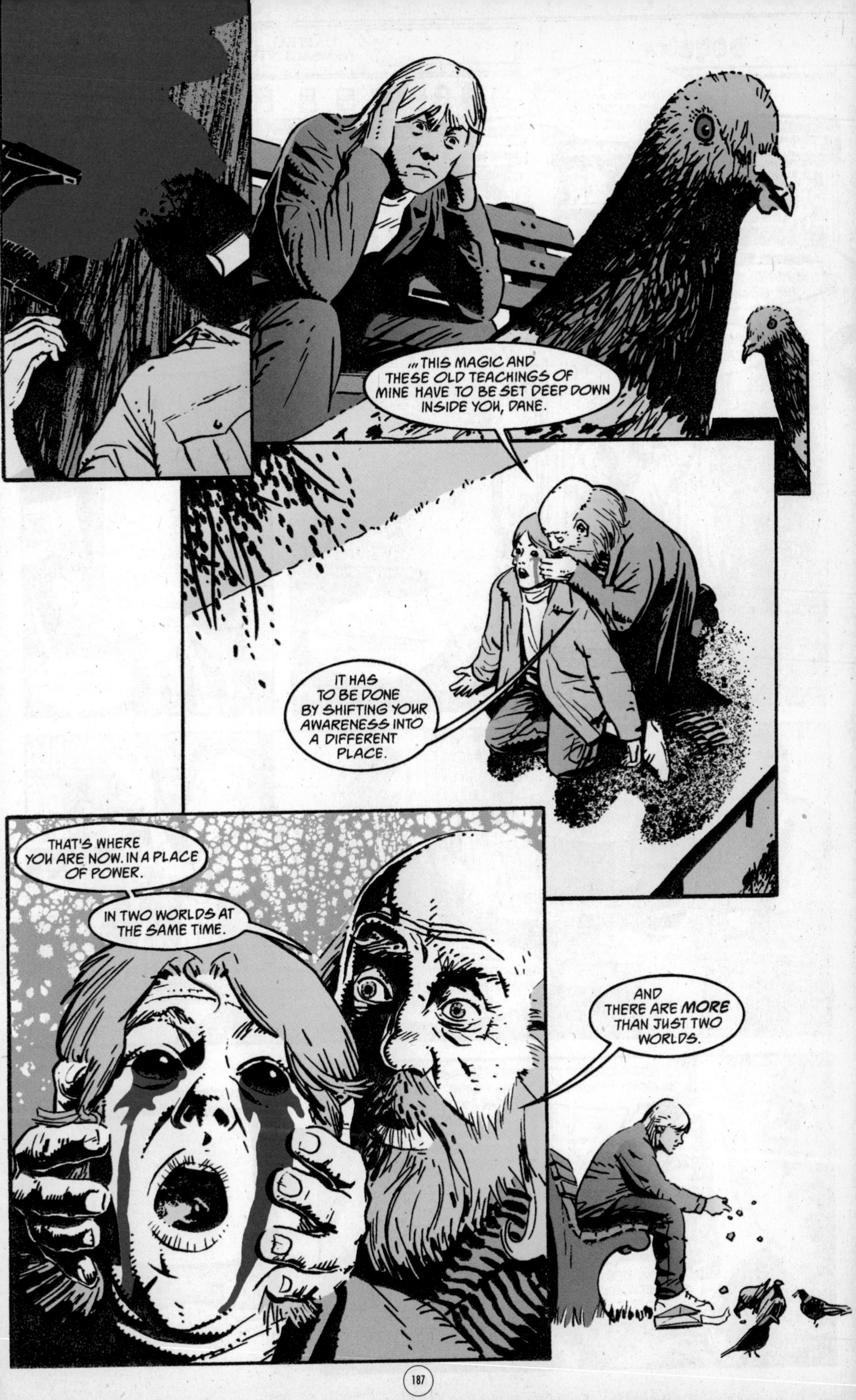
...THIS MAGIC AND THESE OLD TEACHINGS OF MINE HAVE TO BE SET DEEP DOWN INSIDE YOU, DANE.
IT HAS TO BE DONE BY SHIFTING YOUR AWARENESS INTO A DIFFERENT PLACE.
THAT'S WHERE YOU ARE NOW. IN A PLACE OF POWER.
IN TWO WORLDS AT THE SAME TIME.
AND THERE ARE MORE THAN JUST TWO WORLDS.

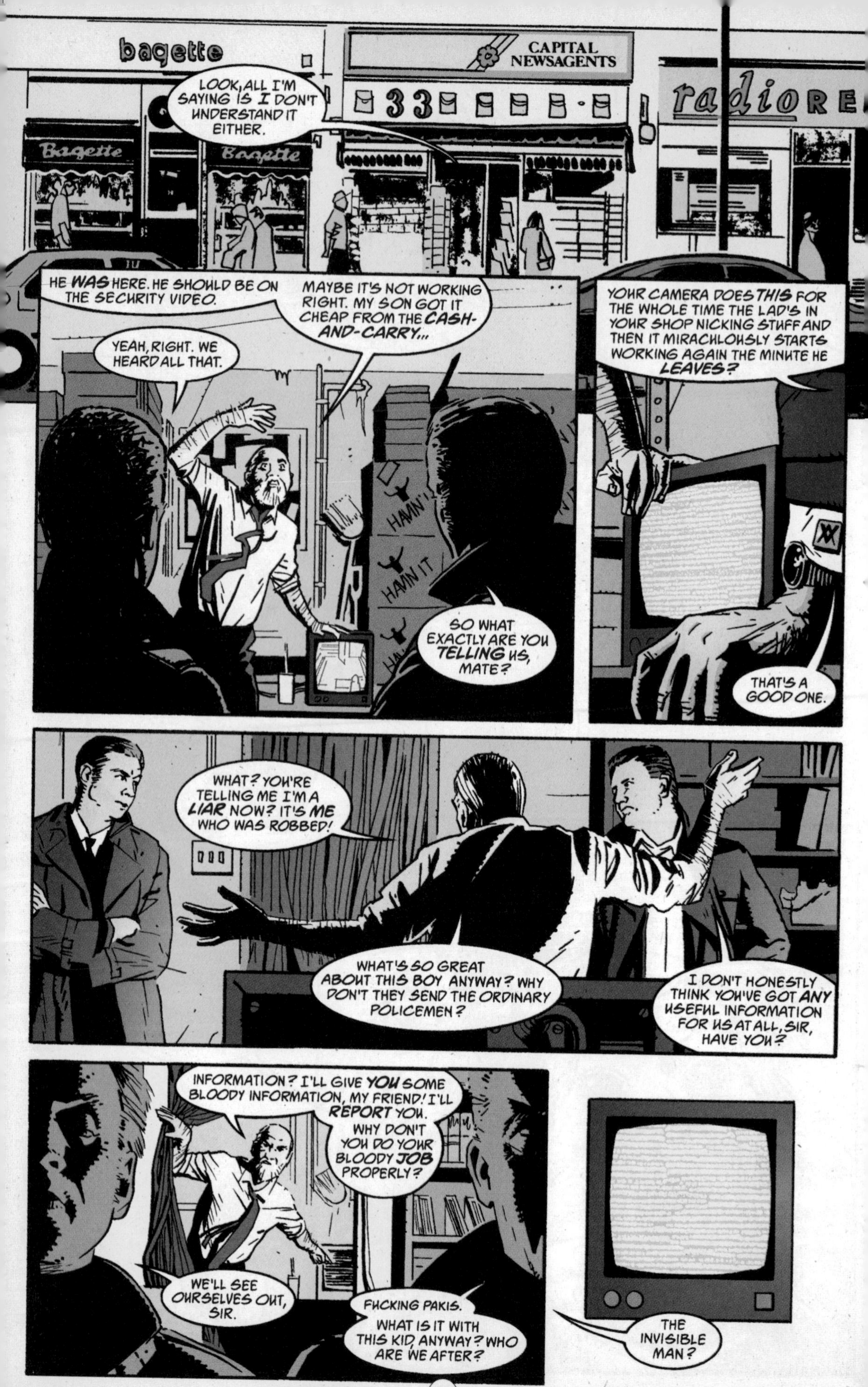

bagette
CAPITAL NEWSAGENTS
33
radiore
LOOK, ALL I'M SAYING IS I DON'T UNDERSTAND IT EITHER.
Bagette
HE WAS HERE. HE SHOULD BE ON THE SECURITY VIDEO.
MAYBE IT'S NOT WORKING RIGHT. MY SON GOT IT CHEAP FROM THE CASH-AND-CARRY...
YEAH, RIGHT. WE HEARD ALL THAT.
SO WHAT EXACTLY ARE YOU TELLING US, MATE?
HAVIN'
HAVIN IT
YOUR CAMERA DOES THIS FOR THE WHOLE TIME THE LAD'S IN YOUR SHOP NICKING STUFF AND THEN IT MIRACULOUSLY STARTS WORKING AGAIN THE MINUTE HE LEAVES?
THAT'S A GOOD ONE.
WHAT? YOU'RE TELLING ME I'M A LIAR NOW? IT'S ME WHO WAS ROBBED!
WHAT'S SO GREAT ABOUT THIS BOY ANYWAY? WHY DON'T THEY SEND THE ORDINARY POLICEMEN?
I DON'T HONESTLY THINK YOU'VE GOT ANY USEFUL INFORMATION FOR US AT ALL, SIR, HAVE YOU?
INFORMATION? I'LL GIVE YOU SOME BLOODY INFORMATION, MY FRIEND! I'LL REPORT YOU.
WHY DON'T YOU DO YOUR BLOODY JOB PROPERLY?
WE'LL SEE OURSELVES OUT, SIR.
FUCKING PAKIS.
WHAT IS IT WITH THIS KID ANYWAY? WHO ARE WE AFTER?
THE INVISIBLE MAN?

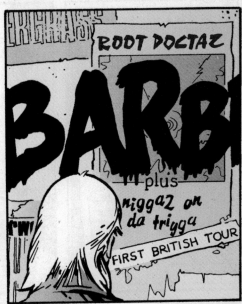

ROOT DOCTAZ

BARB

plus

niggaz on
da trigga

FIRST BRITISH TOUR

BARBELiTH

Pulp

underworld

plt

nigg
da

'At This Stage I Couldn't Say

YOU'LL
REMEMBER EVERY-
THING WHEN THE TIME
IS RIGHT.

WHAT?

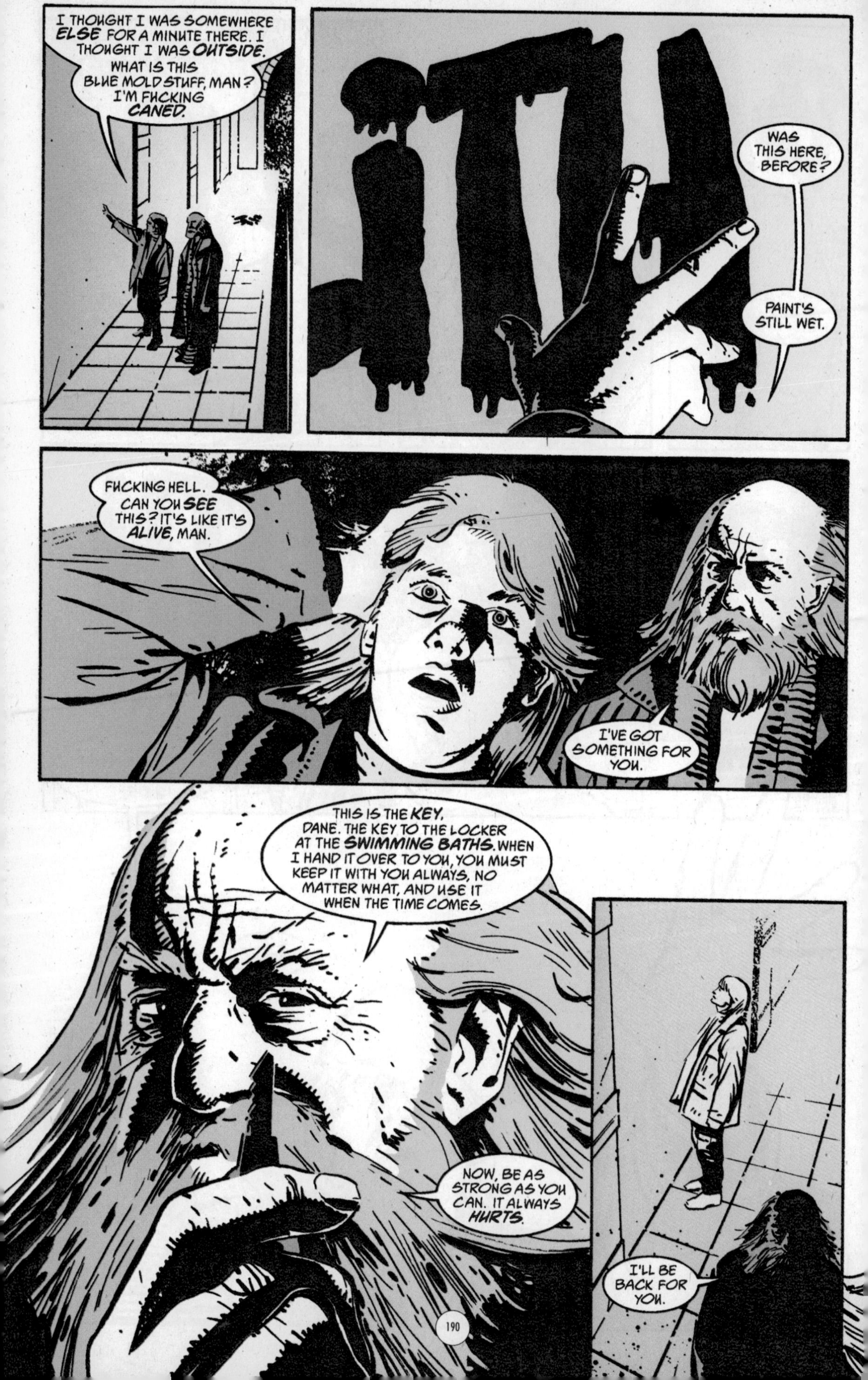
I THOUGHT I WAS SOMEWHERE ELSE FOR A MINUTE THERE. I THOUGHT I WAS OUTSIDE. WHAT IS THIS BLUE MOLD STUFF, MAN? I'M FUCKING CANED.
WAS THIS HERE, BEFORE?
PAINT'S STILL WET.
FUCKING HELL. CAN YOU SEE THIS? IT'S LIKE IT'S ALIVE, MAN.
I'VE GOT SOMETHING FOR YOU.
THIS IS THE KEY, DANE. THE KEY TO THE LOCKER AT THE SWIMMING BATHS. WHEN I HAND IT OVER TO YOU, YOU MUST KEEP IT WITH YOU ALWAYS, NO MATTER WHAT, AND USE IT WHEN THE TIME COMES.
NOW, BE AS STRONG AS YOU CAN. IT ALWAYS HURTS.
I'LL BE BACK FOR YOU.

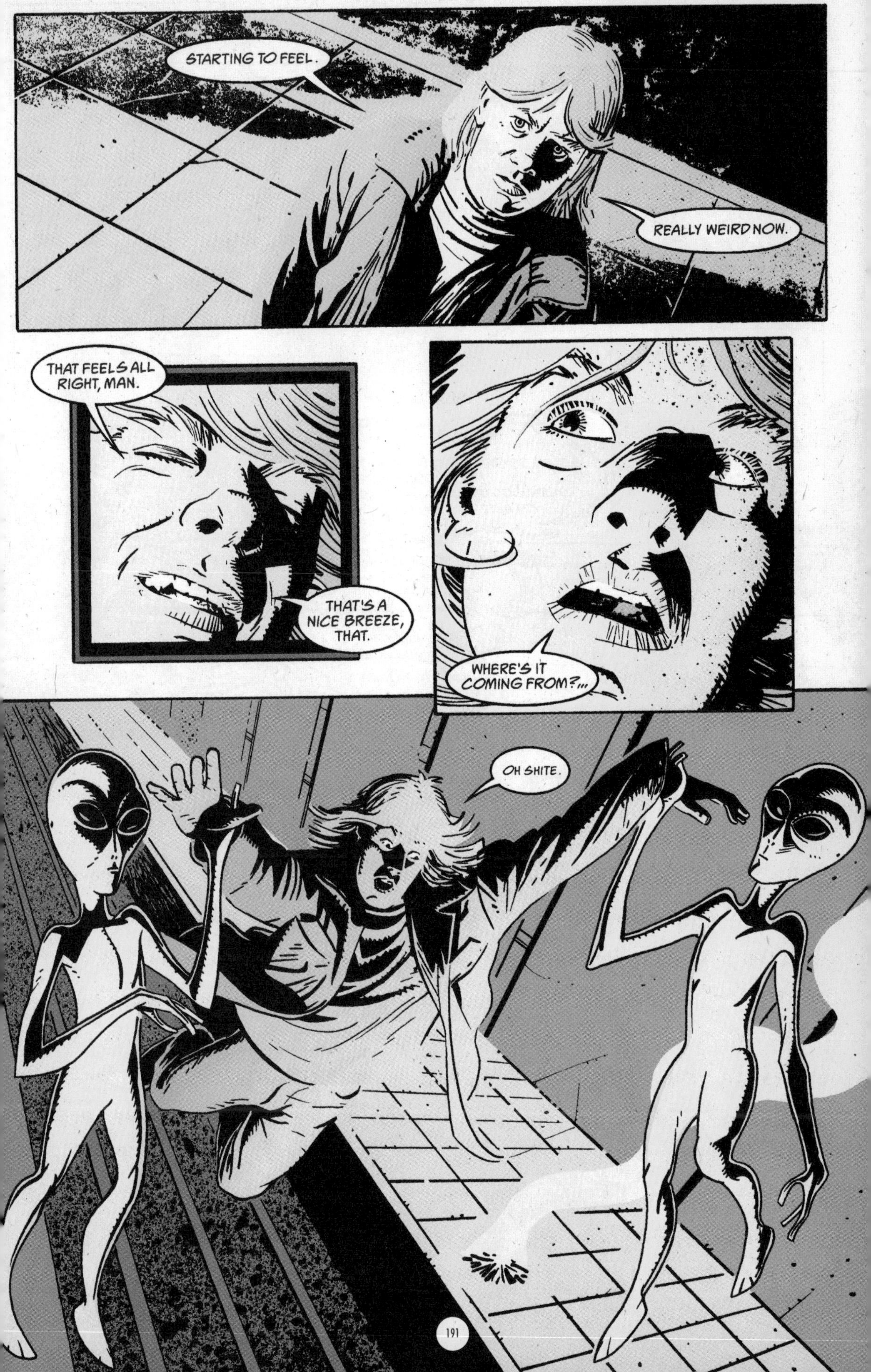
STARTING TO FEEL.
REALLY WEIRD NOW.
THAT FEELS ALL RIGHT, MAN.
THAT'S A NICE BREEZE, THAT.
WHERE'S IT COMING FROM?...
OH SHITE.

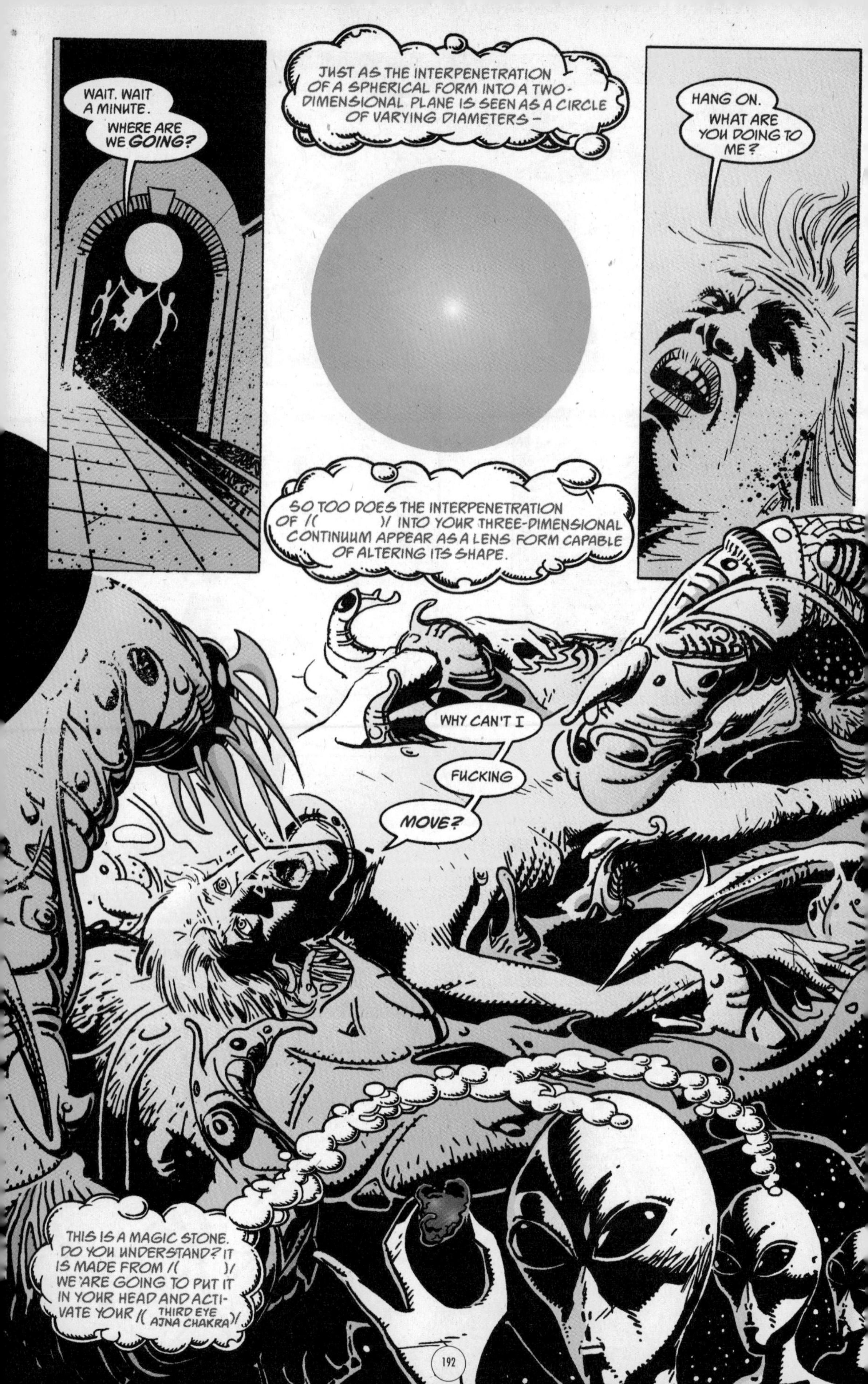
WAIT. WAIT A MINUTE.
WHERE ARE WE GOING?
JUST AS THE INTERPENETRATION OF A SPHERICAL FORM INTO A TWO-DIMENSIONAL PLANE IS SEEN AS A CIRCLE OF VARYING DIAMETERS –
HANG ON.
WHAT ARE YOU DOING TO ME?
SO TOO DOES THE INTERPENETRATION OF //( )// INTO YOUR THREE-DIMENSIONAL CONTINUUM APPEAR AS A LENS FORM CAPABLE OF ALTERING ITS SHAPE.
WHY CAN'T I
FUCKING
MOVE?
THIS IS A MAGIC STONE. DO YOU UNDERSTAND? IT IS MADE FROM //( )// WE ARE GOING TO PUT IT IN YOUR HEAD AND ACTIVATE YOUR //(THIRD EYE AJNA CHAKRA)//

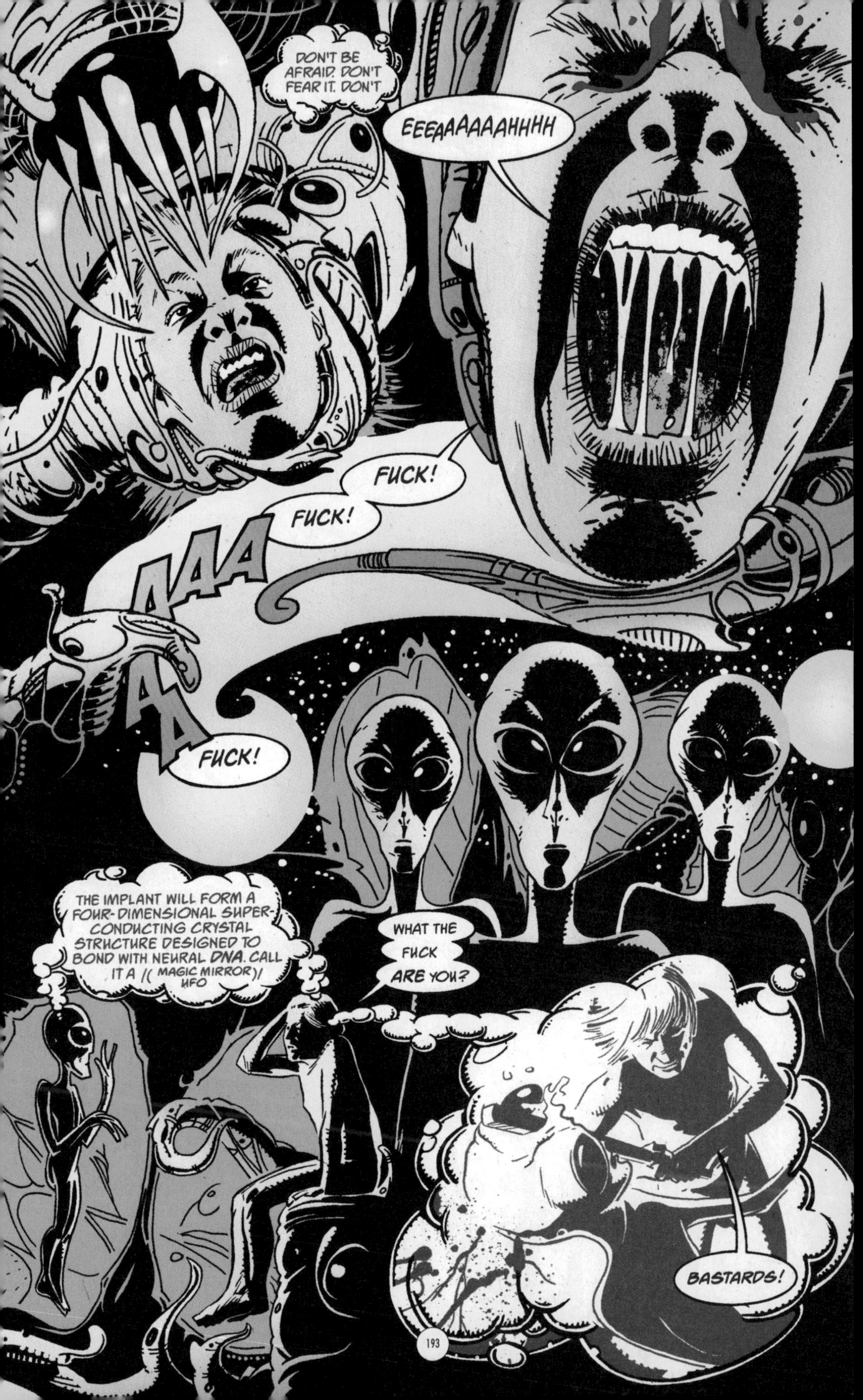
DON'T BE AFRAID. DON'T FEAR IT. DON'T
EEEAAAAAAHHHH
FUCK!
FUCK!
AAA
AA
FUCK!
THE IMPLANT WILL FORM A FOUR-DIMENSIONAL SUPER-CONDUCTING CRYSTAL STRUCTURE DESIGNED TO BOND WITH NEURAL DNA. CALL IT A ((MAGIC MIRROR UFO))
WHAT THE FUCK ARE YOU?
BASTARDS!

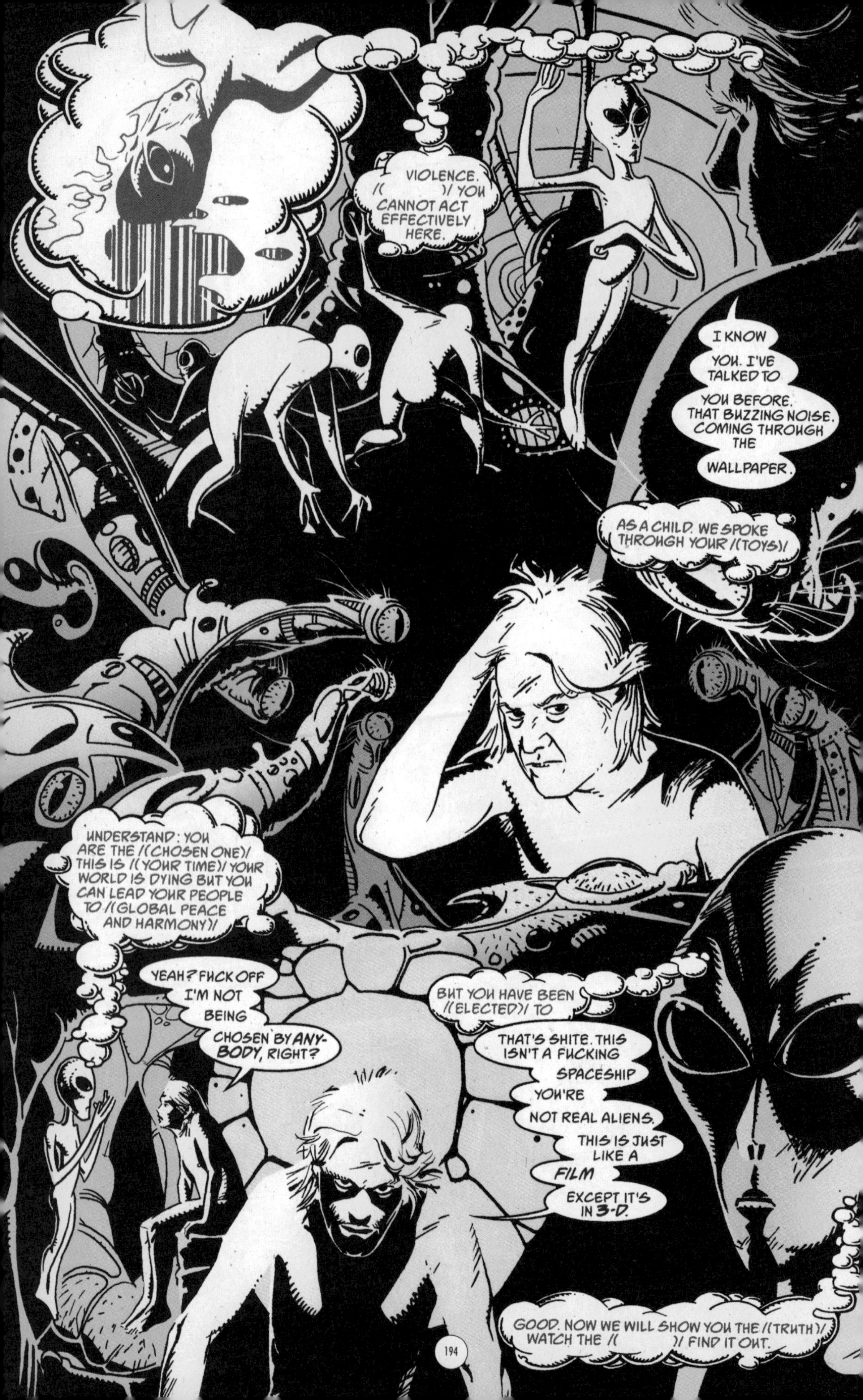
VIOLENCE. /( )/ YOU CANNOT ACT EFFECTIVELY HERE.
I KNOW
YOU. I'VE TALKED TO
YOU BEFORE. THAT BUZZING NOISE. COMING THROUGH THE
WALLPAPER.
AS A CHILD. WE SPOKE THROUGH YOUR /(TOYS)/
UNDERSTAND: YOU ARE THE /(CHOSEN ONE)/ THIS IS /(YOUR TIME)/ YOUR WORLD IS DYING BUT YOU CAN LEAD YOUR PEOPLE TO /(GLOBAL PEACE AND HARMONY)/
YEAH? FUCK OFF
I'M NOT
BEING
CHOSEN BY ANY-BODY, RIGHT?
BUT YOU HAVE BEEN /(ELECTED)/ TO
THAT'S SHITE. THIS ISN'T A FUCKING
SPACESHIP
YOU'RE
NOT REAL ALIENS.
THIS IS JUST LIKE A
FILM
EXCEPT IT'S IN 3-D.
GOOD. NOW WE WILL SHOW YOU THE /(TRUTH)/ WATCH THE /( )/ FIND IT OUT.

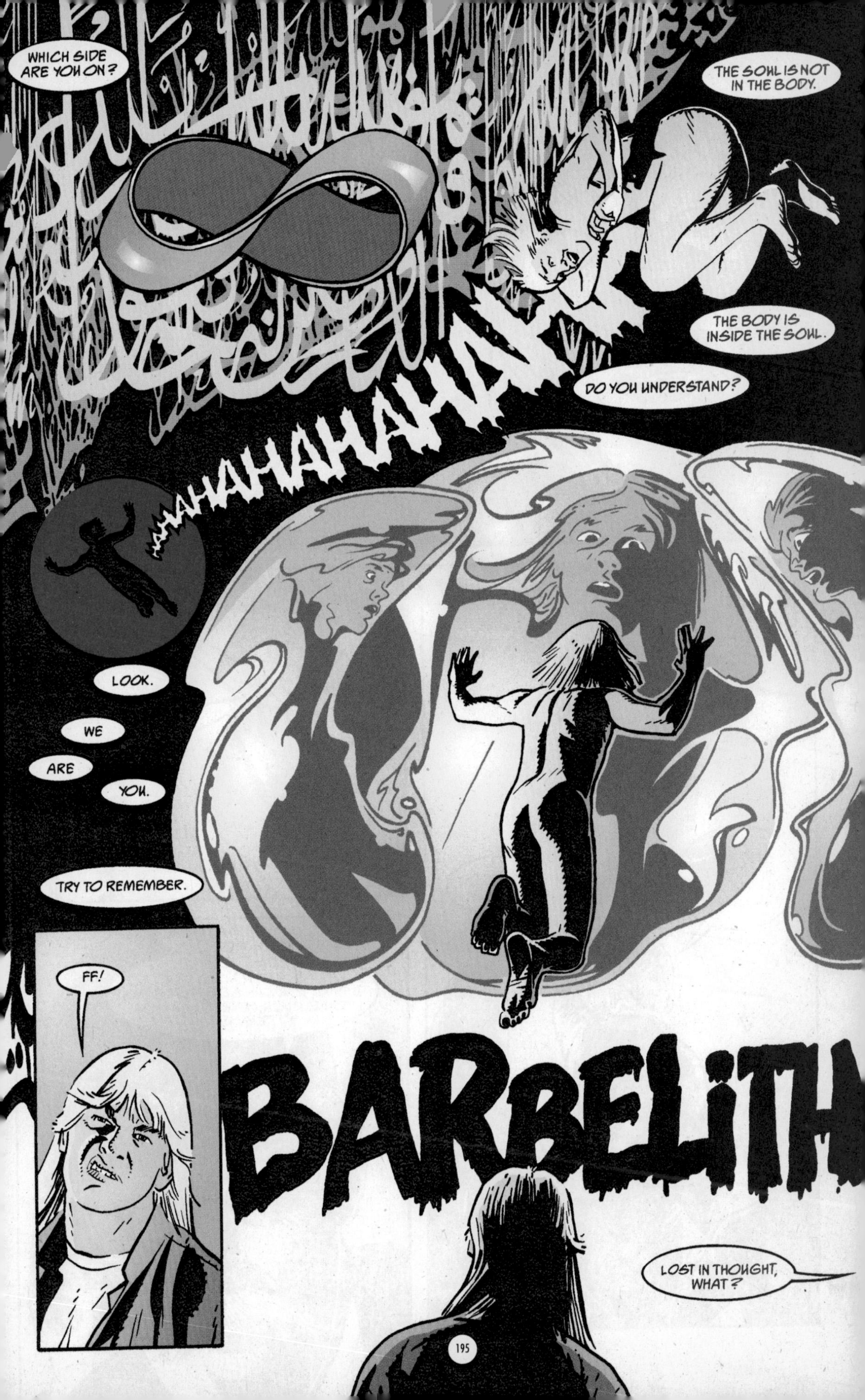
WHICH SIDE ARE YOU ON?
THE SOUL IS NOT IN THE BODY.
THE BODY IS INSIDE THE SOUL.
DO YOU UNDERSTAND?
HAHAHAHAHAHAHAHA
LOOK.
WE
ARE
YOU.
TRY TO REMEMBER.
FF!
BARBELITH
LOST IN THOUGHT, WHAT?

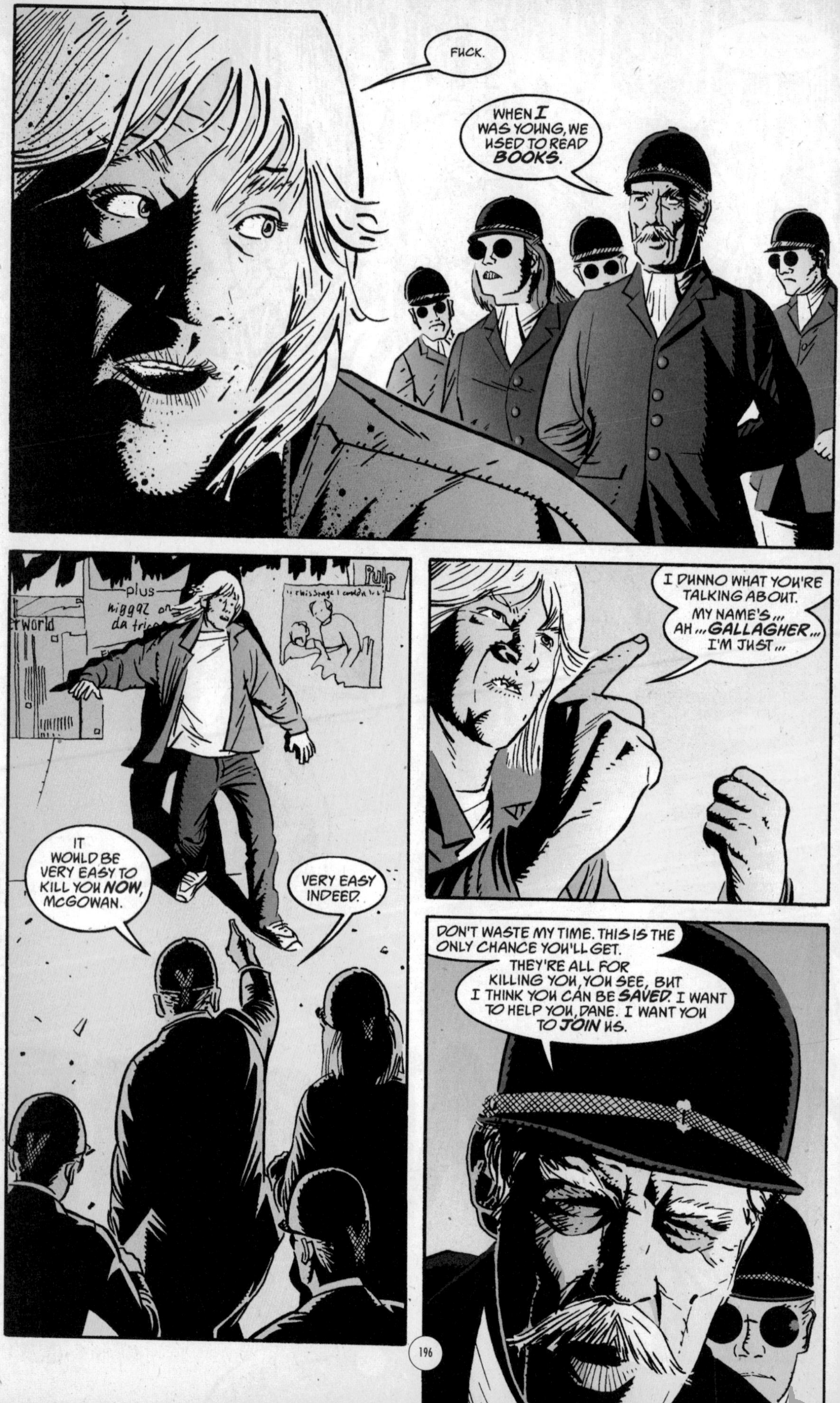

FUCK.
WHEN *I* WAS YOUNG, WE USED TO READ **BOOKS**.
plus
IT WOULD BE VERY EASY TO KILL YOU **NOW**, McGOWAN.
VERY EASY INDEED.
I DUNNO WHAT YOU'RE TALKING ABOUT. MY NAME'S... AH... **GALLAGHER**... I'M JUST...
DON'T WASTE MY TIME. THIS IS THE ONLY CHANCE YOU'LL GET.
THEY'RE ALL FOR KILLING YOU, YOU SEE, BUT I THINK YOU CAN BE ***SAVED***. I WANT TO HELP YOU, DANE. I WANT YOU TO ***JOIN*** US.

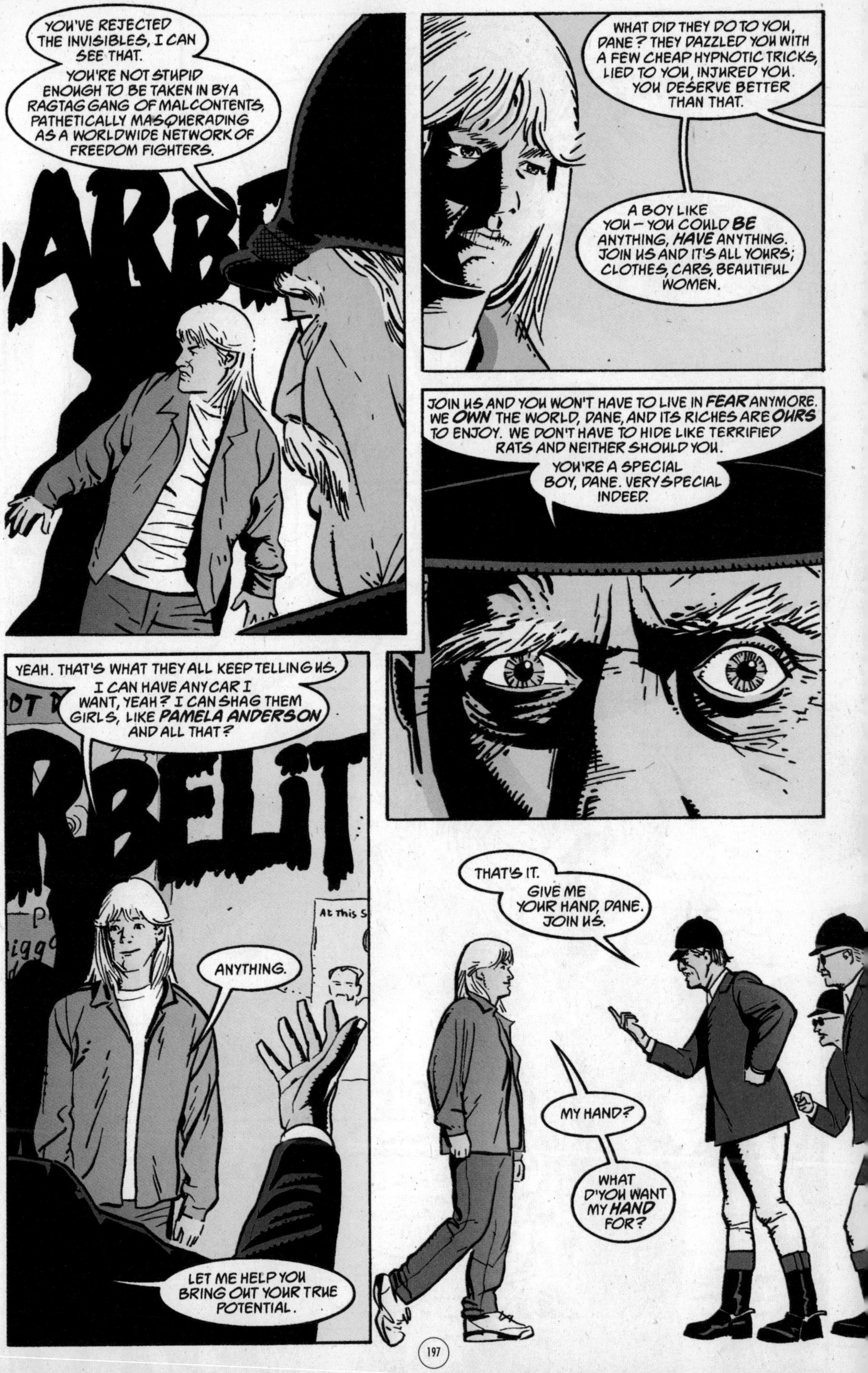
YOU'VE REJECTED THE INVISIBLES, I CAN SEE THAT.
YOU'RE NOT STUPID ENOUGH TO BE TAKEN IN BY A RAGTAG GANG OF MALCONTENTS, PATHETICALLY MASQUERADING AS A WORLDWIDE NETWORK OF FREEDOM FIGHTERS.
WHAT DID THEY DO TO YOU, DANE? THEY DAZZLED YOU WITH A FEW CHEAP HYPNOTIC TRICKS, LIED TO YOU, INJURED YOU.
YOU DESERVE BETTER THAN THAT.
A BOY LIKE YOU – YOU COULD BE ANYTHING, HAVE ANYTHING. JOIN US AND IT'S ALL YOURS; CLOTHES, CARS, BEAUTIFUL WOMEN.
JOIN US AND YOU WON'T HAVE TO LIVE IN FEAR ANYMORE. WE OWN THE WORLD, DANE, AND ITS RICHES ARE OURS TO ENJOY. WE DON'T HAVE TO HIDE LIKE TERRIFIED RATS AND NEITHER SHOULD YOU.
YOU'RE A SPECIAL BOY, DANE. VERY SPECIAL INDEED.
YEAH. THAT'S WHAT THEY ALL KEEP TELLING US.
I CAN HAVE ANY CAR I WANT, YEAH? I CAN SHAG THEM GIRLS, LIKE PAMELA ANDERSON AND ALL THAT?
ANYTHING.
LET ME HELP YOU BRING OUT YOUR TRUE POTENTIAL.
THAT'S IT.
GIVE ME YOUR HAND, DANE. JOIN US.
MY HAND?
WHAT D'YOU WANT MY HAND FOR?

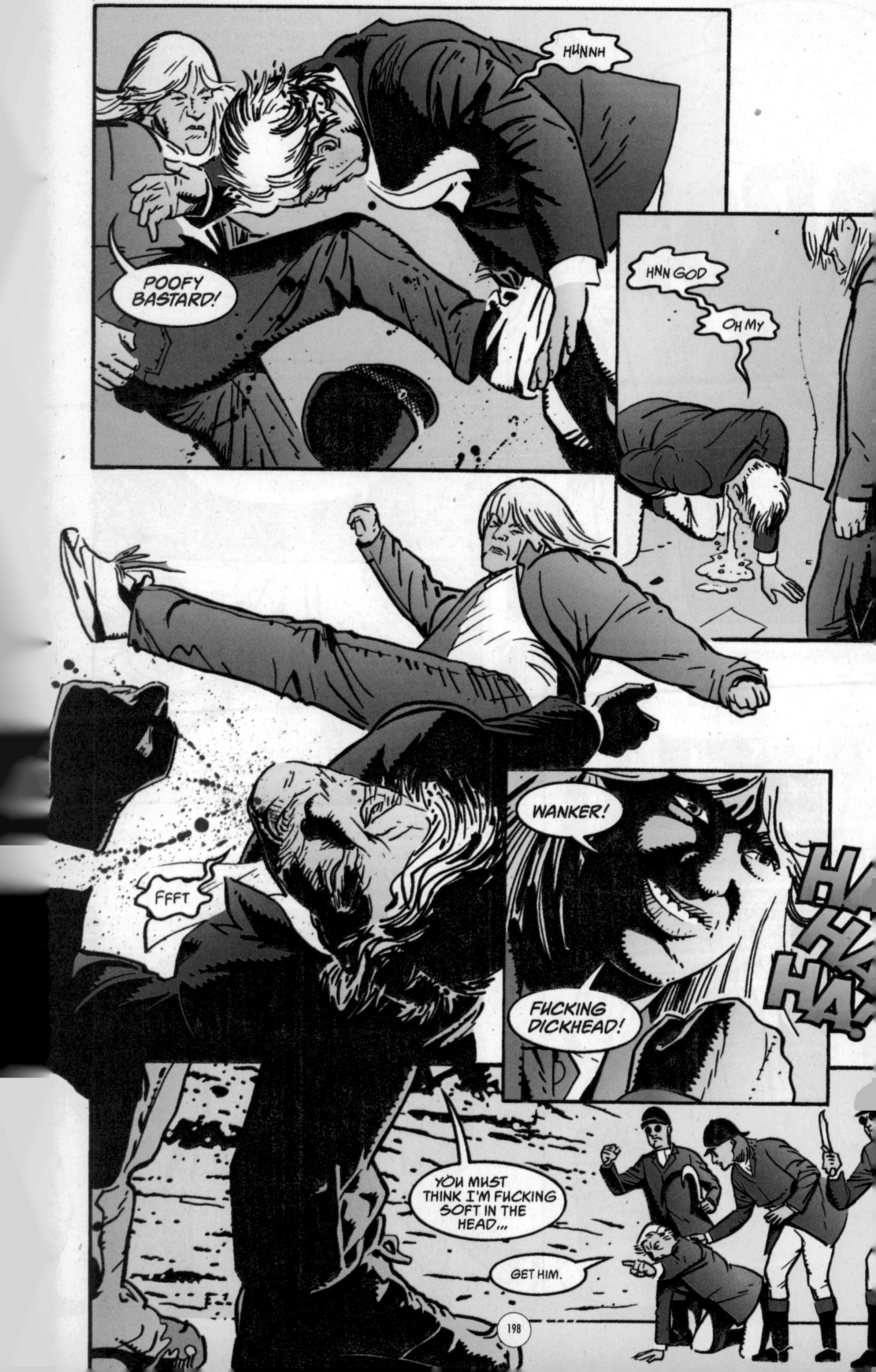
HUNNH
POOFY BASTARD!
HNN GOD
OH MY
FFFT
WANKER!
FUCKING DICKHEAD!
YOU MUST THINK I'M FUCKING SOFT IN THE HEAD...
GET HIM.

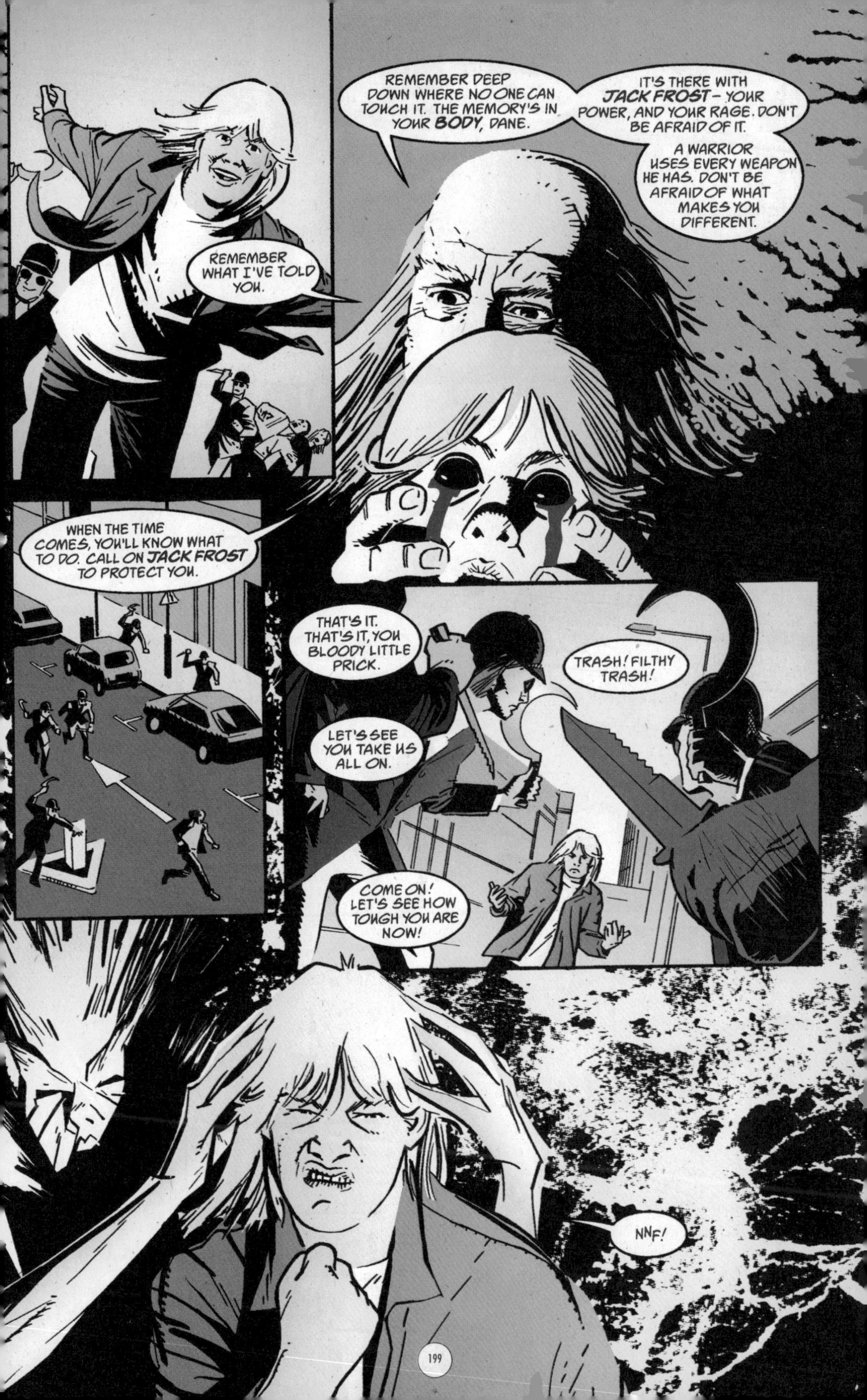
REMEMBER WHAT I'VE TOLD YOU.
REMEMBER DEEP DOWN WHERE NO ONE CAN TOUCH IT. THE MEMORY'S IN YOUR BODY, DANE.
IT'S THERE WITH JACK FROST - YOUR POWER, AND YOUR RAGE. DON'T BE AFRAID OF IT.
A WARRIOR USES EVERY WEAPON HE HAS. DON'T BE AFRAID OF WHAT MAKES YOU DIFFERENT.
WHEN THE TIME COMES, YOU'LL KNOW WHAT TO DO. CALL ON JACK FROST TO PROTECT YOU.
THAT'S IT. THAT'S IT, YOU BLOODY LITTLE PRICK.
TRASH! FILTHY TRASH!
LET'S SEE YOU TAKE US ALL ON.
COME ON! LET'S SEE HOW TOUGH YOU ARE NOW!
NNF!

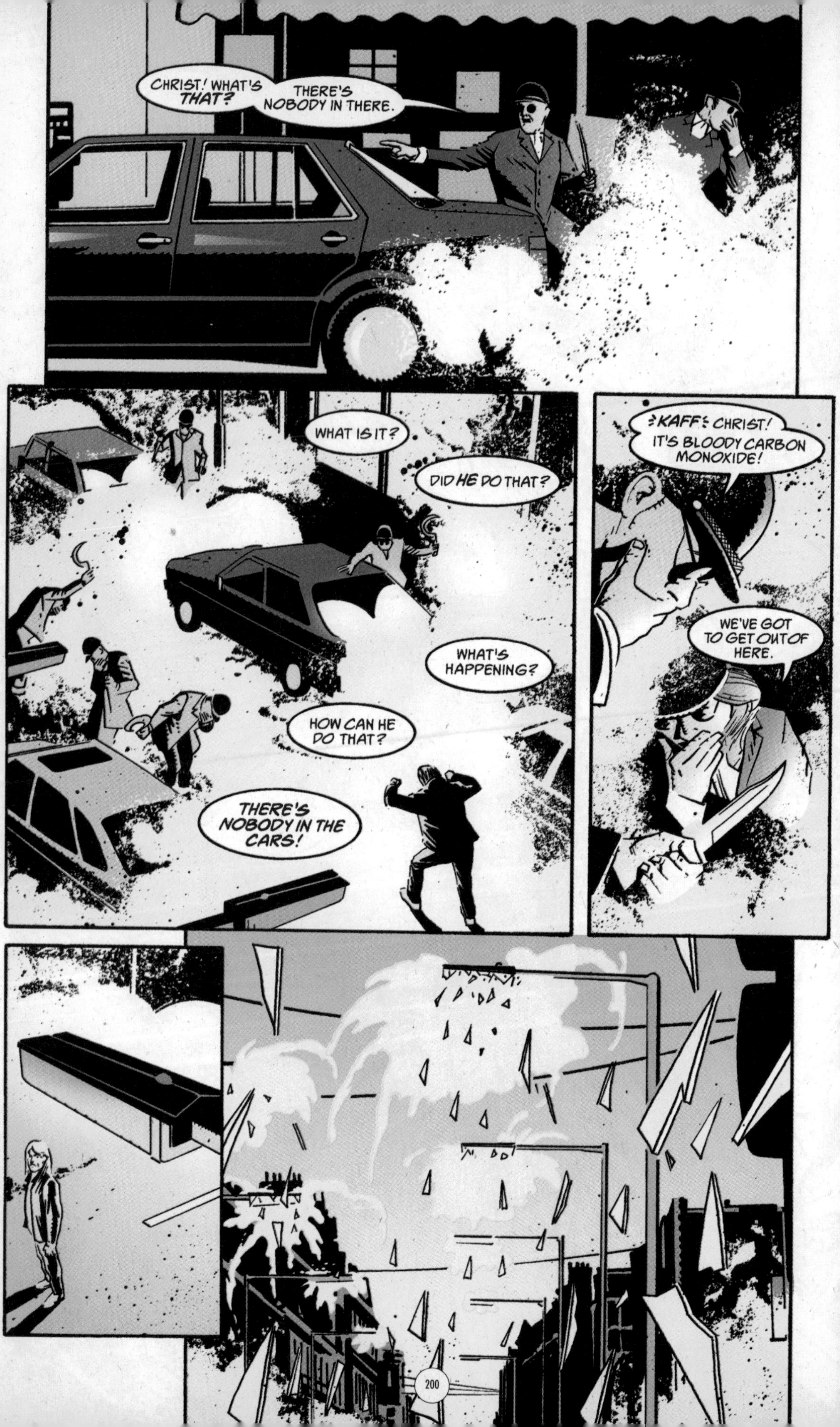
CHRIST! WHAT'S THAT?
THERE'S NOBODY IN THERE.
WHAT IS IT?
DID HE DO THAT?
WHAT'S HAPPENING?
HOW CAN HE DO THAT?
THERE'S NOBODY IN THE CARS!
KAFF CHRIST! IT'S BLOODY CARBON MONOXIDE!
WE'VE GOT TO GET OUT OF HERE.

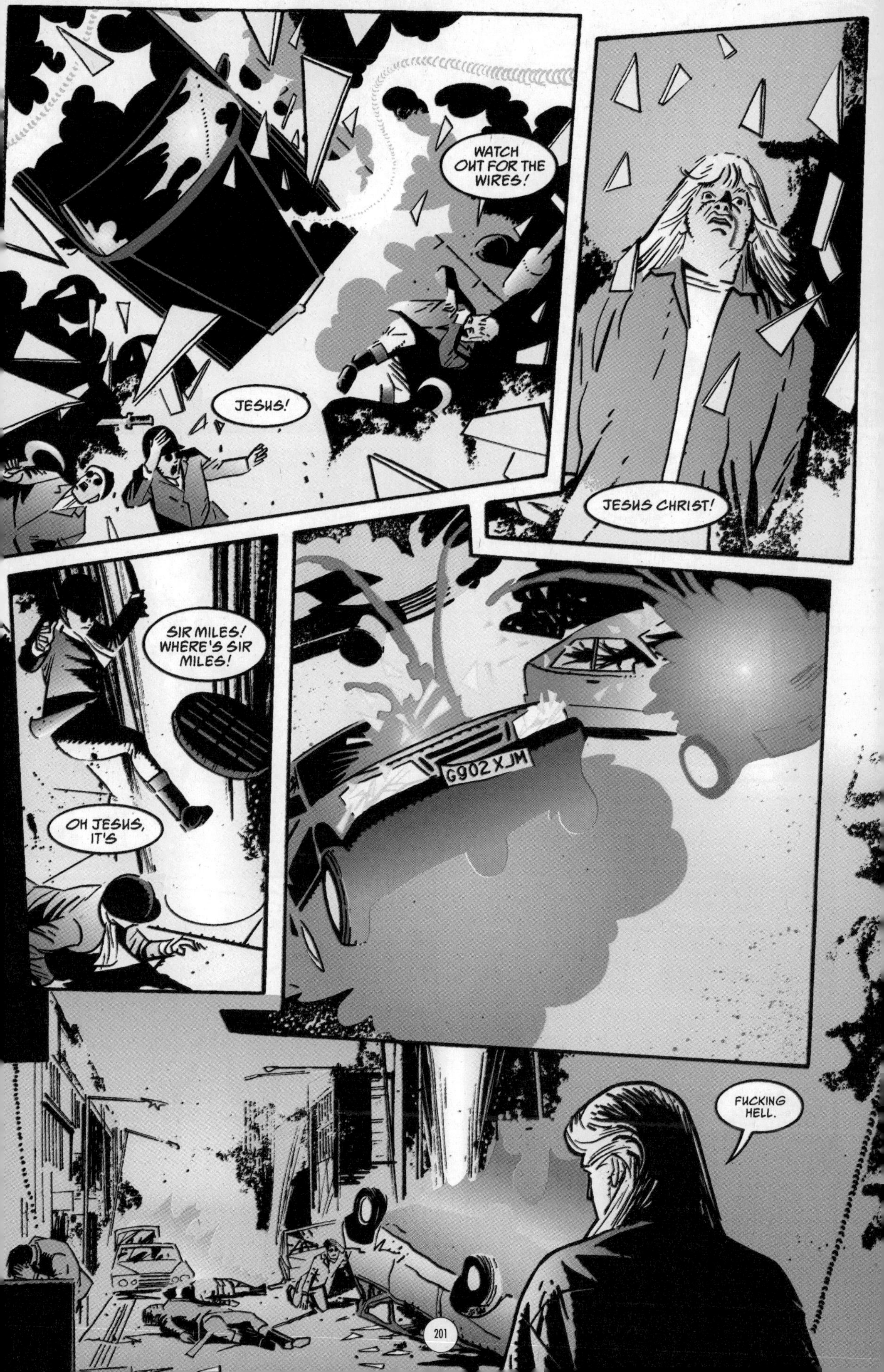

WATCH OUT FOR THE WIRES!
JESUS!
JESUS CHRIST!
SIR MILES! WHERE'S SIR MILES!
OH JESUS, IT'S
G902 XJM
FUCKING HELL.

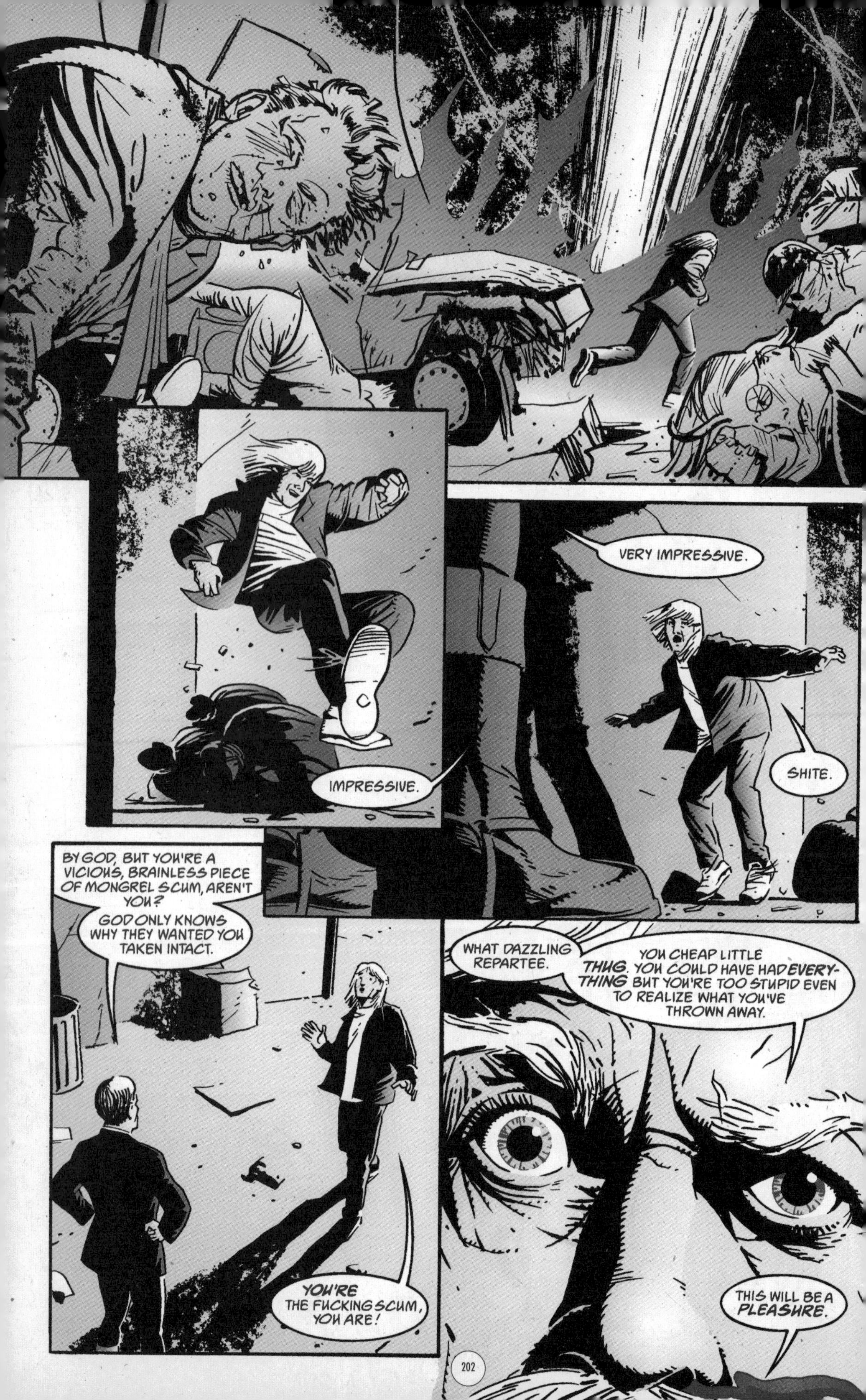
IMPRESSIVE.
VERY IMPRESSIVE.
SHITE.
BY GOD, BUT YOU'RE A VICIOUS, BRAINLESS PIECE OF MONGREL SCUM, AREN'T YOU?
GOD ONLY KNOWS WHY THEY WANTED YOU TAKEN INTACT.
YOU'RE THE FUCKING SCUM, YOU ARE!
WHAT DAZZLING REPARTEE.
YOU CHEAP LITTLE THUG. YOU COULD HAVE HAD EVERYTHING BUT YOU'RE TOO STUPID EVEN TO REALIZE WHAT YOU'VE THROWN AWAY.
THIS WILL BE A PLEASURE.

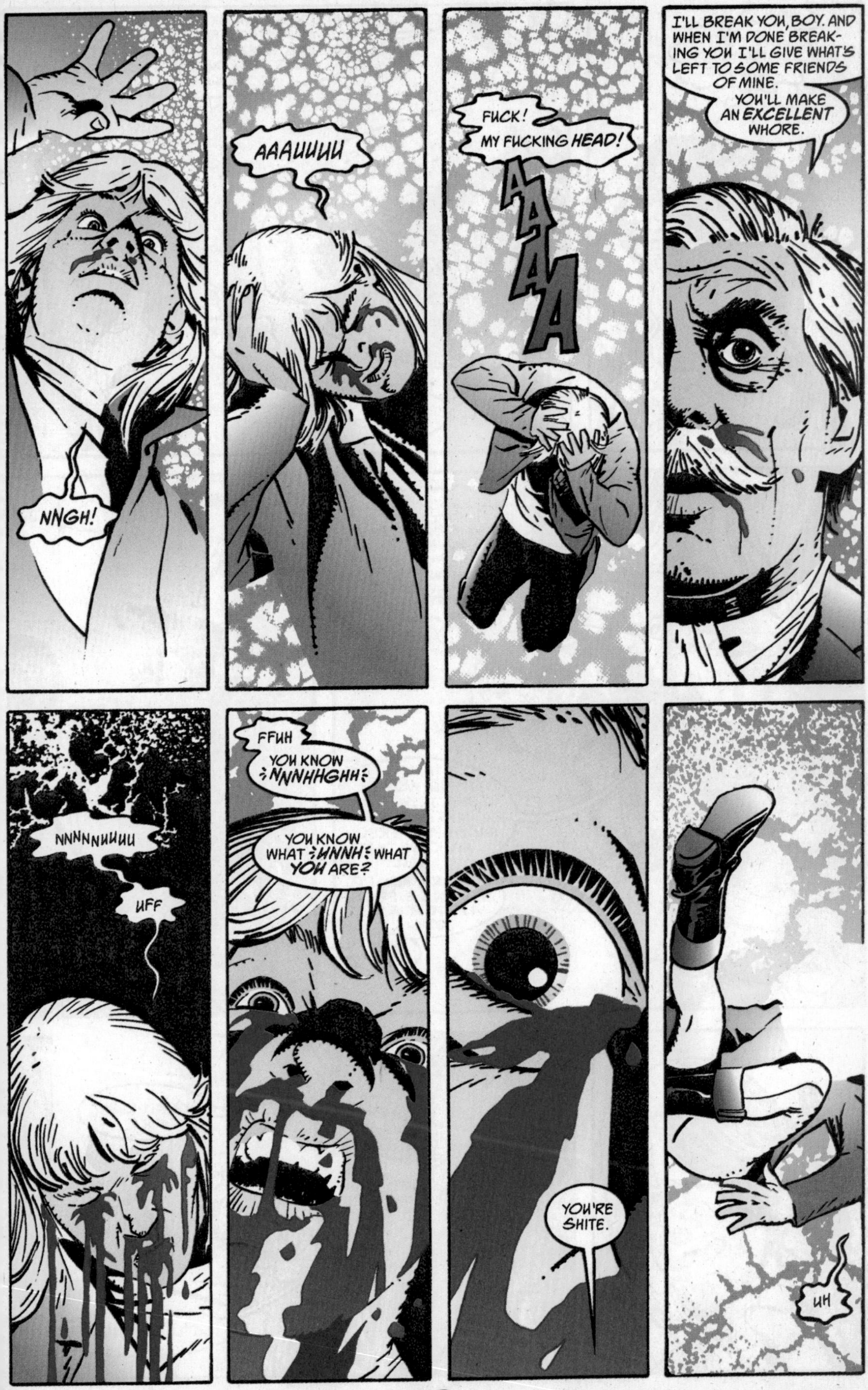
NNGH!
AAAUUUU
FUCK! MY FUCKING HEAD!
AAAA
I'LL BREAK YOU, BOY. AND WHEN I'M DONE BREAKING YOU I'LL GIVE WHAT'S LEFT TO SOME FRIENDS OF MINE.
YOU'LL MAKE AN EXCELLENT WHORE.
NNNNNUUUU
UFF
FFUH
YOU KNOW NNNHHGHH
YOU KNOW WHAT UNNH WHAT YOU ARE?
YOU'RE SHITE.
UH

UHHH

DEAR GOD, WHAT HAVE YOU DONE TO...

≥HOOO AAAK≥

DON'T LOOK SO FUCKING GREAT *NOW*, DO YOU? YOU IN YOUR STUPID FUCKING PONCEY TROUSERS. YOU THINK YOU OWN EVERYBODY AND EVERYTHING BUT YOU CAN'T FUCKING TOUCH *ME*, MAN.

URRRRR

EY, LOOK WHAT I'VE GOT.

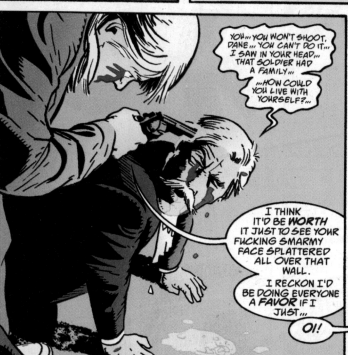

YOU... YOU WON'T SHOOT. DANE... YOU CAN'T DO IT... I SAW IN YOUR HEAD... THAT SOLDIER HAD A FAMILY... ...HOW COULD YOU LIVE WITH YOURSELF?...

I THINK IT'D BE *WORTH* IT JUST TO SEE YOUR FUCKING SMARMY FACE SPLATTERED ALL OVER THAT WALL. I RECKON I'D BE DOING EVERYONE A *FAVOR* IF I JUST...

OI!

HOLD IT RIGHT THERE, YOU!

YOU ALL RIGHT, SIR?

LITTLE BASTARDS!

204

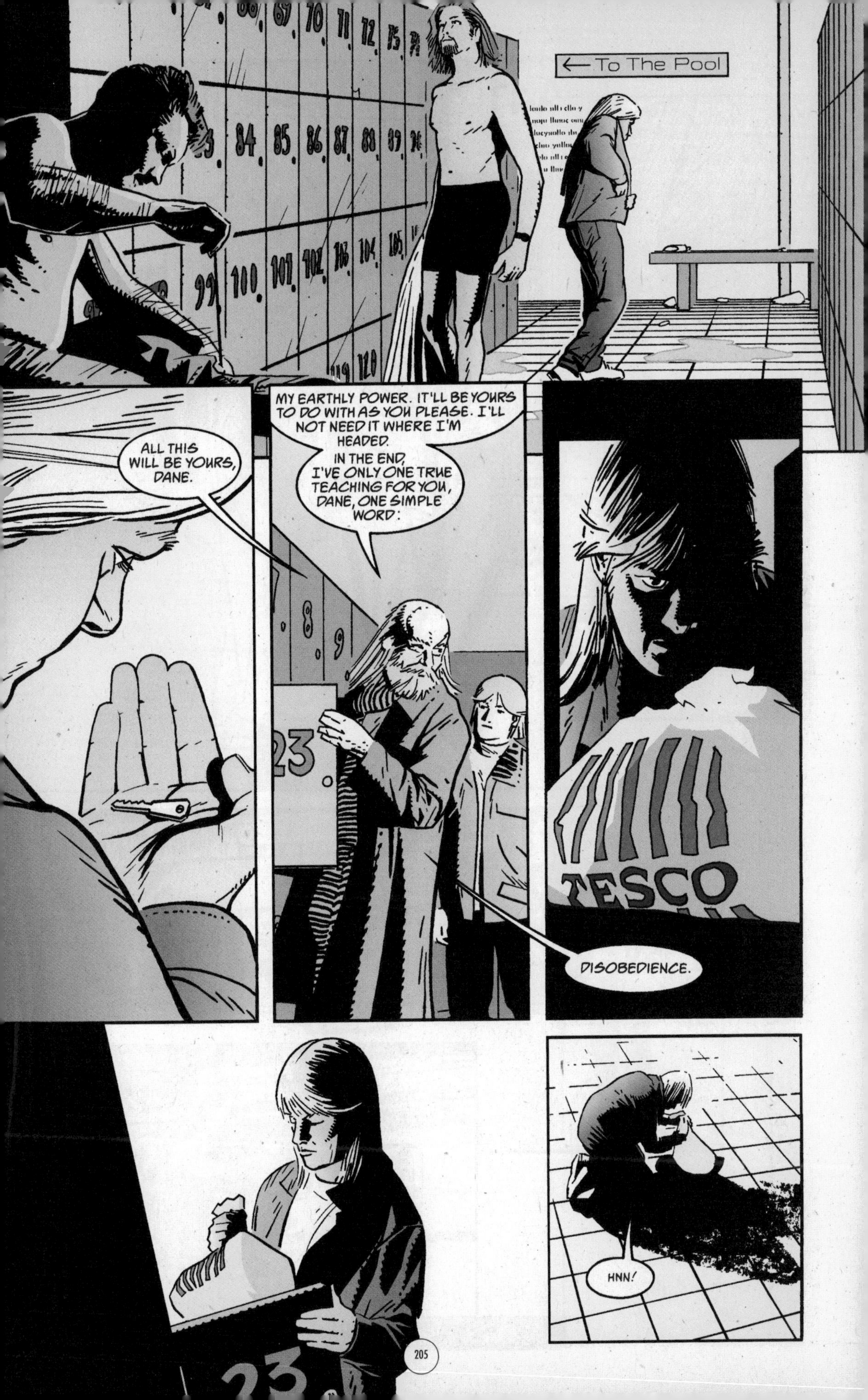

← To The Pool
ALL THIS WILL BE YOURS, DANE.
MY EARTHLY POWER. IT'LL BE YOURS TO DO WITH AS YOU PLEASE. I'LL NOT NEED IT WHERE I'M HEADED.
IN THE END, I'VE ONLY ONE TRUE TEACHING FOR YOU, DANE, ONE SIMPLE WORD:
TESCO
DISOBEDIENCE.
HNN!

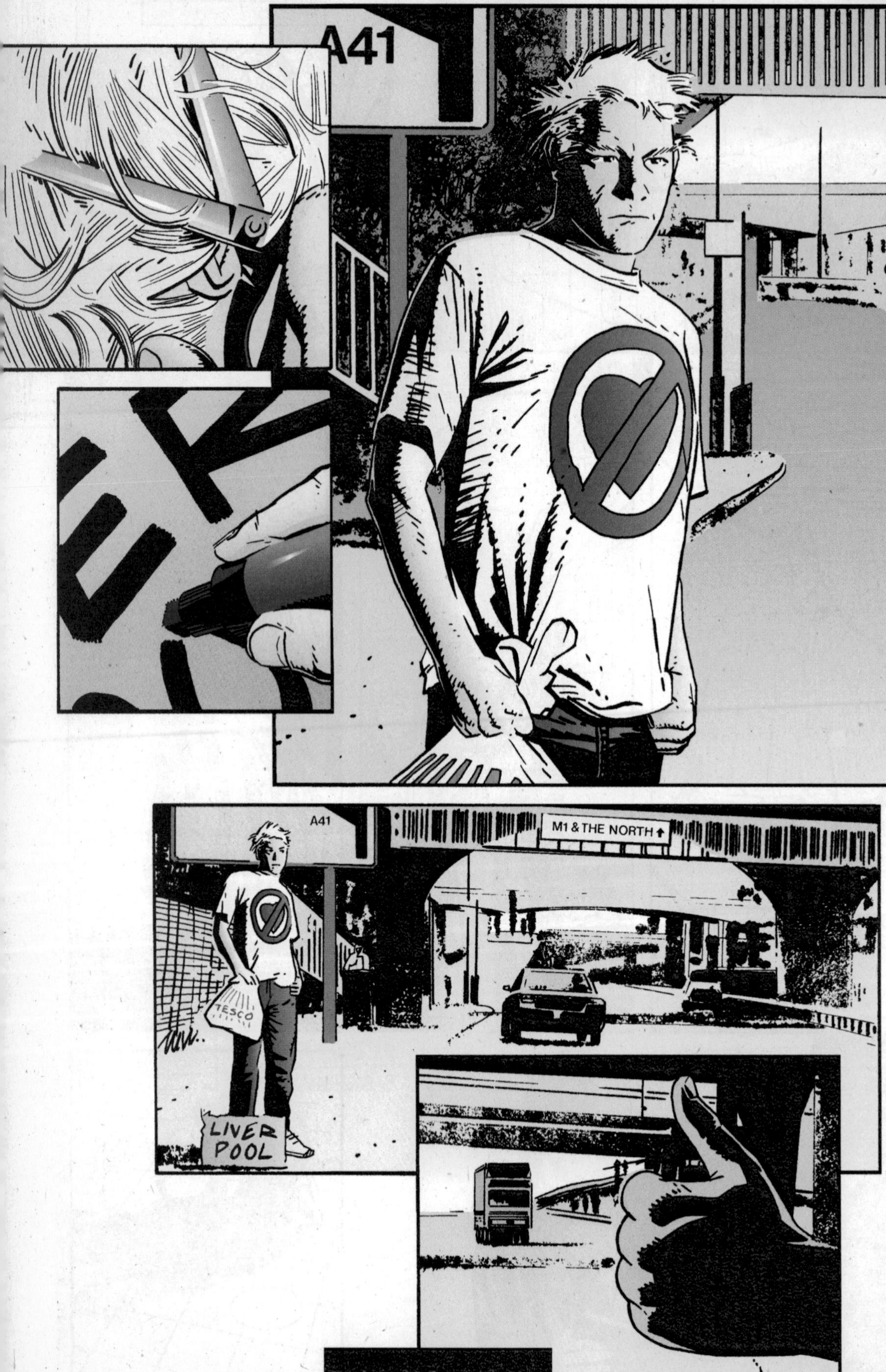
A41
A41
M1 & THE NORTH
TESCO
LIVER
POOL

THE GRANT MORRISON LIBRARY

From VERTIGO. Suggested for mature readers.

ANIMAL MAN

A minor super-hero's consciousness is raised higher and higher until he becomes aware of his own fictitious nature in this revolutionary and existential series.

Volume 1: ANIMAL MAN
With Chas Truog, Doug Hazlewood and Tom Grummett

Volume 2: ORIGIN OF THE SPECIES
With Chas Truog, Doug Hazlewood and Tom Grummett

Volume 3: DEUS EX MACHINA
With Chas Truog, Doug Hazlewood and various

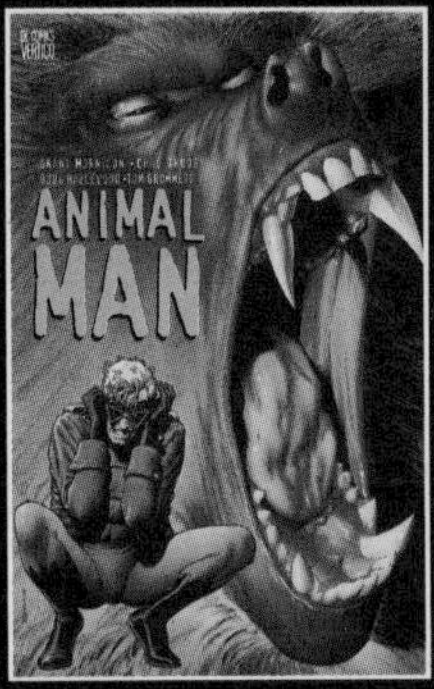
ANIMAL MAN

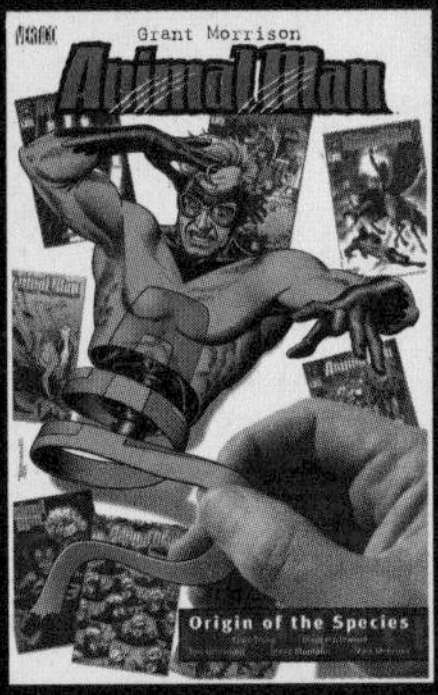
Grant Morrison
Animal Man
Origin of the Species

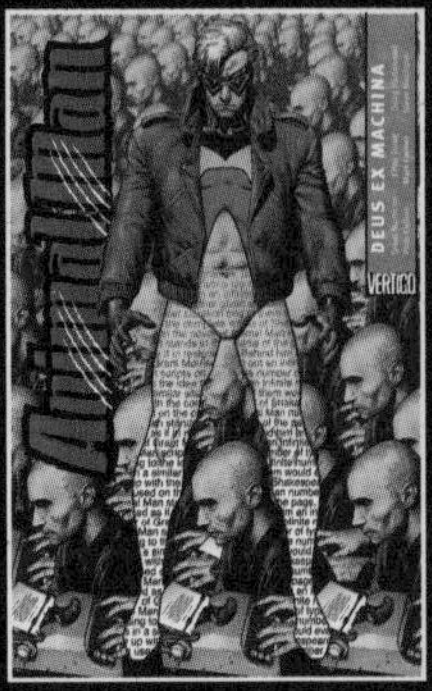
Animal Man
DEUS EX MACHINA
VERTIGO

THE INVISIBLES

The saga of a terrifying conspiracy and the resistance movement combatting it — a secret underground of ultra-cool guerrilla cells trained in ontological and physical anarchy.

Volume 1: SAY YOU WANT A REVOLUTION
With Steve Yeowell and Jill Thompson

Volume 2: APOCALIPSTICK
With Jill Thompson, Chris Weston and various

Volume 3: ENTROPY IN THE U.K.
With Phil Jimenez, John Stokes and various

Volume 4: BLOODY HELL IN AMERICA
With Phil Jimenez and John Stokes

Volume 5: COUNTING TO NONE
With Phil Jimenez and John Stokes

Volume 6: KISSING MR. QUIMPER
With Chris Weston and various

Volume 7: THE INVISIBLE KINGDOM
With Philip Bond, Sean Phillips and various

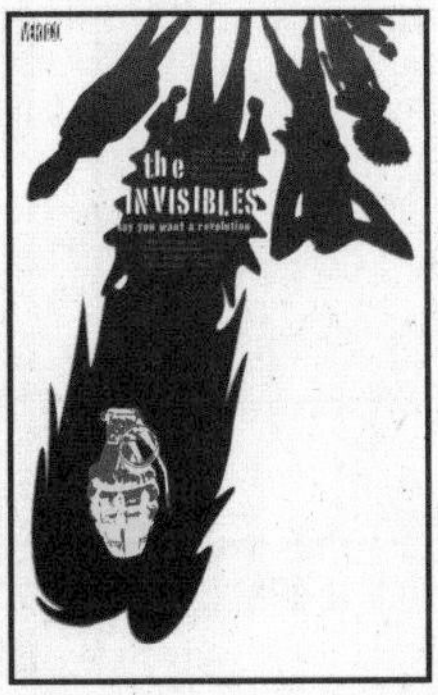
the INVISIBLES

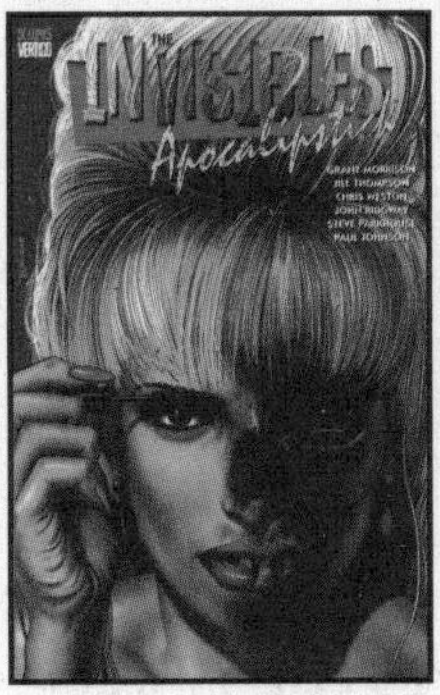
INVISIBLES
Apocalipstick

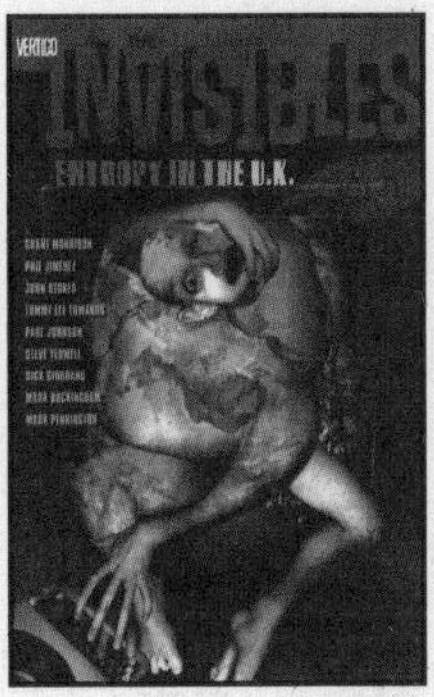
INVISIBLES
ENTROPY IN THE U.K.

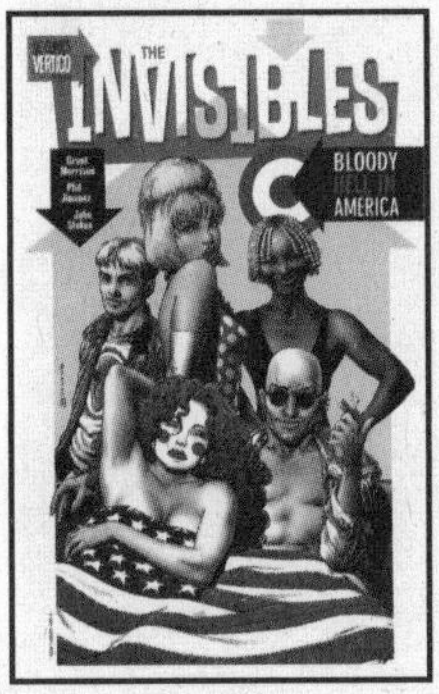
THE INVISIBLES
BLOODY HELL IN AMERICA

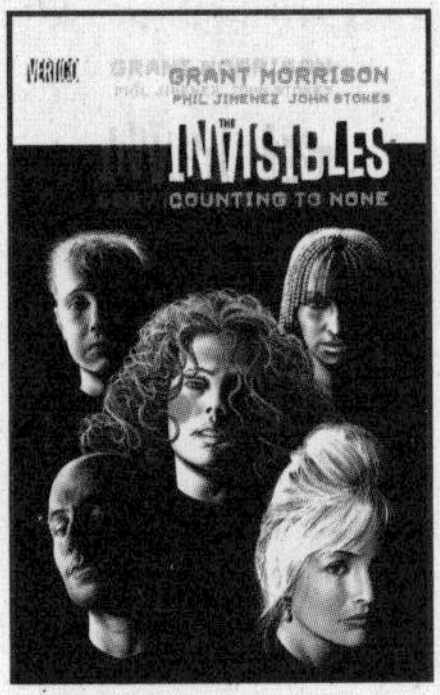
GRANT MORRISON
PHIL JIMENEZ JOHN STOKES
INVISIBLES
COUNTING TO NONE

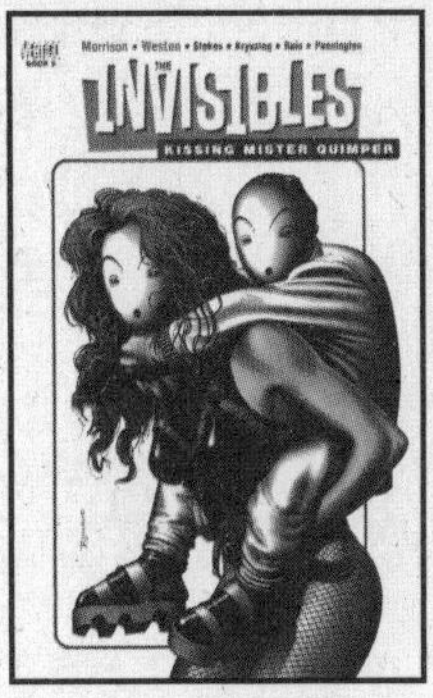
INVISIBLES
KISSING MISTER QUIMPER

SEAGUY
With Cameron Stewart

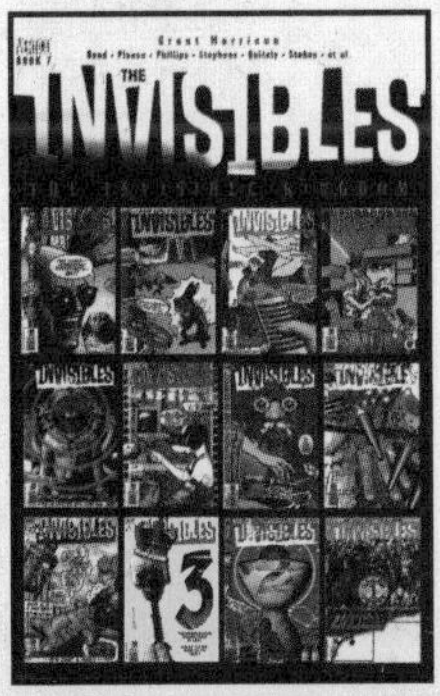
Grant Morrison
THE INVISIBLES

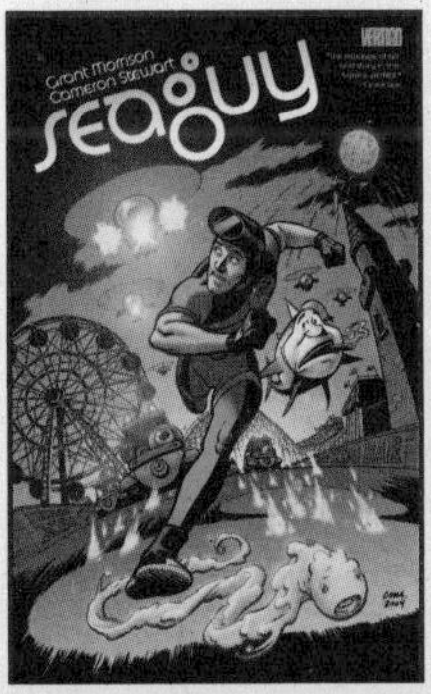
Grant Morrison
Cameron Stewart
seaguy

DOOM PATROL

The World's Strangest Heroes are reimagined even stranger and more otherworldly in this groundbreaking series exploring the mysteries of identity and madness.

Volume 1:
CRAWLING FROM THE WRECKAGE
With Richard Case, Doug Braithwaite, Scott Hanna, Carlos Garzon and John Nyberg

Volume 2:
THE PAINTING THAT ATE PARIS
With Richard Case and John Nyberg

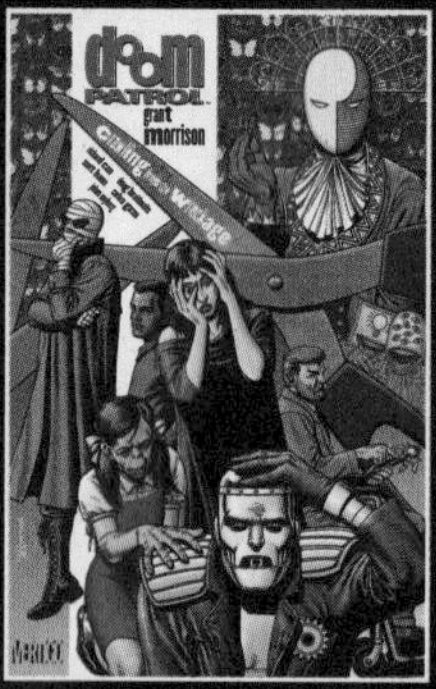
doom
PATROL
grant
morrison

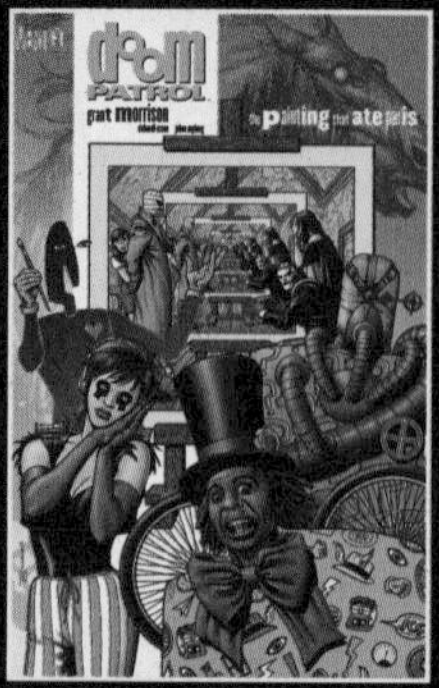
doom
PATROL
grant morrison
the painting that ate paris

THE FILTH
With Chris Weston and Gary Erskine

MYSTERY PLAY
With Jon J Muth

SEBASTIAN O
With Steve Yeowell

From VERTIGO
Suggested for mature readers.

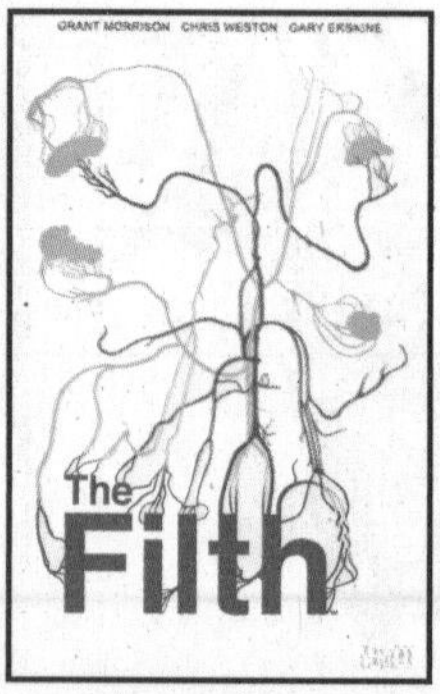
GRANT MORRISON CHRIS WESTON GARY ERSKINE
The
Filth

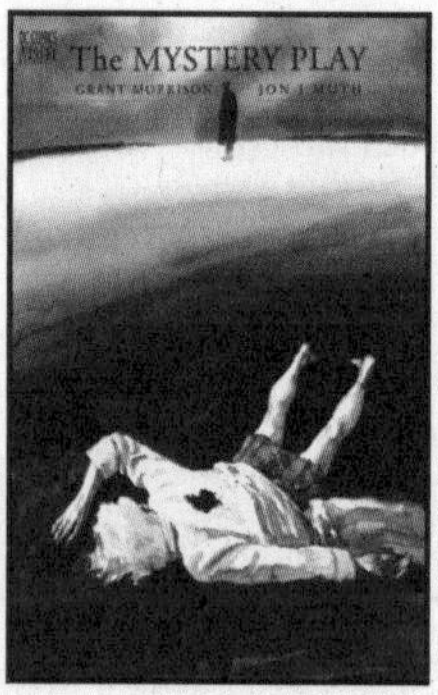
The MYSTERY PLAY
GRANT MORRISON JON J MUTH

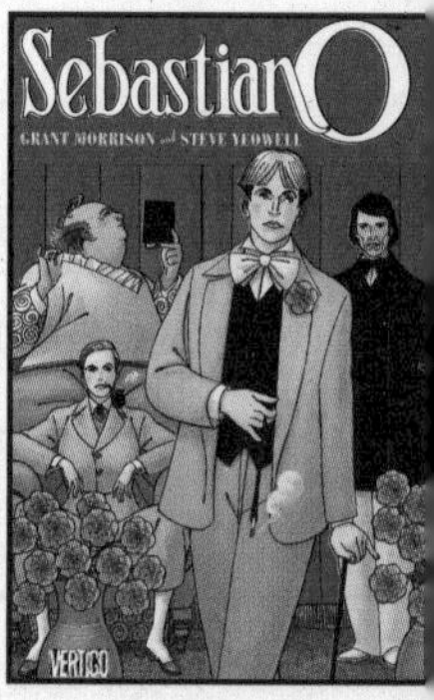
SebastianO
GRANT MORRISON and STEVE YEOWELL
VERTIGO

From DC COMICS

BATMAN: ARKHAM ASYLUM
With Dave McKean

JLA: EARTH 2
With Frank Quitely

JLA: NEW WORLD ORDER
With Howard Porter and John Dell

JLA: AMERICAN DREAMS
With Howard Porter, John Dell and various

JLA: ROCK OF AGES
With Howard Porter, John Dell and various

JLA: ONE MILLION
With Val Semeiks, Prentis Rollins and various

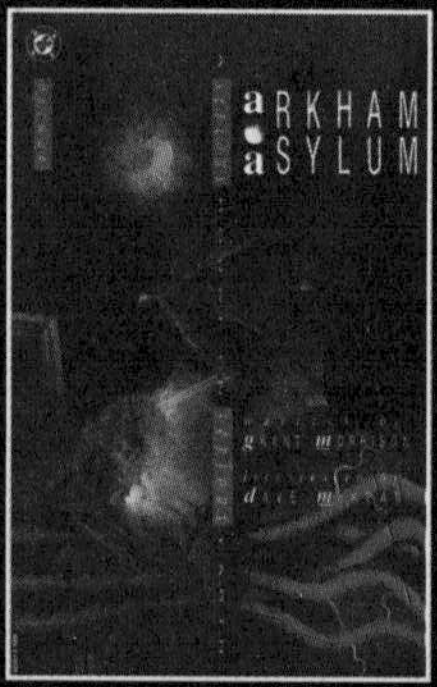
aRKHAM
aSYLUM

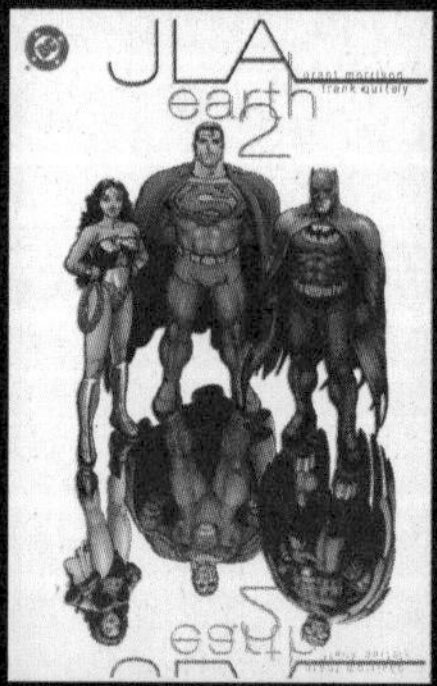
JLA
earth
2

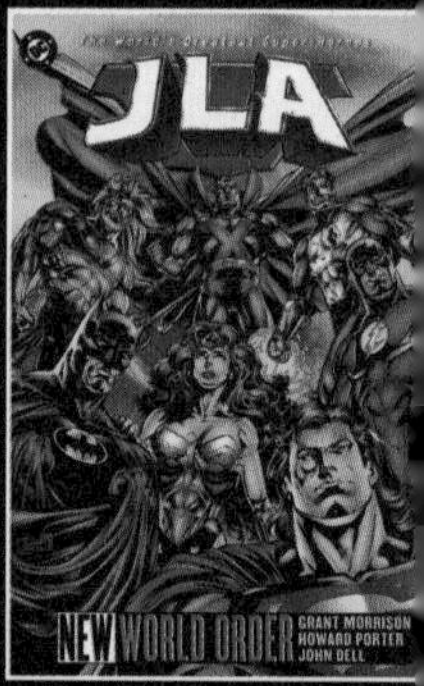
JLA
NEW WORLD ORDER
GRANT MORRISON
HOWARD PORTER
JOHN DELL

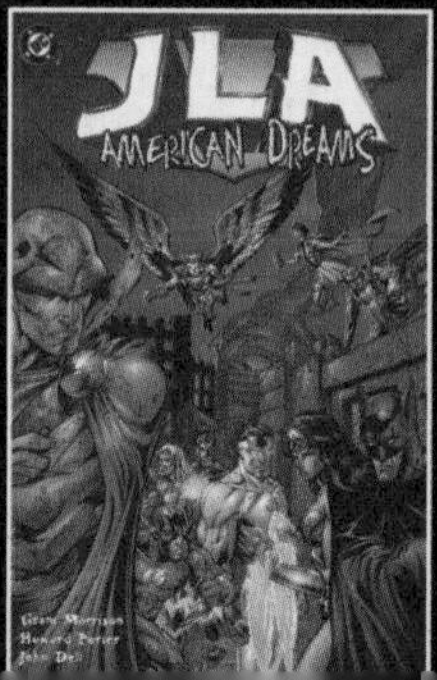
JLA
AMERICAN DREAMS

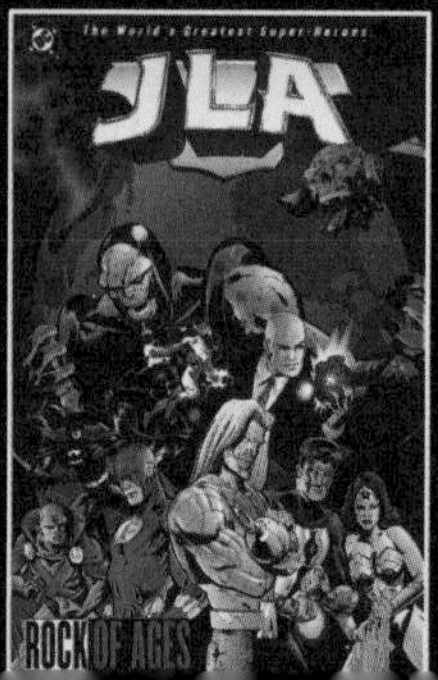
JLA
ROCK OF AGES

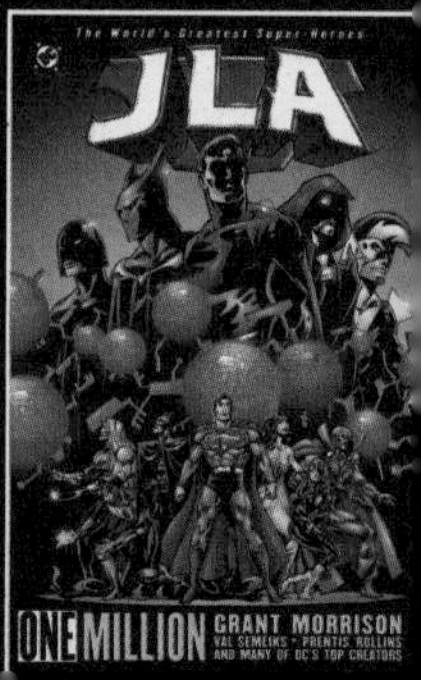
JLA
ONE MILLION
GRANT MORRISON